Lecture Notes in Computer Science 7957

Commenced Publication in 1973
Founding and Former Series Editors:
Gerhard Goos, Juris Hartmanis, and Jan van Leeuwen

Khalil Drira (Ed.)

Software Architecture

7th European Conference, ECSA 2013
Montpellier, France, July 1-5, 2013
Proceedings

 Springer

Volume Editor

Khalil Drira
LAAS-CNRS, Univ. de Toulouse
31031 Toulouse, France
E-mail: khalil@laas.fr

ISSN 0302-9743
ISBN 978-3-642-39030-2
DOI 10.1007/978-3-642-39031-9
Springer Heidelberg Dordrecht London New York

e-ISSN 1611-3349
e-ISBN 978-3-642-39031-9

Library of Congress Control Number: 2013940538

CR Subject Classification (1998): D.2, D.3, F.3, H.4, C.2, K.6

LNCS Sublibrary: SL 2 – Programming and Software Engineering

Typesetting: Camera-ready by author, data conversion by Scientific Publishing Services, Chennai, India

Printed on acid-free paper

Springer is part of Springer Science+Business Media (www.springer.com)

Preface

The 7th European Conference on Software Architecture (ECSA 2013) aimed at bringing together researchers and industry practitioners to exchange the recent and innovative fundamental advances in the state of the art, to identify emerging research topics, and to take part in the next trend in the field of software architecture. This edition of ECSA built upon a history of a successful series of European workshops on software architecture held from 2004 through 2006, and a series of European software architecture conferences from 2007 through 2012.

We received more than 80 submissions in the three main categories: full research and experience papers (64 papers), emerging research papers (10 papers), and research challenge papers (8 papers). The conference attracted papers coauthored by researchers, practitioners, and academics from 46 countries. Each paper, independently of the category, was peer-reviewed by at least three reviewers, and discussed by the Program Committee. Based on the recommendations and the discussions, we accepted 12 full papers out of 64 full papers submitted. The acceptance rate for the full papers is 18.75%. In the Emerging Research category, we accepted a total of 13 papers, 3 of which were originally submitted in this category, and 10 were submitted as full papers. Finally, we accepted 11 papers as Research Challenge (Poster) papers.

In addition to the technical program consisting of academic and industrial keynote talks, a main research track, and a poster session, the scope of ECSA 2013 was broadened by the SESoS 2013 workshop: the Workshop on Software Engineering for Systems-of-Systems.

We are grateful to the members of the Program Committee for helping us to seek submissions and provide valuable and timely reviews. Their efforts enabled us to put together a high-quality technical program for ECSA 2013. We are indebted to the local arrangements team of LIRMM for the successful organization of all conference, social, and co-located events. The ECSA 2013 submission, review and proceedings process was extensively supported by the EasyChair Conference Management System. We also acknowledge the prompt and professional support from Springer, who published these proceedings in printed and electronic volumes as part of the *Lecture Notes in Computer Science* series. Finally, we would like to thank our sponsors ORACLE, Bouygues Telecom, IBM Research, Typesafe, La Région Languedoc-Roussillon, Montpellier Agglomération, and GDR GPL for their support of this conference. Most importantly, we would like to thank all authors and participants of ECSA 2013 for their insightful work and discussions!

April 2013

Khalil Drira
Flavio Oquendo
Marianne Huchard

Organization

Conference Chair

Flavio Oquendo   IRISA - University of South Brittany, France

Program Committee

Program Committee Chair

Khalil Drira   LAAS-CNRS - Université de Toulouse, France

Program Committee Members

Ahmed Hadj Kacem   University of Sfax, Tunisia
Alexander Egyed   Johannes Kepler University, Austria
Andrea Zisman   City University London, UK
Antonia Lopes   University of Lisbon, Portugal
Antony Tang   Swinburne University of Technology, Australia
Bedir Tekinerdoğan   Bilkent Üniversitesi, Turkey
Bradley Schmerl   Carnegie Mellon University, USA
Carlos Cuesta   Rey Juan Carlos University, Spain
Cecilia Rubira   University of Campinas, Brazil
Claudia Maria Lima Werner   Federal University of Rio de Janeiro - UFRJ,
          Brazil
Claudia Raibulet   University of Milano-Bicocca, Italy
Claus Pahl   Dublin City University, Ireland
Cristina Gacek   City University London, UK
Danny Weyns   Linnaeus University - Växjö, Sweden
Darko Huljenic   Ericsson Nikola Tesla, Croatia
David Garlan   Carnegie Mellon University, USA
Dewayne Perry   University of Texas at Austin, USA
Eduardo Santana de Almeida   Federal University of Bahia and RiSE, Brazil
Eila Ovaska   VTT Technical Research Centre of Finland,
          Finland
Elena Navarro   Castilla-La Mancha University, Spain
Elisa Yumi Nakagawa   University of São Paulo, Brazil
Gerald Kotonya   Lancaster University, UK
Henry Muccini   University of L'Aquila, Italy
Ian Gorton   Pacific Northwest National Laboratory, USA

Additional Reviewers

Achraf Ghabi
Alexander Nöhrer
Amal Gassara
Amrita Chaturvedi
Andreas Demuth
Ashish Agrawal
Cédric Eichler
Claudia Susie
  Camargo Rodrigues
Clément Quinton
Codé Diop
Damian Andrew
  Tamburri
Daniel Ståhl
David Allison
Dominique Mery
Francisca Losavio
Francisco Monaco

Håkan Burden
Hala Naja
Hatem Hadj Kacem
Hossein Tajalli
Huy Tran
Ilias Gerostathopoulos
Imen Tounsi
Imene Lahyani
Ioanna Lytra
Ivano Malavolta
Ivo Krka
Jae Young Bang
Jair Leite
Jan Salvador van der Ven
Jessica Díaz
Lauret Jimmy
Liam O'Reilly

Lucas Bueno Ruas
  De Oliveira
M. Pilar Romay
Milena Guessi
Mohamed Nadhmi
  Miladi
Mohamed Tounsi
Mohamed Zouari
Nabil Bachir Djarallah
Nesrine Khabou
Philippe Merle
Pooyan Jamshidi
Riad Belkhatir
Riadh Ben Halima
Séverine Sentilles
Stephany Bellomo

Steering Committee

Steering Committee Chair

Flavio Oquendo   IRISA - University of South Brittany, France

Steering Committee Members

Muhammad Ali Babar   IT University of Copenhagen, Denmark
Ivica Crnkovic   Mälardalen University, Sweden
Carlos E. Cuesta   Rey Juan Carlos University, Spain
Khalil Drira   LAAS-CNRS - Université de Toulouse, France
Ian Gorton   Pacific Northwest Labs, USA
Volker Gruhn   University of Duisburg-Essen, Germany
Rick Kazman   SEI/CMU and University of Hawaii, USA
Tomi Männistö   Aalto University, Finland

Organizing Committee

General Conference Chair

Marianne Huchard   LIRMM, Montpellier, France

Organization Chairs

Roland Ducournau and
   Christophe Dony   LIRMM, Montpellier, France

Local Organization Chairs

Elisabeth Grverie
   and Justine Landais   LIRMM, Montpellier, France

Workshop Chairs

Olivier Zendra   INRIA Nancy, France
Reda Bendraou   Université Pierre et Marie Curie, France
Damien Cassou   Université Lille 1, France
Stéphane Ducasse   INRIA Lille, France
Thierry Monteil   LAAS-CNRS, INSA Toulouse, France

Tutorial Chairs

Naouel Moha   Université du Québec à Montréal, Canada
Jean Privat   Université du Québec à Montréal, Canada
Gergely Varró   Technische Universität Darmstadt, Germany

Doctoral Symposium Chairs

Mireille Blay-Fornarino
   and Philippe Collet   Université de Nice, France

Research Project Symposium Chair

Isabelle Borne   University of South Brittany, France
Ileana Ober   Université de Toulouse, France

Poster and Demo Chairs

Houari Sahraoui   Université de Montréal, Canada
Bernard Carré   Université de Lille, France
Harald Störrle   DTU Informatics, Denmark

Summer School Chairs

James Noble   Victoria University of Wellington, New Zealand
Jan Vitek   Purdue University, USA

Web Chairs

Chouki Tibermacine and
   Clémentine Nebut   LIRMM, Montpellier, France

Social Events Chairs

Clémentine Nebut and
   Chouki Tibermacine   LIRMM, Montpellier, France

Sponsorship and Industrial Relationships Chairs

Jean-Paul Rigault   Université de Nice, France
Abdelhak-Djamel Seriai   LIRMM, Montpellier, France

Student Volunteers Chairs

Jannik Laval   École des mines de Douai, France
Floréal Morandat   Université de Bordeaux, France
Petr Spacek   LIRMM, Montpellier, France

Sponsoring Institutions

ORACLE
Bouygues Telecom
IBM Research
Typesafe
GDR GPL
La Région Languedoc-Roussillon
Montpellier Agglomération

Table of Contents

Architectural and Design Patterns and Models

ADLs and Architectural MetaModels

Architectural Design Decision-Making

Software Architecture Conformance and Quality

Architectural Repair and Adaptation

Short Papers

Composition-Centered Architectural Pattern Description Language

Minh Tu Ton That, Salah Sadou, Flavio Oquendo, and Isabelle Borne

Université de Bretagne Sud
IRISA
Vannes, France
{minh-tu.ton-that,Salah.Sadou,Flavio.Oquendo,Isabelle.Borne}@irisa.fr

Abstract. Architectural patterns are important artefacts containing specialized design knowledge to build good-quality systems. Complex systems often exhibit several architectural patterns in their design which leads to the need of architectural pattern composition. Unfortunately, information about the composition of patterns tend to be vaporized right after the composition process which causes problems of traceability and reconstructability of patterns.

This paper proposes a pattern description language that first, facilitates several types of pattern merging operation and second, allows the traceability of pattern composition. More specifically, the approach consists of a proper description of pattern that supports composition operations and a two-step pattern design process that helps to preserve pattern composition information.

1 Introduction

A key issue in the design of any software system is the software architecture, i.e. the fundamental organization of the system embodied in its components, their relationships to each other and to the environment, and the principles guiding its design and evolution [11]. In particular, from a runtime viewpoint, an architecture description should provide a specification of the architecture in terms of components and connectors and how they are composed together; where components are the units of computation and connectors are the interconnections for supporting interactions between components.

The activity of architecting software systems can benefit from the concept of pattern, therefore providing a general reusable solution to a commonly occurring problem within a given context. It is the case of architectural patterns, a concept that enables to define a group of cohesive elements of a software architecture to solve a particular problem.

However, the current use of architectural patterns has a major shortcoming that needs to be addressed to leverage their use in complex software architectures. More specifically, in real world architectures recurring problems are complex and their solutions can be represented by patterns in complex forms that require the combination and reuse of other existing architectural patterns [5].

K. Drira (Ed.): ECSA 2013, LNCS 7957, pp. 1–16, 2013.
© Springer-Verlag Berlin Heidelberg 2013

Moreover, in a well defined context (a given company) there may be some recurring problems that no classical architectural pattern fits. Thus, two problems emerge: the definition of specific patterns and the construction of patterns by combining existing ones. In the literature, current support for pattern composition consists in fact of using merging operators that are not part of the pattern language [10,3,19,7]. This limitation prevents the traceability as well as the reconstructability of patterns which are essential to solve for software evolution.

For addressing these open issues, we propose an architectural pattern description language, called COMLAN, that has in particular the following properties: (i) it deserves first-class citizenship for both patterns and merging operators; (ii) it supports the design of hierarchical patterns. This language is graphical and can be easily integrated to an Architectural Description Language (ADL) environment.

The remainder of this paper is organized as follows: Section 2 points out the problem via illustrative examples. Section 3 introduces the general approach. Section 4 goes into detail the pattern description language. Section 5 describes the pattern refinement step. Section 6 gives some implementation information. Section 7 discusses related work. Section 8 concludes the paper.

2   Problem Statement

Architectural patterns tend to be combined together to provide greater support for the reusability during the software design process. Indeed, architectural patterns can be combined in several ways. We consider here three types of combination: A pattern can be blended with, connected to or included in another pattern. To highlight the existing problems, we first show an example for each case of architectural pattern composition and then point out issues drawn from them.

2.1   Blend of Patterns

By observing the documented patterns in [5,6], we can see that there are some common structures that patterns share. For example, the patterns *Pipes and Filters* and *Layers* share a structure saying that their elements should not form a cycle.

If we consider to express the constraint that no circle can be formed from filters via a pattern, we can say that the pattern *Pipes and Filters* is composed of two sub-patterns (see Figure 1). We call them *Sequential pattern* and *Acyclic pattern*. The former consists of *Filter* components linked together by *Pipe* connectors and the latter consists of *Acylic components* in a way that no cycle can be formed from them. Thus, *Pipes and Filters* is actually the product of the blend of these two patterns. But unfortunately, it is impossible to reuse the *Sequential pattern* or the *Acyclic pattern* alone because they are completely melted in the definition of the *Pipes and Filters* pattern.

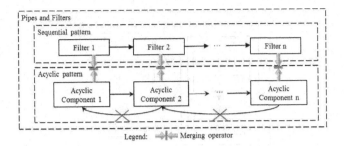

Fig. 1. Pipes and Filters

2.2 Connection of Patterns

A lot of documented patterns formed from two different patterns can be found in [6,2]. For instance, the pattern *Pipes and Filters* can be combined with the pattern *Repository* to form the pattern called *Data-centered Pipeline* as illustrated in Figure 2.

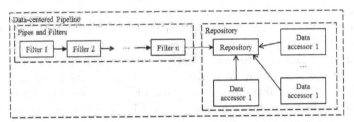

Fig. 2. The Data-centered pipeline pattern

As we can observe, the two patterns are linked together by a special connector which serves two purposes at the same time: convey data from a *Filter* and access to the *Repository*. But once the composed pattern built, it is difficult to identify the sub-patterns used in its constituent patterns.

2.3 Inclusion of Patterns

Architectural patterns themselves can help to build the internal structure of one specific element of another pattern. In [2], we can find several known-uses of this type of pattern composition. An example where the *Layers pattern* becomes the internal structure of *Repository pattern* is shown in Figure 3. Indeed, when we have to deal with data in complex format, the *Layers* pattern is ideal to be set up as the internal structure of the repository since it allows the process of data through many steps. Moreover, the inclusion of patterns can be found at different levels. To be able to model such case, it is necessary to recursively explore patterns through many levels.

Despite the existence of this type of composition, the proposed works have not given the support for it.

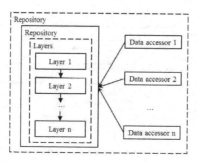

Fig. 3. Layers as internal structure of Repository

2.4   Discussion

As we can observe from the example of subsection 2.2, the *Pipes and Filters* pattern is used as a constituent pattern to build the *Data-centered pipeline* pattern. When we look at the *Pipes and Filters* pattern in this view, we have no idea that it is composed from other patterns as shown in Example 2.1. We think the fact that the border between constituent patterns of a composed pattern is blurred can reduce greatly the pattern comprehensibility. Moreover, since the composed patterns may be then used to build another pattern, knowing the role and the original pattern of every element in the pattern becomes really essential.

Another issue to be taken into consideration is the reconstructability of composed patterns. In the example of subsection 2.1, when one of the two pattens forming the *Pipes and Filters* pattern changes, we should be able to propagate the change to the *Pipes and Filters* pattern. Moreover, since the *Pipes and Filters* pattern has been changed, the *Data-centered Pipeline* in which it participates in Example 2.2 must be also reconstructed.

In the literature, the already proposed approaches such as [10,3,19,7] present pattern merging operators in an *ad-hoc* manner where information about the composition of patterns is vaporized right after the composition process. Thus, they ignore two aforementioned issues.

To realize the inclusion operation like one presented in the example from subsection 2.3, the pattern description language should provide the recursive definition for pattern. More specifically, when specifying an element of a pattern we should be able to add other patterns inside to characterize the element's internal structure. To our knowledge, the proposed pattern description languages [9,18,14] have not given the support to this type of hierarchical composition.

In summary, the examples shown above highlight three problems to solve:

1. *Traceability of constituent patterns*: One should be able to trace back to constituent patterns while composing the new pattern.
2. *Reconstructability of composed patterns*: Anytime there is a change in a constituent pattern, one should be able to reuse the merging operators to reflect the change to the composed pattern.

3. *Support for hierarchical pattern composition*: While constructing a pattern, one should be able to build the internal structure of an element by including another pattern.

3   General Approach

We propose the process of constructing patterns including two steps as illustrated in Figure 4. The first step consists in describing a pattern as a composition graph of unit patterns. Thus, the pattern comprises many blocks, each block represents a unit pattern, all linked together by merging operators.

The second step consists in refining the composed pattern in the previous step by concretizing the merging operators. More specifically, depending on the type of merging operator (see Section 4.1), a new element is added to the composed pattern or two existing elements are mixed together. On the purpose of automating the process of pattern refinement, we use the Model Driven Architecture (MDA) approach [16]. Each pattern is considered as a model conforming to its meta-model in order to create a systematic process thanks to model transformation techniques. Thus, each refined pattern is attached to a corresponding pattern model from step 1 and any modification must be done only on the latter at step 1. At this stage, we offer the architect a pattern description language based on the use of classical architectural elements, architectural patterns and pattern merging operators.

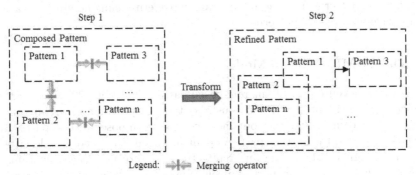

Fig. 4. Overall Approach

We can see that through this two-step process, anytime we want to trace back the constituent patterns of a composed pattern in the second step, we can find them in its corresponding pattern model. Thus, we solve the traceability problem pointed out in the previous section.

We solve the second problem (reusability of merging operators) by the fact that merging operators are first-class entities in our pattern description language. In other words, merging operators are treated as elements of the pattern language where we can manipulate and store them in the pattern model like other elements. Therefore, the composition of patterns is not an *ad-hoc* operation but a part of pattern. This proposal facilitates significantly the propagation of changes in constituent patterns to the composed pattern. Indeed, the latter can thoroughly be rebuilt thanks to the stored merging operators. So, merging operators not only do their job which performs a merge on two patterns but also contain information about the composition process. Thus, we think documenting them is one important task that architects should take into consideration.

Finally, to solve the third problem (support for hierarchical pattern composition), we propose to give pattern itself first-class status in our pattern description language. That means that patterns should play the same role as other elements where we can make connection with, add properties and most importantly, set them up as internal elements. This recursive definition of pattern gives the pattern description language the capacity to describe hierarchical patterns as mentioned in the illustrative example of Section 2.3.

In the two following sections, we describe our pattern description language and the transformation process that produces the refined pattern model from a pattern model.

4   A Pattern Description Language for Hierarchical Pattern and Composition

We introduce our language called COMLAN (Composition-Centered Architectural Pattern Description Language) as a means to realize two main purposes: build complex patterns from more fine-grained patterns using merging operators and leverage hierarchical patterns.

4.1   The COMLAN Meta-Model

In this work, we reuse part of our role-based pattern language [20] which serves for documenting architectural decisions about the application of architectural patterns. As shown in Figure 5, our meta-model is composed of two parts: the structural part and the pattern part. As pointed out in [13,1] and also described in [6], the design vocabulary of an architectural pattern necessarily contains a set of component, connector, port and role. We take these concepts into consideration to build the structural part of our language. More specifically, they are described in our language as follows:

- *Component* is a composite element which, through the *internalElements* relation, can contain a set of component ports or even a sub-architecture with components and connectors
- *Component port* is a simple element through which components interact with connectors. A component port can be attached to a connector role or delegated to another component port in an internal sub-architecture.
- *Connector* is a composite element which, through the *internalElements* relation, can have a set of connector roles or even a sub-architecture with components and connectors.

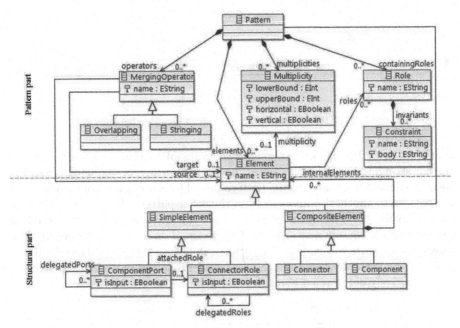

Fig. 5. The COMLAN meta-model

– *Connector role* is a simple element that indicates how components (via component ports) use a connector in interactions. A connector role can be delegated to another connector role in an internal sub-architecture.

The *pattern aspect* part (see Figure 5) of our meta-model aims at providing functionalities to characterize a meaningful architectural pattern. To be more specific, the meta-model allows us to describe a pattern element at two levels: generic and concrete. Via the *multiplicity*, we can specify an element as generic or concrete. A concrete element (not associated with any multiplicity) provides guidance on a specific pattern-related feature. Being generic, an element (associated with a multiplicity) represents a set of concrete elements playing the same role in the architecture. A multiplicity indicates *how many times* a pattern-related element should be repeated and *how* it is repeated. Figure 6 shows two types of orientation organization for a multiplicity: vertical and horizontal. Being organized vertically, participating elements are parallel which means that they are all connected to the same elements. On the other hand, being organized horizontally, participating elements are inter-connected as in the case of the pipeline architectural pattern [5].

Each element in the meta-model can be associated with a *role*. A role specifies properties that a model element must have if it is to be part of a pattern solution model [8]. To characterize a role, we use architectural *constraints*. A constraint made to a role on an element helps to make sure that the element participating in a pattern has the aimed characteristics. Constraints are represented in our approach in form of OCL (Object Constraint Language) [17] rules.

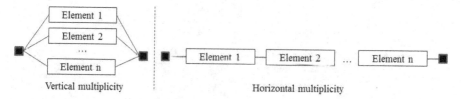

Vertical multiplicity   Horizontal multiplicity

Fig. 6. Orientation organization of generic elements

Similar to [10,3,19], in our language two types of merging operator are supported: stringing and overlapping as shown in Figure 7. A stringing operation means a connector is added to the pattern model to connect one component from one pattern to another component from the other pattern. If an overlapping operation involves two elements, it means that two involving elements should be merged to a completely new element. Otherwise, if an overlapping operation involves a composite element and a pattern, it means that the latter should be included inside the former. In both cases of merging, the participating elements are respectively determined through two references *source* and *target*.

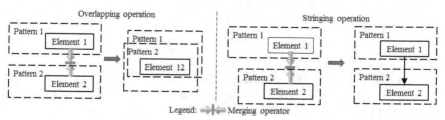

Fig. 7. Two types of merging operation

Pattern can contain all concepts described above and most importantly, it inherits from *Element* which allows a composite element to contain it. This special feature helps our language to include an entire pattern into an element while constructing a pattern. In other words, hierarchical patterns are supported.

4.2   Pattern Definition through an Example

For the purpose of illustration, our pattern definition language will be used to model an example about the pattern for data exploration and visualization as in the Vistrails application's architecture [4]. More specifically, this model represents the first step of the pattern definition process. As shown in Figure 8, this pattern model consists of three main sub-patterns: *Pipes and Filters*, *Client-Server* and *Repository*, all connected together through merging operators. Among these three patterns, the *Repository* pattern is a hierarchical one whose the component of the same name includes the *Layers* pattern.

To explain how the pattern concepts are realized, we go into details for the *Pipes and Filters* pattern. On the upper left corner of Figure 8, we can observe that the *Pipes and Filters* pattern is constructed with the emphasis on the following

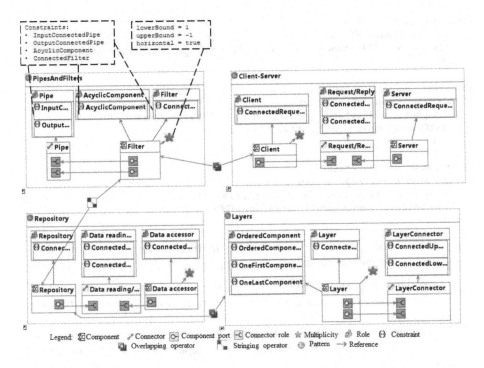

Fig. 8. Example of pattern model

elements: the component *Filter* specified with two roles *Filter* and *AcyclicComponent*, the connector *Pipe* specified with the role *Pipe*. The connector *Pipe* is not assigned with any multiplicity. Otherwise, the component *Filter* is assigned with a multiplicity since it represents many possible filters inter-connected by Pipe connectors. Furthermore, its horizontal multiplicity[1] indicates that there may be many instances of Filters and they must be horizontally connected. The role *Filter* is characterized by the *ConnectedFilter* constraint. To be more specific, it stipulates that a filter cannot stand alone, there must be at least one pipe connected to a filter. Similarly, the constraint *AcyclicComponent* characterizing the role *AcyclicComponent* stipulates that among filters, we cannot form a cycle. Finally, the two constraints *InputConnectedPipe* and *OutputConnectedPipe* say that for a given pipe, there must be a filter as input and a filter as output. The above constraints are presented as OCL invariants as follows:

```
invariant AcyclicComponent:
if role->includes('AcyclicComponent') then
    Component.allInstances()->forAll(role = 'AcyclicComponent' implies not
    self.canFormCycle())
    endif;
```

---

[1] Upperbound = -1 indicates that there's no limited upper threshold for a multiplicity.

```
invariant ConnectedFilter:
if role->includes('Filter') then
    Connector.allInstances()->exists(role = 'Pipe' and isConnected(self))
  endif;

invariant InputConnectedPipe:
if role->includes('Pipe') then
    Component.allInstances()->exists(role = 'Filter' and
    getOutputConnectors().contains(self))
  endif;

invariant OutputConnectedPipe:
if role->includes('Pipe') then
    Component.allInstances()->exists(role = 'Filter'
    and getInputConnectors().contains(self))
  endif;
```

Merging operators are used to link participating patterns together. More specifically, in our pattern model (see Figure 8), three merging operators are used:

- An overlapping operator whose source is the *Filter* component in the *Pipes and Filters* pattern and target is the *Client* component in the *Client-Server* pattern.
- A stringing operator whose source is the *Filter* component in the *Pipes and Filters* pattern and target is the *Repository* component in the *Repository* pattern.
- An overlapping operator whose source is the *Repository* component in the *Repository* pattern and target is the Layers pattern.

These three operators are used as elements of the pattern language and stored along with the other elements.

This example has shown the ability of using our language to describe complex patterns which are combined from different patterns by leveraging merging operators.

5   Pattern Refinement

After being described as the composition of constituent patterns through merging operators, the pattern model will be refined. We consider this second step in the pattern definition process as a model transformation from a pattern model where merging operators are explicitly presented to a pattern model where merging operators are concretized. While realizing this transformation, three important issues need to be taken into account: how to concretize a stringing operator, how to concretize an overlapping operator and how to handle nested patterns.

5.1   Stringing Operator Transformation

Among structural elements in the pattern language, except for components which can be linked by stringing operators, there is no interest to link together other elements like connectors, component ports or connector roles. That is the reason

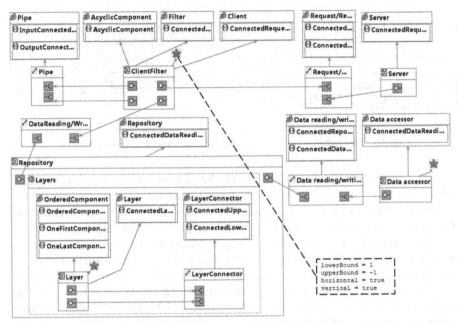

Fig. 9. The refined pattern model

why a stringing operator can only be transformed into a new *connector* to link source component and target component. New component ports are also added to the source component and the target component and attached to new connector roles in the newly created connector. As shown in Figure 9, the stringing operator described in the previous step is now transformed to the connector *DataReading/WritingPipe*. This new connector contains two connector roles, one attached to a component port in the *ClientFilter* component and the other attached to a component port in the *Repository* component.

5.2   Overlapping Operator Transformation

The result of the transformation for an overlapping operator is a new element which carries all the characteristics of the source element and the target element. For composite elements, the composition begins with the fusion of all internal elements. As we can see from Figure 9, the overlapping operator described in the previous step is concretized by the component *ClientFilter*. This component contains all component ports from the source element which is a *Filter* and the target element which is a *Client*. Furthermore, via these component ports, the link from the component to two connectors *Pipe* and *Request/Reply* is also preserved.

The overlapped element plays all the roles of the source element and the target element. Indeed, the *ClientFilter* plays three roles at once: *AcyclicComponent*, *Filter* since it participates as a *Filter* in the *Pipes and Filters* pattern and finally, *Client* since it participates as a *Client* in the *Client-Server* pattern.

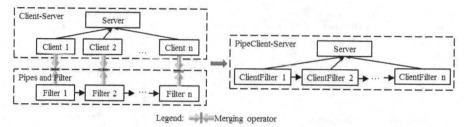

Fig. 10. The merged pattern of Client-Server and Pipes and Filters

The multiplicity is merged as follows: The lower bound of the merged element's multiplicity is the maximum between the lower bound of the source element's multiplicity and the lower bound of the target element's multiplicity. On the contrary, the upper bound of the merged element's multiplicity is the minimum between the upper bound of the source element's multiplicity and the upper bound of the target element's multiplicity. If the source elements multiplicity or the target elements multiplicity is vertical or horizontal then merged elements multiplicity is also vertical or horizontal. In our pattern model (Figure 9), the multiplicity of the merged component *ClientFilter* is both vertical and horizontal since its source component *Client* is vertical and its target component *Filter* is horizontal as illustrated in Figure 10.

In the case of a chain of consecutive overlapping operators in which one continues another, we use a special algorithm which is sketched in Figure 11. Let's say we have n random elements linked together by (n-1) overlapping operators. The algorithm consists of n-1 steps. In the first step, the overlapping operator merges *Element 1* and *Element 2* to create *Element 12*. Next, *Element 2* is replaced by *Element 12*. In the second step, the overlapping operator merges the new *Element 12* and *Element 3* to create *Element 123*. Similarly, *Element 3* is then replaced by *Element 123*. The algorithm continues so on until the $(n-1)$-th step when all elements are merged into the *Element 123..n*. An important remark in this algorithm is that thanks to the replacement mechanism, an element can reflect the merging operation in which it participates. Thus, the merging operation is propagated to every element participating in the merging chain.

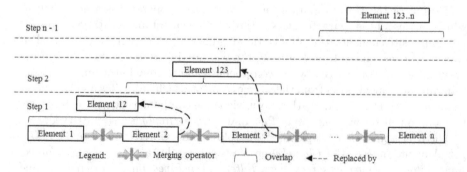

Fig. 11. The algorithm in case of multiple overlapping operators

5.3   Nested Pattern Transformation

If a pattern participates in a merging operation, all of its internal elements will be added in the refined pattern while the pattern itself will not be transformed. As shown in Figure 9, all the three patterns *Pipes and Filters*, *Client-Server* and *Repository* disappear leaving their internal elements in the refined pattern. Otherwise, if a pattern does not participate in any merging operation, a refinement procedure (which is actually a recursive procedure) will be applied to the pattern. Since the *Layers* pattern does not contain any merging operators, the refinement procedure just simply keeps all its internal elements.

6   Implementation Information

To verify the feasibility of our approach, we developed the *COMLAN* tool which allows a graphical use of the COMLAN pattern description language. With the *COMLAN* tool we aim to make concrete the aforementioned concepts. Thus, this tool provides the following functionalities:

1. Create architectural patterns
2. Compose patterns using merging operators
3. Refine the composed pattern

COMLAN is developed based on EMF (Eclipse Modelling Framework)[2]. We choose EMF to realize our tool since we leverage MDA, where models are basic building units, to develop our approach. The tool consists of two Eclipse plug-ins built on existing Eclipse technologies:

- *Pattern creation plug-in* uses EMF and GMF (Graphical Modeling Framework)[3] modeling support in order to allow architects to define *Pattern models* graphically. More specifically, the editor allows to design constituent patterns and compose them using two types of merging operators: stringing and overlapping. Furthermore, hierarchical pattern description is also supported. Besides, the editor allows the automatic propagation of changes in the constituent patterns to the already composed patterns. This editor is based on the *COMLAN Meta-Model* (see figure 5).
- *Pattern refinement plug-in* uses *Kermeta* [15] to implement rules transforming composed pattern model to refined pattern model. This functionality allows the architect to obtain a pattern with all the merging operators concretized, ready to be instantiated in the architectural model.

We applied the *COMLAN* tool to model the pattern of Vistrails's architecture [4]. For a complete tutorial and a video about this tool and the applied example, the reader is invited to visit the following website: http://www-irisa.univ-ubs.fr/ARCHWARE/software/COMLAN/

---

[2] More details about EMF are accessible at: http://www.eclipse.org/modeling/emf/"

[3] More details about GMF are accessible at: http://www.eclipse.org/modeling/gmp/"

7   Related Work

Our work concerns three areas of related work: i) architectural pattern description language, ii) pattern composition, iii) hierarchical pattern composition. In the following we will discuss work related to these three aspects.

7.1   Architectural Pattern Description Language

In the literature there have been some efforts to model architectural patterns and their properties. For instance, there are works focusing on the use of formal approach to specify patterns. In the Wright ADL [1], the authors tend to provide a pattern-oriented architectural design environment where patterns are formally described. In [18], the authors use an ontological approach for architectural pattern modeling based on a description logic language. As opposed to these domain specific languages,in [14] the authors propose to use general purpose languages such as UML to model architectural patterns. Applying a role-based pattern modeling approach, our language is designed to focus specifically on software architectural patterns. However, the genericness of the language is also assured since the pattern concepts used are those synthesized from many different ADLs.

7.2   Pattern Composition

There are mainly two branches of work on the composition of patterns. The first including [10,3,19] proposes to combine patterns at the pattern level which means that patterns are composed before being initialized in the architectural model. On the contrary, the second including [7] proposes to compose pattern at instance level where an architectural entity is allowed to belong to different patterns. However, all of these approaches consider the composition as transient operation which leads to the problems we pointed out in previous sections. By proposing to give composition operators first-class status, our approach helps to prevent these shortcomings. In another work [12], the authors propose a UML profile to attach pattern-related information on merged elements in composed patterns. With this approach, although one can trace back the constituent pattern in which an element participates, a composition view showing how the original pattern is composed is still missing. Our proposal should also be compared with works on architectural constraint composition such as [21]. In this work, a pattern can be generally imposed by a constraint and complex patterns can be expressed through the composition of constraints. With our approach we raise the level of abstraction by using models to describe architectural patterns. Thus, not only the conformance of architectural patterns is assured but the application of patterns is also encouraged.

7.3   Hierarchical Pattern Composition

In [22], the authors propose to use a number of architectural primitives to model architectural patterns. Through the stereotype extension mechanism of UML, one can define primitives (which is equivalent to sub-patterns in our approach) to design a specific element of a pattern. However, the fact that pattern itself is not considered as an element in the pattern construction totally prevents its reusability. In our proposed language, pattern is treated as first-class status which allows not only the modeling of primitives as patterns but also the reusability of patterns to construct more coarse-grained patterns.

8 Conclusion

Through this paper we proposed a language for describing patterns and compose them to build more complex patterns. This language has the particularity to make explicit the pattern composition operators and the constituent patterns. Making these elements explicit allows us to trace back constituent patterns in case of changes and in this way allow the propagation of changes to the container pattern.

The use of the MDA approach in our process of building patterns allowed us to separate the two forms of a pattern: i) its model form which facilitates its construction and its modification, because all of its aspects are explicit; ii) Its operational form which leaves visible only elements that are relevant to its integration into the architecture. This facilitates its use by architects.

We believe that the use of patterns, when building architectures, has a twofold interest: the use of proven solutions to recurring problems, but also insure part of the documentation on the architectural choices. In one of our previous papers [20] we proposed a solution based on the use of patterns to handle the latter issue.

Our pattern description language covers only structural aspects of architectures. Thus, patterns that are based on behavioural aspects of an architecture can not be described using our language. One of our future work is to extend our pattern description language to cover the behavioural aspect of architectures. To validate this extension to behavioural aspects, we plan to use the πADL architecture description language. This is motivated by the fact that some members of our team have participated in its elaboration and thus their experience will be useful.

References

1. Allen, R.: A Formal Approach to Software Architecture. PhD thesis, Carnegie Mellon, School of Computer Science (1997)
2. Avgeriou, P., Zdun, U.: Architectural patterns revisited a pattern language. In: 10th European Conference on Pattern Languages of Programs (EuroPlop 2005), Irsee, pp. 1–39 (2005)
3. Bayley, I., Zhu, H.: On the composition of design patterns. In: Proceedings of the Eighth International Conference on Quality Software, pp. 27–36. IEEE Computer Society (2008)
4. Brown, A., Wilson, G.: The Architecture of Open Source Applications. Lulu.com (2011)
5. Buschmann, F., Meunier, R., Rohnert, H., Sommerlad, P., Stal, M.: Pattern-Oriented Software Architecture: a system of patterns. John Wiley & Sons, Inc. (1996)

6. Clements, P., Bachmann, F., Bass, L., Garlan, D., Ivers, J., Little, R., Merson, P., Nord, R., Stafford, J.: Documenting Software Architectures: Views and Beyond, 2nd edn. Addison-Wesley Professional (2010)
7. Deiters, C., Rausch, A.: A constructive approach to compositional architecture design. In: Crnkovic, I., Gruhn, V., Book, M. (eds.) ECSA 2011. LNCS, vol. 6903, pp. 75–82. Springer, Heidelberg (2011)
8. France, R.B., Kim, D.K., Ghosh, S., Song, E.: A uml-based pattern specification technique. IEEE Transactions on Software Engineering, 193–206 (2004)
9. Garlan, D., Allen, R., Ockerbloom, J.: Exploiting style in architectural design environments. In: Proceedings of the 2nd ACM SIGSOFT Symposium on Foundations of Software Engineering, pp. 175–188. ACM (1994)
10. Hammouda, I., Koskimies, K.: An approach for structural pattern composition. In: Lumpe, M., Vanderperren, W. (eds.) SC 2007. LNCS, vol. 4829, pp. 252–265. Springer, Heidelberg (2007)
11. ISO/IEC/IEEE 42010:2011. Systems and Software Engineering - Architecture Description. ISO, Geneva, Switzerland (2011)
12. Jing, D., Sheng, Y., Kang, Z.: Visualizing design patterns in their applications and compositions. IEEE Transactions on Software Engineering, 433–453 (2007)
13. Kim, J.S., Garlan, D.: Analyzing architectural styles. J. Syst. Softw., 1216–1235 (2010)
14. Medvidovic, N., Rosenblum, D.S., Redmiles, D.F., Robbins, J.E.: Modeling software architectures in the unified modeling language. ACM Trans. Softw. Eng. Methodol., 2–57 (2002)
15. Muller, P.-A., Fleurey, F., Jézéquel, J.-M.: Weaving executability into object-oriented meta-languages. In: Briand, L.C., Williams, C. (eds.) MoDELS 2005. LNCS, vol. 3713, pp. 264–278. Springer, Heidelberg (2005)
16. O.M.G. Model-driven architecture, http://wwww.omg.org/mda
17. OMG. Object Constraint Language, OCL Version 2.0, formal/2006-05-01. Technical report, OMG (2006)
18. Pahl, C., Giesecke, S., Hasselbring, W.: Ontology-based modelling of architectural styles. Inf. Softw. Technol., 1739–1749 (2009)
19. Sabatucci, L., Garcia, A., Cacho, N., Cossentino, M., Gaglio, S.: Conquering fine-grained blends of design patterns. In: Mei, H. (ed.) ICSR 2008. LNCS, vol. 5030, pp. 294–305. Springer, Heidelberg (2008)
20. That, M.T.T., Sadou, S., Oquendo, F.: Using architectural patterns to define architectural decisions. In: 2012 Joint Working IEEE/IFIP Conference on Software Architecture (WICSA) and European Conference on Software Architecture (ECSA), pp. 196–200 (2012)
21. Tibermacine, C., Sadou, S., Dony, C., Fabresse, L.: Component-based specification of software architecture constraints. In: Proceedings of the 14th International ACM Sigsoft Symposium on Component Based Software Engineering, pp. 31–40. ACM (2011)
22. Zdun, U., Avgeriou, P.: A catalog of architectural primitives for modeling architectural patterns. Inf. Softw. Technol., 1003–1034 (2008)

Software Reference Architectures - Exploring Their Usage and Design in Practice

Samuil Angelov[1], Jos Trienekens[2], and Rob Kusters[3]

[1] Software Engineering Team, Fontys University of Applied Sciences,
Eindhoven, The Netherlands
s.angelov@fontys.nl
[2] Information Systems Group, School of Industrial Engineering,
Eindhoven University of Technology, Eindhoven, The Netherlands
j.j.m.trienekens@tue.nl
[3] Management Science Faculty, Open University, Heerlen, The Netherlands
rob.kusters@ou.nl

Abstract. Software reference architectures have been around for quite some years. They have been designed and used with varying success. We have conducted an exploratory survey among software architects and developers to establish the extent to which SRA have penetrated among practitioners and to identify the benefits and problems practitioners face when using and designing SRA. In this article, we present our findings.

Keywords: Reference architecture, software architecture, survey.

1 Introduction

Software reference architectures (SRA) have become one of the ways to address problems in managing complexity, size, and scope of architectures, and in managing the dynamics of the environment in which systems are designed [1]. While comprehensive methods have been defined for the design, evaluation, and application of concrete software architectures, SRA have received relatively less attention in literature [2], [3]. The reasons for this can be probably traced in an assumption that theory on software architectures is directly applicable to SRA.

In our practice, we have faced difficulties in working with SRA [4], [5]. Similar observations inspired several, recent, and with still preliminary results, research efforts [6], [7]. This triggered our interest in finding out what practitioners think of SRA. Do they design and use SRA? Do they benefit from them? Do they face problems in using them? Currently, literature does not provide insights into the status of SRA in the software community. Finding on the use of SRA are discussed in [8], but those are from a local and domain specific nature.

To answer our questions and establish an initial picture for the state of the practice of SRA, we have embarked on conducting an exploratory, cross-sectional, web-based survey on SRA, following the guidelines for data collection in software engineering disciplines discussed in [9-14]. In our survey, we targeted the following objectives:

K. Drira (Ed.): ECSA 2013, LNCS 7957, pp. 17–24, 2013.
© Springer-Verlag Berlin Heidelberg 2013

1. *Building awareness in the community for the global status of SRA.*
2. *Building awareness for differences (or lack of such) in existing practices with SRA on the basis of geographical, experience, etc. specifics.*
3. *Building awareness for problems that practitioners experience and benefits they obtain in their work with SRA.*

In this paper, we present the findings from the survey. We explain our survey methodology in Section 2. In Sections 3, 4, 5, and 6 we present the results from the survey.

2   Survey Methodology, Setup, and Execution

2.1   Data Collection, Target Population, and Sampling

A survey provides a "snapshot of the situation to capture the current status" [12]. Furthermore, "explorative surveys are used as a pre-study to a more thorough investigation to assure that important issues are not foreseen … the information is gathered and analyzed, and the results are used to improve the full investigation" [12]. This fully matched with our goals of investigating the trends and establishing the status of SRA. We have opted for a web-survey as a data collection method as it allows the collection of standardized data from a large, remotely-located population, which can be used for the establishment of the status and trends of SRA. An extensive discussion on the advantages and disadvantages of on-line surveys is provided in [13].

The target population was defined to be software architects and developers as these roles are the major stakeholder roles related to SRA. We aimed at respondents from two tiers of countries as defined in [15], i.e., Tier 1 representing major software exporting nations (e.g., USA, Germany, The Netherlands) and Tier 2 formed by emerging software exporting nations (e.g., Eastern European countries, developed Latin American countries). Our sampling approach was quota sampling (defined by our tier classification) augmented by convenience and snowball sampling [11].

2.2   Survey Design and Execution

The questions in our survey were designed on the bases of existing literature on SRA, e.g., [1, 4, 16]. We have grouped the questions in order to present to the respondents a clear survey structure. Group 1 questions collected information on the respondents' background and context. Group 2 questions contained questions determining the interpretation of the respondents for the term "software reference architecture". Group 3 questions investigated the experience of the respondents with usage of SRA, the benefits that they have obtained, and the problems that they have faced when using them. Group 4, respectively, investigated the design of SRA and the problems accompanying the design process. The latter two groups represented the core of the survey. Finally, we have added in Group 5 questions where the respondents had an opportunity to provide their opinions and thoughts on SRA. After addressing the feedback from four pilot respondents, we ended with 32 questions distributed in the five groups.

For the distribution of the survey, we have used contacts from our network in combination with posting the survey to professional forums. We have received in total 114 responses. The major set of reactions was received through personal contacts and from relatively small but active, professional LinkedIn groups. Thus, the response rate from the directly targeted population was high. The response rate from the indirectly targeted population was poor. Although a low response rate "affects the representativeness of the sample" [9], "if the objective is to understand trends, then low response rates may be fine. The homogeneity of the population, and the sampling technique used also affect the extent to which one can generalize the results of surveys" [9]. As we discuss in Section 3, the population was relatively homogeneous and our goal was indeed understanding trends, rather than establishing precise percentages.

3   Results from the Introductory Questions (Groups 1 and 2)

From the total number of responses, we have filtered out the responses that did not fit in our target population. This resulted in 90 valid responses[1]. We received 61 responses from 11 countries from Tier 1 (Netherlands dominating the set of responses) and 29 responses from 5 countries from Tier 2 (dominated by Bulgaria and Chile) giving a reasonable response from each tier. The size of the companies of the respondents were equally distributed among large (>500 employees), medium (50-500), and small (<50). Respondents from Tier 1 were predominantly from larger organizations and respondents from Tier 2 from smaller organizations (which is a characteristic of the tiers). The major group of respondents were employed by a "Software and services" organization (59%), followed by "Financials" (13%), and other. The respondents were relatively experienced with architectures, with a mean value of 10 years of experience. On the basis of the answers of the respondents for their occupation, we have classified the respondents into: 70 architects and 20 developers.

We have used the definition provided by Wikipedia (alternative definitions are discussed in [16]) and asked whether the respondents agree with it: *"A reference software architecture is a software architecture where the structures and respective elements and relations provide templates for concrete architectures in a particular domain or in a family of software systems."* Out of the 90 respondents, 66 (73%) felt experienced with the term and agreed with the definition (of which 8 had minor remarks), 17 agreed with the definition, but indicated that to them the term was not too clear before reading the definition, 7 indicated that they were not aware of the term SRA. To improve the survey representativeness, the latter respondents were filtered out from the rest of the survey results. The high percentage of respondents experienced with the term indicates the deep penetration of the term in the architecting community. Notably, 5 of the 7 respondents unaware of the term SRA had less than 5 years of experience.

Six more respondents from the target population (but excluded from subsequent percentage calculations) agreed also with the definition. However, at a later, control

---

[1] Available at `https://sites.google.com/site/samuilangelov/ECSAvalid.xls`

question, these six respondents gave examples for SRA that did not fit in the definition, referring to frameworks, methods, modelling techniques (Zachman, TOGAF, ARIS, COBIT, ITIL). We concluded that although professionals tend to agree around a definition on SRA, the high abstraction of the definition, and the numerous related terms lead to differences in the interpretation of the term.

4   Results from the Questions on Usage of SRA (Group 3)

Propagation of SRA. Out of the 61 respondents who have answered the questions on the usage of SRA, 5 have indicated to have never used a SRA in their career (8%). All other respondents have used a SRA in their work at least 1-3 times (33%), 3-10 times (31%), and more than 10 times (28%). This leads us to conclude that SRA have become a popular tool used in the design of software architectures.

Scope and Origin of Used SRA. SRA with different scopes are used in practice with a preponderance of SRA defined specifically for the organization of the respondent (49%) or defined for a complete domain (43%). Intriguingly, professionals make use predominantly of SRA defined by their own organization (63%), followed by reference architectures defined by standardization (37%), IT-consultancy (27%), consortium (20%), software house (18%), or governmental organization (16%). The least used SRA are those defined from research organizations (4%). These results imply:

- Professionals have mostly used SRA defined for their own organization and by their own organization. However, some of these SRA were defined by the organization to be applied at a wider scope, e.g., the complete domain.
- Research organizations have a minimal contribution to the design of used SRA.

Goals When Using SRA and Benefits Obtained. Based on literature, we have defined a set of benefits introduced by reference architectures and asked the respondents to select those sought by them when using SRA and those that they have actually obtained from using SRA. In addition to our list of possible benefits (see Table 1), respondents have indicated also "education and training", "risk reduction", and "assessment tool". Twelve respondents indicated that they are not currently using a SRA. Since we preferred recent and therefore more relevant experiences for this question, these respondents were cut from the sample, leaving 49 respondents.

A limited number (16%) of the respondents saw little or no benefits of the usage of reference architectures. For a number of aims (indicated as "n/a" in Table 1), we considered that achieving them is a direct consequence from the actual usage of the SRA. The question for the benefit achieved was therefore not asked in these cases. In all measured aims, the actual benefits scored substantially lower than those initially expected - the difference (reduction) is fairly stable at 20%. We have also surveyed the overall estimation on the improvement of the quality of the architectures and architecting processes when using a SRA - 43% of respondents saw improvements in the architecture quality and 37% in the architecting process. In only 29% of the cases, do SRA improve both the architecture quality and process – a rather low result given the fact that following best practices is leading when implementing SRA.

Table 1. Sought and actual benefits from the usage of SRA (percentages reflect the % of respondents who have mentioned a particular reason)

Goals when using SRA	Benefit sought	Benefit achieved
To follow best practices	78%	n/a
To speed up design work	61%	35%
To establish a common architecture strategy/vision	61%	41%
To ensure reusability	57%	37%
To ensure interoperability with other systems	55%	37%
To structure work (follow guidelines)	47%	n/a
To comply with a standard	45%	n/a
To improve communication in the organization	45%	22%
To decrease costs	31%	10%
To get inspiration	18%	n/a
To make use of the most novel design solutions	12%	n/a
For political reasons (externally imposed)	10%	n/a

Problems with Using SRA. Out of 56 responders to this question, 9 respondents (16%) did not experience any problems with the usage of reference architecture (all of them from Tier 1 countries, and 8 of them from a large organization) and 11 (from both Tiers) experienced only minor problems (20%). The major problems faced by the respondents were that SRA are often too abstract (34%), the lack of common interpretation of the term SRA (34%), bad documentation of SRA (23%), poor quality of SRA (16%), and being too specific/limiting (14%). With respect to the documentation, out of the 13 respondents who have indicated problems with it, 69% missed guidelines for the application of the SRA, 62% missed one or more viewpoints in the documentation, 54% missed the quality attributes aimed at by the SRA, 39% had difficulties with interpreting SRA, 23% saw the notation used as improper, 15% had problems with the extensive volume of the documentation of SRA and 7% with the incompleteness of the documentation. Last but not least, 7% (4 respondents) indicated other problems in free text. Remarkably, they had a common core: inability to apply the SRA due to the SRA complexity and/or reluctance by the stakeholders due to lack of clear benefits and therefore of motivation. While being a low percentage, this common response has been given in free text and therefore raises a question for its relevance to other respondents. This is further strengthened by the conclusions drawn in [8]. In conclusions, we infer that complexity, abstraction, documentation of SRA, and reluctance of stakeholders to consider SRA due to lack of clear benefits are problems when applying SRA. Also, the observation made earlier on the lack of common interpretation of the SRA concept in the domain receives a confirmation.

5   Results from the Questions on Design of SRA (Group 4)

Number of SRA Designed. Many practitioners declared that they have designed SRA - 35 out of the 53 respondents to this group of questions (32 of them were in an architect role). Most respondents have designed 1-2 architectures (30%) but also 3-5 architectures collected a substantial number of votes (23%).

Scope and Origin of SRA Designs. The respondents have designed SRA for their own organization (58%), a specific external organization (32%), a set of external organizations (29%), and a complete domain (16%).

Goals When Designing SRA. The stated goals for the design of reference architectures are manifold (see Table 2). The table shows a definite agreement on many of the goals, with 7 of them scoring more than 50%, and with 'Providing best practices' peaking at 71%. An important misalignment between designing SRA and using them is "To provide a high quality design solution for an innovative application". In other words, although many designers aim at it, innovation is not really appreciated by stakeholders embarking on the application of SRA. "Improving communications" and "decreasing costs" stand out as even more distant if we compare aims of designers with the actual benefits obtained from using SRA.

Table 2. Goals when designing SRA versus goals when using SRA (based on 31 respondents that have recently used and designed a SRA)

Goals when designing SRA	When designing SRA	When using SRA
To provide best practices	71%	77%
To promote reusability	58%	55%
To promote interoperability	58%	55%
To set up a common architecture strategy/vision	58%	65%
To improve communications	58%	55%
To set up a standard	52%	55%
To structure the work of designers	52%	45%
To speed up design work	48%	61%
To provide a high quality design for an innovative application	42%	7%
To decrease costs	36%	23%
To provide an inspiration tool to designers	13%	16%
For political reasons (externally imposed)	13%	10%

Usage of Designs. About 40% of the respondents could not estimate the usage of the SRA they have designed and 13% were not aware of any usage of some of the SRA they have designed. This disconnection prevents designers from getting feedback on their designs and on maintaining and improving the architectures.

Problems with Design SRA. The answers of the 35 respondents to this question depict a multitude of problems when designing SRA (Figure 1). Problems with stakeholders' involvement led in the responses. They are followed by the lack of suitable

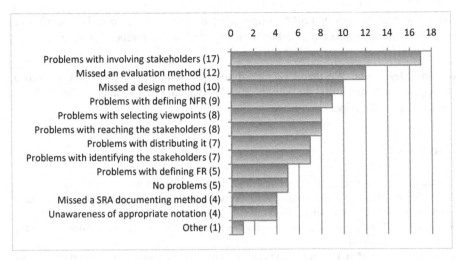

Fig. 1. Problems encountered during the design of SRA

methods for the design and evaluation of reference architectures. Only 14% did not report on experiencing problems. Figure 1 leads to the conclusion that professionals face multiple challenges during the design of SRA and existing theory and practices are not sufficient to facilitate their work.

6   Results from Questions on Status and Future (Group 5)

Predominantly, the respondents think that more and more SRA are being designed (51% of the respondents to this question, where 17% expressed the counter opinion). Similarly, 55% of the respondents in the last group of questions expect that the role of SRA will become more important in the future and only 13% expect that it will become less important. The majority of the respondents indicated that they are interested in the outcomes of the survey and that they are ready to be approached for clarification questions. From this, we conclude that there is an interest in the community in SRA and practitioners believe that SRA may even further grow in their importance.

7   Concluding Remarks

The survey improves the awareness in the community on state of the practice of SRA and the strengths and weaknesses of SRA. It indicates that SRA are widely recognized and used by practitioners but that there is still a lack of clear and commonly accepted definition of SRA which undermines progress in the field. The results delineate the leading benefits sought and obtained when using SRA as well as the problems encountered during the design and usage SRA. Some of the problems observed in the results are the misalignment between SRA design goals, usage goals, and eventual benefits obtained and the underperformance of SRA in terms of architecture quality and documentation. Stakeholder involvement and lack of design and evaluation methods lead in the reported SRA design problems. No statistically valid specifics of the clusters in our population could be derived based on the number of responses.

Acknowledgements. We thank D. Greefhorst, M. Schuur, R. Seguel, M. Comuzzi for helping in distributing the survey and W. van der Beek, and R. Hilliard for commenting on the paper.

References

1. Muller, G.: A Reference Architecture Primer. Repport: Gaudi Project (2008)
2. Taylor, R., Medvidovic, N., Dashofy, E.: Software Architecture: Foundations, Theory, and Practice. Wiley, John & Sons (2009)
3. Bass, L., Clements, P., Kazman, R.: Software Architecture in Practice. Addison-Wesley Professional (2003)
4. Angelov, S., Grefen, P.: An E-contracting Reference Architecture. The Journal of Systems and Software 81(11), 1816–1844 (2008)
5. Angelov, S., Trienekens, J.J.M., Grefen, P.: Towards a Method for the Evaluation of Reference Architectures: Experiences from a Case. In: Morrison, R., Balasubramaniam, D., Falkner, K. (eds.) ECSA 2008. LNCS, vol. 5292, pp. 225–240. Springer, Heidelberg (2008)
6. Galster, M., Avgeriou, P.: Empirically-grounded Reference Architectures: A Proposal. In: QoSA+ISARCS 2011, Boulder, Colorado, USA, June 20-24. ACM (2011)
7. Martínez-Fernández, S., Ayala, C., Franch, X.: A Reuse-Based Economic Model for Software Reference Architectures. Repport: ESSI-TR-12-6, Departament d'Enginyeria de Serveis i Sistemes d'Informació, Barcelona, Spain (2012)
8. Galster, M., Avgeriou, P., Tofan, D.: Constraints for the Design of Variability-Intensive Service-Oriented Reference Architectures – An Industrial Case Study. Information and Software Technology 55(2), 428–441 (2013)
9. Shull, F., Singer, J., Sjøberg, D.: Guide to Advanced Empirical Software Engineering. Springer (2007)
10. Fink, A.: The Survey Handbook, 2nd edn. Sage Publications, Inc. (2002)
11. Pfleeger S., Kitchenham, B.: Principles of Survey Research, parts 1-6. ACM Sigsoft, Software Engineering Notes 26(6), 16–18, 27(1), 18–20, 27(2), 20–24, 27(3), 20–23, 27(5), 17–20, 28(2), 24–27 (2001-2003)
12. Wohlin, C., Runeson, P., Höst, M., Ohlsson, M.C., Regnell, B., Wesslén, A.: Experimentation in Software Engineering. Springer (2012)
13. Punter, T., Ciolkowski, M., Freimut, B., John, I.: Conducting On-Line Surveys in Software Engineering. In: Proceedings on the International Symposium on Empirical Software Engineering 2003, pp. 80–88 (2003)
14. Pfleeger, S.: Experimental Design and Analysis in Software Engineering, parts 1-5. ACM Sigsoft, Software Engineering Notes 19(4), 16–20, 20(1), 22–26, 20(2), 14–16, 20(3), 13–15, 20(5), 14–17 (1995)
15. Carmel, E.: Taxonomy of New Software Exporting Nations. The Electronic Journal on Information Systems in Developing Countries 13(2), 1–6 (2003)
16. Angelov, S., Grefen, P., Greefhorst, D.: A Framework for Analysis and Design of Software Reference Architectures. Information and Software Technology 54(4), 417–431 (2012)

Concurrent Object-Oriented Development with Behavioral Design Patterns

Benjamin Morandi[1], Scott West[1], Sebastian Nanz[1], and Hassan Gomaa[2]

[1] ETH Zurich, Switzerland
`firstname.lastname@inf.ethz.ch`
[2] George Mason University, USA
`hgomaa@gmu.edu`

Abstract. Architectural modeling using the Unified Modeling Language (UML) can support the development of concurrent applications, but the problem of mapping the model to a concurrent implementation remains. This paper defines a scheme to map concurrent UML designs to a concurrent object-oriented program. Using the COMET method for the architectural design of concurrent object-oriented systems, each component and connector is annotated with a stereotype indicating its behavioral design pattern. For each of these patterns, a reference implementation is provided using SCOOP, a concurrent object-oriented programming model. Given the strong execution guarantees of the SCOOP model, which is free of data races by construction, this development method eliminates a source of intricate concurrent programming errors.

1 Introduction

Writing concurrent applications is challenging because of the complexity of concurrent software architectures and the hazards associated with concurrent programming, such as data races. For object-oriented applications, support for the architectural design of concurrent software is fortunately available. Standard notations, such as the Unified Modeling Language (UML), can provide such support when used with a method for developing concurrent applications, such as COMET [1]. The remaining difficulty is the mapping of the concurrent object-oriented model to an implementation that avoids common concurrency pitfalls.

This paper describes a development method that starts with a concurrent UML design, annotated with behavioral stereotypes, and maps the design systematically to an implementation that is guaranteed to be data-race free. Each component and connector in the UML model is given a behavioral role, based on COMET. For each of COMET's component and connector types, this paper defines a mapping to an implementation in SCOOP (Simple Concurrent Object-Oriented Programming) [2,3], a concurrent object-oriented programming model. Choosing this model over others simplifies concurrent reasoning [4] and offers strong execution guarantees: by construction, the model is free of data races [2]; also, a mechanism for deadlock avoidance is available [5]. To evaluate the approach, the development process is applied to a case study of an ATM system that covers all important connector and component patterns.

K. Drira (Ed.): ECSA 2013, LNCS 7957, pp. 25–32, 2013.

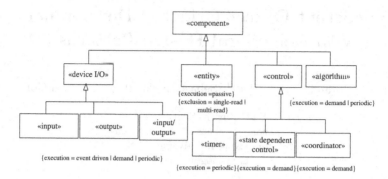

Fig. 1. Classification of components using stereotypes

A companion technical report [6] contains additional material. The remainder of the paper is structured as follows. Section 2 describes behavioral design patterns of the COMET method in UML. The implementation of the design patterns is described in Section 3. Section 4 presents the case study. Section 5 presents a survey of related work, and Section 6 draws conclusions.

2   Behavioral Design Patterns

Behavioral design patterns used by the COMET method [1, 7] address design issues in concurrent and distributed applications. There are two main categories: component patterns and connector patterns.

Component Patterns. Component patterns address concurrent component design. Each component is depicted from two different perspectives, its role in the application and the behavioral nature of its concurrency. Models of the design use UML stereotypes to depict the decisions made by the designer. The stereotype depicts the component's role criterion, which describes the component's function in the application such as «I/O» or «control». A UML constraint is used to describe the type of concurrency of the component, which is based on how the component is activated. For example, a concurrent «I/O» component could be activated by an external event or a periodic event, whereas an «entity» component is passive and access to it is mutually exclusive or by means of multiple readers and writers. Components are categorized using the component stereotype classification hierarchy in Figure 1. Separate stereotypes can be used to depict the component role and the type of concurrency.

Connector Patterns. Connector patterns describe the different types of message communication between the concurrent components. In both distributed and non-distributed applications, connector patterns include asynchronous communication and synchronous communication with or without reply.

   A connector can be designed for each connector pattern to encapsulate the details of the communication mechanism. The *message buffer* and *message buffer*

(a) Message buffer connector for synchronous communication without reply

(b) Message queue connector for asynchronous communication

(c) Message buffer and reply connector for synchronous communication with reply

(d) Message queue and callback connector for asynchronous communication with callback

Fig. 2. Connectors for communication patterns

and reply connectors respectively implement the synchronous communication pattern without reply and with reply; the *message queue* and *message queue and callback* connectors implement the corresponding asynchronous communication patterns. These connectors can also be categorized using stereotypes.

Figure 2a depicts a synchronous communication without reply pattern, in which the concurrent producer component sends a message to a concurrent consumer component via a message buffer connector, and waits for the consumer to accept the message. Figure 2b depicts an asynchronous message communication pattern in which a producer communicates with a consumer through a message queue connector that encapsulates the details of the asynchronous communication by: (1) adding a message from the producer to a FIFO message queue and only suspending the producer if the queue is full (2) returning a message to a consumer or suspending the consumer if the queue is empty. Figure 2c depicts a synchronous communication with reply pattern in which the client component sends a message to a service component and waits for the reply via a message buffer and reply connector. Figure 2d depicts an asynchronous communication with reply pattern, in which the client sends a message to a service via a message queue and callback connector, continues executing and later receives the service response from the connector. In this pattern, the client needs to provide an id or callback handle to which the response is returned.

3   Implementation of Design Patterns

This section describes the SCOOP implementation of the behavioral design patterns with examples, and highlights the most relevant implementation properties. The full implementation is available online [8].

Implementing Components. Components are implemented by providing a class hierarchy mirroring the component taxonomy in Figure 1. Specialized components in the end user application inherit from the appropriate abstract class.

To remove ambiguity, the term *component object* will be used to denote an instance of the *component class*, which is the implementation of the design pattern component.

We examine the implementation of the periodic task in detail. It is implemented as a pair of classes: one class represents the job to be done, the other represents a "pacemaker", which periodically calls an instance of the first class to perform its task. The instances of each class reside on two distinct processors.

The basic interface to PERIODIC defines:

- a single iteration (step),
- an indicator that the task is finished (is_done),
- integration with the pacemaker: notify executes a step then asks the pacemaker to schedule another call to notify (unless is_done).

This design increases the availability of the PERIODIC object to other processors. If the waiting were to occur directly within the PERIODIC object, that object's processor would be unavailable for the duration of the waiting time; other objects would be unable to ask the periodic task simple queries such as is_done. This is why the pacemaker does the waiting and calls to the task after an appropriate delay. The interaction between the pacemaker and the periodic task allows the processor containing the periodic task to remain unoccupied between step executions.

Implementing Connectors. Each of the connectors is implemented using three dependent pieces: the sender endpoint, the receiver endpoint, and the conduit(s). These are implemented as a cohesive unit to guarantee the communication takes place correctly. Conduits are data channels; they sit as a bridge between endpoints, with the endpoints responsible for using the conduit correctly (e.g., ensuring synchronous access). We use the term *connector objects* to denote the combination of *endpoint objects* and *conduit objects*, which are the realization of a particular connector.

An example of a simple connector is the synchronous message buffer. It holds a single message, and the sender does not proceed until the receiver has received the message. The usage of this connector can be seen in the object diagram in Figure 3a, which is the SCOOP implementation of Figure 2a.

Another example is an asynchronous message queue with callback, where the sender sends its message, continues on, and then waits for a reply. The connector is implemented using two independent conduits; one conduit is responsible for carrying outgoing messages and the other for replies (this pattern is common in connectors with a reply). This is seen in the implementation given in Figure 3b, which is the SCOOP implementation of Figure 2d. The sender uses the conduits in two basic ways:

- Sending a message, along with its identity. This allows the receiving end to send a message back to it.
- Receiving the callback from the other end. The sender's identity is used once again to select the correct message to receive.

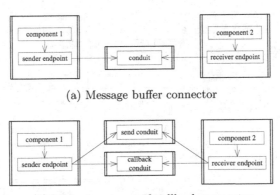

(a) Message buffer connector

(b) Message queue and callback connector

Fig. 3. Object diagrams for conduit and endpoints

Since connector objects come in three parts: sender/receiver endpoints and the conduits, any component object that wants to use a connector must have access to the connector's endpoint functionality. This can either be done by creating an endpoint object, or inheriting from the appropriate endpoint class. Because the conduits are an implementation detail of the endpoints, component objects do not need a direct reference to the conduits.

4   Case Study

This section applies the suggested development method to an ATM system [1], shown in Figure 4a and available at [8].

Applying the Design Pattern Implementations. Figure 4b shows the result of applying the design pattern implementations to Figure 4a. Active components become component objects handled by separate processors; passive components become component objects handled by one of the processors for an active component object. The class of a component object inherits from the framework class that corresponds to the component's stereotype. Connectors become conduit objects on separate processors and endpoint objects on existing processors.

Implementing Interconnections. The root object sets up the objects representing control components, i.e., the server object and the ATM objects. It first creates the conduit objects that connect these control component objects. It then creates the control component objects using the conduit objects; the component objects then create local endpoint objects. After creation, the root object starts the new component objects. Each object representing a controlled component gets created by the controlling object. To do so, the control object first creates the conduit objects for the connectors along with local endpoint objects. It then creates the controlled object using the conduit objects.

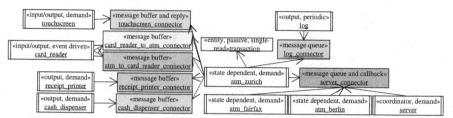

(a) Design of the ATM system. Only one ATM with one customer is detailed; however, the server can be connected to multiple ATMs. To save space, the arrows omit the direction of the communication as done in Figure 2; instead, the names contain this information.

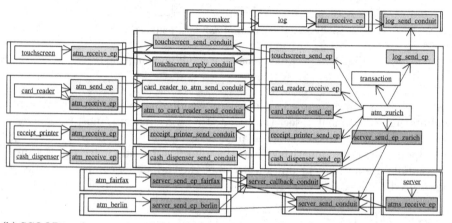

(b) SCOOP implementation of the ATM system. The boxes group objects handled by the same processor. Endpoint objects have the suffix **ep**. The names of the endpoint and conduit objects indicate the direction of the communication; for example, the atm_receive_ep object queries the touchscreen_send_conduit object to receive a message from the ATM. The colors link the connectors in Figure 4a to the resulting connector objects here.

Fig. 4. Design and implementation of the ATM system

Implementing Interactions. The interactions between components can be implemented in the **start** features of the component objects. For instance, an ATM object executes a loop; each iteration begins with a message from the card reader object. Upon receiving this message, the ATM object proceeds according to the customer's choice. The server object executes a similar loop: it waits for messages from one of the ATM objects and acts accordingly.

Discussion. The case study was a manual effort; the development method has however potential for automation, using the following steps:

1. Generate one class for each component. The class inherits from the framework class corresponding to the component's stereotype. For each of the component's connectors, the class has a non-separate attribute for the connector's endpoint object; for each passive component, the class has a nonseparate attribute as well. The class has a creation procedure to initialize

these attributes. For each connector, the creation procedure takes the connector's conduit objects as arguments and uses them to initialize the endpoint object. Finally, the creation procedure creates a non-separate component object for each passive component.

2. Generate one root class. The root object first creates the conduit objects for each connector. It then creates component objects on separate processors for each active component. It links the component objects according to the design by passing the conduit objects during construction. Lastly, the root object triggers the execution of all created component objects.

3. In each component class, add code for the component's interactions.

The first and second steps can be automated; the design contains the necessary information. However, it does not contain the data for the third step.

5   Related Work

Software design patterns provide a tried and tested solution to a design problem in the form of a reusable template, which can be used in the design of new software applications. Software architectural patterns [9] address the high-level design of the software architecture [10, 11], usually in terms of components and connectors. These include widely used architectures [12] such as client/server and layered architectures. Design patterns [13] address smaller reusable designs than architectural patterns in terms of communicating objects and classes customized to solve a general design problem in a particular context. The patterns described in this paper are aimed at developing concurrent applications and are hence different from patterns for sequential applications.

Component technologies [11] have been developed for distributed applications. Examples of this technology include client-side Java Beans and server-side Enterprise Java Beans (EJB). Patterns for concurrent and networked objects are comprehensively described in [14]. However, these patterns are not used to systematically derive a concurrent program from a design, as it is the case in our approach. Pettit and Gomaa [15] represent UML models using colored Petri nets to conduct behavioral analyses (e.g., timing behavior). Our work focuses on obtaining an executable system with built-in behavioral guarantees.

6   Conclusion

With the increasing need of concurrency, offering adequate support to developers in designing and writing concurrent applications has become an important challenge. The approach taken in this paper is to base such support on widely used architectural modeling principles, namely UML with the COMET method, which should simplify adoption in industrial settings. We defined a mapping of COMET's behavioral design patterns into SCOOP programs and demonstrated with a case study that using this approach entire concurrent UML designs can be systematically mapped to executable programs.

For future work, it would be interesting to integrate our method with other approaches based on UML and the COMET method, giving rise to a more comprehensive framework with additional analyses of concurrent designs. In the long term, we would also like to provide an automated method to translate UML concurrent software architecture designs to an implementation.

Acknowledgments. This work was funded in part by the ERC under the EU's Seventh Framework Programme (FP7/2007-2013) / ERC Grant agreement no. 291389, the Hasler Foundation, and ETH (ETHIIRA). Hassan Gomaa thanks Bertrand Meyer for the opportunity to work, during his sabbatical, with the Chair of Software Engineering group at ETH.

References

1. Gomaa, H.: Designing Concurrent, Distributed, and Real-Time Applications with UML. Addison-Wesley (2000)
2. Meyer, B.: Object-Oriented Software Construction, 2nd edn. Prentice-Hall (1997)
3. Nienaltowski, P.: Practical framework for contract-based concurrent object-oriented programming. PhD thesis, ETH Zurich (2007)
4. Nanz, S., Torshizi, F., Pedroni, M., Meyer, B.: Design of an empirical study for comparing the usability of concurrent programming languages. In: ESEM 2011, pp. 325–334 (2011)
5. West, S., Nanz, S., Meyer, B.: A modular scheme for deadlock prevention in an object-oriented programming model. In: Dong, J.S., Zhu, H. (eds.) ICFEM 2010. LNCS, vol. 6447, pp. 597–612. Springer, Heidelberg (2010)
6. Morandi, B., West, S., Nanz, S., Gomaa, H.: Concurrent object-oriented development with behavioral design patterns. Technical report (2012), http://arxiv.org/abs/1212.5491
7. Gomaa, H.: Software Modeling and Design: UML, Use Cases, Patterns, and Software Architectures. Cambridge University Press, Cambridge (2011)
8. SCOOP implementations of design patterns (2013), https://github.com/scottgw/scoop_design_patterns
9. Buschmann, F., Meunier, R., Rohnert, H., Sommerlad, P., Stal, M.: Pattern-Oriented Software Architecture: A System of Patterns. John Wiley & Sons (1996)
10. Shaw, M., Garlan, D.: Software Architecture: Perspectives on an Emerging Discipline. Prentice-Hall (1996)
11. Taylor, R.N., Medvidovic, N., Dashofy, E.M.: Software Architecture: Foundations, Theory, and Practice. Wiley (2009)
12. Bass, L., Clements, P., Kazman, R.: Software Architecture in Practice, 2nd edn. Addison-Wesley (2003)
13. Gamma, E., Helm, R., Johnson, R., Vlissides, J.: Design Patterns: Elements of Reusable Object-Oriented Software. Addison-Wesley (1995)
14. Schmidt, D., Stal, M., Rohnert, H., Buschmann, F.: Pattern-Oriented Software Architecture: Patterns for Concurrent and Networked Objects. Wiley (2000)
15. Pettit IV, R.G., Gomaa, H.: Modeling behavioral design patterns of concurrent objects. In: ICSE 2006, pp. 202–211. ACM (2006)

Building Correct by Construction SOA Design Patterns: Modeling and Refinement

Imen Tounsi, Mohamed Hadj Kacem, and Ahmed Hadj Kacem

ReDCAD-Research Unit, University of Sfax, Sfax, Tunisia
{imen.tounsi,mohamed.hadjkacem}@redcad.org, ahmed.hadjkacem@fsegs.rnu.tn

Abstract. Modeling SOA design patterns with a standard formal notation avoids misunderstanding by software architects and helps endow design methods with refinement approaches for mastering system architectures complexity. In this paper, we propose a formal architecture-centric approach that aims to model message-oriented SOA design patterns with the SoaML standard language. Pattern models are developed in a stepwise manner which are then automatically translated into Event-B specifications that can be proved using the Rodin theorem prover. These two steps are performed before undertaking the effective coding of a design pattern providing correct by construction solutions. Our approach is experimented through pattern examples.

Keywords: Design patterns, SoaML modeling, Event-B method, Pattern transformation.

1 Introduction

The communication and integration of the heterogeneous applications poses great challenges to computer science research works. Several research have been made to face these challenges and find out a solution to the issue. Although, many methods and technologies have been used such as message-oriented middleware and Enterprise Application Integration (EAI), no decisive success has been achieved up to now.

Service-oriented architectures (SOA) offer a model and an opportunity to solve these problems [4]. Nevertheless these architectures are subject to some quality attribute failures (e.g., reliability, availability, and performance problems). *Design patterns*, as models that provide tested solutions to specific design problems, have been widely used to solve these weaknesses.

Most design patterns are proposed in an informal way, and this could raise ambiguity and lead to their incorrect usage. Patterns, proposed by the SOA design pattern community, are described with a proprietary notation [4]. So they require modeling with a standard notation and then formalization. The intent of our approach is to model and formalize message-oriented SOA design patterns. These two steps are performed before undertaking the effective coding of a design pattern, so that the pattern in question will be correct by construction.

K. Drira (Ed.): ECSA 2013, LNCS 7957, pp. 33–44, 2013.

Our approach allows developers to reuse correct SOA design patterns, hence we can save effort on proving pattern correctness.

In this paper, we propose a formal architecture-centric approach that consists mainly on three steps. In the first step, SOA design patterns are modeled graphically with the semi-formal Service oriented architecture Modeling Language (SoaML) in a stepwise manner. This modeling step is proposed in order to attribute a standard notation to SOA design patterns. In the second step, the resulting graphical diagrams are translated into Event-B specifications in refinement steps with respect to transformation rules implemented with the XSLT language [11]. We provide both structural and behavioral features of SOA design patterns in the modeling phase as well as in the specification phase. Structural features of a design pattern are generally specified by assertions on types of components in the pattern. The configuration of the elements is also described, in terms of the static relationships between them. Behavioral features are defined by assertions on the temporal orders of the messages exchanged between the components. The resulting model is enriched by invariants describing relevant properties that will be proved in the third step using the Rodin tool that generates Proof Obligations belonging to Event-B models. The third step checks the syntax of resulting SOA design pattern specifications as well as their correctness. In this paper we present the first and the second steps.

The remainder of the paper is organized as follows. In section 2, we present the modeling of SOA design patterns based on the SoaML meta-modeling. In section 3 we present the transformation of the modeled patterns into Event-B specifications. In section 4, we examine related works dealing with pattern identification, pattern modeling, pattern specification and pattern reuse. Ultimately, in section 5, we present conclusions and future works.

2   Patterns Modeling

We provide a modeling solution for describing SOA design patterns using a visual notation based on the graphical SoaML language. SoaML[1] [9] is a specification developed by the OMG that provides a standard way to architect and model SOA solutions.

SoaML consists of a UML profile and a meta-model that extends the UML 2.0 (Unified Modeling Language) meta-model to support an explicit service modeling in distributed environments. This extension is perfectly applied to the modeling of SOA design patterns. We model structural features of design patterns with «Participant» diagram, «ServiceInterface» diagram, «MessageType» diagram and we model behavioral features with the UML2.0 sequence diagram. To model these diagrams, we use the part of the SoaML meta-model presented in Figure 1. Gray classes represent abstract metaclasses and white classes represent stereotypes. Hereinafter, we only present the basic concepts that we use in the pattern modeling.

---

[1] http://www.omg.org/spec/SoaML/

Entities, that make up the architecture of an SOA design pattern, can be either «Participants» or «Agents». A «Participant» represents a subclass of *Component* that provides and/or consumes services. «Agents» extend «Participants» with the ability to be active (their needs and capabilities may change over time). Entities can have «Ports» that constitute interaction points with their environment. These «Ports» are related to one or more *provided* or *required* *Interfaces* and their types can be either «Service» or «Request». «ServiceInterfaces» are used to describe provided and required operations to complete services functionality, they can be used as protocols for a service port or a request port. The communication path between *Services* and *Requests* within an architecture is called «ServiceChannel», it extends the metaclass *Connector*.

The «MessageType» is used to specify information exchanged between services, it extends the metaclass *DataType*. An «Attachment» is a part of a message that is attached to it, it extends the metaclass *Property*. The stereotype «Property» extends the metaclass *Property* with the ability to be distinguished as an identifying property ("primary key" for messages).

A «Capability» is the ability to produce an outcome that achieves a result, it extends the metaclass *Class*. A «Participant» can realize zero or several capabilities with the link «CapabilityRealization».

In some SOA design patterns entities are organized in various ways across many orthogonal dimensions, for example they can be organized by service layers or by physical boundaries. «Catalogs» provide a means of classifying and organizing elements by «Categories» for any purpose, they extends the metaclass *Package* and specializes the stereotype «NodeDescriptor». «Categories» are related to «Catalogs» with the relation «Belongs_to». A collection of related entities are characterized by a «Category». Applying a «Category» to an entity by using a *Categorization* places that entity in the «Catalog».

We develop SoaML diagrams in a stepwise manner. In the first step, an abstract pattern model is defined. In the next step, we add to the model an architecture entity and its connections to the model. In a later refinement step, we add all pattern entities.

3   Patterns Transformation

The graphic transformation of the SOA design pattern models seeks to automatically generate Event-B specifications. We define transformation rules to translate the different elements in the SoaML design pattern models to their respective concepts in Event-B notation.

3.1   Participant Diagram Mapping

In the Participant diagram we specify entities that constitute the pattern's architecture, their types and their dependencies (connections). This diagram is the static part of the defined pattern. It is specified in the *Context* part. The transformation of the Participant diagram is based on four major rules allowing the transformation of a graphical model into an Event-B specification.

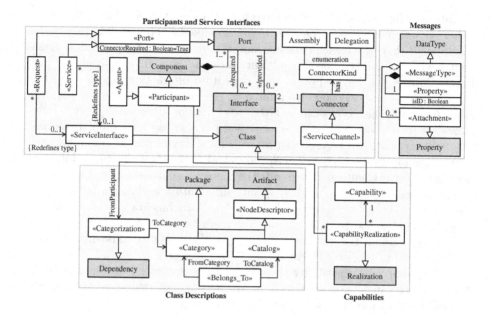

Fig. 1. SOA design patterns Meta-model

R1. Architecture Entities Transformation Rules. Entities that constitute the architecture of the pattern can be Participants or Agents. Figure 2 shows how to transform the architecture entities.

R1.1 Transformation Rule. This rule transforms entity types into new Event-B entity types by specifying in the context *PCi* the entities as constants. The set *Entity* is composed of the set of all *Participants* and the set of all *Agents* ($Entity = Participant \cup Agent \land Participant \cap Agent = \varnothing$). This is specified by using a partition in the AXIOMS clause (*Entity_partition*).

R1.2 Transformation Rule. This rule transforms Participants name P_i into constants in the CONSTANTS clause. The set of participants is composed of all participants name. This is transformed formally to a partition (*Participant_partition*) i.e. $Participant = \{P_1,...,P_n\} \land P_1 \neq P_2 \land ... \land P_{n-1} \neq P_n$.

R1.3 Transformation Rule. This rule transforms Agents name A_i into constants in the CONSTANTS clause in the Event-B specification. Also the set of agents is specified using a partition in the AXIOMS clause (*Agent_partition*), that is $Agent = \{A_1,...,A_n\} \land A_1 \neq A_2 \land ... \land A_{n-1} \neq A_n$.

R2. Connections Transformation Rules. In the SoaML modeling, a «ServiceChannel» $PushE_iE_j$ is a connection between two architecture entities, it can be between two participants ($PushP_iP_j$), two agents ($PushA_iA_j$) and between

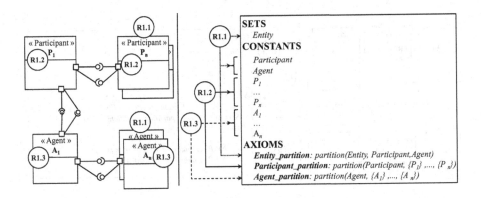

Fig. 2. Architecture entities transformation rules

a participant and an agent. In the last case, if the direction of the connection is from a participant to an agent, it is named $PushP_iA_j$ and if it is from an agent to a participant, it is named $PushA_iP_j$. Figure 3 shows how to transform a service channel.

R2.1 Transformation Rule. This rule define the graphical connection with an Event-B relation between two entities (ServiceChannel).

R2.2 Transformation Rule. This rule transforms ServiceChannels name $PushE_iE_j$ into constants in the **CONSTANTS** clause. The set of ServiceChannels is composed of all ServiceChannel's name. This is transformed formally into a partition (*ServiceChannel_partition*).

R2.3 Transformation Rule. This rule generates *Domain* and *Range* axioms for each service channel specified in R2.2 transformation rule to define its source and its target.

R3. Class Descriptions Transformation Rules. In some SOA design patterns entities are organized in various ways across many orthogonal dimensions, for example they can be organized by service layers or by physical boundaries. In the SoaML modeling «Catalogs» provide a means of classifying and organizing elements by «Categories» for any purpose. A collection of related entities are characterized by a «Category». Applying a «Category» to an entity by using a *Categorization* places that entity in the «Catalog». Figure 4 shows how to transform class descriptions.

R3.1 Transformation Rule. This rule transforms catalog type to a new Event-B catalog type and catalogs name C_i into constants in the **CONSTANTS** clause. The set of Catalogs is composed of all catalogs name. This is transformed formally to a partition (*Catalog_partition*).

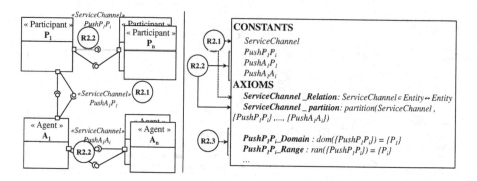

Fig. 3. Service Channels transformation rules

R3.2 Transformation Rule. This rule transforms category type to a new Event-B category type and categories name Ca_i into constants in the CONSTANTS clause. The set of Categories is composed of all Categories name. This is transformed formally to a partition (*Category_partition*).

R3.3 Transformation Rule. This rule transforms the relation of containment of a Catalog with Categories. This is transformed to the relation *Belongs_to*.

R3.4 Transformation Rule. This rule transforms the link of *Categorization* to a relation between a Category and an Entity.

R4. Capabilities Transformation Rules. A Capability is the ability to produce an outcome that achieves a result. Each Participant is comprised of a set of capabilities. Figure 5 shows how to transform capabilities.

R4.1 Transformation Rule. This rule transforms capability type to a new Event-B capability type and capability name Cp_i into constants in the CONSTANTS clause. The set of Capabilities is composed of all capabilities name. This is transformed formally to a partition (*Capability_partition*).

R4.2 Transformation Rule. This rule transforms the link between a Participant and a capability to a relation *Provide*.

3.2 MessageType Diagram Mapping

The MessageType diagram model messages exchanged between the different entities of the architecture. This diagram is specified with the Event-B method in the CONTEXT clause.

R5. MessageType Transformation Rule. MessageType is the type of messages exchanged between different entities.

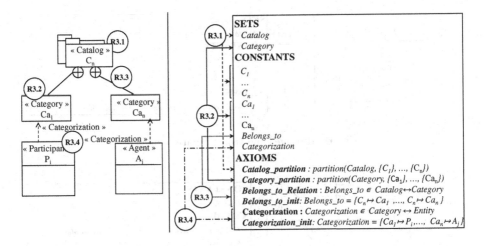

Fig. 4. Class descriptions transformation rules

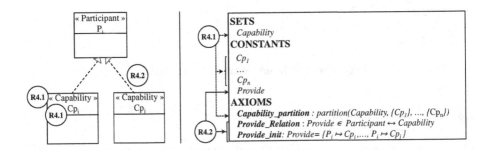

Fig. 5. Capabilities transformation rules

R5.1 Transformation Rule. This rule transforms message type to a new Event-B message type and messages name M_i into constants in the CONSTANTS clause. Then messages name are attributed with their type with a partition in the AXIOMS clause (*Message_partition*).

3.3 Service Interface Diagram Mapping

The Service Interface diagram models entities interfaces and their relations with messages. We don't do the mapping for all the elements of this diagram to the event-B specifications, but we do it to know only what entity can send what message.

R6.1 Service Interface Transformation Rule. This rule defines the relation Can_Send and initiates it.

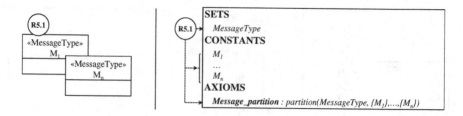

Fig. 6. MessageType transformation rule

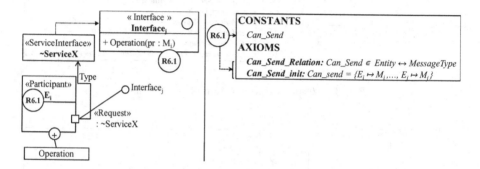

Fig. 7. Service Interface transformation rule

3.4   Sequence Diagram Mapping

The sequence diagram is a way to describe interactions. It provides a graphical notation for modeling behavioral features of a pattern by describing interactions between its several entities. It constitute the dynamic part of the pattern, it is specified with the Event-B method in the MACHINE part. A machine of a pattern specification PMi has a state defined by means of a number of variables and invariants. From this diagram, we can extract for each transition the `Transition_Name` (which is composed of two elements; `Transition_Id` and `Message_Name`), the `Message_Sending_Instance` and the `Message_Receiving_Instance`.

R7.1 Transformation Rule. This rule extracts from Transition_Names the set of variables. Some of variables can be general like the variable *Send*, which denotes the sent message and the variable *Process*, which denotes the message process. If the variable is general, the invariant that defines it can be automatically generated. For example, the variable *Send* is defined with the invariant *Send_Relation* ($Send \in ServiceChannel \leftrightarrow MessageType$) which specify that *Send* is a relation between a *ServiceChannel* and a *MessageType* so we know the sender, the receiver and the sent message. The variable *Process* is defined with the invariant *Process_Function* ($Process \in Participant \nrightarrow MessageType$) which specify that *Process* is a function between a *Participant* and a *MessageType* so we know which participant is processing which message.

R7.2 Transformation Rule. This rule transforms each transition to an Event-B event. Transition_Name is transformed to an event_name. Each pattern has its own behavior but some events can be general like the event of sending a message *Sending_M$_i$* and the event of processing a message *Processing_M$_i$*.

```
Event   Sending_Mᵢ
   when
      grd : G(v)
   then
      act : Send := Send ∪ {PushEᵢEⱼ ↦ Mᵢ}
   end
```

```
Event   Processing_Mᵢ
   when
      grd : G(v)
   then
      act : Process := Process ⩤ {Pᵢ ↦ Mᵢ}
   end
```

3.5   Pattern Refinement

The specification of a pattern P will be too complicated and error prone if it is done in one shot. In order to handle this complexity, we define specification levels by using a step-wise development approach. Models are developed in a stepwise manner which are then automatically translated into Event-B specifications. In the first level, we create a very abstract model (a context $PC0$ and a machine $PM0$). In the next levels, we use the horizontal refinement techniques to gradually introduce detail and complexity into our model until obtaining the final pattern specification. By applying an horizontal refinement, we extend the state of a pattern model by adding new variables. We can strengthen the guards of an event or add new guards. We also add new actions in an event. Finally, it is possible to add new events [1]. Our refinement strategy is explained in Figure 8. When we move from Level(i) to Level(i+1), we add a new entity and its connections to the model. In Level(i+1), the context PCi is extended with the context $PC(i+1)$ and the machine PMi is refined with the machine $PM(i+1)$. The refined machine sees the extended context. The Event-B specifications are proved by theorem provers at each refinement step.

4   Related Work

In the literature, several research [5], [6], [4] identify design patterns. Erl [4] has proposed a set of design patterns for service-oriented architecture. Each pattern is presented with a proprietary notation represented in a symbol legend. Hohpe and Woolf [6] have proposed a set of design patterns which are dealing with enterprise integration using messaging. Similarly to Erl's patterns, these design patterns are represented with a visual notation using their proprietary notation. These works present their identified patterns with no standard notations and in order to understand these patterns, we have to form a knowledge on the pattern-related terminology and notation. Gamma et al. [5] reduce these problems by

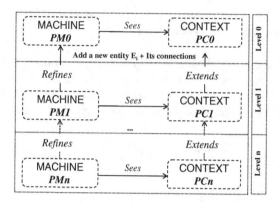

Fig. 8. Refinement strategy

proposing a set of design patterns in the field of object-oriented software design described with the graphical OMT (Object Modeling Technique) notation. So, the two first steps of the pattern definition (pattern identification and pattern modeling) are combined. Nevertheless, this approach propose modeled patterns without any formal specification.

Most proposed patterns are described using a combination of textual description and a graphical proprietary notations in order to make them easy to read and understand. However, using these descriptions makes patterns ambiguous and may lack details. There have been many research that define pattern specifications using formal techniques [12], [10], [3], [7], [2] but research that model design patterns with semi-formal languages are few [8].

Zhu et al. [12] specify design patterns and pattern composition formally. They specify 23 GoF patterns. Zhu et al. use the first order logic induced from the abstract syntax of UML defined in the Graphic Extension of BNF (GEBNF) to define both structural and behavioral features of design patterns. Taibi et al. [10] develop a language called Balanced Pattern Specification Language (BPSL) to formally specify patterns, pattern composition and instances of patterns. This language is used as a formal basis to specify structural features of design patterns in the First-Order Logic (FOL) and behavioral features in the Temporal Logic of Action (TLA). Taibi et al. use as a case study the Observer-Mediator pattern composition proposed by GoF. Kim et al. [7] present an approach to describe design patterns based on role concepts. First, they develop an initial role meta-model using an existing modeling framework, Eclipse Modeling Framework (EMF), then they transform the meta-model to Object-Z using model transformation techniques in order to specify structural features. Behavioral features of patterns are also specified using Object-Z and integrated in the pattern role models. Kim et al. also use GoF patterns as examples to represent their approach. Blazy et al. [2] propose an approach for specifying design patterns and how to reuse them formally. They use the B-method to specify structural features of design patterns. Nevertheless, this work do not consider the specification of their behavioral features.

All these works are dealing with object oriented design patterns, in our work we are interested in SOA design patterns [4]. Up to now, our research works deal with the first major step (pattern definition), we use the SoaML language for the pattern modeling and the Event-B formal method for the pattern specification. Like the work of Kim et al. [7], we propose a transformation approach from a meta-modeling language to a specification method. We use the Event-B method, which is an extension to the B method, to define both structural and behavioral features of design patterns.

5   Conclusions

In this paper, we presented a formal architecture-centric approach supporting the modeling and the transformation of message-oriented SOA design patterns to formal specifications. The modeling phase allows to represent SOA design patterns with a graphical standard notation using the SoaML language. The formalization phase allows to formally characterize both structural and behavioral features of these patterns at a high level of abstraction, so that they will be correct by construction. Generated specifications are imported under the Rodin platform in order to check their correctness. Currently, we are working on generalizing our approach in order to examine the other categories and formally specify pattern compositions.

Acknowledgments. This paper is done with the support of the Ministry of Higher Education and Scientific Research of Tunisia within the Tunisian-French scientific cooperation (DGRS/CNRS).

References

1. Abrial, J.-R.: Modeling in Event-B: System and Software Engineering, 1st edn. Cambridge University Press, New York (2010)
2. Blazy, S., Gervais, F., Laleau, R.: Reuse of specification patterns with the B method. CoRR, abs/cs/0610097 (2006)
3. Dong, J., Alencar, P.S.C., Cowan, D.D.: A behavioral analysis and verification approach to pattern-based design composition. Software and System Modeling, 262–272 (2004)
4. Erl, T.: SOA Design Patterns, 1st edn. The Prentice Hall Service-Oriented Computing Series from Thomas Erl. Prentice Hall PTR (2009)
5. Gamma, E., Helm, R., Johnson, R.E., Vlissides, J.: Design Patterns: Elements of Reusable Object-Oriented Software. Addison-Wesley, Reading (1995)
6. Hohpe, G., Woolf, B.: Enterprise Integration Patterns - Designing, Building, and Deploying Messaging Solutions. Addison-Wesley (2003)
7. Kim, S.-K., Carrington, D.A.: A formalism to describe design patterns based on role concepts. Formal Asp. Comput. 21(5), 397–420 (2009)
8. Mapelsden, D., Hosking, J., Grundy, J.: Design pattern modelling and instantiation using DPML. In: 40th International Conference on Tools Pacific: Objects for Internet, Mobile and Embedded Applications, CRPIT 2002, pp. 3–11. Australian Computer Society, Inc. (2002)

9. OMG: Service oriented architecture Modeling Language (SoaML) Specification. Technical report (2012)
10. Taibi, T., Ngo, D.C.L.: Formal specification of design pattern combination using BPSL. Information and Software Technology 45(3), 157–170 (2003)
11. Tounsi, I., Hrichi, Z., Hadj Kacem, M., Hadj Kacem, A., Drira, K.: Using SoaML Models and Event-B Specifications for Modeling SOA Design Patterns. In: 15th International Conference on Enterprise Information Systems, ICEIS 2013 (to appear, 2013)
12. Zhu, H., Bayley, I.: Laws of pattern composition. In: Dong, J.S., Zhu, H. (eds.) ICFEM 2010. LNCS, vol. 6447, pp. 630–645. Springer, Heidelberg (2010)

Towards an Architecture for Managing Big Semantic Data in Real-Time[*]

Carlos E. Cuesta[1], Miguel A. Martínez-Prieto[2,3], and Javier D. Fernández[2,3]

[1] VorTIC3 Research Group, Dept. of Comp. Languages and Systems II,
Rey Juan Carlos University, Madrid, Spain
[2] DataWeb Research, Dept. of Computer Science,
University of Valladolid, Segovia & Valladolid, Spain
[3] Dept. of Computer Science, University of Chile, Santiago, Chile
carlos.cuesta@urjc.es, {migumar2,jfergar}@infor.uva.es

Abstract. Big Data Management has become a critical task in many application systems, which usually rely on heavyweight batch processes to process large amounts of data. However, batch architectures are not an adequate choice for the design of real-time systems, where expected response times are several orders of magnitude underneath. This paper outlines the foundations for defining an architecture able to deal with such an scenario, fulfilling the specific needs of real-time systems which expose big RDF datasets. Our proposal (SOLID) is a tiered architecture which separates the complexities of Big Data management from their real-time data generation and consumption. Big semantic data are stored and indexed in a compressed way following the RDF/HDT proposal; while at the same time, real-time requirements are addressed using NoSQL technology. Both are efficient layers, but their approaches are quite different and their combination is not easy. Two additional layers are required to achieve an overall high performance, satisfying real-time needs, and able to work even in a mobile context.

1 Introduction

Big Data is one of the buzzwords in the current technological landscape. A widely accepted definition says that Big Data is *"when the size of the data itself becomes part of the problem"* [11]. It basically states the most obvious dimension of Big Data: the **volume**. However, any definition is incomplete without considering **velocity** and **variety**. These *three V's* [8] comprises the most accepted Big Data characterization:

Volume: large amounts of data are gathered and stored in massive datasets created for different uses and purposes. *Storage* is the first scalability challenge in Big Data management since preserving the data must be our first responsibility. In turn, storage impacts in data *retrieval*, *processing* and *analysis*.

Velocity means how data flow, at high rates, in increasingly distributed scenarios. Two data streams can be distinguished: i) streams of new data (potentially generated in different ways and sources) being progressively integrated into existing (big)

---

[*] This work has been partially funded by the Spanish Ministry of Economy and Competitiveness through Projects TIN2012-31104, TIN2009-13838 and TIN2009-14009-C02-0; and also by Chilean Fondecyt Grant 1-110066, the Regional Government of Castilla y Leon and the ESF.

K. Drira (Ed.): ECSA 2013, LNCS 7957, pp. 45–53, 2013.
© Springer-Verlag Berlin Heidelberg 2013

datasets, and ii) streams of query results (potentially large) to user requests. Thus, velocity means how fast data is produced, demanded and served.

Variety refers to various degrees of structure (or lack thereof) within the Big Data [9]. This dimension is motivated by the fact that Big Data may integrate multiple sources: *e.g.* any kind of sensor network, web server logs, politics, or social networks, among others. Obviously, each source describes its own semantics, resulting in different data schemas which are hardly integrable in a single model. Thus, Big Data variety demands a logical model enabling effective data integration.

These three V's provide a good description of Big Data, but the volume dimension must be revised from a practical perspective. Although one could think in terabytes, petabytes or exabytes talking about Big Data, few gigabytes may be enough to collapse an application running on a mobile device or even in a personal computer. Thus, the term Big Data is used, in this paper, to refer any dataset whose size is greater than the computational resources available for its storage and processing in a given system.

An architecture designed for managing Big Data [3] must consider all the dimensions above. However, its intended purpose restricts which one is first addressed. For instance, storage could be more critical for a mobile application than for another one running on a powerful server, whereas data retrieval speed is a priority for a real-time system but may not for a batch process. Thus, the dimensions must be prioritized in such a way that the resulting architecture covers effectively its requirements.

We design our proposal on a strong assumption: the more data are integrated, the more interesting knowledge may be generated, increasing the resulting dataset **value**. Thus, we *promote data variety over volume and velocity*. This decision is materialized through the model used for logical data organization. We choose a graph-based model because it can reach higher levels of variety before data become unwieldy. This allows more data to be linked and queried together [16]. The most practical trend, in this line, relies on the use of the Resource Description Framework (RDF) [12] as data model.

RDF is a cornerstone of the Semantic Web [5], whose basic principles are materialized by the emergent Web of Data. It reaches all its potential when it is used in conjunction with vocabularies providing data semantics, so we will use the term *big semantic data* to refer big RDF datasets. Note that choosing RDF as data model is a variety decision which does not discriminate any kind of software managing big semantic data. However, it restricts how these data are finally structured, stored, and accessed, so *it influences on volume and velocity dimensions*. Under this consideration, we design SOLID as a high-performance architecture for real-time systems consuming RDF data.

SOLID *(Service-OnLine-Index-Data architecture)* tackles this scenario through a tiered configuration which separates complexities of real-time data generation and Big Semantic Data consumption. On the one hand, the dataset must be preserved as compact as possible in order to save storage and processing resources. Thus, Big Data is stored and indexed in compressed way, enabling significant spatial savings and efficient query resolution (compression allows more data to be processed in main memory). These responsibilities are managed in the *Data* and *Index* layers, which are built around the RDF/HDT [13,7] features. However, these optimized representations are costly to update online. It means that, on the other hand, the pieces of RDF generated in real-time must be processed in a third layer which enables efficient data updates and also provides competitive query resolution. This *Online* layer is implemented using NoSQL technology. Although both approaches are efficient by themselves, two additional layers are required to achieve an overall high performance: i) the *Merge* layer leverages RDF/HDT features for integrating the "online data" into the big semantic data; and ii) the *Service* layer supports efficient query resolution, by merging results retrieved from the Index and the Online layers using SPARQL [15].

The rest of the paper is organized as follows. Section 2.1 summarizes the current "RDF world". Section 3 describes the architecture SOLID, whereas Section 4 realizes it using different technologies from the state of the art. Finally, Section 5 concludes about our achievements and devises the SOLID evolution towards its final implementation.

2 Motivation

This section provides a brief review about *the RDF world* and introduces the main RDF features. More detailed information about this topic, and some examples about its current use, can be found in [10]. Then, we illustrate a use case highlighting the core requirements of managing big semantic data in practice.

2.1 The RDF World

The Resource Description Framework (RDF) [12] is an extremely simple data model in which an entity (also called resource) is described in the form (subject, predicate, object). For instance, describing a transaction (in the following example): chek-in#1, which was made the day 01/01/2013 in station#123, involves the triples: (chek-in#1, date, "01/01/2013") and (chek-in#1, in_station, station#123). An RDF dataset can be seen as a graph of knowledge in which entities and values are linked via labeled edges. These labels (the predicates in the triples) own the semantic of the relation, hence it is highly recommendable to use standard vocabularies or to formalize new ones as needed.

RDF has been gaining momentum since its inception thanks to its adoption in diverse fields, such as bioinformatics, social networks, or geographical data. The Linked Open Data project plays a crucial role in the RDF evolution [10]. It leverages the Web infrastructure to encourage the publication of such semantic data [4], providing global identity to resources using HTTP URIs. Moreover, integration between data sources is done at the most basic level of triples, that is, to connect two data sources can be as easy as making connection between resources. For instance, a new triple: (station#123, location, <http://dbpedia.org/page/Canal_Street>), enables all information stored in DBpedia[1] about *Canal Street* to be directly accessed from the aforementioned station.

This philosophy pushes the traditional document-centric perspective of the Web to a data-centric view, emerging a huge interconnected cloud of data-to-data hyperlinks: the

---

[1] DBpedia: http://dbpedia.org, is a partial RDF conversion of Wikipedia.

Web of Data. Latest statistics[2] pointed that more than 31 billion triples were published and more than 500 million links established cross-relations between datasets.

It is worth noting that, although each piece of information could be particularly small (the *Big Data's long tail*), the integration within a subpart of this Web of Data can be seen as big semantic data. RFID labels, Web processes (crawlers, search engines, recommender systems), smartphones and sensors are potential sources of RDF data, such as in our running example. Automatic RDF streaming, for instance, would become a hot topic, specially within the development of smart cities [6]. It is clear that Linked Data philosophy can be applied naturally to these *Internet of Things*, by simply assigning URIs to the real-world things producing RDF data about them via Web.

2.2   Running Example

Each time we use a metro card, the transaction is recorded. A register may include, at least, an anonymous identifier, the date and time of the transaction, and the checked station. Let us consider an information system storing and serving all this information for a city such as New York (NYC), having 468 stations, 5 millions rides per weekday and a total 1,640 millions rides per year[3]. It conforms a really interesting Big Data to query and analyze, subject to integration with other data (such as subway and city facilities, events or services), but increasingly growing minute by minute. After, five years of gathering, this huge information system will store 8,000 millions records and it has to be able to serve queries efficiently for a wide range of purposes, such as prediction and other logistic processes related to the metro management and NYC organization, statistics, business intelligence, etc. Under this scenario, thousand of records are generated every couple of minutes, which has to be integrated into the full knowledge base. On the one hand, it makes no sense to perform continuously insertions, as this would imply to regenerate the (huge) indexes to more than 8,000 millions records, suffering a significant performance degradation of the tasks running in the system. On the other hand, we could not afford an offline batch insertion (typically at the end of the day) as some of the processes, such as prediction, requires the latest records to perform real-time processes.

Let us describe how this decision applies to the previous example. We consider, for instance, that the check-in transaction is enhanced with data about breakdowns in other transports, meteorology or information about cultural and sporting events held in New York. These new data can be the glue to understand different displacement patterns, allowing better service plans to be adopted or increasing security in days of massive traffic, among other possible decisions. Although it is out of the scope of this paper, the first step is to design a specific vocabulary for transaction modeling. Once the vocabulary is agreed, each transaction is represented as a small piece of RDF which must be integrated into the dataset. Thus, a competitive throughput must be provided to integrate all these pieces of data since no transactions may be lost. Besides, continuous data streams of breakdowns, weather or events are also received, but these additional data can be considered as "small data", so we can process them efficiently. Moreover, all the data must be available for querying and these requests must be resolved efficiently.

---

[2] http://www4.wiwiss.fu-berlin.de/lodcloud/state/ (September, 2011).
[3] NYC statistics 2011, http://mta.info/nyct/facts/ridership/index.htm

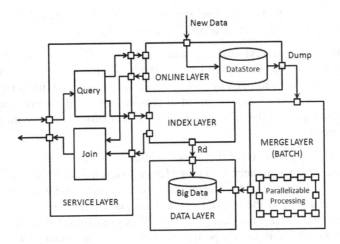

Fig. 1. Layered configuration of the SOLID architecture

3   The SOLID Architecture

Our solution for the stated problem –to be able to reconcile the requirements of Big Data processing and the need to consider the flow of incoming real-time information– is to define a generic architecture able to simultaneously deal with both approaches. The problem could seem rather specific, but it actually applies to a large set of applications; indeed, there are even some architectural approaches which tackle a similar problem, such as Lambda [14]. Our proposal, however, emphasizes the use of semantic technologies, and has a different setting. Apart from that, this architecture has been designed not to depend on any particular domain or technology.

Our proposal consists of a specific architecture, named SOLID after the enumeration of its main components: *Service-OnLine-Index-Data*, which gathers lessons learned from batch architectures, real-time overlays, and high-performance semantic datastores. It can be described as a 3-tier architecture, in which the middle tier is also subdivided in three layers (*OnLine*, *Index* and *Data*), defining a multi-tiered, layered architecture. It is summarized in Fig. 1, and its five layers are quickly mentioned in the following.

Online Layer. The top layer of the architecture, which is also the one which specifically deals with real-time needs. It captures the incoming flow of new data in a high-speed datastore, which is used for temporary storage. It works as a large buffer for real-time incoming data: what is not (still) in the main database is located here.

Data Layer. The bottom layer of the architecture, which contains the main datastore, *i.e.* the Big Data repository. It is designed as a storage layer, able to maintain large sets of information, their organization and their semantics - but it needs not to be inherently fast, just self-descriptive.

Index Layer. The middle layer, which provides an *index* for the Data Layer, therefore turning it into a high-speed datastore. It is built using the semantic metadata in the lower layer, and designed to provide a fast access to the information it contains: all queries to the main datastore are performed using this index. This way we are able to maintain a large, stable datastore with a quick access.

Service Layer. The most external tier, which presents a façade to the outside user. All queries are performed through this layer, which multiplexes them adequately, and forwards it to both the Online and Index Layers. Each layer provides the corresponding result set; these are joined and combined to provide an unified answer. The internal modules in this layer can therefore be described as mediators, and have themselves a pipe-filter structure.

Merge Layer. The most internal tier, which provides one of the key steps of our approach. In some chosen moment, the Online Layer *dumps* the contents of its datastore. The Merge Layer receives and transforms this input and combines it with existing data, producing a fresh copy of the Big Data store, which is fed into the Data Layer, without altering its structure, *i.e.* maintaining immutability properties. This process requires much computational effort, so it is performed in batch as a massively parallel process using, for instance, MapReduce-based computation.

Therefore, in summary: the data architecture uses a large datastore for Big Data, which is indexed to allow a fast access. At the same time, the flow of real-time data is stored in a temporary datastore, until it is eventually merged in the main store by using a massive-parallel batch process. When the architecture receives a query, it is forwarded to the two datastores, and the corresponding result sets are merged to provide a federated answer, in a completely user-transparent way.

This "abstract" architecture has to make certain decisions to be applied to a concrete case - such as the nature of the datastores, or the different implementations. The next section is devoted to explain this sort of compromises.

4   SOLID in Practice

Once we have characterized the SOLID layers, we are able to devise its implementation. First, we analyze practical decisions made around the data-centric layers: *Data*, *Index*, and *Online*, which are designed by leveraging possibilities of binary RDF. Then, we outline *Merge* and *Service* layers, emphasizing how their processes can also take advantage of binary RDF for improving performance.

4.1   Data-Centric Layers

One main decision when managing RDF data is the underneath format, since the RDF data model does not restrict its concrete representation. RDF/XML [2] was originally recommended as the RDF syntax. It restructures the RDF graph to be encoded as a XML tree, preserving a document-centric view which is not acceptable when big semantic data must be serialized. The potential of huge RDF is seriously underexploited due to the large space they take up [13]. Some other syntaxes has been proposed later [10], but RDF/HDT[4] [13,7] was the first designed bearing in mind final serialization sizes.

---

[4] HDT is W3C Member Submission from 2011:
http://www.w3.org/Submission/2011/03/

RDF/HDT is a binary syntax which reduces verbosity in favor of machine-under-standability. It allows Big Semantic Data to be efficiently managed within the common workflows of the Web of Data, being an ideal choice for storage and transmission (it takes up to 15 times less space than traditional RDF syntaxes [7]). In addition, the RDF/HDT specification comprises specific configurations of compact data structures which enable to easily parse and load Big Semantic Data in compressed space.

The **Data Layer** stores the Big Semantic Data serialized in RDF/HDT. It enables large spatial savings and guarantees data immutability in compressed space. Besides, it allows big datasets to be efficiently mapped to the memory hierarchy by using the RDF/HDT data structures. This feature is the SOLID core for accessing Big Semantic Data because any RDF triple can be retrieved without prior decompression. Thus, this layer assumes the complexity of Big Data storage and set the basis for the Index Layer.

The **Index Layer** exploits the Data Layer features for supporting efficient query res-olution over the Big Semantic Data storage. It implements the HDT-FoQ (HDT *Focused on Querying*) proposal [13] which, basically, builds two lightweight indexes on top of the RDF/HDT representation. These structures enable fast lookups over the Data Layer, and it results in efficient SPARQL resolution reporting competitive performance with respect to the state of the art of RDF stores [13].

The **Online Layer** assumes the complexity of managing data generated in real-time, keeping the Data Layer immutable. In fact, this philosophy perfectly fits the lower lay-ers, as RDF/HDT was thought to be read-only and updates are costly. On the one hand, the Online Layer must allow fast write operations in order to insert all new generated data. On the other hand, it must resolve SPARQL in an efficient way, although scalabil-ity issues are minimized in this case by considering that this Layer only stores a small subset of data (for instance, in the running example, the check-in transactions generated in the current day). This layer implementation depends on the computational resources available. We suggest to use general-purpose NoSQL technology or any native RDF store, because these report the best numbers for managing RDF [1].

4.2 Processing-Centric Layers

These two layers play intermediary roles between the data-centric layers. Both ones leverage RDF/HDT features for implementing their processing tasks.

The **Merge Layer** implements the batch process which merges the Big Semantic Data (from the Data Layer), and the data recorded in the Online Layer. It is a time-consuming process which requires a high-performance configuration. As explained, it can be realized using Map-Reduce. Whereas the Big Semantic Data from the Data Layer is already in RDF/HDT, the data dumped from the Online Layer must be firstly converted to RDF/HDT; this conversion can take place in the Merge Layer, or it can be held in the Online Layer. In any case, the new Big Semantic Data is not obtained from the scratch because the process leverages internal RDF/HDT ordering for efficient merging. It results in a cost proportional to the smallest dataset size, isolating possible Big Data drawbacks. This process finishes delivering a new Big Semantic Data rep-resentation which replaces the previous one in the Data Layer. This fact triggers two additional operations: i) the Index Layer updates its structures according to the new data and ii) the Online Layer clears all data currently integrated into the Data Layer.

The **Service Layer** relies on the SPARQL expressiveness to satisfy all possible queries. Its inner pipeline first duplicates the corresponding query and sends the copies to the filters responsible for interacting with the Service and Index Layers. Each layer resolves the query independently and delivers its results to the last filter, which finally computes the results. In practice, results from the Service Layer are first obtained, and then there is room for optimization. They can be processed to obtain a hash structure which allows to efficiently join both result sets before final delivery.

5 Conclusions and Future Work

This paper proposes SOLID, a new architecture for managing Big Semantic Data in real-time. It is designed upon the property of complexity isolation allowing the main concerns to be resolved independently. On the one hand, we rely on binary RDF/HDT features for storing and indexing RDF in compressed space. On the other hand, we use NoSQL technology for recording real-time data. The overall dataset is queried through a pipeline-based layer which asks to the big and online representations, retrieves results, and then merges them for delivering. Online and Big Data are merged programmatically by performing a parallel process: *e.g.* Map-Reduce.

The empirical results reported by each technology considered in SOLID bodes well for our future work. We are currently implementing the different layers and their interfaces to obtain an optimized prototype for servers. Besides, we are working on a lightweight SOLID version designed for mobile devices because our spatial savings enable more data to be processed in these limited devices. Nevertheless, their practical requirements are different and, for instance, the merge layer is discarded because its functionality is not directly required.

References

1. Abadi, D., Marcus, A., Madden, S., Hollenbach, K.: Scalable semantic Web data management using vertical partitioning. In: Proc. of VLDB, pp. 411–422 (2007)
2. Beckett, D. (ed.): RDF/XML Syntax Specification. W3C Recommendation (2004)
3. Begoli, E., Horey, J.: Design Principles for Effective Knowledge Discovery from Big Data. In: Proc. 2012 Joint WICSA/ECSA Conference, pp. 215–218. IEEE (August 2012)
4. Berners-Lee, T.: Linked Data: Design Issues (2006),
   http://www.w3.org/DesignIssues/LinkedData.html
   (retrieved on March 01, 2013)
5. Berners-Lee, T., Hendler, J., Lassila, O.: The Semantic Web. Scientific American (2001)
6. De, S., Elsaleh, T., Barnaghi, P., Meissner, S.: An Internet of Things Platform for Real-World and Digital Objects. Scalable Computing: Practice and Experience 13(1) (2012)
7. Fernández, J., Martínez-Prieto, M., Gutiérrez, C., Polleres, A., Arias, M.: Binary RDF representation for publication and exchange (HDT). Journal of Web Semantics (in press, 2013),
   http://dx.doi.org/10.1016/j.websem.2013.01.002
8. Genovese, Y., Prentice, S.: Pattern-Based Strategy: Getting Value from Big Data. Gartner Special Report (June 2011)
9. Halfon, A.: Handling Big Data Variety,
   http://www.finextra.com/community/fullblog.aspx?blogid=6129
   (retrieved on March 01, 2013)

10. Heath, T., Bizer, C.: Linked Data: Evolving the Web into a Global Data Space. Morgan & Claypool (2011)
11. Loukides, M.: Data Science and Data Tools. In: Big Data Now, ch. 1. O'Reilly (2012)
12. Manola, F., Miller, E. (eds.): RDF Primer. W3C Recommendation (2004)
13. Martínez-Prieto, M.A., Arias Gallego, M., Fernández, J.D.: Exchange and Consumption of Huge RDF Data. In: Simperl, E., Cimiano, P., Polleres, A., Corcho, O., Presutti, V. (eds.) ESWC 2012. LNCS, vol. 7295, pp. 437–452. Springer, Heidelberg (2012)
14. Marz, N., Warren, J.: Big Data: Principles and Best Practices of Scalable Realtime Data Systems. Manning (2013)
15. Prud'hommeaux, E., Seaborne, A. (eds.): SPARQL Query Language for RDF. W3C Recommendation (2008), http://www.w3.org/TR/rdf-sparql-query/
16. Styles, R.: RDF, Big Data and The Semantic Web, http://dynamicorange.com/2012/04/24/rdf-big-data-and-the-semantic-web/ (retrieved on March 01, 2013)

Controlled Experiment on the Supportive Effect of Architectural Component Diagrams for Design Understanding of Novice Architects

Thomas Haitzer and Uwe Zdun

Research Group Software Architecture
University of Vienna
Austria
{thomas.haitzer,uwe.zdun}@univie.ac.at

Abstract. Today, architectural component models are often used as a central view of architecture descriptions. So far, however, only a very few rigorous empirical studies relating to the use of component models in architectural descriptions of software systems have been conducted. In this paper, we present the results of a controlled experiment regarding the supportive effect of architectural component diagrams for design understandability. In particular, the goal of the experiment was to determine whether architectural component diagrams, provided in addition to a non-trivial software system's source code, have a supportive effect on the ability of novice architects to answer design and architecture related questions about that system. Our study provides initial evidence that architectural component diagrams have a supportive effect for understanding the software design and architecture, if a direct link from the component diagram's elements to the problem that requires understanding can be made. If such a direct link cannot be made, we found evidence that it should not be assumed that architectural component diagrams help in design understanding, for instance only by providing a big picture view or some general kind of orientation.

Keywords: Software Architecture, Architectural Component Diagrams, Design and Architecture Understanding, Empirical Study, Controlled Experiment.

1 Introduction

Today a software architecture description is usually comprised of multiple views [5, 19, 20]. The component and connector model (or component model for short) of an architecture is a view that is often considered to contain the most significant architectural information [5]. This view deals with the components, which are units of runtime computation or data-storage, and the connectors which are the interaction mechanisms between components [5, 29]. An architectural component model is a high-level abstraction of the entities in the source code of the software system, as the software architecture concerns only the major design decisions about a software system, and abstracts from irrelevant details [21].

While much research work has been done in component-related research areas such as modelling languages for component and connector models, component implementation technologies, component composition, and the formal semantics of components,

K. Drira (Ed.): ECSA 2013, LNCS 7957, pp. 54–71, 2013.

only a very few rigorous empirical studies relating to the use of component models in architectural descriptions of software systems have been conducted. Such foundational research is however essential to provide guidelines and tools to software architects, based on sound evidence, to help them understand how to design component models that are appropriate for the architectural understanding of a software system.

In this paper, we present the results of a controlled experiment regarding the supportive effect of architectural component diagrams for design understandability. In particular, the goal of the experiment was to determine whether architectural component diagrams, provided in addition to a non-trivial software system's source code, have a supportive effect on the ability of novice architects to answer design and architecture related questions about that system. This goal is interesting to study, as today it is unclear whether component diagrams alone are sufficient to help architects to understand complex architectural relationships in a given system in a better way than just studying the source code of that system. While the literature suggests a supportive effects of component diagrams (see e.g. [5, 31]) for design understanding, there is little empirical evidence so far.

In addition, many existing approaches seem to assume seasoned architects as their main target group. Assuming that component diagrams alone are a useful help to gain a better architectural understanding of a system, as some of the software architecture literature suggests, it is unclear whether this effect can also be observed for novice architects. As software architecture has the goal to convey the big picture of a software system and novices who start on a new project especially require help to gain such a big picture quickly, it is highly interesting whether there is indeed a supportive effect on design understanding for them. Hence, we particularly focus on novice architects.

The experiment presented in this paper studies the experiment goal by letting 60 students with medium programming experience answer seven questions about the design and architecture of a given software system (the computer game FreeCol). One half of the participants, the control group, received the source code of that system as the main source of information, while the other half of the participants, the experiment group, additionally received architectural component diagrams for FreeCol. By showing that the quality of the answers improves for certain questions, our study provides initial evidence on how architectural component diagrams help in understanding the design and architecture of software systems. The results indicate that architectural component diagrams are especially useful if a direct link from the component diagram's elements to the problem that requires understanding can be made and that they have in such cases indeed a supportive effect for software design and architecture understanding. In contrast, if no such direct link can be made, we found evidence that it should not be assumed that architectural component diagrams help in design understanding, for instance only by providing a big picture view or some general kind of orientation.

This paper is organized as follows: In Section 2 we briefly discuss the related work. Next, in Section 3 we introduce our experiment, including the goal, the hypotheses, the parameters and variables, the experimental design, and the execution. Section 4 describes the statistical analysis and the testing of the hypotheses. Section 5 provides the validity evaluation. Finally, Section 6 concludes and discusses possible future research directions.

2 Related Work

The general notion of empirical studies in software architecture has been studied by Falessi et al. [8]. They conclude from their study that a greater synergy between empirical software engineering and software architecture would support the emergence of a body of knowledge consisting of more widely accepted and well-formed theories on software architecture and the empirical maturation of the software architecture area.

Only a few of the empirical studies in the area of software architecture are directly related to architecture design or design understanding. Boucke et al. [4] introduce an approach that explicitly supports compositions of models, together with relations among models in an architecture description language. In an empirical study they show that their approach reduces the number of manually specified elements and manual changes.

van Heesch et al. study in two surveys the reasoning process of architects, one with students [16] and one with professionals [18]. A related study performs a controlled experiment about the supportive effect of patterns in architecture decision recovery [17].

Many empirical studies in the field of software architecture study other aspects, like quality aspects or other views. For instance, a number of studies related to evaluating architectures have been conducted. Barbar et al. [2] performed an empirical study aiming at understanding the different factors involved in evaluating architectures in industry. The influence of software visualization on source code comprehensibility was studied by Umphress et al. [35] based on control structure diagrams and complexity profile graphs. Biffl. et al. [3] study the impact of experience and team size on the quality of scenarios for architecture evaluation. A number of empirical studies aim at better understanding the relation of architecture and requirements [11, 26]. Various empirical studies relating architecture to certain qualities or metrics have been conducted. For example, Hansen et al. study the relation of product quality metrics and architecture metrics [15].

A number of papers focus on the comprehension of UML diagrams. Some focus on dynamic models [28], while others focus on specific diagrams or models like sequence diagrams [13], state charts [7], or class diagrams [30]. The influence of the level of detail in class and sequence diagrams on the maintainability of software has been studied by Fernández-Sáez et al. [10]. These papers focus on factors that influence the understandability of the diagrams itself, while we focus on the effects of component diagrams on the architecture understanding of novice architects.

Even though we found no rigorous empirical studies of architectural component model understandability so far, aspects like reuse or fault density of components have been studied empirically before. Fenton and Ohlsson have studied the relations of fault density and component size in a large telecom system [9]. Mohagheghi et al. provide a study comparing software reuse with defect density and stability [27]. Their study is based on historical data on defects, modification rate, and software size. Malaiya and Denton provide an analysis of a number of studies and identify the component partitioning and implementation as influencing, competing factors to determine the "optimal" component size with regard to fault density [24]. Graves et al. have studied the software change history of components to create a fault prediction model [14]. Our experiment and these studies have in common, that they make a link between component models and software quality, but in contrast to our experiment they only study aspects that can solely be studied using the software systems and their historical data. In contrast, we consider the (novice) architect's perception of understandability as well as expert opinions on their results. In addition, in those other studies components are understood as implemented software modules, rather than architectural abstractions.

A number of approaches suggest that other aids are needed to gain a better understanding of the design or architecture, such as architectural views [5, 19, 20] or architectural decision models [23, 34, 38], which would contain or augment component models. Both research directions only focus on complementing component models with additional knowledge, but do not research on the effects of the component models on the understandability of a software architecture or design. Other literature suggests that it might be hard to understand the source code only with models, and traceability links [1] between components and code are needed to make the connection [12].

3   Experiment Description

For the design of the experiment we followed the guidelines by Kitchenham et al. [22] and Wohlin et al. [37]. In our experiments, the guidelines by Kitchenham et al. were primarily used in the planning phase of the experiments, while the advice by Wohlin et al. was used as a reference for the analysis and interpretation of the results.

3.1   Goal and Hypotheses

The goal of the experiment was to determine whether architectural component diagrams, provided in addition to a non-trivial software system's source code, have a supportive effect on the ability of novice architects to answer questions about the design and architecture of that system. Depending on the question asked, the guidance or help provided by architectural component diagrams can vary greatly. The two extreme cases are that component diagrams readily provide the answer without any need to study other information (like the source code) and that component diagrams provide no clue for answering the question. Intentionally we left out these two extreme cases and studied the shades of grey in between. In particular, we further distinguished the following three types of questions in our experiment:

- $QT1$: A question about the software system's design and architecture for which the component diagrams provide some guidance or help, but the information in the component diagrams alone is not enough to answer the question fully.
- $QT2$: A question about the software system's design and architecture for which the component diagrams provide some guidance or help, but the same information is easily visible from the source code.
- $QT3$: A question about the software system's design and architecture for which the component diagrams provide no direct guidance or help, only vague orientation in related components and connectors; digging in the source code is required for answering the question.

Hypotheses: We postulate the following three hypotheses about the effects of architectural component diagrams (in addition to the source code) on the quality of answers that novice architects provide to questions about a software system's design and architecture.

- In case of $QT1$, i.e. if the component diagrams provide architectural guidance for answering the question,
    - the null hypothesis is that the quality does not improve, $H_{0\_QT1} : \mu \leq \mu_0$;
    - the alternative hypothesis is that the quality improves, $H_{QT1} : \mu > \mu_0$.
- In case of $QT2$, i.e. if the component diagrams provide architectural guidance for answering the question, but the same information is visible from the source code,
    - the null hypothesis is that the quality does not improve, $H_{0\_QT2} : \mu \leq \mu_0$;
    - the alternative hypothesis is that the quality improves, $H_{QT2} : \mu > \mu_0$.
- In case of $QT3$, i.e. if the component diagrams provide no direct guidance or help, only vague orientation in related components and connectors,
    - the null hypothesis is that the quality does not improve, $H_{0\_QT3} : \mu \leq \mu_0$;
    - the alternative hypothesis is that the quality improves, $H_{QT3} : \mu > \mu_0$.

Expectations: Our expectations for the three hypotheses are:

- For design questions of type $QT1$, we *expect that the null hypothesis can be rejected.* That is, component diagrams have a supportive effect on the answers that novice architects provide to questions about a software system's design and architecture, if the component diagrams provide architectural guidance for answering the question.
- For design questions of type $QT2$, we expect that the *null hypothesis can not be rejected.* That is, component diagrams are helpful, but that novice architects with medium software development experience are able to see the same information in the source code, if it is easily visible. However, this expectation might be wrong as possibly the visual information in the component diagrams might be more readily accessible to novice architects than the easily visible information in the source code.
- For design questions of type $QT3$, we expect that the *null hypothesis can not be rejected,* as there is no direct relation between the question and the additional information provided by the component diagrams. However, this might be wrong as component diagrams might have an indirect supportive effect, for instance by providing some kind of general orientation that helps in answering this type of questions.

3.2 Parameters and Variables

Dependent Variable. One dependent variable was observed during the experiment, as shown in Table 1: the quality of the answer to the design question. The quality of the answers was assessed by three independent software architecture researchers with multiple years of practical software development and architecture experience (later also referred to as analysts) using an interval scale, ranging from 0 (worst) to 10 (best). The interval scale nature of the rating system was explained to the analysts before their analysis (i.e., that equal distances between the points on the scale can be assumed), as this is important for applying parametric statistical tests [33]. The analysts were assigned per question, and each analyst rated each of the assigned questions completely in both experiment and control group, to make sure that each question is homogeneously assessed. Two analysts rated two of the questions, and one analyst rated three of the questions. Each of the analysts studied the two software systems used in the experiments before their analysis in depth and reference answers were created before the evaluation to ensure fair evaluation. The ratings were left to the analysts' own experience and interpretation, but they were asked to specifically take the displayed architectural understanding into account. The participants of the experiments were also reminded before the beginning of the experiments that they should focus on the architectural dimension of the questions.

Independent Variables. Table 1 also shows other variables that could influence the dependent variables. They concern characteristics and previous experiences of the participants.

Table 1. Observed Variables

Type	Description	Scale Type	Unit	Range
Dependent Variable	Quality of the answer to design question	Interval	Points	0 (worst) to 10 (best)
Independent Variable	Group	Nominal	N/A	Possible values: *experiment group, control group*
	Programming experience	Ordinal	Years	4 classes: 0-1, 1-3, 3-6, >6
	Commercial programming experience in industry	Ordinal	Years	4 classes: 0, 0-1, 1-3, >3
	Experience in programming computer games	Ordinal	Years	4 classes: 0, 0-1, 1-3, >3

3.3   Experiment Design

To test the hypotheses, we conducted the experiment in the context of the Software Architecture course at the Faculty of Computer Science, University of Vienna in spring 2012.

Subjects. The subjects of the experiment are 60 students of the Software Architecture course. The subjects were randomly assigned into two equally sized groups of 30 students: experiment group and control group.

Objects. The basis of the experiment is the source code of the Freecol computer game[1], an open source version of the classic computer game Colonization (a turn-based strategy game) with multi-player support, implemented in Java. Both experiment group and control group were provided with access to the complete source code of Freecol. In order to avoid any bias caused by complex Integrated Development Environments (IDEs) or code editors, source code access was only provided using the Browser-based code navigation tool that is integrated with our locally hosted installation of Gitorious[2].

---

[1] See http://www.freecol.org/
[2] See http://www.gitorious.org/

Instrumentation. The participants of both groups received the following materials: The Browser-based access to the source code of Freecol was provided in a Lab environment on prepared computers. All other materials were provided on paper. The participants received a questionnaire about the independent variables regarding the participants' experiences. Both groups also received 7 different questions about the design and architecture of Freecol (see below). In addition, the experiment group received an additional document with 6 UML component diagrams showing: a FreeCol Architecture Overview, the FreeCol Server Architecture, the FreeCol Client Architecture, a Detailed View: FreeCol Server - Control, the FreeCol MetaServer Architecture, and a Detailed View: FreeCol Commons. The component diagrams have been created in an architectural reconstruction of FreeCol that took place before the experiment and was independent of the experiment.

In the experiment we have tested 7 different questions about the design and architecture of Freecol. The questions have been confirmed by the independent analysts as being relevant questions for understanding Freecol's design and architecture. The questions and their classifications are shown in Table 2. We have classified the questions into the question types from Section 3.1 as follows:

– $QT1$: For 3 questions ($Q1$, $Q5$, $Q7$) the component diagrams provide direct guidance or help to better understand Freecol's design and architecture, but the information in the component diagrams alone is not enough to answer the question fully.
– $QT2$: For 1 question ($Q2$) the answer can be deduced both from the component diagrams and the source code organization (in packages) alike.
– $QT3$: For 3 questions ($Q3$, $Q4$, $Q6$) the component diagrams provide no obvious information, only vague orientation, and digging in the source code is required to answer the question.

We asked 3 questions of type $QT1$ and 3 questions of type $QT3$, so clearly those two question types are our main focus. We also checked $QT2$, but only once, as it is a rather seldom occurring option somewhat in between $QT1$ and $QT3$ that some design aspects are directly visible from the source code organization. To illustrate the difference between the two extremes in our experiment, $QT1$ and $QT3$, and let us briefly explain the difference in the level of detail modelled:

– *Example for Type QT3:* For question $Q3$ of type $QT3$ there is only a component *AI* visible in the FreeCol Server Architecture model. It has a single connector with the interface *AIPlayer* to the *Model* component. This provides only *vague orientation* for answering question $Q3$, as it enables the participants to know that AI concerns are implemented in the server packages and that there is a link to the model classes, but it does not provide details for answering the question.
– *Example for Type QT1:* For question $Q1$ of type $QT1$ there are significantly more details and links to all important aspects of the question in the component diagrams. First of all in the FreeCol Client Architecture model, we can see a component *Controller* that is linked through a connector with an interface *GameControl* to the *Actions* component and through another connector with an interface *UpdateHandler* to the *GUI* component. This enables participants to understand how GUI Actions

use *InGameController* (and another class *ConnectController*) to perform model, game, etc. updates using basic controls. It also makes it easy to find various basic control tasks in the game's client, which can then easily be found in the source code. The *Controller* also has a connector to a port with the *Model* interface, which links to details in the Commons and Server Architecture component models. In the server, the *Model* component is linked to another *Control* component which is modelled in a detailed view, the FreeCol Server: Control component diagram. This enables participants to understand (1) the client-server relationship for control and the synchronization through models and (2) the event handling for changes through model messages.

Clearly, the level of detail for question type $QT1$ is much higher. We hope this example helps to illustrate what we mean by *"providing direct guidance or help"* for $QT1$ in contrast to *"vague orientation"* for $QT3$.

3.4   Execution

The experiment was executed in the context of the Software Architecture course at the Faculty of Computer Science, University of Vienna in the summer semester 2012/2013. Before the experiment took place, the participants were randomly assigned to experiment group and control group. Each of the two groups consisted of 30 participants (total participant number: 60).

Figure 1 shows the previous experience of the participants for the control group and the experiment group. In particular, the figure shows the programming experience of the participants, which is quite comparable in the two groups, with slightly more participants with longer experience in the experiment group. The industry programming experience is low in both groups, with a few participants with 1, 1-3, or even more than 3 years of industry experience in both groups. Finally, the very few participants with game programming experience are equally present in both groups.

Before the experiment started, the materials explained in Section 3.3 were handed out to the participants and the tasks were briefly explained to both groups. After 15 minutes of introduction, the participants were given time to fill out the questionnaire about their experiences. After all participants were ready, the answering of the questions started. The answers were provided by the participants on paper. This main phase of the experiment lasted for two hours.

The data collection was performed as planned in the design. No participants dropped out and no deviations from the study design occurred.

The experiment took place in a controlled environment. The experiment was conducted for both groups in different rooms, equipped with computers to which the participants had logins. At least one experimenter was present in each room during the whole experiment time to assure that participants behaved as expected. After the experiment, all materials were collected by the experimenters before any of the participants left the room. There were no situations in which participants behaved unexpectedly.

Table 2. Questions and Classification of Questions

ID	Type	Question	Classification Details
Q1	QT1	Explain the role of the class "InGameController" in the Package "net.sf.freecol.client.control". What is its purpose?	Component diagrams provide detailed orientation through related components and connectors, and also hint at interesting architectural concerns not easily seen from the source code. Connection to the source code must be made for providing the full answer.
Q2	QT2	How many and which independent executable programs belong to this game?	Component diagrams provide detailed orientation. The answer can be deduced from component model, but also from the package structure in the source code.
Q3	QT3	Explain how the computer players (AI) are integrated into the game. Which classes are responsible for the integration and implementation of the AI players? In which of the executable program(s) (see Q2) do they run?	Component diagrams provide vague orientation through components. The source code is the main source of information.
Q4	QT3	What is the role of the class "DOMMessage" in the "net.sf.freecol.common.networking" Package? How is it used in the game?	Component diagrams provide no details for answering the question, only vague orientation. The source code is the main source for getting the required information.
Q5	QT1	What is the role of classes in the package "net.sf.freecol.metaserver"?	Component diagrams provide detailed orientation through related components and connectors. Connection to the source code must be made for providing the full answer.
Q6	QT3	What are the roles of the classes in the packages "net.sf.freecol.server.model", "net.sf.freecol.client.control", "net.sf.freecol.common.model"? How are they related to each other?	Component diagrams are useful for basic orientation, but not for answering the question. The source code is the main source of information.
Q7	QT1	In order to show a consistent game state to all players, the programs of the different players must be updated regularly. How and by which classes is this mechanism realized? Sketch the control flow from one class (or object) to the next one.	Component diagrams show related components and connectors, and a few details helpful for answering the question. Component diagrams also hint at the architectural big picture not easily seen only from the source code.

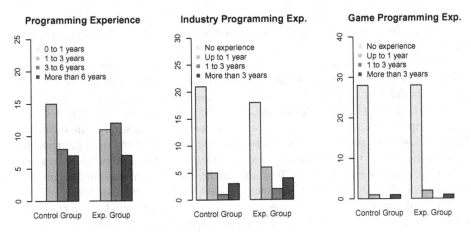

Fig. 1. Experience of the Participants

4   Analysis

4.1   Descriptive Statistics

Figure 2 shows the medians and means for the quality of the answers given to the seven questions $Q1$–$Q7$ for both control group and experiment group (the values can also be seen below in Table 4). As can be seen, the medians and means for questions of type $QT1$ ($Q1$, $Q5$, $Q7$) are always higher in the experiment group than those in the control group. For the question of type $QT2$ ($Q2$) the control group yields a slightly better result. The medians and means for questions of type $QT3$ ($Q3$, $Q4$, $Q6$) of the experiment group show the same or slightly better results than those of the control group.

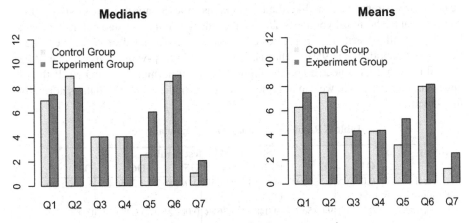

Fig. 2. Medians and means for the seven questions

4.2   Data Set Reduction

The deviations from the means for the ratings of all questions are in a corridor that roughly corresponds to our previous experiences from other exercises with participants in our courses. Hence, we did not want to exclude individual participants from the data set, as excluding data points would have introduced a potential vulnerability for the study results.

An interesting outlier in the medians and means for the seven questions is Question $Q7$, where both groups performed rather poorly. Hence, we studied the answers for this question in depth to understand whether it is necessary to exclude Question $Q7$ from the further analysis, for instance because it was too hard to answer or simply because the participants did not have enough time for answering the question (which was the last question). First we checked the protocols of the experiment and most participants have finished before the end of the 2 hours slot, so the limited time frame does not seem to be the cause of the poor results. To study whether the question was too difficult, we did an in depth study of answers without knowledge whether the individual answers were from the control group or the experiment group. The results are: Indeed, Question $Q7$ seems to be a difficult question that requires complex design and architecture understanding and making connections across multiple parts of the FreeCol system's design and architecture. Most participants failed and reached 0-3 points. Very few participants are in the middle ranks of 4-6 points. Only 6 out of the 60 participants managed to provide a sufficient answer to the question (with a score > 6 points). As this means that 10% of the participants were able to answer the question sufficiently, it does not seem impossible for novice architects to answer Question $Q7$, just difficult. Hence, we decided to not exclude the question from further analysis but rather view it as a case to study a difficult question of type $QT1$.

4.3   Hypotheses Testing

Testing the Normality of the Data.   As a first step in analysing the data, we tested the normality of the data by applying the Shapiro-Wilk test [32], in order to see whether we can apply parametric tests like the t-test that assume the normal distribution of the analysed data. The null hypothesis H_0 for the Shapiro-Wilk test states that the input data is normally distributed. H_0 is tested at the significant level of $\alpha = 0.05$ (i.e., the level of confidence is 95%). That is, if the calculated p-value is lower than 0.05 the null hypothesis is rejected and the input data is not normally distributed. If the p-value is higher than 0.05, we can not reject the null hypothesis that the data is normally distributed.

Table 3. Results of the Shapiro-Wilk normality test

Group	N	Shapiro-Wilk test p-value						
		Q1	Q2	Q3	Q4	Q5	Q6	Q7
Control Group	30	0.06505	6.528e-05	0.07345	0.0852	0.005865	7.255e-05	1.362e-06
Experiment Group	30	0.01998	9.035e-05	0.04852	0.3658	0.0002576	3.028e-05	0.0007023

In the Table 3 the p-values for the Shapiro-Wilk normality test for the seven questions $Q1$–$Q7$ for both control group and experiment group are shown. As can be seen, most questions do not have a normal distribution (i.e., hypothesis H_0 is rejected). Some other questions show a p-value right above 0.05 which means a very weak tendency of being normally distributed. In order to test the normality of the variables with a p-value above 0.05, we graphically examined how well these variables fit the normal distribution using the normal Q-Q plot. Q-Q plot is a graphical method for comparing two probability distributions by plotting their quantiles against each other [36]. Normal Q-Q plot is a method for graphically comparing the probability distribution of the given data sample with the normal distribution. While some of the resulting plots fit the normal distribution pretty well, for none of the questions both control group and experiment group showed a strong tendency to be normally distributed. Based on these considerations of normality, we decided to pursue non-parametric statistical tests with our data.

Comparison of the Means between Two Variables. To compare the means of the variable for the control group and experiment group of a question, we applied the Wilcoxon rank-sum test [25]. The Wilcoxon rank-sum test is a non-parametric test for assessing whether one of two data samples of independent observations is stochastically greater than the other. The null hypothesis of the one-tailed Wilcoxon test (appropriate for the hypotheses in our experiment) is that the means of the first variable's distribution is less than or equal to the means of the second variable's distribution, so that we can write $H_0 : A \leq B$. The Wilcoxon rank-sum test tries to find a location shift in the distributions, i.e., the difference in means of two distributions. The corresponding alternative hypothesis H_A could be written as $H_A : A > B$. If a p-value for the test is smaller than 0.05 (level of significance), the null hypothesis is rejected and the distributions are shifted. If a p-value is larger than 0.05, the null hypothesis can not be rejected, and we can not claim that there is a shift between the two distributions.

Table 4. Results of the Wilcoxon rank-sum test

ID	Control Group: Mean	Experiment Group: Mean	Control Group: Median	Experiment Group: Median	p-value
Q1	6.3	7.466667	7	7.5	0.02021
Q2	7.466667	7.1	9	8	0.4818
Q3	3.866667	4.3	4	4	0.263
Q4	4.266667	4.333333	4	4	0.494
Q5	3.133333	5.266667	2.5	6	0.01512
Q6	7.9	8.066667	8.5	9	0.2212
Q7	1.166667	2.433333	1	2	0.006899

In the Table 4 the p-values for the Wilcoxon rank-sum test are shown, together with means and medians. The raw material for these results can be downloaded from https://swa.univie.ac.at/CDE. Based on the obtained p-values, we can assess that the following distributions show a statistically significant shift between each other: $Q1$, $Q5$, and $Q7$. None of the other variables shows a statistically significant shift.

Testing Hypothesis H_{QT1}. In our experiment, we have introduced 3 questions related to H_{QT1}: $Q1$, $Q5$, and $Q7$. Each of the three questions shows a significant location shift in their distributions, and in each of them the experiment group shows better results than the control group in their means and medians. This provides evidence that H_{0_QT1} can be rejected. That is, indeed there is evidence that augmenting the source code with architectural component diagrams *improves the quality* of answers that novice architects provide to questions about a software system's design and architecture, if the component diagrams provide architectural guidance for answering the question.

It is interesting to note that the difficult Question $Q7$ shows the same result (even with the highest significance level) as Questions $Q1$ and $Q5$ (of medium difficulty). While many of the participants in the experiment group failed as well, all but one of the sufficient answers were in the experiment group. This result seems to indicate that component diagrams can be especially helpful for problems that require making complex design and architecture connections across multiple parts of the system.

Testing Hypothesis H_{QT2}. In our experiment, we have introduced 1 question related to H_{QT2}: $Q2$. For this question we can observe higher means and medians for the control group than for the experiment group, however the location shift is not statistically significant. Therefore H_{0_QT2} can *not* be rejected. As expected, there is *no evidence* that augmenting the source code with architectural component diagrams does improve the quality of answers that novice architects provide to questions about a software system's design and architecture, *if the component diagrams provide architectural guidance for answering the question, but the same information is visible from the source code.*

Testing Hypothesis H_{QT3}. In our experiment, we have introduced 3 questions related to H_{QT3}: $Q3$, $Q4$, and $Q6$. The medians and means of the experiment group show the same or slightly better results than those of the control group. None of the three questions shows a significant location shift in their distributions so H_{0_QT3} *can not be rejected*. As expected, there is *no evidence* that augmenting the source code with architectural component diagrams does improve the quality of answers that novice architects provide to questions about a software system's architecture, *if the component diagrams provide no direct guidance or help, only vague orientation in related components and connectors.*

5   Validity Evaluation

Several levels of validity have to be considered in this experiment. We consider the classification scheme for validity in experiments by Cook and Campbell [6].

Internal Validity. The internal validity is the degree to which conclusions can be drawn about cause-effect of independent variables on the dependent variables.

- The subjects' experiences in the two groups have approximately the same degree with regard to programming, industrial, and game programming experience. Of course, a certain differences in experience between the two groups can not be entirely excluded.

- All subjects' have at least medium programming experiences and have passed several courses on programming and design at our university. Hence, we consider their responses as valid, keeping in mind that our goal was to analyse the supportive effects component diagrams have on novice architects.
- The experiment lasted about 2 hours so fatigue effects were not considered relevant.
- The experiment happened in a controlled environment in separate rooms under supervision of at least one experimenter. While it is not possible to completely exclude misbehaviour or interaction among participants, it is not very likely that misbehaviour or interactions have had a big influence on the outcomes of the experiment.
- Possibly the analysts could have been biased towards the experiment group in some way. We tried to exclude this threat to validity by not revealing to the analysts the identity of the participants or in which of the two groups they have participated. Hence, it is rather unlikely that this threat occurred.

External Validity. The external validity is the degree to which the results of the study can be generalized to the broader population under study. The greater the external validity, the more the results of an empirical study can be generalised to software engineering practice.

- We used students of our software architecture lecture as subjects. As discussed, they have medium programming and design experience, but limited professional experience. Hence, we believe them to be well representative for the target group of novice architects, but if and how the results can be translated to more experienced architects is open to future study. We plan to replicate the experiment with other target groups.
- The instrumentation and object in the experiment might have been unrealistic, not representative, or too simple to allow generalization. For instance, FreeCol as an open source game might be too simple or no representative software system for typical architectural studies. The component diagrams used might not be representative or unrealistic. Or the questions asked might not be typical design or architecture questions. All these considerations might impede the generalizability of our results. We do not think that this is the case as FreeCol is a widely used, non-trivial software system implemented in Java. The component diagrams were created in an architectural reconstruction effort that took place before the experiment and was independent of the experiment. The questions have been confirmed by the independent analysts as being relevant questions for understanding design and architecture of FreeCol.
- The experimenters could have biased the measurements of the independent variables. We mitigated this risk by assigning the quality ratings to independent analysts that had no knowledge about the goals of the experiment. Furthermore the analysts did not know the identities nor the groups of the participants.

Conclusion Validity. The conclusion validity defines the extent to which the conclusion is statistically valid. The statistical validity might be affected by the size of the sample (60 participants, 30 in each group). The size can be increased in replications of the study in order to reach normality of the obtained data. We plan to replicate the study with different systems and by engaging subjects who work in industry in our future work.

Construct Validity. The construct validity is the degree to which the independent and the dependent variables are accurately measured by their appropriated instruments. As only one object, the FreeCol implementation and associated component diagrams, was used in the experiment, there is the risk that the cause construct is under-represented. Possibly, the results could look different if multiple systems and sets of diagrams would be used for the recovery. We assume that the used system is representative for large and medium-size object-oriented systems. This threat, however, can not totally be ignored. Another potential threat to validity is that we only used one variable to measure the quality of answers. This does not allow cross-checking the results with different measures.

6 Conclusions

Our study provides initial evidence on how architectural component diagrams help in understanding the design and architecture of software systems. The results indicate that architectural component diagrams are especially useful if a direct link from the component diagram's elements to the problem that requires understanding can be made. Component diagrams seem to help in such cases to understand the bigger architectural connections that are hard to see from studying the source code alone and/or they provide orientation in the source code to understand such problems. However, there is a different situation for problems that are readily solvable by looking at the source code (like the question of type $QT2$ in our experiment) or for problems that are only vaguely linked to what is depicted in the component diagrams (like the question of type $QT3$ in our experiment). As expected, we found no evidence that architectural component diagrams help, for instance, just by providing a big picture view or providing some general kind of orientation.

We can conclude for the design of architectural component diagrams that they should be designed with specific important architectural problems in mind and that elements of the component diagrams should explicitly represent links to those problems. That is, components, connectors, and other model elements for providing an abstract understanding of the design that resolves the problem should be shown in the diagrams. The component models related to questions of type $QT1$ in our experiment achieve this by leaving out irrelevant details and showing high-level connections of system parts that are hard to reconstruct by just studying the low-level source code classes. It also seems to be important that these links from component models to the problem in focus are modelled in enough detail. Only vaguely showing a problem-related component in its context of other components and connectors that are not related to the problem is not enough.

It seems plausible, based on our results, that such details could also be provided through other architectural views or through architectural knowledge models. Further, it seems that making links to the source code is important for the supportive effect revealed in our study. Such links can be made explicit through traceability links. Hence, it also seems plausible that establishing traceability links between architectural component models and code might have a further supportive effect. We plan to study these aspects in further studies in our future work. From the combined results of this and future studies we plan to develop design guidelines for architectural component diagrams. Regarding generalizability, our results are strictly limited to the target group of novice architects with medium programming experience. We expect that similar results will also show for seasoned architects, but potentially they can make more use of vague information in architectural component diagrams. Again, we plan to investigate this in our future research.

Acknowledgement. This work was partially supported by the Austrian Science Fund (FWF), Project: P24345-N23.

References

[1] IEEE Standard Glossary of Software Engineering Terminology. Tech. rep. (1990)

[2] Babar, M.A., Bass, L., Gorton, I.: Factors influencing industrial practices of software architecture evaluation: An empirical investigation. In: Overhage, S., Ren, X.-M., Reussner, R., Stafford, J.A. (eds.) QoSA 2007. LNCS, vol. 4880, pp. 90–107. Springer, Heidelberg (2008)

[3] Biffl, S., Ali Babar, M., Winkler, D.: Impact of experience and team size on the quality of scenarios for architecture evaluation. In: Proceedings of the 12th International Conference on Evaluation and Assessment in Software Engineering, EASE 2008, pp. 1–10. British Computer Society, Swinton (2008)

[4] Boucké, N., Weyns, D., Holvoet, T.: Composition of architectural models: Empirical analysis and language support. J. Syst. Softw. 83(11), 2108–2127 (2010)

[5] Clements, P., Garlan, D., Bass, L., Stafford, J., Nord, R., Ivers, J., Little, R.: Documenting Software Architectures: Views and Beyond. Pearson Education (2002)

[6] Cook, T.D., Campbell, D.T.: Quasi-Experimentation: Design and Analysis Issues for Field Settings. Houghton Mifflin (1979)

[7] Cruz-Lemus, J.A., Genero, M., Manso, M.E., Morasca, S., Piattini, M.: Assessing the understandability of uml statechart diagrams with composite states–a family of empirical studies. Empirical Softw. Engg. 14(6), 685–719 (2009)

[8] Falessi, D., Babar, M.A., Cantone, G., Kruchten, P.: Applying empirical software engineering to software architecture: challenges and lessons learned. Empirical Softw. Engg. 15(3), 250–276 (2010)

[9] Fenton, N.E., Ohlsson, N.: Quantitative analysis of faults and failures in a complex software system. IEEE Trans. Softw. Eng. 26(8), 797–814 (2000)

[10] Fernández-Sáez, A.M., Genero, M., Chaudron, M.R.V.: Does the level of detail of uml models affect the maintainability of source code? In: Kienzle, J. (ed.) MODELS 2011 Workshops. LNCS, vol. 7167, pp. 134–148. Springer, Heidelberg (2012)

[11] Ferrari, R., Miller, J.A., Madhavji, N.H.: A controlled experiment to assess the impact of system architectures on new system requirements. Requir. Eng. 15(2), 215–233 (2010)

[12] Galster, M.: Dependencies, traceability and consistency in software architecture: towards a view-based perspective. In: Proceedings of the 5th European Conference on Software Architecture: Companion Volume, ECSA 2011. ACM (2011)

[13] Genero, M., Cruz-Lemus, J.A., Caivano, D., Abrahão, S., Insfran, E., Carsí, J.A.: Assessing the influence of stereotypes on the comprehension of uml sequence diagrams: A controlled experiment. In: Czarnecki, K., Ober, I., Bruel, J.-M., Uhl, A., Völter, M. (eds.) MoDELS 2008. LNCS, vol. 5301, pp. 280–294. Springer, Heidelberg (2008)

[14] Graves, T.L., Karr, A.F., Marron, J.S., Siy, H.: Predicting fault incidence using software change history. IEEE Trans. Softw. Eng. 26(7), 653–661 (2000)

[15] Hansen, K.M., Jonasson, K., Neukirchen, H.: Controversy corner: An empirical study of software architectures' effect on product quality. J. Syst. Softw. 84(7), 1233–1243 (2011)

[16] van Heesch, U., Avgeriou, P.: Naive architecting - understanding the reasoning process of students: a descriptive survey. In: Babar, M.A., Gorton, I. (eds.) ECSA 2010. LNCS, vol. 6285, pp. 24–37. Springer, Heidelberg (2010)

[17] van Heesch, U., Avgeriou, P., Zdun, U., Harrison, N.: The supportive effect of patterns in architecture decision recovery - a controlled experiment. Sci. Comput. Program. 77(5), 551–576 (2012)

[18] van Heesch, U., Avgeriou, P.: Mature architecting - a survey about the reasoning process of professional architects. In: Proceedings of the 2011 Ninth Working IEEE/IFIP Conference on Software Architecture, WICSA 2011, pp. 260–269. IEEE Computer Society, Washington, DC (2011)

[19] Hofmeister, C., Nord, R., Soni, D.: Applied Software Architecture. Addison-Wesley (2000)

[20] ISO: ISO/IEC CD1 42010, Systems and software engineering — Architecture description (January 2010)

[21] Jansen, A., Bosch, J.: Software architecture as a set of architectural design decisions. In: Proceedings of the 5th Working IEEE/IFIP Conference on Software Architecture, WICSA 2005, pp. 109–120. IEEE Computer Society, Washington, DC (2005)

[22] Kitchenham, B.A., Pfleeger, S.L., Pickard, L.M., Jones, P.W., Hoaglin, D.C., El Emam, K., Rosenberg, J.: Preliminary guidelines for empirical research in software engineering. IEEE Transactions on Software Engineering 28(8), 721–734 (2002)

[23] Kruchten, P., Lago, P., van Vliet, H.: Building up and reasoning about architectural knowledge. In: Hofmeister, C., Crnkovic, I., Reussner, R. (eds.) QoSA 2006. LNCS, vol. 4214, pp. 43–58. Springer, Heidelberg (2006)

[24] Malaiya, Y.K., Denton, J.: Module size distribution and defect density. In: Proceedings of the 11th International Symposium on Software Reliability Engineering, ISSRE 2000, pp. 62–71. IEEE Computer Society, Washington, DC (2000)

[25] Mann, H.B., Whitney, D.R.: On a test of whether one of two random variables is stochastically larger than the other. Annals of Mathematical Statistics 18(1), 50–60 (1947)

[26] Miller, J.A., Ferrari, R., Madhavji, N.H.: An exploratory study of architectural effects on requirements decisions. J. Syst. Softw. 83(12), 2441–2455 (2010)

[27] Mohagheghi, P., Conradi, R., Killi, O.M., Schwarz, H.: An empirical study of software reuse vs. defect-density and stability. In: Proceedings of the 26th International Conference on Software Engineering, ICSE 2004, pp. 282–292. IEEE Computer Society, Washington, DC (2004)

[28] Otero, M.C., Dolado, J.J.: Evaluation of the comprehension of the dynamic modeling in uml. Information and Software Technology 46(1), 35–53 (2004)

[29] Perry, D.E., Wolf, A.L.: Foundations for the study of software architecture. SIGSOFT Softw. Eng. Notes 17(4), 40–52 (1992)

[30] Purchase, H.C., Colpoys, L., McGill, M., Carrington, D., Britton, C.: Uml class diagram syntax: an empirical study of comprehension. In: Proceedings of the 2001 Asia-Pacific Symposium on Information Visualisation, APVis 2001, vol. 9, pp. 113–120. Australian Computer Society, Inc., Darlinghurst (2001)

[31] Rozanski, N., Woods, E.: Software Systems Architecture: Working With Stakeholders Using Viewpoints and Perspectives. Addison-Wesley Professional (2005)

[32] Shapiro, S.S., Wilk, M.B.: An analysis of variance test for normality (complete samples). Biometrika 3(52) (1965)

[33] Stevens, S.: On the theory of scales of measurement. Science 103(2684), 677–680 (1946)

[34] Tyree, J., Akerman, A.: Architecture decisions: Demystifying architecture. IEEE Software 22, 19–27 (2005)

[35] Umphress, D.A., Hendrix, T.D., Cross II, J.H., Maghsoodloo, S.: Software visualizations for improving and measuring the comprehensibility of source code. Science of Computer Programming 60(2), 121–133 (2006)

[36] Wilk, M.B., Gnanadesikan, R.: Probability plotting methods for the analysis of data. Biometrika 55(1), 1–17 (1968)

[37] Wohlin, C.: Experimentation in Software Engineering: An Introduction. Kluwer Academic (2000)

[38] Zimmermann, O., Koehler, J., Leymann, F., Polley, R., Schuster, N.: Managing architectural decision models with dependency relations, integrity constraints, and production rules. Journal of Systems and Software 82(8), 1249–1267 (2009)

Software Architecture Documentation for Developers: A Survey

Dominik Rost[1], Matthias Naab[1], Crescencio Lima[2],
and Christina von Flach Garcia Chavez[2]

[1] Fraunhofer Institute for Experimental Software Engineering
Kaiserslautern, Germany
{dominik.rost,matthias.naab}@iese.fraunhofer.de
[2] Fraunhofer Project Center on Software and Systems Engineering
Software Engineering Laboratory, Department of Computer Science
Federal University of Bahia, Bahia, Brazil
{crescencio,flach}@dcc.ufba.br

Abstract. Software architecture has become an established discipline in industry. Nevertheless, the available documentation of architecture is often not perceived as adequate by developers. As a foundation for the improvement of
methods and tools around architecture documentation, we conducted a survey
with 147 industrial participants, investigating their current problems and wishes
for the future. Participants from different countries in Europe, Asia, North and
South America shared their experiences. This paper presents the results of the
survey. The results confirmed the common belief that architecture documentation is most frequently outdated and inconsistent and backed it up with data.
Further, developers perceive difficulties with a "one-size-fits-all" architecture
documentation, which does not adequately provide information for their specific task and context. Developers seek for more interactive ways of working with
architecture documentation that allow finding needed information more easily
with extended navigation and search possibilities.

Keywords: Software architecture, documentation, developers, implementation,
industry, survey.

1   Introduction

1.1   The Practical Problem

Software architecture is accepted as an integral part of software engineering and an
enabler for efficient and effective software development. Increasing system size and
complexity, as well as the employment of multiple, globally distributed development
teams pose new challenges and increase the importance of documenting software
architecture.

Nevertheless, many industrial organizations still do not have *any architecture documentation in place*. A main reason for this is that creation of architecture documentation is inherently cost intensive. As a consequence, their software development suffers
from growing communication and alignment effort, which makes implementation

K. Drira (Ed.): ECSA 2013, LNCS 7957, pp. 72–88, 2013.

increasingly inefficient, inconsistent, and incompliant to the architecture. During system evolution, this leads to architecture erosion [1] which can prevent the achievement of essential system qualities and leads to a decreasing maintainability. This holds true even for the initial development of the system [2].

However, we also observe organizations that *have architecture documentation but are not able to leverage the potential* that lies in it. The reasons for this are diverse. For instance, the information provided in architecture documentation is often too unspecific for a concrete usage or task. Software architects create models and documents when they design the system and provide these as a comprehensive architecture documentation to all software developers. Developers then have to understand the complete architecture documentation to extract the information relevant for the local scope of their task and adapt it to their context. Another problem is inconsistencies in content and form, making finding and understanding relevant architecture information a challenge. Very often, the effectiveness of architecture documentation decreases over time, because it is not kept up to date. The cost-benefit ratio of such architecture documentation may found the decision to stop investing in architecture in general.

These challenges should be addressed by applied research on architecture documentation. Enhanced methods and tools shall support architects in creating and maintaining architecture documentation that allows highly efficient and effective implementation for software developers. To collect empirical facts for backing up our project experiences and as a foundation for improving methods and tools, we conducted a survey with developers in industry and asked them about their work with architecture documentation. In total, 147 developers from different countries in Europe, Asia, North and South America participated, working in organizations from two to more than 100,000 employees. In this paper, we report on the creation and results of the study and discuss our main findings.

1.2 This Study

In this study, we focused on software architecture documentation for developers to complement our experiences from industry projects with the views of software developers. By this, we aim to create a basis for future improvement of methods and tools for architecture documentation, to make implementation more efficient and effective. So, we defined the overall goal of the study according to the GQM template [3] as:

"Characterizing the current situation and improvement potential of software architecture documentation with respect to architectural information and its representation from the perspective of developers in industry as the basis for developing practically applicable methods and tools to make implementation work more efficient and effective."

There are some aspects that need to be emphasized in this goal statement: Our main focus is software developers. While methods and tools might target architects in the creation of documentation, in this study we ask developers about their view as users of the documentation. A second aspect is that we separate two dimensions: (1) architecture information vs. representation and (2) characterization of the current situation vs. requirements for the future. The combination of both dimensions gives us four areas in which we ask developers about their views. And the last aspect is that this study constitutes the basis for the improvement of methods and tools for advanced architecture documentation that shall help developers to fulfill their implementation tasks in less time, with high quality results.

From the goal statement following the two dimensions, we derived four research questions that are the source of the structure and content of the survey:

- *RQ1: Which architectural information do developers currently receive for implementation activities and which problems do they perceive?*
- *RQ2: Which representation of architectural information do developers currently receive for implementation activities and which problems do they perceive?*
- *RQ3: Which architectural information would developers like to get for their implementation activities?*
- *RQ4: Which representation of architectural information would developers like to get for their implementation activities?*

1.3   Related Studies

In 2003, Lethbridge, Singer, and Forward published the results of three studies on how software engineers use documentation [4]. Unlike the work presented in this paper, their studies were not focused on architecture documentation only. Most of their main findings confirm our experiences in industry projects. They state: *"documentation of all types is frequently out of date"*, *"much mandated documentation is so time consuming to create that its cost can outweigh its benefits"*, and *"A considerable fraction of documentation is untrustworthy"*. We were interested in whether there has been any improvement in the past ten years concerning these factors. To investigate this, we asked questions like *"How often is architecture documentation up to date?"* or *"How much architecture documentation do you have typically available in development projects?"* and specifically replicated the question of *"in your experience, when changes are made to a software system, how long does it take for the architecture documentation to be updated to reflect the changes?"*. It is fair to say that the problems from one decade ago persist to a large extent until today.

In 2006, Koning and van Vliet reported on their study of four architecture descriptions from industry and their distances to the IEEE Standard 1471 in [5]. Specifically, they studied which parts of the documents were relevant to which stakeholder concern. They stated that *"Our research makes it very understandable that readers complain about too much information."* as well as *"Almost none of the stakeholders is interested in the full report."* This supports our assumption that unspecific architecture is a factor for inefficient and ineffective implementation activities. We included questions in our survey concerning the amount and specificity of architecture documentation provided to developers, like *"Please rate your agreement to the statement: "The architecture documentation I work with contains a lot of unnecessary (overhead) information.""*.

In 2012, Malavolta et al. reported results on their study on the industrial usage of architecture description languages in [6]. Main findings of their study include *"Organizations (even in domains involving critical systems) prefer semi-formal and generic ALs than formal- and domain-specific ones like ADLs"* and *"[...] Code generation is not often required. Link to requirements (elicitation and specification) is important as well".* We included questions about the usage of formal ADLs in our survey, as well as about developers' wishes concerning the features of architecture documentation. Besides this, as we found it quite compelling, we adopted to a large extent their paper's structure.

The remainder of this paper is structured as follows: In Section 2 we introduce fundamental work on architecture documentation. In Section 3 we describe our research methodology. In Section 4, we describe the participants of our study. In Section 4.2 we present the results and our main findings. In Section 5 the main findings are discussed together with threats to the validity of the study and conclusions.

2   Architecture Documentation

Making software architecture explicit and persistent is a key factor of utilizing the potential that it offers. This is reflected by the fact that almost all comprehensive approaches for software architecture also cover documentation. Examples are [7] or [8]. There is even a standard in place for the description of software architectures [9].

Architecture views have been introduced to address the need to deal with the complexity of software systems and are still one of the central concepts of the discipline. They help to separate different concerns of the software systems according to the needs of different stakeholders. Several different view sets have been presented since then and some of the most known and applied ones include Kruchten's 4+1 View model [10], the Siemens Four Views model [11], or the SEI's Views and Beyond approach [12]. However, the usage of different architecture view types is not sufficient anymore to handle the complexity of modern software systems and to describe them in an adequate form for different stakeholders. The amount of information can be so high that efficient working is still hampered, making studies as ours necessary.

For description languages, different ways are used and have been proposed in practice and research. This reaches from simple whiteboard sketches to formal architecture description languages. Thereby, the degree of formality is the main varying factor. In research, high levels of formality are typically valued in architecture description languages, as they allow sophisticated analyses and automated processing of information. Examples are ACME [13] or AADL [14]. In contrast, practice values fast creation and understandability, as it is mainly used as a vehicle for information exchange. The predominant description language for architectures is UML [15]. Often UML diagrams are complemented with descriptions in natural language. Accordingly, also the format, in which architecture documentation is distributed, varies. This includes electronic documents and presentation files, webpages, but also model files, created with modeling tools like Sparx System's Enterprise Architect [16].

Recent research brought up the relatively new discipline of architecture knowledge management to explicate and persist architecture information. Farenhorst and de Boer published a state of the art survey on this topic [17] and observed four main directions of architecture knowledge management: 1. *Sharing architecture knowledge,* to make architecture information efficiently available to stakeholders, like in [18] or [19]. 2. *Aligning architecting with requirements engineering,* to create a between architecture information and requirements, like in [20]. 3. *Towards a body of knowledge*, for the creation of a comprehensive encyclopedia of architecture info, like in [21]. 4. *Intelligent support for architecting*, for efficient working with architecture and its documentation, like in [22]. However, architecture knowledge management methods are currently not applied to a large extent in practice.

3   Research Methodology

For our research, we distinguish the following phases: planning the survey, designing and conducting the survey, and analyzing the data.

3.1   Planning the Survey

We defined the overall goal of the survey the four research questions as introduced in Section 1.2. Based on these, we planned and designed the survey and derived the concrete survey questions for the participants.

The target group for the survey was software developers in industry. Thereby it was not important whether they actually had software architecture documentation available in their implementation work, because asking them about their wishes for the future was possible in either way. To invite participants we decided to use e-mail, however we did not want to just contact random software companies. To increase the chances for a high response rate, we compiled a list of fitting past and current customers and project partners from industry. As we typically have only one or two contact persons, we contacted them directly and asked to distribute the information about the survey internally to software developers in their organization with the request to participate. In this way we contacted 92 IT organizations from Europe, Asia, North and South America, ranging from two to around 130,000 employees. Additionally BITKOM[1], the German Association for Information Technology, Telecommunications and New Media and the Software Foren Leipzig[2] assisted by distributing the information via their mailing lists.

3.2   Designing and Conducting the Survey

The 4 research questions (see Section 1.2) provided the framework for the derivation of our survey questions. Fig. 1 depicts the resulting structure of survey questions as a matrix. The key distinctions are between architectural information and its representation and the distinction between the as-is situation for the participant and wishes for a to-be situation related to architecture documentation. Additionally, we asked for information about the participants' background (e.g. on their company, see Section 4.1). In Fig. 2, the flow of survey questions is presented. It starts with a question about the preferred language for conducting the survey. As this research was done in a German-Brazilian cooperation with many participants from Germany and Brazil expected, we offered the languages German, Portuguese and in addition, English.

---

[1] http://www.bitkom.org
[2] http://www.softwareforen.de

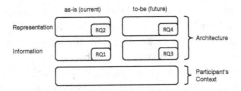

Fig. 1. Structure of survey questions and relationship to research questions

Then, we asked about the availability of architecture documentation for the participants and their tasks as a developer. This question had an impact on the further flow of survey questions: Only if a participant indicated that architecture documentation was available, the questions about the as-is situation were asked, otherwise they were not visible for the participant.

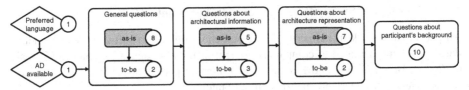

Fig. 2. Flow of questions in the survey. Grey blocks are only asked in case of architecture documentation available. The circled number indicates the number of questions.

The main part of the survey were three pages of questions, each visually separated into a set for the as-is situation and a set for the to-be situation: First, general questions about architecture documentation were asked, not differentiating between the aspects of information and their representation. Second, questions with a focus on architectural information in architecture documentation were asked. Third, questions about the representation of architecture information were asked. Finally, a set of questions about the participant's background were asked (cf. Section 4.1). We had two types of questions: First, questions with a fixed set of answers, partially single and partially multi selection ones. Second, there were questions with a free text answer.

We created an online questionnaire by using the Enterprise Feedback Suite by questback[3], containing 42 questions. We conducted the survey in the period from December 1st, 2012 to January 31st, 2013.

3.3 Analyzing the Data

Only a subset of the participants starting the survey actually finished it. We considered the survey as finished when the participants clicked the submit button. For the analysis and evaluation, when we talk about participants we refer to the ones having finished the survey.

A total of 147 participants (N=147) have been included in the data analysis. Nevertheless, we did not have a complete data set for each question, as not all questions were mandatory. That is, for each question the sample varies.

---

[3] http://www.questback.com/solutions/market-research/

As described, we asked about the availability of architecture documentation and excluded respective questions if there was none. Not all participants had architecture documentation available for their tasks. Thus, for the questions about current architecture documentation we have only answers of a subset of the participants (N=109).

For questions with fixed answers we counted the results in the analysis. For the evaluation of free text results, we grouped the answers into coherent categories with an appropriate name to cover the full range of answers. Then we additionally aligned these answer categories across questions where it was meaningful.

Due to space limitations, we did not present all questions and answers in this paper[4].

4   Results

4.1   Overview of Survey Participants and Their Context

All participants work in industry and are somehow related to software development. Participants are affiliated to companies in eight different countries, mainly in Germany (59%), Brazil (23%), and Finland (13%). Further participants come from France, Japan, Sweden, Switzerland, and the United States.

The survey aims at the development perspective on software architecture. Nevertheless, many participants with a slightly different focus in their own position contributed to the survey. Fig. 3 depicts the distribution of participants' occupational positions. The largest group is developers (46%), followed by architects (23%) and managers (20%). The participant's position was asked as free text, thus we consolidated the answers into the depicted categories.

Fig. 3. Current position of the participants in their companies

In order to judge the professional experience of the participants we asked for the number of years they already are in their or a similar position. The answers, grouped from an open question, were the following: 0 to 3 years – 27%, 4 to 7 years – 34%, 8 to 11 years – 17%, 12 to 15 years – 10%, more than 15 years – 12%.

In order to characterize the companies the participants are affiliated with, we asked for the industry sectors they work in (see Fig. 4). Most participants work for companies that have software development for multiple industries (27%) as their main business. The other companies are developing software for customers of a dedicated sector or for their own business units. Other strong sectors in our survey are building construction management (10%), automotive (8%), energy (8%), and finance (8%). While the survey in general was anonymous, we asked the participants at the end

---

[4] We provide the complete data set upon request.

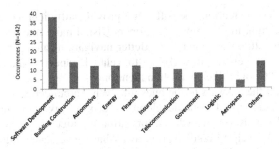

Fig. 4. Sectors of the participants' companies

whether they agree with publishing their company's name in the study. Participating companies included among others: Accenture, Deloitte Consulting GmbH, Denso, KSB, msg systems AG, Murex, SAP AG, Software AG, Talend, T-Systems, Tekla.

There are significant differences, in the participants' companies in the number of people contributing to software development. 41% reported less than 100 people in software development, 41% reported 100 to 1000, 11% reported 1000 to 5000, and 7% reported more than 5000 people in software development.

The majority (50%) of the participants develops software according to a combination of agile and conventional development processes. 33% work completely with agile development processes, 7% work with purely conventional development processes. 10% do not use a structured development process at all.

Finally, we asked the participants to rate the size of the product they are contributing to. 22% contribute to a very large product, 32% contribute to a large product. 34% contribute to a medium-size product, 11% contribute to a small product and 1% to a very small product. How the product size was estimated was left to the participants for simplicity of answering the question.

4.2   Main Findings

This section describes the results of the survey. Please note that the results of the *general* questions are consistently integrated into this structure. We identified 5 main findings, which are summarized below and discussed in Section 5.

1. Architecture documentation is often not up-to-date and thus strongly lacks utility. In particular, architecture documentation is not kept up-to-date with changes in requirements or changes in the source code.
2. Architecture documentation is often provided in a "one-size-fits-all" manner. Consequently, it does not provide the right information for the specific stakeholders and their current tasks. Developers in particular have strongly varying needs in information and the level of detail, which can only be covered with more specific architecture documentation.
3. Architecture documentation is often inconsistent. Inconsistency comes in different forms like inconsistent structure in and across documents, inconsistent notations, or contradicting information. A higher level of consistency is desirable for developers in order to easier understand the architecture and to come up with a higher quality implementation.

4. Architecture documentation does often not provide sufficient navigation support to easily find the right information. Developers wish a more interactive way of working with architecture documentation: Better navigation (along the hierarchical decomposition and general traceability to related aspects) and powerful search functionality ("Google-like" was often mentioned).
5. Aggregating all the answers to the question "What architecture information do you need for best support of your development tasks?" gives in our opinion a very complete and mature picture what information architecture documentation should contain. This is a helpful confirmation that what we see as architecturally relevant is also demanded by developers. Nevertheless, it has to be taken into account that architecture documentation should be strongly tailored to the concrete usage.

4.3   Architectural Information: The as-is Situation

In the *general questions*, we asked "What do you consider as the main problems with the architecture documentation you work with?" and received with respect to architectural information the following most frequent questions:

- Outdated architecture documentation (25 [occurrences])
- Inadequate level of granularity (19)
- Implementation not in sync with architecture any more (17)
- Not specific for stakeholders and concrete situation (10)

We asked about the amount of architecture documentation available and its up-to-dateness. The results are depicted in Fig. 5. This also confirms that architecture documentation is often not up-to-date and if at all updated with a strong delay. This supports the findings reported in [4].

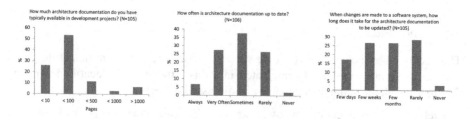

Fig. 5. Amount and up-to-dateness of architecture documentation

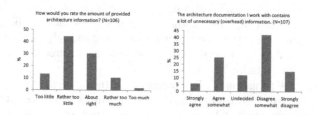

Fig. 6. Adequacy of amount of architecture documentation provided

We asked the participants to rate their perceived adequacy of the amount of architecture information provided (see Fig. 6). A tendency can be observed that there is rather too little architectural information available. Some participants agree that there is also necessary information but most participants rather see no unnecessary information provided. Keeping in mind that many participants have too little architecture information, it is no surprise that they do not see much overhead. When architecture documentation becomes extensive, the need for better orientation and specific tailoring arises.

4.4   Representation of Architectural Information: The as-is Situation

In the *general questions*, we asked "What do you consider as the main problems with the architecture documentation you work with?" and received with respect to representation of architectural information the following most frequent questions:

- Inconsistencies and missing structure (15)
- Information scattered across documents (8)
- Missing traceability to other artifacts (5)

In order to get some more insights into the problems with the representation of architecture information, we asked the question described in Table 1. The answers received, confirm and detail the answers to the general question described before. We summarized further, non-categorized answers as "other".

Table 1. What problems do you see in the way how architecture information is described?

Answer Category	Occurrences	% (N=42)
Missing common formats and structures	6	14,3
Targets too many groups and thus not specific	5	11,9
Unnecessary information	5	11,9
Wrong or varying degree of abstraction	4	9,5
Missing traceability to external information	3	7,1
Missing details in the written description	3	7,1
Hard to consistently update	3	7,1
Missing information about business logic, focus only on infrastructure	2	4,8
Other	6	14,3

We asked about the main formats in which architecture documentation is provided. Architecture documentation is mostly provided as electronic documents, like Word or pdf (87%), model files (50%), and web pages (45%).

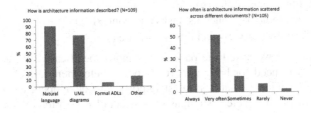

Fig. 7. Notation of architecture documentation and scattering across documents

The two key notations for the description of software architecture are natural language and UML (see Fig. 7). Formal ADLs are used very rarely. This confirms the findings of [6]. Mentioned under other, informal diagrams in Visio or Powerpoint are also used. Another result is that architecture information is typically not consolidated in a single source of information but scattered across documents (see Fig. 7).

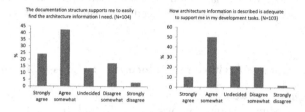

Fig. 8. Perceived adequacy of representation of architecture information

We asked the participants how they perceive the support of their architecture documentation to find specific information and to conduct their development tasks. Fig. 8 depicts the results, showing that there is a tendency that the participants perceive the representation as adequate. To refine the insights about problems finding the needed architecture information, we asked the question described in Table 2.

Table 2. What problems do you see in terms of finding the architecture information you need?

Answer Category	Occurrences	% (N=56)
Missing clarity in structure	13	23,2
Information scattered across documents	11	19,6
Missing strong search functionality	10	17,9
Missing traceability (inside and to other artifacts)	8	14,3
Documents not up-to-date	8	14,3
Inconsistent terminology and notation	5	8,9
Too much information	4	7,1
Missing information	4	7,1
Other	6	10,7

4.5   Architectural Information: The to-be Situation

In the *general questions*, we asked "What are your wishes in general for the future of architecture documentation?" and received with respect to architectural information the following most frequent questions:

- Up-to-date (19)
- In sync with implementation (18)
- Specific for stakeholders, concerns, tasks and contexts (14)
- Providing a system overview and the big picture (11)

For a deeper insight we asked the participants more specifically "What architecture information do you need for best support of your development tasks?" From the answers it becomes evident, that it is most important to developers to get an overall understanding of the complete system, as well as detailed information on components in their scope together with interfaces and relationships to other components. Table 3 shows an overview.

Table 3. What arch. information do you need for best support of your development tasks?

Answer Category	Occurrences	% (N=103)
Components, interfaces, relationships, decomposition	44	42,7
Big picture	20	19,4
Mapping to implementation	12	11,7
Functional modularization	11	10,7
Data model and data flow	11	10,7
Deployment and deployment alternatives	9	8,7
Patterns and best practices	9	8,7
Project context	9	8,7
Technologies, frameworks and standards	9	8,7
(Discarded) Architecture decisions and rationale	8	7,8
Architecture drivers	8	7,8
Behavior	7	6,8
Other	17	16,5

Additionally, we asked the participants how much architecture documentation they perceive as optimal. This question is a bit provocative and as expected, the most frequent answer was: "It depends". But mainly it depends on the target group and task, but also on the system and context. However the answers also suggest that a reduction of the information to the indispensable amount is desirable. Table 4 shows the results.

Table 4. How much architecture documentation is optimal?

Answer Category	Occurrences	% (N=83)
Depends on target group and task	16	19,3
Depends on project / system	15	18,1
Enough to provide an overview of the system and context	9	10,8
As minimal as possible	9	10,8
Other	42	50,6

4.6 Representation of Architectural Information: The to-be Situation

In the *general questions*, we asked the question "What are your wishes in general for the future of architecture documentation?" and received with respect to representation of architectural information the following most frequent questions:

- Easy creation, handling, updating, and maintenance (20)
- Connected and integrated information, artifacts and tools (16)
- Readable and understandable (12)
- Consistent and systematically structured and described (11)

For a deeper insight, we asked the participants more specifically "In what format should architecture documentation be provided in the future?". Table 5 shows an overview. It can be noted that webpages, electronic documents and diagrams are the predominant wishes. UML also plays a significant role, formal ADLs do not. Additionally, participants frequently voted for standard formats, for which no specific (reader) tool has to be installed.

We asked "What means should architecture documentation provide to help you in finding the information you need?" It can be observed that developers wish for interactive ways of working with architecture documentation, where it is possible to search information in different ways and navigate through hierarchical structures and related

Table 5. In what format should architecture documentation be provided in the future?

Answer Category	Occurrences	% (N=117)
Webpages	25	21,4
Electronic documents	24	20,5
Diagrams	23	19,7
UML	19	16,2
Natural language	17	14,5
Standard formats	11	9,4
Architecture models	10	8,5
Wikis	9	7,7
Other	44	37,6

Table 6. What means should architecture documentation provide to help you in finding the information you need?

Answer Category	Occurrences	% (N=84)
Interactive search functionality	25	29,8
Links and navigation	24	28,6
Traces to artifacts	15	17,9
Directories	10	11,9
Clear structure	9	10,7
Mapping to implementation	8	9,5
Other	28	33,3

elements. Also traces to other artifacts, like requirements documents have been rated as important. Table 6 shows an overview of the result data.

Finally we asked how architecture should be described to make it more useful for the developer's implementation task. Table 7 shows the results. It becomes evident, that clarity and structure are of highest importance, in diagrams and language.

Table 7. How should arch. information be described to make it more useful for your dev. tasks?

Answer Category	Occurrences	% (N=71)
Self-explaining, simple diagrams	15	21,1
Clear, concise, uniform, consistent	10	14,1
Clear terminology and language	6	8,5
Other	32	45,1

5   Discussion

In the following sections we discuss the survey result as well as threats to the validity of the study and present our conclusions and next steps.

5.1   Survey Results

With this study we wanted to confirm our experiences from many industrial projects and to lay the foundation for innovative and practically applicable architecture documentation methods for improved implementation. From this perspective we revisit our main research questions and the responses we received from the participants.

Concerning *architectural information*, it became evident that one of the participants' main concerns is up-to-dateness. Architecture documentation suffers significantly from outdated in the majority of cases, making it less relevant and useful for developers. To improve this situation, the maintenance of architecture documentation has to be simplified and be made more efficient. Centralization of architecture information is the most feasible way we see to achieve this. But this requires powerful tooling that allows efficient and automated creation of architecture documentation that is tailored to the needs of individual developers. Such specific architecture information was another of the main aspects, mentioned by the participants. General and all-encompassing architecture documentation seems not adequate anymore to face the size and complexity of modern software systems and development situations. Developers ask for architecture information specific for their scope, task, and context. Analogously to the aspect mentioned before, centralization of architecture information and automatic generation may be feasible strategies to address this. We outlined a first idea of such an approach in [23]. In terms of needed architectural information, developers mainly ask for a system overview, providing the big picture of the system and its basic principles, complemented with detailed information within their scope, like components, interfaces, relationships, data, patterns, deployment, technologies, architectural drivers, etc. However, it is of major importance to reduce the amount of overhead information to the necessary minimum, but without leaving needed aspects out. In general we can say that the closer to the scope of the developer, the more details are needed, and analogously, the more details need to be left out, the farer away from the scope. And finally, a clear, easy to understand and to follow connection between architecture information and the implementation is a major concern of developers. While with model driven development and code generation techniques, such a connection can be established for detailed design, for architecture in general this is currently not possible. Here we see the potential for further research and development of advanced tool support.

Concerning the *representation of architecture information*, consistency and uniform structure were two of the main concerns of developers. More effort might be needed to establish internal standards and a common terminology within organizations. But also extended automation, for example with generation techniques might contribute to achieve this goal. This fits also quite well to the need for a single source of information, that developers mentioned repeatedly. Besides this, developers predominantly asked for interactive documentation that allows easy navigation and searching. We understand that static architecture documents as they are common are not adequate to serve the needs of developers. Future research needs to concentrate on such forms of documentation. And finally, readability and understandability need to be increased, in which we see another argument for standardization and clarity through reduction of information.

5.2   Validity

In this section, we describe threats to validity and limitations of the survey.

- Not all participants finished the study and submitted their results. As described in Section 4.3, we found that the answers of the participants having not finished considerable diverged from the participants having finished. However, we decided not to include unfinished surveys as they are not confirmed by the participants.

- The survey included questions that are not mandatory. Thus, not all participants filled in all questions. We always took the number of answers given as the reference and typically indicated how many results we got.
- We did not restrict the number of participants in a single company. This leads to the effect that some companies are represented by a single participant while others are represented by multiple participants. However, contexts and projects in larger companies are so different that we see it as valuable to get multiple contributions.
- Our survey is mainly targeted at developers, as indicated in the research question. Although we clearly put this in the survey invitation, several participants indicated that their main role is rather architect or manager. However, we nevertheless see this as valuable input and assume that these participants took a developer perspective (currently doing actual implementation work, having done it earlier, or supervising people that do implementation work).
- The questions we raised in the survey are not fully disjoint. So we received partially similar answers to our questions. However, this confirmed the general tendencies and top results fairly well.
- For free text questions, we derived categories from the participants' answers for aggregation. These categories might depend on our background. However, we see a good match of these categories and typical topics in literature.
- The study is related to further own research [23] Although we tried to maintain neutrality, we might have been biased in survey design and analysis.

5.3 Conclusions

We conducted an international study on the as-is and to-be situation of software architecture documentation from the perspective of developers. We are happy having received contributions from as much as 147 participants from industry to this research.

The study confirmed that software architecture is a very important topic in industrial software development and that many companies are successfully engaged in it. Aggregating the answers what practitioners wish as architectural support for their development activities is an impressing list, covering nearly the whole literature topics on software architecture documentation. We identified a lot of interesting improvement opportunities how software architecture can become even more helpful.

Our main findings are that architecture documentation has to become up-to-date and consistent in order to better serve the developers' needs. Additionally, developers demand for more specific architecture documentation, targeted at their concrete context and tasks. Such an architecture documentation should be complemented by improved navigation and search possibilities.

As researchers of Fraunhofer, we strongly aim at improving the industrial applicability of software architecture methods and tools. We conducted this survey to complement our own experiences from projects and discussions with practitioners. The survey confirms that architects need more tool support for the creation of adequate architecture documentation. For the near future we plan to extend tools and increase the level of automation as next steps towards the identified improvement potentials.

Acknowledgements. This survey has been conducted in the context of the Fraunhofer Germany-Brazil cooperation between Fraunhofer IESE and UFBA. We would like to thank all the participants that contributed by answering our questions. Additionally, we would like to thank our colleagues, business partners, and networks (Bitkom, Softwareforen Leipzig) who supported us in inviting and reaching so many participants for the study. We thank our colleagues Jessica Jung for her help on the empirical aspects and Jens Knodel for reviewing the paper.

References

1. Perry, D.E., Wolf, A.L.: Foundations for the study of software architecture. ACM SIGSOFT Software Engineering Notes 17, 40–52 (1992)
2. Knodel, J.: Sustainable Structures in Software Implementations by Live Compliance Checking. Fraunhofer Verlag (2011)
3. Basili, V.R., Rombach, H.D.: The TAME project: towards improvement-oriented software environments. IEEE Transactions on Software Engineering 14, 758–773 (1988)
4. Lethbridge, T.C., Singer, J., Forward, A.: How software engineers use documentation: the state of the practice. IEEE Software 20, 35–39 (2003)
5. Koning, H., van Vliet, H.: Real-life IT architecture design reports and their relation to IEEE Std 1471 stakeholders and concerns. Automated Software Engg. 13, 201–223 (2006)
6. Malavolta, I., Lago, P., Muccini, H., Pelliccione, P., Tang, A.: What Industry Needs from Architectural Languages: A Survey (2012),
   http://www.computer.org/csdl/trans/
   ts/preprint/tts2012990044-abs.html
7. Bass, L., Clements, P., Kazman, R.: Software Architecture in Practice. Addison-Wesley Professional (1998)
8. Rozanski, N., Woods, E.: Software Systems Architecture: Working With Stakeholders Using Viewpoints and Perspectives. Addison-Wesley Professional (2005)
9. International Organization of Standardization: ISO/IEC/IEEE 42010:2011 - Systems and software engineering – Architecture description (2011)
10. Kruchten, P.: The 4+1 View Model of Architecture. IEEE Software 12, 42–50 (1995)
11. Hofmeister, C., Nord, R., Soni, D.: Applied Software Architecture. Addison-Wesley Professional (1999)
12. Clements, P., Bachmann, F., Bass, L., Garlan, D., Ivers, J., Little, R., Merson, P., Nord, R., Stafford, J.: Documenting Software Architectures: Views and Beyond. Addison-Wesley Professional (2002)
13. Garlan, D., Monroe, R.T., Wile, D.: Acme: architectural description of component-based systems. In: Foundations of Component-based Systems, pp. 47–67 (2000)
14. Feiler, P., Gluch, D., Hudak, J.: The Architecture Analysis & Design Language (AADL): An Introduction (2006)
15. OMG: UML Superstructure Specification 2.4.1 (2011)
16. Sparx Systems: Enterprise Architect, http://www.sparxsystems.com/
17. Farenhorst, R., De Boer, R.C.: Knowledge Management in Software Architecture: State of the Art. In: Ali Babar, M., Dingsøyr, T., Lago, P., van Vliet, H. (eds.) Software Architecture Knowledge Management, pp. 21–38. Springer, Heidelberg (2009)
18. Farenhorst, R., Izaks, R., Lago, P., van Vliet, H.: A Just-In-Time Architectural Knowledge Sharing Portal. In: Seventh Working IEEE/IFIP Conference on Software Architecture (WICSA 2008), pp. 125–134. IEEE (2008)

19. Babar, M.A., Gorton, I.: A Tool for Managing Software Architecture Knowledge. In: SHARK/ADI 2007: ICSE Workshops 2007 Second Workshop on Sharing and Reusing Architectural Knowledge - Architecture, Rationale, and Design Intent, p. 11. IEEE (2007)

20. Pohl, K., Sikora, E.: COSMOD-RE: Supporting the Co-Design of Requirements and Architectural Artifacts. In: 15th IEEE International Requirements Engineering Conference (RE 2007), pp. 258–261. IEEE (2007)

21. Babu, T.L., Seetha Ramaiah, M., Prabhakar, T.V., Rambabu, D.: ArchVoc–Towards an Ontology for Software Architecture. In: Second Workshop on Sharing and Reusing Architectural Knowledge - Architecture, Rationale, and Design Intent, SHARK/ADI 2007: ICSE Workshops 2007, p. 5. IEEE (2007)

22. Tang, A., Liang, P., van Vliet, H.: Software Architecture Documentation: The Road Ahead. In: 2011 Ninth Working IEEE/IFIP Conference on Software Architecture, pp. 252–255. IEEE (2011)

23. Rost, D.: Generation of task-specific architecture documentation for developers. In: Proceedings of the 17th International Doctoral Symposium on Components and Architecture - WCOP 2012, p. 1. ACM Press, New York (2012)

Analysis Support for TADL2 Timing Constraints on EAST-ADL Models

Arda Goknil[1], Jagadish Suryadevara[2], Marie-Agnès Peraldi-Frati[1],
and Frédéric Mallet[1]

[1] AOSTE Team, UNS-I3S-INRIA, Sophia-Antipolis, France
[2] Formal Modeling and Analysis Group, Mälardalen University, Västerås, Sweden
arda.goknil@inria.fr, jagadish.suryadevara@mdh.se,
{map,frederic.mallet}@unice.fr

Abstract. It is critical to analyze characteristics of real-time embedded systems, such as timing behavior, early in the development. In the automotive domain, EAST-ADL is a concrete example of the model-based approach for the architectural modeling of real-time systems. The Timing Augmented Description Language v2 (TADL2) allows for the specification of timing constraints on top of EAST-ADL models. In this paper we propose a formal validation & verification methodology for timing behaviors given with TADL2. The formal semantics of the timing constraints is given as a mapping to the Clock Constraint Specification Language (CCSL), a formal language that implements the MARTE Time Model. Based on such a mapping, the validation is carried out by the simulation of TADL2 specifications. The simulation allows for a rapid prototyping of TADL2 specifications. The verification is performed based on a TADL2 mapping to timed automata modeling using the UPPAAL model-checker. The whole process is illustrated on a Brake-By-Wire application.

1 Introduction

Non-Functional properties and time are central concerns in real-time embedded systems. The increasing complexity of automotive systems requires the early identification of specification problems and the use of common/standard formalisms to cover all aspects of the systems. In the automotive domain, EAST-ADL [9] is a concrete example of the model-based approach for the architectural modeling of safety-critical embedded systems. EAST-ADL has been developed to provide a standard architecture description language aligned with Autosar [10]. The new release of EAST-ADL (v2) has recently adopted the timing model proposed in the Timing Augmented Description Language (TADL) [19]. TADL allows for expressing and composing basic timing constraints such as repetition rates, end-to-end delays, and synchronization constraints.

The TIMMO-2-USE project [2] goes one step beyond TADL by recently introducing TADL2 [19]. The time model of TADL2 specializes the time model of the UML Profile for MARTE (Modeling and Analysis of Real-Time and Embedded systems) [18]. It elaborates on TADL and adds constructs borrowed from the MARTE companion language, the Clock Constraint Specification Language (CCSL) [8], a formal language dedicated to the specification of temporal and causality constraints. In particular, it adds

K. Drira (Ed.): ECSA 2013, LNCS 7957, pp. 89–105, 2013.
© Springer-Verlag Berlin Heidelberg 2013

new modelling capabilities such as the explicit notion of time base and the ability to use symbolic timing expressions in timing constraints.

In this paper, we propose a formal validation and verification methodology for timing constraints specified using TADL2. The validation is carried out by the simulation of TADL2 specifications, based on a mapping of TADL2 to CCSL. With such a mapping the simulation of TADL2 timing constraints becomes possible through TIMESQUARE [11], the framework dedicated to the analysis of CCSL specifications. This mapping gives a semantic reference interpretation for TADL2 constraints and the simulation with CCSL allows for a rapid prototyping of TADL2 specifications. Complementary to the simulation, the formal verification is performed by model checking, based on a mapping of TADL2 to timed automata (TA) for using the UPPAAL model-checker [17]. We use a Brake-By-Wire (BBW) application as a running example to illustrate and compare the results of those mappings.

The remainder of the paper is organized as follows. Section 2 introduces the BBW system used as a running example. Section 3 gives a brief overview of TADL2. Section 4 describes the mapping between TADL2 and CCSL and the analysis results provided by TIMESQUARE. In Section 5, we present the mapping between TADL2 and TA as well as the verification results using the UPPAAL model-checker. Section 6 discusses the benefits of using both the analysis approaches together. In Section 7, we discuss the related work. We conclude the paper in Section 8.

2   Running Example: Brake-By-Wire Application

A distributed Brake-By-Wire (BBW) application with an anti-lock braking functionality illustrates our approach. The BBW application is one of the validator proposed by Volvo Technology in the TIMMO-2-USE project [2].

The structural decomposition of the braking functionality is shown in Figure 1. It gives the BBW functional design architecture in East-ADL: the parts denote subfunctions and the connectors represent data dependencies. The BBW is composed of two mains functions. First, the brake controller reads the wheel speed sensors and the brake pedal sensor. The brake controller computes the desired brake torque applied to the wheels. In addition to this basic brake controller functionality, a second function Anti-lock Braking System (ABS) adapts the brake force on each wheel if the speed of one wheel is significantly smaller than the estimated vehicle speed. The brake force is reduced on that wheel until it regains the speed that is comparable with the estimated vehicle speed. The braking functionality has the following components (Fig. 1):

– *BrakePedalSensor* (BPS) reads the pedal position percentage on port *EISignal*.
– *BrakeTorqueCalculator* (BTC) receives the pedal position percentage from BPS and computes the desired global torque.
– The wheel sensors—*RearRightWheelSensor* (RRWS), *RearLeftWheelSensor* (RLWS), *FrontRightWheelSensor* (FRWS) and *FrontLeftWheelSensor* (FLWS)— read the speed values for each wheel.
– *GlobalBrakeController* (GBC) receives the speed values measured by the wheel sensors and the global torque calculated by *BrakeTorqueCalculator*. It calculates the torque required for each wheel.

- The ABS components—*ABSatRearRightWheel* (ABSrrw), *ABSatRearLeft-Wheel* (ABSrlw), *ABSatFrontRightWheel* (ABSfrw) and *ABSatFrontLeftWheel* (ABSflw)—control the wheel braking to prevent locking the wheels.
- The brake actuators—*RearRightBrake* (RRB), *RearLeftBrake* (RLB), *FrontRight-Brake* (FRB) and *FrontLeftBrake* (FLB)—apply the brake force on each wheel.

Sensors, actuators and the Electronic Control Units (ECUs) are distributed through a unique Controller Area Network (CAN).

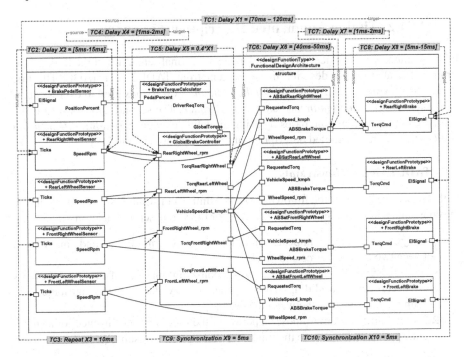

Fig. 1. Brake-By-Wire functional view augmented with TADL2 timing constraints

Table 1. The main timing constraints for the functional architecture of the BBW

ID	Constraint Description
TC1	Four **delays** X1 are measured from the brake pedal stimulus (*EISignal* on *BPS*) to the brake actuator responses (the *EISignal* ports on *RRB*, *RLB*, *FRB* and *FLB*). The delays are bounded with a minimum value of **70** ms and a maximum value of **120** ms.
TC3	The acquisition of the wheel sensors (the *Ticks* ports on *RRWS*, *RLWS*, *FRWS*, *FLWS*) must be done **periodically** every X3=**10** ms.
TC5	Four **delays** X5 are measured from the wheel rpm signal (the *RRW_rpm*, *RLW_rpm*, *FRW_rpm* and *FLW_rpm* ports on *GBC*) to the brake torque calculation (the *TRRW*, *TRLW*, TFRW, *TFLW* ports on *GBC*). The delay constraint X5 applied on the global brake controller is 40 percent of the initial time budget **X1** given in **TC1**.
TC10	First and last wheel brake actuations (the *EISignal* ports on *RRB*, *RLB*, *FRB*, *FLB*) must follow each other by no more than X10 =**5** ms.

This functional decomposition is augmented with thirty one TADL2 timing constraints. Figure 1 and Table 1 reflect the main types of timing constraints attached to the BBW architecture and provide an intuitive description of them. Some of these constraints are about a periodic sensor acquisition (see *TC3*). The distributed nature of the system generates some potential de-synchronizations. Therefore, some synchronization constraints that represent the temporal consistency of events (*TC9* and *TC10*) are introduced in the BBW timing specification. Delays on the ports are represented by delay constraints (*TC1*, *TC2*, *TC4*, *TC5*, *TC6*, *TC7* and *TC8*).

3 TADL2: Timing Augmented Description Language

In this section, we introduce TADL2 and give an informal semantics of the timing constraints. We also briefly describe the increment from TADL2 over TADL. The first improvement with TADL2 concerns *symbolic timing expressions* used to express durations such as *maximum/minimum delay* and *tolerance*. The second improvement is the ability to define explicit time bases by using modeling elements: *TimeBase*, *Dimension* and *Unit*. For a more detailed description of TADL2 please refer to [19].

3.1 TADL2 Timing Constraints

In this paper, we consider the following TADL2 timing constraints, sufficient to capture the constraints described in Figure 1 (See [9] for the whole set of constraints):

- `DelayConstraint` imposes duration bounds (minimum and maximum) between two events *source* and *target*.
- `SynchronizationConstraint` is a constraint on a set of events. All events must occur within a sliding window, specified by the *tolerance* attribute, i.e., maximum allowed skew between the events.
- `RepeatConstraint` imposes a period of the successive occurrences of a single event. *upper* and *lower* give the time interval between two subsequent occurrences.

The TADL2 timing constraints mostly constrain the identifiable state changes formulated as *Events*. The causally related events are contained as a pair by *EventChains*. Based on *Events* and *EventChains*, it is possible to represent data dependencies and critical execution paths as additional constraints for an EAST-ADL functional architecture model, and to apply timing constraints on these paths.

Timing attributes like *tolerance*, *upper* and *lower* are given as *Timing Expressions*. There are three types of timing expressions: *Value*, *Variable* and *Symbolic*. *Variable Timing Expressions* stand for free variables and constants. *Symbolic Timing Expressions* integrate basic arithmetic and relation operators associated with timing values.

3.2 TimeBase, Dimension and Unit in TADL2

TimeBase represents a discrete and totally ordered set of instants. An instant can be seen as an event occurrence called a tick. It may represent any repetitive event in the system. Events may refer to the classical time dimension or to some evolution of a hardware part (e.g., rotation of crankshaft, distance). The type of *TimeBase* is *Dimension* with a kind that represents the nature of *TimeBase*. *Time*, *Angle* and *Distance*, often used in automotive specifications, are proposed as a predefined dimension kind.

Dimension has a set of units to express durations measured on a given *TimeBase*. Each Unit is related to another Unit with *factor*, *offset* and *reference* to enable conversions. Only linear conversions are allowed. Because *Timebase* is a discrete set of instants, a discretization step is specified with *precisionFactor* and *precisionUnit*. Listing 1.1 gives examples of TADL2 declarations for Dimension and TimeBase. The *physicalTime* dimension has three units where 1 *second* is equal to 10^6 *micros* and 1 *ms* is equal to 10^3 *micros* (lines 2-4). *universal_time* is declared based on *physicalTime* (lines 7-8).

```
1  Dimension physicalTime {
     Units { micros{factor 1.0 offset 0.0},
3        ms{factor 1000.0 offset 0.0 reference micros},
         second{factor 1000000.0 offset 0.0 reference micros}  }
5    kind Time
   }
7  TimeBase universal_time { dimension physicalTime  precisionFactor 1
              precisionUnit micros  }
```

Listing 1.1. Declaration of Dimension and TimeBase in TADL2

3.3   BBW Example in TADL2

Listing 1.2 gives some of the BBW timing constraints in TADL2. For the complete TADL2 specification of the BBW example, please refer to [1].

```
1   Event brakePedalSensorActivation {}  Event positionPercent {}
2   Event firstWheelBrakeActuation {}   Event firstWheel_rpm {}
    Event firstWheelSensorAcquisition {} Event torqFirstWheel {}
4
    EventChain ec1 {
6     stimulus brakePedalSensorActivation     response firstWheelBrakeActuation
      eventChains ec1a, ec1b, ec1c, ec1d, ec1e, ec1f, ec1g
8   }
    EventChain ec1a {stimulus brakePedalSensorActivation     response
        positionPercent}
10
    var X1min ms on universal_time := 70.0
12  var X1max ms on universal_time := 120.0
    DelayConstraint tc1a {
14    source brakePedalSensorActivation     target firstWheelBrakeActuation
      lower = X1min      upper = X1max
16  }
18  var X3 ms on universal_time := 10.0
    RepeatConstraint tc3a {
20    event firstWheelSensorAcquisition    lower = X3      upper = X3      span = 1
22  }
    var X5min ms on universal_time := (X1min*0.40)
24  var X5max ms on universal_time := (X1max*0.40)
    DelayConstraint tc5a {
26    source firstWheel_rpm    target torqFirstWheel    lower = X5min    upper =
        X5max
28  }
    SynchronizationConstraint tc10 {
30    events firstWheelBrakeActuation, secondWheelBrakeActuation,
          thirdWheelBrakeActuation, fourthWheelBrakeActuation
32    tolerance = (5.0 ms on universal_time)  }
```

Listing 1.2. Some BBW Timing Constraints in TADL2

In Listing 1.2, we give only a part of events and event chains (lines 1-3). *ec1* gives the execution path between the activation of the brake pedal sensor and the actuation of the first wheel brake (lines 5-8). It contains other event chains ec1a, ... , ec1g (line 7) which give the intermediate executions. *ec1a* states that *positionPercent* is provided just after the activation of the brake pedal sensor (line 9). Each event is attached to a port in EAST-ADL. *brakePedalSensorActivation* and *firstWheelBrakeActuation* are attached to *EISignal* of *BPS* and *EISignal* of *RRB* in Figure 1 respectively.

We have variable declarations as *variable timing expression* (e.g., lines 11-12). All delay and repeat constraints in Figure 1 are replicated for the four wheels. *tc1a*, *tc3a* and *tc5a* (*TC1*, *TC3* and *TC5*) are only for the first wheel. The lower and upper bounds of *tc5a* (line 25) are computed by using symbolic timing expressions ("X1min*0.40" and "X1max*0.40" in lines 23-24). *tc3a* describes the occurrences of the first wheel sensor acquisition with a period (*lower* and *upper*). *tc10* is about the maximum tolerated time difference among the wheel brake actuations (*TC10*). Its *tolerance* attribute is equal to a value timing expression ("5 ms on universal_time" in line 32).

4   TADL2 to MARTE/CCSL: Simulation Approach

The TADL2 timing constraints are described informally in the previous section. However, to conduct validation and verification it is required to rely on a formal semantics. In this section, we use CCSL to capture the semantics of those constraints. We then rely on the CCSL operational semantics to execute the BBW example. This is the first part of our proposal to make TADL2 specifications executable. CCSL was selected because it supports both kinds of constraints available in TADL2: causal ones (event chains) and temporal ones (delay, synchronization, repeat). After a brief introduction to CCSL, we give a mapping from TADL2 to CCSL. At the end, we illustrate our proposed validation framework for TADL2.

4.1   The Clock Constraint Specification Language (CCSL)

MARTE is the UML profile for Modeling and Analysis of Real-Time and Embedded systems [18,7]. It defines a broadly expressive formal *Time Model* [8] that provides a generic timed interpretation for UML models through the notion of *clock*. A clock c (not to be confused with the UPPAAL clocks) denotes particular UML events on which we want to impose a constraint. Clocks (events) are ordered sets of instants (event occurrences), $\mathcal{I}$. When the set is discrete, $c[i]$ denotes the ith occurrence of event c. The Clock Constraint Specification Language (CCSL) was defined as a non-normative annex of MARTE as a language to build causal and timed constraints on clocks. CCSL considers two kinds of binary instant relations: *precedence* (denoted $\prec$) and *coincidence* (denoted $\equiv$). Given two instants i and $j \in \mathcal{I}$, $i \prec j$ denotes that the event occurrence i must be observed before j, whereas $i \equiv j$ denotes that i and j must be observed simultaneously. A labeling function $\lambda : \mathcal{I} \rightarrow T$ associates instants with a time tag.

Based on these two primitive relations on instants, CCSL derives relations on clocks. We only describe here the clock relations pertinent to our running example. Eq.1 gives an example of a *non-functional* clock relation where $mic\_universalTime$ is a logical clock, such that $\forall i \in \mathbb{N}^\star, \lambda(mic\_universalTime[i]) = i * 0.000001$, it models a discrete clock of period 1 *mic* (1 microsecond) since *IdealClock* is defined relative to the unit *second*.

$$mic\_universalTime = IdealClock \texttt{ discretizedBy } 0.000001 \qquad (1)$$

Eq.2 gives an example of *synchronous* clock relation that defines a new discrete logical clock ms such that $\forall i \in \mathbb{N}^\star, ms[i] \equiv micro\_universalTime[(i-1) * 1000 + 1]$.

$$ms \texttt{ isPeriodicOn } mic\_universalTime \textbf{ period } 1000 \qquad (2)$$

A basic asynchronous constraint is given by the clock relation $\texttt{precedes}$. "*a* precedes *b*" (symbolically denoted by $a \; \boxed{\prec} \; b$) specifies that for all natural number k, the kth instant of *a* precedes the kth instant of *b*: $\forall k \in \mathbb{N}^\star, a[k] \prec b[k]$.

Some clock constraints mix *precedence* and *coincidence* relations. "*a* causes *b*" or "*b* dependsOn *a*" (both denoted $a \; \boxed{\preccurlyeq} \; b$) specifies that for all natural number k, the kth instant of *a* precedes or is coincident with the kth instant of *b*: $\forall k \in \mathbb{N}^\star, a[k] \prec b[k] \vee a[k] \equiv b[k]$).

CCSL also provides expressions to build new clocks from existing ones. For instance, the CCSL expression $c = \texttt{inf}(a, b)$ builds a new clock c such that c is the slowest clock that is faster than both a and b: $(\forall k \in \mathbb{N}^\star, c[k] \equiv a[k] \texttt{ if } a[k] \prec b[k], c[k] \equiv b[k] \texttt{ otherwise})$. Similarly, "$d = \texttt{sup}(a, b)$" is the fastest clock slower than both a and b: $\forall k \in \mathbb{N}^\star, d[k] \equiv b[k] \texttt{ if } a[k] \prec b[k], d[k] \equiv a[k] \texttt{ otherwise}$. Most of the time, *inf* and *sup* are neither *a* nor *b*. *inf* and *sup* are easily extended to sets of clocks.

Finally, the expression $\texttt{delayedFor}$ builds a delayed clock."$c = a \texttt{ delayedFor }$ n on *b*" imposes c to tick synchronously with the nth tick of *b* following a tick of *a*. It is considered as a mixed constraint since *a* and *b* are not assumed to be synchronous.

TimeSquare. TimeSquare [11] is a software environment (set of Eclipse plugins) dedicated to the analysis of MARTE time model and CCSL specifications. It has four main functionalities: 1) interactive clock-related specifications, 2) clock constraint checking, 3) generation of a solution and 4) displaying and exploring waveforms. The second functionality relies on a constraint solver that yields a satisfying execution trace for CCSL clocks. The traces are given as waveforms written in VCD (Value Change Dump) format [14]. The solver intensively uses Binary Decision Diagrams (BDD) to compose symbolically boolean equations induced by CCSL clock constraints.

4.2 Modelling TADL2 Constraints in CCSL

We first give the MARTE time model as a representation of basic TADL2 elements *TimeBase*, *Dimension* and *Unit* in CCSL. Then we express the semantics of *Event*, *EventChain* and some of the TADL2 constraints in CCSL.

4.2.1 TimeBase, Dimension and Unit

Each *Unit* of a *Dimension* in a *TimeBase* represents a set of ticks. Hence, we represent each *Unit* in a given *TimeBase* as a CCSL *clock*. The reference unit in a dimension is a special unit whose corresponding clock is derived by discretizing *IdealCLK*. Eq.1 defines a discrete chronometric clock *mic_universalTime* for the *micro* Unit of *physical-Time* in *universal_time* in Listing 1.1.

Clocks for other units in the *TimeBase* are defined as a subclock of the reference unit clock with a period. Eq.2 defines *ms* as a subclock of *mic_universalTime* with period 1000 (*factor* of the *ms* unit) for the *ms* unit of *universal_time*.

4.2.2 Timing Constraints

Each TADL2 *Event* on which we want to attach timing constraints is associated with a CCSL *Clock*. An event denotes something that occurs (e.g., the start of an action, the receipt of a message.). Therefore, a CCSL clock represents the set of instants at which the related event occurs.

An *EventChain* in TADL2 contains causally related events. It is mapped to the *causes* relation in CCSL. For instance, we have the following clock constraints for *ec1* and *ec1a* event chains: (*bpsa* $\preccurlyeq$ *fwba*) and (*bpsa* $\preccurlyeq$ *pp*) where the CCSL clocks *bpsa*, *fwba* and *pp* correspond to the TADL2 events *brakePedalSensorActivation, first-WheelBrakeActuation* and *positionPercent* respectively.

DelayConstraint. It specifies an *end-to-end* delay between the *source* and *target* events where the attributes *lower* and *upper* denote minimum and maximum values of the delay respectively. `tc1a` (Listing 1.2) specifies the permissible delay between the source event *brakePedalSensorActivation* and the target event *firstWheelBrakeActuation*. Eqs. 3-6 give the corresponding CCSL clocks and clock constraints for `tc1a`.

$$\text{Clock } bpsa, \, fwba \tag{3}$$

$$\text{Clock } lower \, = \, bpsa \; \texttt{delayedFor} \; 70 \; \text{on } ms \tag{4}$$

$$\text{Clock } upper \, = \, bpsa \; \texttt{delayedFor} \; 120 \; \text{on } ms \tag{5}$$

$$\left(lower \; \boxed{\preccurlyeq} \; fwba \right) \wedge \left(fwba \; \boxed{\preccurlyeq} \; upper \right) \tag{6}$$

Eq.3 declares two CCSL clocks for the source and target events *brakePedalSensorActivation* (bpsa) and *firstWheelBrakeActuation* (fwba). The CCSL constraint *delayedFor* delays an initial clock (*bpsa*) for a given duration. Combining *delayedFor* and *causes* allows for specifying distances between two clocks. Eqs. 4-5 build two clocks *lower* and *upper* delayed for 70 and 120 ms respectively from the source event clock *bpsa*. Eq. 6 enforces the target event clock *fwba* to tick between the corresponding ticks of the clocks *lower* and *upper*.

SynchronizationConstraint. It specifies the bounds on the delay among event occurrences specified by the attribute *tolerance*. `tc10` (see Listing 1.2) specifies the output synchronization among the four brake actuators that must occur within the specified time duration. Eqs. 7-10 give the corresponding CCSL clocks and constraints for `tc10`.

$$\text{Clock } fwba, \ swba, \ twba, \ ftwba \qquad (7)$$

$$\text{Clock } fastest = inf(fwba, \ swba, \ twba, \ ftwba) \qquad (8)$$

$$\text{Clock } slowest = sup(fwba, \ swba, \ twba, \ ftwba) \qquad (9)$$

$$slowest \boxed{\preccurlyeq} \ (fastest \ \texttt{delayedFor} \ 5 \ on \ ms) \qquad (10)$$

The constraint concerns the distance from the earliest event to the latest event. It has four events, one for each wheel. Eq. 7 declares clocks for events *firstWheelBrakeActuation* (fwba), *secondWheelBrakeActuation* (swba), *thirdWheelBrakeActuation* (twba) and *fourthWheelBrakeActuation* (ftwba). In Eqs. 8-9 we get the fastest/slowest clocks among all clocks slower/faster than *fwba*, *swba*, *twba* and *ftwba*. Eq. 10 states that *slowest* must not tick later than 5 *ms* after the respective ticks of *fastest*.

RepeatConstraint. It specifies the periodic occurrence of an event. The duration of the period is specified by the attributes *lower*, *upper* and *span*. This constraint defines the basic notion of repeated occurrences. If the *span* attribute is 1 and the *lower* and *upper* attributes are equal, the accepted behaviors must be strictly periodic. If *lower* is less than *upper*, the event occurrences may deviate from a strictly periodic one in an accumulating fashion. tc3a (Listing 1.2) specifies the strictly periodic nature of the sensor value acquisition, for one of the four wheels. Eqs.11-14 give the corresponding CCSL clocks and clock constraints for tc3a.

$$\text{Clock } fwsa \qquad (11)$$

$$lower \ \texttt{isPeriodicOn} \ ms \ \textbf{period} \ 10 \qquad (12)$$

$$upper \ \texttt{isPeriodicOn} \ ms \ \textbf{period} \ 10 \qquad (13)$$

$$\left(lower \ \boxed{\preccurlyeq} \ fwsa \right) \wedge \left(fwsa \ \boxed{\preccurlyeq} \ upper \right) \qquad (14)$$

Eq. 11 declares the CCSL clock *fwsa* for the event *firstWheelSensorAcquisition*. Eqs. 12-13 build two clocks *lower* and *upper* of period 10 from *ms*. Eq. 14 enforces the event clock *fwsa* to tick between the corresponding ticks of the clocks *lower* and *upper*. Since *lower* and *upper* have the same period, *fwsa* ticks every 10 ticks of *ms*. We defined both *lower* and *upper* clocks to propose an exhaustive transformation in case lower and upper bounds differ.

4.3   Executing TADL2 Specification with TimeSquare

Based on the mapping presented in Section 4.2, we obtain an executable CCSL specification from the Brake-By-Wire TADL2 description. A simulation trace produced by TimeSquare is partially shown in Figure 2. The focus here is on the constraint *TC10*. The dashed (blue) arrows are the *precedence* relations, whereas the vertical plain (red) connectors are the *coincidence* relations between two instants. The first entry shows the fastest (*fastest*) of the four wheel brake actuator events (*fwba*, *swba*, *twba*, *ftwba*). It is followed by the four events. The sixth entry is the slowest of the four events (*slowest*). Coincidence relations show that there is always one occurrence of each of

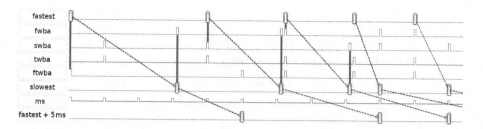

Fig. 2. CCSL Simulation focusing on the constraint TC10 of the BBW Example

the four actuator between an occurrence of $fastest$ and an occurrence $slowest$. Additionally, it also shows that $slowest$ always occur before the deadline, which is 5 ms after $fastest$. The deadline is shown as the last entry of the simulation.

In TimeSquare *runs* consist of multiple execution steps. At each step, the CCSL solver builds a boolean solution and computes a set of all the valid configurations. A configuration is a set of *enabled* clocks, i.e., clocks that are allowed to tick at the given step. If the CCSL specification is deterministic, there is only one valid configuration. If it is nondeterministic, for each step the simulator fires one of the valid configurations. This selection is based on a scheduling policy. When TimeSquare manages to produce a valid trace, this means there is a way to satisfy the constraints. If the system is not deterministic there may be other runs that do not satisfy all the constraints. This is why such a tool must be complement with exhaustive analyses when possible. However, it must be noted that in the general case it is not possible to conduct exhaustive analyses of CCSL specifications, whose state-space can be infinite. In such cases, TimeSquare provides an early support to validate and refine the specification. When focusing on TADL2 timing constraints (delay, repeat and synchronizations) the state-space is bounded and can be explored by model-checking. However, event chains with indeterminate delays may cause problems and need to be further refined. This is discussed in the next section.

On this example, TimeSquare has found one possible run that satisfies the TADL2 specification meaning that the specification is consistent and a solution exists. In the following section, UPPAAL shows that there also may be runs such that the synchronization constraint TC10 is violated (see eq. 20).

5   TADL2 to Timed Automata/UPPAAL: Verification Approach

In this section, we present a formal verification approach for TADL2 specifications. For this, we have chosen UPPAAL [17], a model-checking tool, and present a mapping for a subset of TADL2 into timed automata, the modeling language of UPPAAL.

5.1   UPPAAL Model-Checker: An Overview

UPPAAL extends timed automata (TA), originally introduced by Alur and Dill [6], with a number of features, such as, global and local (bounded) integer variables, arithmetic operations, arrays, and a C-like programming language. The tool consists of three parts: a graphical editor for modeling timed automata, a simulator for trace generation, and a verifier for symbolic (exhaustive) verification of a system modeled as a network of timed automata. A subset of CTL (computation tree logic) is used as the input language for the verifier.

A timed automaton (TAn) is a tuple $< L, l_0, C, A, E, I >$, where L is a set of *locations*, $l_0 \in L$ is the initial location, C is the set of clocks, A is the set of actions, co-actions and the internal τ-action, $E \subseteq L \times A \times B(C) \times 2^C \times L$ is a set of edges between locations with an action, a guard, a set of clocks to be reset, and $I : L \rightarrow B(C)$ assigns clock *invariants* to locations. A location can be marked *urgent* (u) or *committed* (c) to indicate that the time is not allowed to progress in the specified location(s), the latter being stricter form indicating further that the next transition can only be taken from the corresponding locations. Synchronization between two automata is modeled by *channels* (e.g., **x**! and **x**?) with *rendezvous* or broadcast semantics.

Semantically, the *state* of a TAn represents the current location (several in case of a network of TA) and current evaluation of all the variables. An *enabled* edge (that is, when the guard becomes *true*) indicates a *transition* that may be taken in the current state. The semantics of a TAn defines transitions between locations as well as the time progress; an *enabled* edge at a current location may be taken (non-deterministically in case of many), when the invariant at the corresponding target location is preserved, otherwise no transition is taken and the time is allowed to progress as long as the invariant at the current location holds. For further details, we refer the reader to the UPPAAL tutorial [17].

5.2   Modeling TADL2 in UPPAAL

To begin with, we present the TA modeling of basic time (chronometric) aspects in TADL2, such as, *timebase*, *dimension* and *unit*. Next, we will show that the timing constraints in TADL2 can be modeled as TA.

5.2.1   TimeBase, Dimension and Unit

In the semantics of TA, time progresses symbolically, that is, through construction of so-called "region-graphs" [1]. Hence, we represent a time *dimension* and a given time *unit* in TADL2, corresponding to a given time base, as a single *step* of (chronometric) time progress in TA *clocks*. Concretely, a *timebase* can be modeled as a TAn using a *clock* variable which implicitly represents the associated *dimension* and the corresponding *unit*. As a timebase, the automaton is a *reference* clock for a TADL2 timing specification (or part of it, in case of multiple time bases in the specification).

In Figure 3, we present the TAn for the universal_time in BBW specification, a timebase as defined in Listing 1.1. The corresponding *dimension*, that is, the physical_time and the time unit ms (Eqs. 1 and 2) are implicitly represented by the *clock* variable 'x'. The duration of the time unit is represented by the invariant x<=1 and the guard x>=1 at the *location* L0; it represents a single step of the discrete time progress or tick' of the universal_time. The time progress can be observed by the successive ticks of ut_tick (modeled as a broadcast *channel*) during simulation.

---

[1] Makes reachability analysis *decidable* by transforming otherwise an infinite-state timed automaton into finite-state.

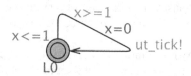

Fig. 3. universal_time: a timebase automaton

5.2.2 Timing Constraints

Timing constraints can be specified for *Event* and *EventChain* in TADL2. An event chain can be modeled as a TAn with synchronization channels representing the corresponding events. For instance, in Fig. 4(a), we present the TA modeling of the event-chain ec1 (Listing 1.2). It consists of events *brakePedalSensorActivation (bpsa)* as the source (stimulus) event and *firstWheelBrakeActuation (fwba)* as the target (response) event, modeled as synchronization channels. The causality among the events is modeled by the receiving(?) and sending(!) signals of the corresponding channels respectively.

DelayConstraint. In Figure 4(b), we present the TA modeling of the delay constraint tc1, for the event chain ec1. The transition from L0 is taken when the source event *bpsa* occurs. At *location* L1, the permissible delay, specified in terms of the invariant and the guard (on outgoing edge) using clock variable x, is allowed before the target event *fwba* occurrence. It can be observed that the TA modeling of the delay constraint tc1 is a time constrained model of the corresponding event-chain automaton (Fig. 4(a)).

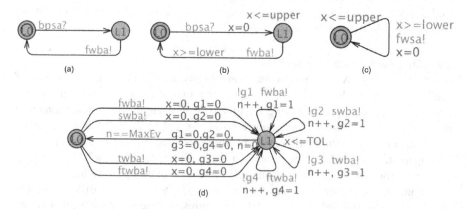

Fig. 4. TADL timing constraints as TA: (a) EventChain *ec1* (b) DelayConstraint *tc1* (c) RepeatConstriant *tc3a* (d) SynchronizationConstraint *tc10*

SynchronizationConstraint. In Figure 4(d), we present the TA modeling of the synchronization constraint tc10 (Listing 1.2). It consists of two *locations* L0 and L1; the edges between the locations contain synchronization channels (receiving signals) corresponding to the events of the specified event group, that is, $firstWheelBrakeActuation(fwba)$, $secondWheelBrakeActuation(swba)$, $thirdWheelBrakeActuation(twba)$ and $fourthWheelBrakeActuation(ftwba)$; corresponding transition is taken when anyone of these occur first. At location L1, the other three events need to occur, before the transition back to L0 is taken, within the specified *tolerance* value denoted by the invariant x <= TOL.

RepeatConstraint. In Figure 4(c), we present the TA modeling of the constraint tc3a (Listing 1.2). When *span* is 1, and *upper* is equal to *lower*, the specified event is periodically generated. Thus the event $fwsa$ (*firstWheelSensorAcquistion*) periodically occurs with the specified period.

5.3   Verification Results

For a TADL2 specification, the corresponding network of TA models is an executable specification that can be simulated and verified. However, to support the verification, we further extend the composed model to enable verification. For example, for event chains with no associated delay constraint, we make the non-initial locations *urgent* to skip indeterminate delays. Further, we introduce a synchronization pattern (Fig. 5 (a) and (b)), for event chains with common response event. Also, we use an observer TAn, e.g. Fig. 5 (c), to verify delay constraints. To begin with, we can verify general properties, such as, well-formedness as discussed below:

- *well-formedness* : we define a TADL2 specification as *well-formed*, if every location in the composed TAn is *reachable*. For example, we can verify a location L in an automaton T is reachable by verifying that the property E<> T.L is satisfied (i.e., there exists a path where the boolean predicate T.L *eventually* holds).

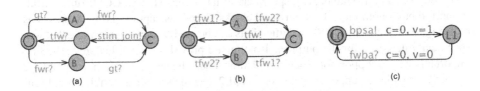

Fig. 5. (a) *join_stimulus*   (b) *join_response*   (c) Observer TA to verify '*tc1a*'

We have verified TADL2 timing constraints, presented in Table 1. And, the constraints are verified in isolation, to keep the statespace minimal. Verification of the delay constraints, using the property (15) shows that there is no deadlock. And, property (16), a liveness property using *leads_to*, implemented as --> in UPPAAL, shows that the event '*bpsa*' always leads_to (⤳) the corresponding response event '*fwba*'. Further, we can verify that the *DelayConstraints* are consistent. In TADL2 specification of BBW example [1], the event chain *ec1a* is defined in terms of *ec1a*, ... , *ec1g* (Listing 1.2). From this, we can verify the timing behavior of *ec1a* given by *tc1a* w.r.t. the combined timing/causality behavior of *ec1a*, ... , *ec1g* (Fig. 1). For the verification, we compose the specification model with an observer TAn (for *tc1a*), using a boolean variable v and a clock variable c (Fig. 5 (c)). The corresponding properties (17) and (18) show the timing property $tc1a$ is *not* satisfied.

$$A[] \text{ not deadlock} \qquad //satisfied \qquad (15)$$

$$tc1a.L1 \text{ --> } tc1a.L0 \qquad //satisfied \qquad (16)$$

$$A[] \ v \text{ imply } c >= 70 \qquad //satisfied \qquad (17)$$

$$A[] \ v \text{ imply } c <= 120 \qquad //not \ satisfied \qquad (18)$$

$$E <> \ v1 \text{ imply } c1 <= 5 \qquad //satisfied \qquad (19)$$

$$A[] \ v1 \text{ imply } c1 <= 5 \qquad //not \ satisfied \qquad (20)$$

To verify the output synchronization constraint *TC10*, we have extended the corresponding TAn with variables $c1$ and $v1$ (similar mechanism as in observer TAn in Fig. 5(c) for verifying $tc1a$). Verification using (19), a *reachability* property, shows the existence of a solution satisfying *TC10*, which confirms the TimeSquare simulation results presented in Section 4.3. However, Property (20) shows that the constraint is not satisfied for all execution paths. This means that the TADL2 specification needs to be constrained further w.r.t a refined description of the system behavior.

6 Discussion of the Approach

This section discusses the benefits of combining two formal models CCSL and Timed Automata to offer a complete support for the analysis of TADL2 specifications. First it should be noted that one major extension of TADL2 over TADL is the addition of explicit references to time bases. Such time bases can be either logical or physical. This extension took a direct inspiration from the MARTE Time model. It recognizes the importance of logical clocks in high-level specifications where information about physical time is not always available. As a specification language, MARTE CCSL offers a full support to build both logical and physical clocks as well as capturing time expressions referring to such clocks. CCSL specifications can be analyzed by TimeSquare that was specifically designed for the purpose. TimeSquare provides several features. The first important one is a support for model simulation. Thus, the transformation from TADL2 to CCSL provides a support for making TADL2 specifications executable directly inside a UML environment (like Papyrus). Other features of TimeSquare offer support for exhaustive analyses of CCSL specifications. Those features mainly focus on logical aspects and offer little or no benefit for the exhaustive analysis of physical-based constraints such that those shown in this paper. Timed Automata, however, are a powerful formalism to handle physical time constraints through the UPPAAL clocks. By offering a transformation to Timed Automata, we then provide a support for the exhaustive analysis of physical-based constraints. This is why the two formalisms are used in a complementing way, CCSL to support model execution and analysis of logical time aspects, Timed Automata/UPPAAL for the exhaustive analysis of physical time constraints. However, having a coordinated analysis of mixed logical and physical constraints is out of the scope of this paper and is still an on-going research work.

Furthermore, exhaustive verifications can only be conducted with finite specifications. However, early specifications may remain incomplete and therefore may not be sufficiently refined to be bounded. For instance, event chains with indeterminate delays are typical unbounded specifications (the time may progress arbitrarily without any upper bound constraint). As discussed in the previous sections, we had to complete the event chains to conduct the analysis with UPPAAL.

7   Related Work

A number of approaches in the literature address modeling and analyzing timing constraints. Klein and Giese [16] present Timed Story Scenario Diagrams (TSSD), a visual notation for scenario specifications that takes structural system properties into account. In TSSD it is possible to specify *Time Constraints* that allow setting *lower* and *upper* bounds for delays. There is no mention of analysis support for TSSD. Alfonso et al. [5] present VTS, a visual language to define complex event-based constraints like freshness, bounded response, and event correlation. VTS does not support the notion of explicit time units coded as time bases. A mapping between VTS and timed automata is provided to model and analyze VTS scenarios. Aegedal [4] presents a general modelling language for Quality of Service (QoS). The language uses a time model where different clocks can be specified.

In the context of EAST-ADL, several approaches have been proposed for TA-based modeling. Qureshi et al. [20] present TA templates for EAST-ADL timing constraints. These modeling templates model various error scenarios and are based on informal semantics of the EAST-ADL architectural models. In comparison, the automata templates presented in this paper specify event chains and associated causality and temporal behavior. Kang et al. [15] present a method for formal modeling of EAST-ADL models, for verification using UPPAAL. And, Enoiu et al. [13], provided a tool support for EAST-ADL models, also limited aspect of timing verification. In comparison to these works, in this paper, we have addressed the analysis of timing specifications based on the explicit notion of timebases and the timing constraints. We have also presented the complimentary use of different analysis approaches for timing specifications.

8   Conclusions

In this paper, we have presented both simulation and model-checking approaches for formal analysis of TADL2 specifications. We have mapped TADL2 specifications into CCSL for simulations in TimeSquare and to timed automata for exhaustive verifications using UPPAAL model-checker. In addition to well-formedness and consistency checking, we have also verified the TADL2 timing constraints. The main limitation of the verification approach is the statespace explosion problem with model-checking. However, this may be addressed by using compositional techniques for event chains in TADL2 specifications.

We have used a real industrial example proposed by Volvo Technology in the TIMMO-2-USE project [2] to show the capability of our approach for handling timing behavior of industrial systems. However, a natural question arises about the scalability and the efficacy of the proposed analysis approach on larger case studies. As future work, we plan to apply the proposed analysis techniques on larger case studies. We also plan to consider a detailed comparison of analysis benefits of using both TimeSquare and UPPAAL for TADL2 specifications. Further, the mappings can be extended to multiple timebases and timebase relationships in TADL2, for specification and verification of timing constraints for distributed embedded systems, i.e., systems with multiple ECUs, with each ECU has its own timebase. The mappings provide a basis for automated model transformations from TADL2 specifications to CCSL and UPPAAL. The automated model transformation from TADL2 to CCSL [3] is already implemented with QVTo [12]. Currently, we are working on the model transformation from TADL2 to UPPAAL.

Acknowledgement. This was a joint work by AOSTE Research Group at INRIA (Sophia-Antipolis) and Formal Modeling and Analysis Group at Mälardalen University, Sweden. The work was funded by the PRESTO project (ARTEMIS-2010-1-269362) under the ARTEMIS Joint Undertaking Programme, the TIMMO-2-USE project in the framework of the ITEA2, the Swedish Research Council (VR) through ARROWS project and Mälardalen University in Sweden.

References

1. BBW Spec in TADL2,
   http://www-sop.inria.fr/members/Arda.Goknil/bbw/
2. ITEA TIMMO-2-USE Project, http://timmo-2-use.org/
3. TADL2-CCSL QVTo Transformation,
   http://www-sop.inria.fr/members/Arda.Goknil/bbw/
4. Aegedal, J.: Quality of service support in development of distributed systems. PhD Thesis (2001)
5. Alfonso, A., Braberman, V.A., Kicillof, N., Olivero, A.: Visual timed event scenarios. In: ICSE 2004, pp. 168–177 (2004)
6. Alur, R., Dill, D.L.: A theory of timed automata. Theoretical Computer Science 126(2), 183–235 (1994)
7. André, C.: Syntax and semantics of the Clock Constraint Specification Language (CCSL). Research Report 6925, INRIA (May 2009)
8. André, C., Mallet, F., de Simone, R.: Modeling time(s). In: Engels, G., Opdyke, B., Schmidt, D.C., Weil, F. (eds.) MoDELS 2007. LNCS, vol. 4735, pp. 559–573. Springer, Heidelberg (2007)
9. ATESST (Advancing Traffic Efficiency through Software Technology). East-ADL2 specification (March 20, 2008), http://www.atesst.org
10. Autosar Consortium. AUTOSAR specification, release 4.0 (2009),
    http://www.autosar.org/
11. DeAntoni, J., Mallet, F.: Timesquare: Treat your models with logical time. In: Furia, C.A., Nanz, S. (eds.) TOOLS Europe 2012. LNCS, vol. 7304, pp. 34–41. Springer, Heidelberg (2012)
12. Dvorak, R.: Model transformation with operational qvt. In: EclipseCon 2008 (2008)
13. Enoiu, E.P., Marinescu, R., Seceleanu, C.C., Pettersson, P.: Vital: A verification tool for EAST-ADL models using uppaal port. In: ICECCS 2012, pp. 328–337 (2012)
14. IEEE Standards Association. IEEE Standard for Verilog Hardware Description Language. Design Automation Standards Committee, IEEE Std 1364TM-2005 (2005)

15. Kang, E.-Y., Schobbens, P.-Y., Pettersson, P.: Verifying functional behaviors of automotive products in EAST-ADL2 using uppaal-port. In: Flammini, F., Bologna, S., Vittorini, V. (eds.) SAFECOMP 2011. LNCS, vol. 6894, pp. 243–256. Springer, Heidelberg (2011)
16. Klein, F., Giese, H.: Joint structural and temporal property specification using timed story scenario diagrams. In: Dwyer, M.B., Lopes, A. (eds.) FASE 2007. LNCS, vol. 4422, pp. 185–199. Springer, Heidelberg (2007)
17. Larsen, K.G., Pettersson, P., Yi, W.: UPPAAL in a Nutshell. Int. Journal on Software Tools for Technology Transfer 1(1-2), 134–152 (1997)
18. OMG. UML Profile for MARTE, v1.0. Object Management Group (November 2009) (formal/2009-11-02)
19. Peraldi-Frati, M.A., Goknil, A., DeAntoni, J., Nordlander, J.: A timing model for specifying multi clock automotive systems: The timing augmented description language v2. In: ICECCS 2012, pp. 230–239 (2012)
20. Qureshi, T.N., Chen, D.-J., Törngren, M.: A timed automata-based method to analyze EAST-ADL timing constraint specifications. In: Vallecillo, A., Tolvanen, J.-P., Kindler, E., Störrle, H., Kolovos, D. (eds.) ECMFA 2012. LNCS, vol. 7349, pp. 303–318. Springer, Heidelberg (2012)

SysADL: A SysML Profile for Software Architecture Description

Jair Leite[1], Flávio Oquendo[2], and Thais Batista[1]

[1] UFRN – Federal University of Rio Grande do Norte, Natal, Brazil
{jair,thais}@dimap.ufrn.br
[2] IRISA – University of South Brittany, Vannes, France
flavio.oquendo@irisa.fr

Abstract. In this paper we propose SysADL, a SysML profile for expressing architecture descriptions using the well-known and consolidated abstractions from the ADL community. We present the SysADL constructs for describing architectures and demonstrate its use in the context of a case study.

Keywords: Architecture Description Language, SysML, Profile, Components, Connectors, Configuration.

1 Introduction

In the last decades, software architecture [1] has become a key activity for software and systems development and considerable progress has been done in two complementary approaches. On one side, a plethora of Architecture Description Languages (ADL) [1] has been proposed by both industry and academia, for describing the architecture as a composition of interacting components. Although different ADLs present particular approaches to specify software architecture, the taxonomy presented by Medvidovic and Taylor [4] states that components, connectors, and configuration are the main abstractions used to represent an architecture. On the other side, OMG (Object Management Group) has proposed standardized modeling languages such as UML (Unified Modeling Language) [3] and SysML (Systems Modeling Language) [2], which have high acceptance by the software development community. To date, there are a number of tools and developers skilled in using the UML notation. SysML is a customized version of UML for systems engineering, and it is being increasingly used by systems engineers and inheriting the popularity of UML.

Although the popularity of the OMG modeling languages, they do not support the high-level architectural description as ADLs do, using the CCC (component, connector, configuration) concepts. On the other hand, ADLs do not support multiple views, which are essential for the distinct involved stakeholders, and none of them have a broad adoption as the OMG modeling languages. Thus, it is clear that the integration of the two strands of modeling languages holds significant potential, providing an unique language that has the advantages of the OMG modeling standards and allow the high-level description of the architecture using the ADLs main concepts. In fact,

K. Drira (Ed.): ECSA 2013, LNCS 7957, pp. 106–113, 2013.
© Springer-Verlag Berlin Heidelberg 2013

the marriage of the modeling capabilities enables the ADL community and the OMG modeling language users to exploit the powerful of both modeling worlds.

In this paper we propose SysADL, a SysML profile for expressing architecture description using the well-known and consolidated abstractions from the ADL community. A profile is a lightweight extension of a language that allows specializing its syntax using stereotypes that represents both a well-defined syntactic element and a set of additional semantic constraints for each stereotyped metaclass. We decided to use SysML as it is an OMG standard that focuses on systems and software. This is important as it provides a systemic view of the software architecture, meaning that the software will be integrated with the other system elements such as hardware, stakeholders, and information, which are important for the architecture analysis. As UML, SysML can be easily customized for expressing the architectural concerns.

This paper is structured as follows. Section 2 presents SysML and architecture description main concepts. Section 3 presents SysADL. Section 4 illustrates the use of SysADL. Section 5 discusses related work. Section 6 presents our final remarks.

2   Background

In this section we briefly present the main concepts of SysML and ADLs that are the basis to understand our profile.

SysML [2] is a standardized modeling language for systems engineering that extends UML. We do not use all SysML elements in our profile. The elements used in SysADL are the ones that have architectural concerns: blocks, ports, flow, and connectors. *Blocks* are the generalization of the UML class concept to modularly represent system description, allowing the description of system decomposition, interconnection, and properties. SysML blocks may include both structural and behavioral features and also an ability to define internal connectors. There are two types of block diagrams in SysML: (i) *Block definition diagrams (bdds)*, used to define blocks in terns of properties and operations, and relationships; (ii) *Internal block diagrams (ibds)*, used to model the internal structure of each block, which can include parts, ports, connectors. SysML blocks include several notational extensions. We use in this work the notation with multiple optional compartments, which can partition the features according to various criteria. Some standard compartments are defined by SysML, such as: flow properties, operations, and constraints. *Ports* and *flows* support the design of blocks with clearly defined ways of connecting and interacting with their context of use. *Ports* define the interactions among blocks and parts. They are a special class of property used to specify allowable types of interactions between blocks. *Connectors* in SysML are used to define relationships between parts or other properties of the same containing block. They can be typed by associations, which can specify more detail about the links between parts or other properties of a system, along with the types of the connected properties. Connectors establish a bind between elements. SysML has its own extension mechanisms to support extensions: stereotypes and profiles. *Stereotypes* add new language concepts, extending existing SysML language concepts with additional properties and constraints. They are defined by either extending a metaclass or subclassing a stereotype. Profiles are represented in packages grouping the stereotypes.

In terms of architecture description concepts, in this paper we follow the taxonomy presented by Medvidovic and Taylor [4], which states that components, connectors, and configuration are the abstractions used to represent an architecture. A *component* is the loci of computation and state [1]. It has a clearly defined interface specification and it distinguishes between *components types* and *instances*. Interfaces are commonly represented with the notion of *ports* and can have attributes and constraints. Component types are abstract components that can be instantiated multiple times in an architecture specification. A *connector* is the element responsible for mediating the interaction among components, establishing rules that govern those interactions. It is a first-class architectural concern in ADLs. Although connectors have been neglected in several languages and tools for software modeling, such as in the first versions of UML, for instance, it has an important role in software architecture descriptions as an element that mediate the interactions among components. A connector's interface is a set of interactions points between it and the components attached to it. The interfaces of connectors are similar to component interfaces are referred under different names such as *ports* or *roles*. An *architectural configuration* defines the associations among components and connectors, shaping the topology of the architecture, specifying the overall behavior of the composed elements, and properly defining the architecture of the system. In the configuration, part of the architectural description, components' ports are attached to connectors' interfaces.

3   SysADL

In this section, we introduce SysADL, our proposal to model basic architectural concepts extending the System Modeling Language. SysADL specializes few SysML elements to describe the software architecture concepts described in Section 2 – components, connectors and configurations. All others SysML elements can be used in SysADL models. Figure 1 illustrates the SysADL extension of SysML. The SysADL profile imports some elements of SysML. Figure 2 details the stereotypes defined in the SysADL profile.

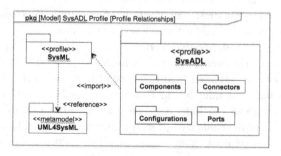

Fig. 1. SysADL extension of SysML

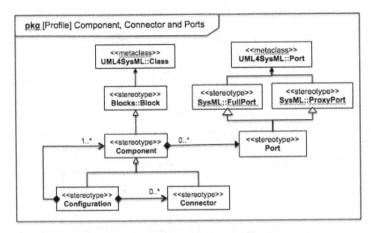

Fig. 2. The SysADL profile stereotypes

Components. A SysADL *component* is a stereotype that specializes a block with a subset of its properties. A component can have a set of features that specify its definition. The features are parts, references, values, constraints and properties. These features enable a system and software architect to model each component at the level of detail that is appropriate for an architectural description. Features represent characteristics, roles or usages in the context of the component or its environment. Features can describe the state of the component, including relations between elements that define its structure (parts and references), constraints, properties types and values that apply to them. *Parts* specify the other elements that compound the component. They can be other components or connectors. *References* specify the elements that are used by the component. The difference between parts and reference is that the former is a composition and the latter is an aggregation in UML/SysML terms. *Values* specify the values of particular properties in a component that characterize it. *Constraints* are properties that specify particular characteristics of the component. The property feature can be used to define general properties of the component. The behavior of a component is specified in terms of its interfaces as defined by its ports and corresponding protocols. We describe ports later in this paper.

In SysADL, we represent a component using the SysML block graphical notation with the stereotype indication. The notation is a rectangle that can have optional compartments. The upper label in a rectangle should have the name <<component>> to indicate that it is a stereotype. Figure 3(a) depicts possible representations of components. A simple rectangle is used to identify a component in a model. In Figure 3(a), to specify the properties of a *Component1* we use a rectangle with compartments. *Component1* has several properties – parts, constraints, references, values, and properties. *Component2* and *Component3* are shown in short notations when it is not relevant to present the details. *Component4* has a port *p* of type *Port1*.

The SysML block definition diagram (*bdd*) is used to define components and its relationships with other elements. BDD diagrams have a diagram frame, which has a *header* and a *content*. The header describes the kind of diagram, the diagram name,

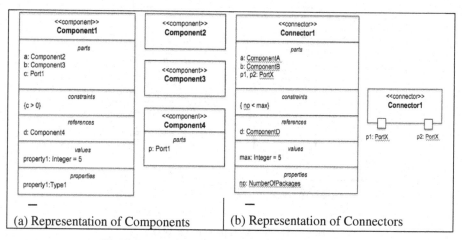

(a) Representation of Components | (b) Representation of Connectors

Fig. 3. Representation of Components and Connectors

and some contextual information. The content are the place define describe the components in the model. Composition and aggregation relationships between components are also specified in a BDD.

Connectors. A *Connector* in SysADL is a stereotype that specializes a SysADL component to represent the interactions between components, as shown in Figure 2. In SysADL, we are promoting connectors to be first-class elements and they can have all features that a component has. Components and connectors have different roles in system architecture. Connectors have the role to mediate interactions – communication and control – between components. The specification of a connector is very similar to a component. The example in Figure 3(b) defines a connector type composed of *a* and *b* components, and a *p* port. It also uses a *d* component. The connector has two ports: *p1* and *p2*. A property type *NumberOfPackages* is defined and is used to constrain that the connector transmits e.g. a maximum of 5 packages at a time. Figure 3(b) also shows a simple representation of the same connector with its two ports. The SysADL connector is different from the SysML connector that simply binds elements. In SysADL a connector follows the idea of Shaw and Garlan [1], containing a protocol specification that makes explicit the rules about the types of interactions.

Configurations. A configuration defines the structure of a system as a composition of components and connectors. In a configuration, component ports are linked to connector ports using SysML connectors. Both ports need to be of the same type. A SysML connector provides a bind between ports. In SysADL, a configuration is a specialization of a component. Figure 2 shows the representation of a configuration in the SysADL profile. Both configuration and connectors are specialization of component. As a composite, a configuration is composed by one or more components, and, in extension, by connectors and other configurations. Because component and connectors can be composite elements and can have a configuration themselves, the internal block diagram (*ibd*), as depicted in Figure 4 can be used to define the configuration of a component and a software architecture configuration. The Figure 4 shows a configuration of two components *c1* and *c2* and one connector. An unnamed instance of *CS-Connector* links *c1* and *c2*. The connector is linked to the components by SysML connectors. It is important to differentiate SysADL and SysML connectors. In SysML, a connector in a direct association between blocks. It binds them linking their ports. In SysADL, a connector has several features that allow the definition of properties, parts, constraints and values. However, in SysADL we use SysML connectors to bind a component and a connector. In other words, a SysML connector binds SysADL components and connectors using their ports. Figure 4 also shows the two types of connectors.

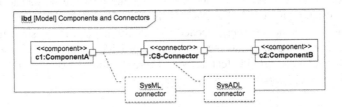

Fig. 4. An example of configuration using an IBD diagram

Ports. A Port is an interface that specifies services in both components and connectors. Services can be functionalities or information required or provided by components and connectors. A SysADL Port is a specialization of a SysML Port. The specification of a SysADL port in the profile is depicted in Figure 2. Both components and connectors can have ports. Component and connectors are linked using SysML binding connectors to their specific ports. The two ends ports of a binding connector must have the same type to assure their compatibility. *Required and provided features* can be services and non-flow information that a component provides for other components or requires of others components. They are defined as required and provided interfaces. For example, a component might provide a data sorting service to other components in one port and the availability state information in other port. Flowports can also be specified.

4   Case Study

The case study consists of a *Central Conditioner System* (CCS) composed of elements that supports the automatic control of the mechanical parts of the system. The parts are: (i) the User Interface; (ii) the Temperature Sensor; (iii) the Condenser; and (iv) the Fan. These elements are integrated to provide an automatic control the desired temperature. Using the *User Interface* component the user can set the desired temperature, and get current temperature (*setTemp* and *getTemp*). The *Temperature Sensor* component continuously gets the ambient temperature to inform it to the *Controller* component. The *Controller* component receives the parameters from both the *User Interface* component and the *Temperature Sensor* and decides which parameters (*Pressure* and *Fan)* are to be sent to the *Condenser* component and to the *Fan* component in order to reach the user desired temperature. Figure 5 represents the detailed configuration of CCS, a connected graph including all components, ports, and connectors. The *User Interface* component contains two ports represented by the provided features *SetTemp* and *GetTemp*. They are provided to the user respectively set and get the temperature. It has also a port *ITemperature* that requires and provides the temperature *SetT* and *GetT*, represented by required features used to connect this component to the *Controller* component. The *Controller* component contains a port that provided features – *SetT* and *GetT* – and three required features ports *GetCurTemp, SetPress, SetSpeed*. The *GetCurTemp* port is used to get the current temperature from the *Temperature Sensor* component. The *setPress* is used to connect this component to the *Condenser* component, to set the pressure needed to achieve the user desired temperature. The *SetSpeed* is used to connect this component to the *Fan* component, to set the air *Speed* needed to quickly achieve the desired temperature. The *Condenser* component has the *setPressure* provide feature port. The *Fan* component has the *setSpeed* provide feature port. There are four connectors: *IUC connector, CTS connector, CC connector*, and *CF connector*.

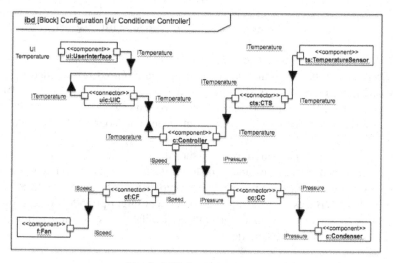

Fig. 5. CCS Configuration

5   Related Work

We briefly discuss some works in terms of profiles for the OMG modeling languages. Medvidovic et al [7] conducted a pioneering work in evaluating the use of UML for modeling software architectures in the manner in which existing ADLs model architectures. They concluded that UML lacks support for capturing and exploiting certain architectural concerns and also that UML lacks direct support for modeling and exploiting architectural styles, explicit software connectors, and local and global architectural constraints. Although new versions of UML were released after that publication, to date UML still neglects the idea of using components, connectors and configuration to represent an architecture description, as ADLs do. Our profile addresses this gap and enriches SysML with ADL-related concepts. Behjati et al. [5] propose the ExSAM profile (*Extended SysML for Architecture Analysis Modeling*) that consists in a SysML extension including concepts of the Architecture Analysis and Design Language (AADL). Our proposal is different as we create a generic and simple SysML profile to support architecture description. DesyreML [6] is a SysML profile for the formal description of heterogeneous embedded systems. The proposal of this work is different from ours. It focuses on formal description of embedded system and our goal is to provide a generic SysML-based ADL to model any kind of system. In addition, it is verbose, in comparison with our proposal, as it creates a number of stereotypes to allow the definition of embedded components with different models of computation.

6   Final Remarks

In this paper we defined SysADL, a SysML profile that incorporates in SysML consolidated concepts from ADLs, allowing the high-level description of the architecture using the ADLs main concepts As SysADL is a lightweight extension of an existing standard, it can be easily adopted by the OMG modeling language community, both from academy and industry, which can use an unique language with tool support to exploit the power of two complementary modeling languages. We investigated the applicability of SysADL through a case study of a Central Conditioner System and we concluded that the consensual structural concepts of ADLs are fully covered by SysADL. As future work we are developing an architectural-driven execution platform using the Action Language for Foundational UML (ALF) [8] that will allow dynamic analysis of system behavioral properties at design time.

References

1. Shaw, M., Garlan, D.: Software Architecture: Perspectives on an Emerging Discipline. Prentice Hall (1996)
2. OMG Systems Modeling Language, http://www.omgsysml.org
3. OMG UML, http://www.omg.org/spec/UML/
4. Medvidovic, N., et al.: A Classification and Comparison Framework for Software Architecture Description Languages. IEEE Trans. Software Eng. 26(1), 70–93 (2000)
5. Behjati, R., et al.: An AADL-Based SysML Profile for Architecture Level Systems Engineering: Approach, Metamodels, and Experiments. ModelME! Tech. Report 2001-03 (2011)
6. Ferrari, A., et al.: DesyreML: A SysML Profile for Heterogeneous Embedded System. In: Embedded Real Time Software and Systems (ERTS), Toulouse, France (2012)
7. Medvidovic, N., et al.: Modeling Software Architecture in the Unified Modeling Language. ACM Trans. on Software Eng. and Methodology (TOSEM) 11(1), 2–57 (2002)
8. OMG 2012. Action Language For Foundational UML – ALF (2012), http://www.omg.org/spec/ALF/

A Lightweight Language for Software Product Lines Architecture Description

Eduardo Silva, Ana Luisa Medeiros, Everton Cavalcante, and Thais Batista

DIMAp – Department of Informatics and Applied Mathematics
UFRN – Federal University of Rio Grande do Norte
Natal, Brazil
{eduafsilva, analuisafdm, evertonranielly, thaisbatista}@gmail.com

Abstract. The architecture description of a software product line (SPL) is essential to make it clear how the architecture realizes the feature model and to represent both the domain and application engineering architectural artefacts. However, most architecture description languages (ADLs) for SPL have limited support regarding variability management and they do not express the relationship between features and the architecture, besides the lack of tools for graphical and textual modelling and a non-clear separation between the domain and application engineering activities. In order to overcome these deficiencies, this paper presents LightPL-ACME, an ADL whose main goal is to be a simple, lightweight language for the SPL architecture description, and enable the association between the architectural specification and the artefacts involved in the SPL development process, including the relationship with the feature model and the representation of both domain and application engineering elements.

Keywords: Software product lines architectures, Architecture description languages, ACME, LightPL-ACME.

1 Introduction

Software product lines (SPLs) [1] consist of an approach for deriving applications that shares a specific set of common features (commonalities) and have variabilities that distinguish the specific applications, thus supporting the development of a product family. The SPL development process follows two main activities: (i) *domain engineering*, which aims to systematize the gathering, organization, and storage of reusable and consistent information in the form of artefacts, thus exploring similarities while preserving the ability to build different products, and; (ii) *application engineering*, which aims to specify and customize different products from the artefacts generated by the domain engineering activity.

The architectural description is one of the activities involved in the development of an SPL that enables to anticipate important decisions regarding the system design and represent architectural characteristics of the SPL. In the software architecture context, *architecture description languages* (ADLs) [2] provide

K. Drira (Ed.): ECSA 2013, LNCS 7957, pp. 114–121, 2013.
© Springer-Verlag Berlin Heidelberg 2013

abstractions for representing architectures through *components*, *connectors*, and *configurations*. Components represent software functionalities, connectors are communication elements, and configurations describe the relationship between components and connectors.

Although there are some ADLs for describing SPL architectures [3–5], most of them have limited support regarding the management of variabilities since they only focus on documenting SPL concepts (similarities and variabilities) and architectural elements rather than the relationship and traceability between the variabilities represented in the feature model and the architecture of an SPL. Moreover, these ADLs do not express the relationship between features and the architecture and suffer from the following limitations: (i) high verbosity that makes the architectural description confusing and difficult to understand; (ii) complexity for instantiating products; (iii) lack of tools for graphical and textual modeling; and (iv) lack of a clear separation between the domain and application engineering activities in the SPL development process.

In this context, this paper presents *LightPL-ACME*, an ADL that aims to provide a lightweight strategy for describing architectures of SPLs in order to overcome the abovementioned limitations. We have chosen the ACME ADL [6] as basis of the proposed ADL since ACME provides generic structures to cope with a wide range of systems and includes a language based on first-order predicate logic called Armani [7], which is used to design architectural constraints. The main features of LightPL-ACME are: (i) semantic enrichment of ACME elements originally used to specify the SPL architecture, the so-called *base architecture*; (ii) elements designed to enable the definition of the *referenced architecture*, which is a base architecture whose elements refer to the features of the SPL; and (iii) products instantiation, which is based on the architectural description of the SPL and the referenced architecture. In this paper, we illustrate the main elements of the LightPL-ACME ADL with the *GingaForAll* [8] SPL for *Ginga* [9], the middleware adopted by the Brazilian Digital Television System (SBTVD).

This paper is structured as follows. Section 2 describes the basic concepts regarding SPLs and provides an overview about the ACME/Armani ADL. Section 3 presents LightPL-ACME and its application for describing the *GingaForAll* SPL. Section 4 presents the LightPL-ACME Studio tool. Section 5 presents related work. Finally, Section 6 contains final remarks and future works.

2   Background

2.1   Software Product Lines

Software product lines (SPLs) [1] enable the creation of a *family* (or *product line*) of similar products by using a common software infrastructure to mount and configure parts designed to be reused among products and following two main activities, namely *domain engineering* and *application engineering* [11]. The construction of a software product, also called *instantiation* or *derivation*, is made from a configuration of core assets, which consists of an arrangement of the software artefacts that implement the product.

In the SPL development, the members of a family have a basic set of common functionalities and associated variants that individualize each one of these members. Typically, similarities and variabilities among products of a family are modelled in terms of *features*, which are concepts that may be a requirement, a function, or a non-functional feature [1]. Features are organized in *feature models*, which that represent similarities, variabilities, and constraints related to the variations between features and their relationships. In general, feature models have a tree structure in which features are represented by nodes of the tree and the variations between features are represented by edges and feature groups, so that the hierarchical organization of the diagram describes the key concept from more general to more specific concepts as they descend the tree. Furthermore, features can be [10]: (i) *mandatory*, i.e. the feature must be included in a product; (ii) *optional*, i.e. the feature may or may not be included if the feature from which it derives is selected; (iii) *inclusive-or*, i.e. among the set of related features at least one of them must be selected, and; (iv) *alternative*, i.e. among the set of related features exactly one of them must be selected.

2.2 ACME/Armani

ACME [6] is a generic ADL that provides a basis for developing new domain-specific ADLs. A system is described in ACME by seven basic elements: *Component, Connector, System, Attachment, Port, Role*, and *Representation*. *Components* are computational entities that can have multiple interfaces called *Ports*. The ports of a component are bound to the ports of other components through *Connectors*, which can have multiple interfaces called *Roles*. *Systems* are abstractions that represent configurations of components and connectors including a set of *Component* elements, a set of *Connector* elements, and a set of *Attachment* elements that describe the topology of the system in terms of *Port–Role* associations. *Representations* are alternative architecture views of an element or more detailed decompositions of a given element (component, connector, port or role). Furthermore, architectural elements can be annotated in order to represent behavioral and non-functional properties by using *Property* elements. *Properties* have the form of <*name, type, value*> triples and can be used in any of the ACME elements. ACME also enables to define architectural styles in order to increase reuse and expressiveness, which is done through the *Type* and *Family* elements. In ACME, an architectural style defines a family of systems, through *Family* element, in terms of a structural organization pattern that contains a vocabulary of element types and a set of constraints that indicate how these elements can be combined, and the *Type* element is used to define a vocabulary of abstract types of ACME elements. In turn, Armani [7] is an ACME extension and consists of a predicate language based on first-order logic used to express architectural *constraints* over ACME elements. Such constraints are defined in terms of *invariants*, design constraints that must be fulfilled, and *heuristics*, design constraints that may or may not be fulfilled.

3   LightPL-ACME

LightPL-ACME is an ADL proposed as an ACME extension that aims to provide a lightweight, simple language for SPL architecture description, so that it is possible to associate such description with the artefacts related to the domain engineering and application engineering activities in the SPL development process. It supports the separation of these SPL activities by creating specific abstractions for features (related to the domain engineering activity) and products (related to the application engineering activity). Moreover, LightPL-ACME was designed envisioning the representation of the architecture and its relationship with the features. The following subsections present the main elements of the LightPL-ACME ADL.

3.1   *ProductLine*, *Feature*, and *Product* Elements

The *ProductLine* element has similar characteristics to the ACME *Family* element, which is semantically and syntactically enriched in order to represent the SPL, thus enabling the user to describe its specific elements, such as features and products. Within the *ProductLine* element, the *Feature* element is defined to represent the features that compose the SPL and is specified by the definition of an identifier and an associated type related to the types of features that may occur in an SPL: (i) *Mandatory*, which represents mandatory features; (ii) *Optional*, which represents optional features; (iii) *Alternative*, which represents alternative features, and; (iv) *InclusiveOr*, which represents inclusive-or features. Additionally, the *extends* mechanism provided by ACME enables to establish an inheritance relationship between two features.

Fig. 1 illustrates the definition of the *Demultiplexer*, *Hardware*, and *Software* features for the *GingaCC ProductLine* element and its corresponding feature model. The *Demultiplexer* feature is mandatory (line 3), and the *Hardware* and *Software* features are alternative and derived from the *Demultiplexer* feature (lines 4 and 5).

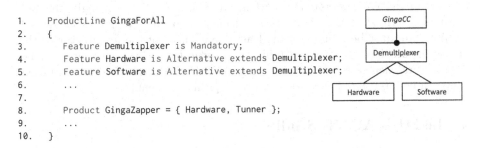

```
1.    ProductLine GingaForAll
2.    {
3.        Feature Demultiplexer is Mandatory;
4.        Feature Hardware is Alternative extends Demultiplexer;
5.        Feature Software is Alternative extends Demultiplexer;
6.        ...
7.
8.        Product GingaZapper = { Hardware, Tunner };
9.        ...
10.   }
```

Fig. 1. Features and product description in a *ProductLine* element and its corresponding depiction as a feature model

In order to complement the description of the features in an SPL, LightPL-ACME provides Armani [7] functions for specifying constraints between *Feature* elements in a *ProductLine* element, namely the *requires* (for dependency) and *excludes* (for mutual exclusion) functions, which receive as parameters the identifiers of the *Feature* elements included in the relationship.

Finally, the *Product* element corresponds to the concept of products that can be generated by an SPL. The specification of this element consists of an identifier regarding the product that is being specified and a set of identifiers regarding the *Feature* elements that compose this product. The inclusion of *Feature* elements also occurs by hierarchy, so that the inclusion of a *Feature* element in a *Product* element includes all of its direct dependencies, which take place through the inheritance relationship.

3.2   Referenced Architectures

In LightPL-ACME, *referenced architectures* are artefacts related to the system architecture and consist of a description of the base architecture that is enriched with references to the *Feature* elements previously described in a *ProductLine* element. This notion of referenced architectures in terms of mapping architectural elements to features is part of the well-known concept of *configuration knowledge* [11], which represents all available information used to support the product derivation process and includes this mapping between SPL artefacts and features.

In LightPL-ACME, the mapping mechanism between architectural elements and features in order to compose the referenced architecture is made by using the keyword *MappedTo* followed by a set of *Feature* elements and can be added to the specification most of the conventional ACME elements after their names. In order to make *Feature* elements (that represent the features) accessible in the referenced architecture, it is necessary that the *System* element that represents the complete system has been adhered to the architectural style described by a *ProductLine* element. Fig. 2 illustrates the mapping between the base architecture and the *GingaForAll* SPL architectural description in order to compose the referenced architecture, which is represented by the *GingaFull System* that adheres to the *GingaForAll ProductLine*. It is important to highlight that all features described in the *ProductLine* element associated with the referenced architecture must be mapped to at least one element of the architecture, otherwise the architecture does not fulfill the *ProductLine*. However, there may be architectural elements that are not being mapped to *Feature* elements and then they can be interpreted as implementation-specific elements.

4   LightPL-ACME Studio

LightPL-ACME Studio[1] [12] is a tool developed as an Eclipse IDE plug-in that was designed to assist the SPL development and support the textual specification and graphical representation of architectures described in LightPL-ACME.

---

[1] The LightPL-ACME Studio tool is available as free download from:
http://www.dimap.ufrn.br/lightplacmestudio/downloads.php

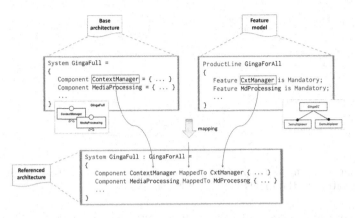

Fig. 2. Mapping to the referenced architecture in LightPL-ACME

The tool enables to specify architectural descriptions, create and edit LightPL-ACME elements (e.g. *ProductLine*), and represent referenced architectures, besides maintaining an automatic correspondence between textual and graphic descriptions. Fig. 3 illustrates a partial textual description of the *GingaForAll* SPL in LightPL-ACME and its corresponding graphical representation in the LightPL-ACME Studio tool.

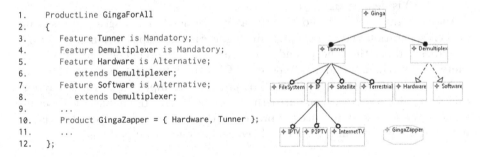

Fig. 3. Partial textual description of the *GingaForAll ProductLine* (left) and its corresponding graphical representation

Furthermore, LightPL-ACME Studio also enables to define the mapping between elements in the base architecture and features of the SPL by accessing the properties of the architectural element and choosing the features to which such element will be mapped, as exemplified in Fig. 4.

5   Related Work

In this section we present some proposals of the literature regarding ADLs to SPL architectural description. In ADLARS [3] the relationship between features and the architectural description is explicitly done through conditional expressions, so that a *Component Template* specifies the collection of possible component

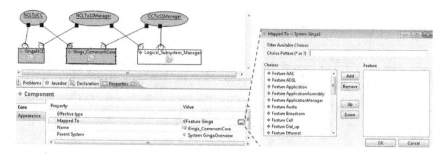

Fig. 4. Mapping from the *Ginga_CommonCore* component in the base architecture to the *Ginga* feature in the LightPL-ACME Studio tool

configurations and associates these components to the features. xADL 2.0 [4] specifies the architecture using XML (*eXtensible Markup Language*) schemas, but this ADL does not define specific elements for representing SPL architectures, thus hampering the identification of the variation points and their relation with the system architecture. In turn, PL-AspectualACME [5] represents variabilities by purely using the conventional ACME abstractions. It combines *Representation* elements for identifying product variations and *Port* elements for representing the mechanism of variability selection, features are described as *Component Type* elements, and the type of a feature (mandatory, optional or alternative) is defined through properties.

Unlike LightPL-ACME, none of the abovementioned languages addresses an explicit separation between the domain engineering and application engineering activities and has the concept and representation of the referenced architecture. Moreover, xADL 2.0 and PL-AspectualACME architectural descriptions tend to be verbose, whereas LightPL-ACME provides a simple, lightweight way for describing SPL architectures. Furthermore, LightPL-ACME enables the description of any sort of system since the proposed ADL is a general-purpose language, unlike ADLARS, which is a specific language for embedded systems.

6   Final Remarks

This paper presented *LightPL-ACME*, a simple, lightweight ADL for describing SPL architectures that introduces three essential elements (*ProductLine, Feature*, and *Product*) in order to reduce the verbosity and complexity in the description of SPL concepts and enrich elements present in the ACME ADL for SPL description and enable the description of the *referenced architecture*, a key concept that denotes a base architecture with references to the features described in the SPL. Finally, the LightPL-ACME strategy promotes a clear separation between the domain engineering and application engineering activities that are involved in the SPL development process. and maintains characteristics related to generality, simplicity, expressiveness, and extensibility inherited from ACME by using the existing abstractions of this ADL and avoiding the addition of many new abstractions. The proposed language has also an associated tool called

LightPL-ACME Studio, which provides textual and graphical support for representing SPL architectures specified in this ADL.

LightPL-ACME was evaluated by a controlled experiment with a real-world case study, the *GingaForAll* SPL, as available at http://www.dimap.ufrn.br/lightplacmestudio/experiments.php. In this experiment, it was possible to observe that LightPL-ACME is able to express important elements of an SPL (such as features and the products that can be generated from them) in a simple, lightweight, clear, and objective way. As directions to future work, we intend to use the LightPL-ACME ADL within a model-driven development strategy in order to automatically generate customized source code from product models and also check the correlation between the source code and the architectural model.

References

1. Clements, P., Northrop, L.: Software product lines: Practices and patterns. Addison-Wesley, USA (2001)
2. Medvidovic, N., Taylor, R.N.: A classification and comparison framework for software architecture description languages. IEEE Trans. on Software Engineering 26(1), 70–93 (2000)
3. Bashroush, R., et al.: ADLARS: An architecture description language for software product lines. In: 29th Annual IEEE/NASA Software Engineering Workshop, pp. 163–173. IEEE Computer Society, USA (2005)
4. Dashofy, E.M., et al.: A highly-extensible, XML-based architecture description language. In: 2001 Working IEEE/IFIP Conf. on Software Architecture, pp. 103–112. IEEE Computer Society, USA (2001)
5. Barbosa, E.A., Batista, T., Garcia, A., Silva, E.: PL-AspectualACME: An aspect-oriented architectural description language for software product lines. In: Crnkovic, I., Gruhn, V., Book, M. (eds.) ECSA 2011. LNCS, vol. 6903, pp. 139–146. Springer, Heidelberg (2011)
6. Garlan, D., et al.: ACME: An architecture description interchange language. In: 1997 Conf. of the Centre for Advanced Studies on Collaborative Research, pp. 169–183. IBM Press (1997)
7. Monroe, R.: Capturing software architecture expertise with Armani. Technical report, School of Computer Science, Carnegie Mellon University, USA (1998)
8. Saraiva, D., et al.: Architecting a model-driven aspect-oriented product line for a digital TV middleware: A refactoring experience. In: Ali Babar, M., Gorton, I. (eds.) ECSA 2010. LNCS, vol. 6285, pp. 166–181. Springer, Heidelberg (2010)
9. Ginga Middleware, http://www.ginga.org.br/en
10. Kang, K.C., et al.: Feature-oriented domain analysis (FODA) feasibility study. Technical report, Software Engineering Institute, Carnegie Mellon University, USA (1990)
11. Czarnecki, K., Eisenecker, U.: Generative Programming: Methods, tools, and applications. ACM Press/Addison-Wesley, USA (2000)
12. LightPL-ACME Studio, http://www.dimap.ufrn.br/lightplacmestudio/
13. Batista, T., et al.: Aspectual connectors: Supporting the seamless integration of aspects and ADLs. In: XX Brazilian Symposium on Software Engineering, pp. 17–32. SBC, Brazil (2006)

Towards a Multi-scale Modeling
for Architectural Deployment Based on Bigraphs

Amal Gassara[1], Ismael Bouassida Rodriguez[1,2,3], and Mohamed Jmaiel[1]

[1] ReDCAD, University of Sfax, B.P. 1173, 3038 Sfax, Tunisia
{amal.gassara,bouassida}@redcad.org,
mohamed.jmaiel@enis.rnu.tn
[2] CNRS, LAAS, 7 Avenue du colonel Roche, F-31400 Toulouse, France
[3] Univ de Toulouse, LAAS, F-31400 Toulouse, France

Abstract. With the evolution of distributed systems in size and complexity, software deployment remains a challenging task. Despite the existence of several approaches, most of them use informal models that lack a solid mathematic foundation. In this paper, we propose a bigraphical based approach for modeling and formalizing the deployment of distributed applications. This approach relies on multi-scale modeling. So, we start by modeling the first scale with a bigraph. This bigraph is enriched, through a series of reaction rules, until reaching the last scale that represents the deployment architecture.

Keywords: Deployment, Multi-scale modeling, Bigraphs.

1 Introduction

With significant advances in software development, software applications become more and more complex, and distributed over a large network. These applications need to deal with hardware constraints and user requirements during the execution. Thus, software components must be placed on the suitable hosts among the distributed target environment to run the application properly. We called this process software deployment.

By placing software components on hardware nodes, we can have several deployment architectures. So, it is necessary to select the more efficient one in terms of QoS. Consequently, the designer needs to specify the possible deployment architectures in order to select the suitable one. This process remains a challenging task. In this paper, we focus on the modeling of the deployment architectures. In future work, we will analysis these models in qualitative and quantitative way allowing the selection of the appropriate deployment architecture.

Despite the efficiency of existing models, most of them are informal and lack of a solid mathematic foundation. Since bigraphs have a highly logical algebraic language, we use it as a formal model. So, the aim of this paper is to propose a bigraphical based approach for modeling and formalizing the deployment for distributed applications. We follow a multi-scale modeling approach. So, we start

K. Drira (Ed.): ECSA 2013, LNCS 7957, pp. 122–129, 2013.
© Springer-Verlag Berlin Heidelberg 2013

with modeling the first scale which is defined by a bigraph. This bigraph is enriched using bigraphical reactive system (BRS) to reach the scales one by one. At the last scale, we obtain bigraphs that represent the deployment architectures. The latter includes hosts and software components. The enriching rules are defined through a series of reaction rules.

The remainder of this paper is organized as follows. In Section 2, we explain our proposal for the formal modeling of deployment architecture. In this section, we present also overviews of bigraphs and multi-scale modeling. Then, we present in the section 3 a case study called "Smart Home" which illustrates the feasibility of our approach. We briefly review most related work in Section 4. Finally, Section 5 concludes this paper and presents future work.

2   The Proposed Approach

We propose an approach aiming the modeling and the formalizing of deployment for distributed applications. This approach performs three steps to generate deployment architectures. In this paper, we focus only on the two first steps.

- **Step 1: Modeling** The designer starts with defining the different scales. Then, he models the first scale using bigraphs.
- **Step 2: Enriching** The models specified by the designer are enriched by applying reaction rules to reach the scales one by one. At the end of this step, we obtain the set of the possible deployment architectures.
- **Step 3: Selecting** Each deployment architecture obtained at the previous step is quantified in order to select the suitable one.

2.1   Overview of Bigraphs

The Static Structure. Bigraphs [1], proposed by Milner, formalise distributed systems by emphasising both locality and connectivity. We use Fig. 1 to introduce bigraphs informally. A bigraph consists principally of hyperedges and nodes which can be nested and have ports. Each hyperedge can connect many ports on different nodes (for example, v_0, v_1 and v_2 are joined by e_1). A bigraph combines two graphical structures, a *place graph* and a *link graph*, hence the term bigraph. Fig 2 depicts the *place* and *link* graphs of the bigraph G.

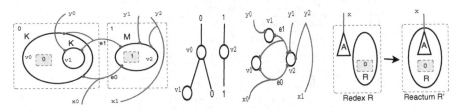

Fig. 1. A Bigraph G   **Fig. 2.** *place* and *link* graphs   **Fig. 3.** A reaction rule

Place Graph. The *place graph* is a hierarchical tree that describes the locality of the nodes. In this graph, branches establish the nesting relationship of nodes in the bigraph. Trees of are rooted by regions represented by dashed rectangle. Within the *place graph*, in addition to nodes and regions, there can also be sites, represented as grey rectangles. A site is a hole that can host new nodes.

Link Graph. The *link graph* is a hyper-graph that describes the connectivity of nodes. Within this graph, there can be outer names (Fig. 2 y_0, y_1, y_2) and inner names (Fig. 2 x_0, x_1) represented as open links. These names define the connection points at which coincident names may be fused to form a single link. So, they give bigraphs the possibility to be composed by joining the inner names of one bigraph with the corresponding outer names of another bigraph.

Control and Signature. Each node in the bigraph is assigned a control. Controls (in this example K and M) indicate the node ports' number through the arity and how it behaves dynamically through the status which is either active or passive or atomic. An atomic node cannot contain any node and a non atomic node can be active or passive which means whether reactions may take place within the node. We can use the notation "X-node", which means a node that has been assigned the control X. The set of controls forms the signature.

The Dynamic Structure. A BRS is a set of bigraphs and a set of reaction rules that may be applied to rewrite these bigraphs. Each reaction rule consists of two bigraphs: a *Redex R* and a *Reactum R'*. The application of the rule consists of identifying the image of R in a bigraph and replacing it by the corresponding R'. For example in Fig. 3, the rule allows an A-node to enter a R-node which is placed in the same region. The site (grey rectangle) in the *Redex* represents all other possible occupants of the R-node which are unchanged after applying this rule. The graphical representation used above is handy for modeling, but unwieldy for reasoning. Fortunately, bigraphs have an associated term language [2]. The corresponding algebraic expression (using details in table 1) of this rule is:

$$A_x \mid R.d_0 \rightarrow R.(A_x \mid d_0)$$

Table 1. The term language for Bigraphs

Algebraic expression	Meaning
U||V	Juxtaposition of roots
U|V	Juxtaposition of nodes
U.V	Nesting (U contains V)
K_x	K-Node linked to an outer name x
d_i	Site numbered i
1	The *barren* (empty) root
/x.U	U with outer name x replaced by an edge

2.2 Multi-scale Modeling

Our approach is based on multi-scale modeling [3]. In fact, a scale is a generic model that provides additional details of the design and describes a level or a layer in a system. Multi-scale methodologies are based on the fundamental principle: model each phenomenon across the most relevant. For this, these methodologies have two key points: the first is to distinguish between different scales and the second is to model the relationships between these different scales.

Multi-scale Modeling with Bigraphs. In our approach, a scale is represented as a bigraph, where nodes correspond to deployment nodes (i.e., physical environment, hosts, devices, etc) or software components, edges represent interaction between linked nodes. Moreover, the transition from one scale to another is considered as bigraphical reactive system. This transition is an enriching performed through a series of **meta-reaction** rules. In fact, a meta-reaction rule contains nodes having a variable control (i.e., a variable can represent any control from the signature). Thus, the meta-reaction rule can be instantiated to several ones with different controls.

3 Case Study: Smart Home

In order to illustrate our approach, we consider an example of an M2M application named "Smart Home" denoted in the Fig. 4. A smart home is composed of rooms. Each room can be equipped with heterogeneous devices (sensors like thermometer, presence sensor, light sensor, etc and actuators like air conditioner, lamp, etc). Between these devices, there is a need of communication. Sensors monitor and record information related to the environment such as rooms luminosity, human presence, temperature, etc. These information are transmitted to a control unit. Once received, the control unit, by analyzing them, makes the appropriate decisions to configure the devices and propagate these decisions. Now we apply our approach on Smart Home.

3.1 Step 1: Modeling

This step allows the designer to determine the application scales. Until now, our approach enables the deployment of the software entities ensuring the

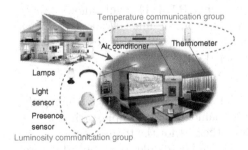

Fig. 4. Smart Home

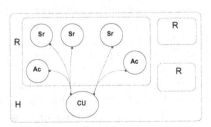

Fig. 5. Deployment infrastructure scale

communication of an application. So, we propose three scales: the deployment infrastructure scale, the communication scale and the deployment scale. After that, the designer models the first scale using a bigraph.

Scale 0: Deployment Infrastructure Scale. This scale includes physical environment, hosts, devices, etc. The bigraph defined in the Fig. 5 illustrates this scale for a smart home. The nodes H and R represent the home and a room respectively. Whereas, the nodes CU, Sr and Ac represent the control unit, a sensor and an actuator respectively. Initially, these nodes are empty. A hyperedge depicts a need of communication. For example, the hyperedge at right depicts the temperature communication group between the air conditioner (Ac-node) and the thermometer (Sr-node) and the control unit. The other hyperedge depicts the luminosity communication group.

3.2   Step 2: Enriching

Scale 1: Communication Scale. This scale represents explicitly the entities that take part in the communication. Each communication group is formed by a set of senders and receivers. So, the bigraph defined in the first step (Fig. 5), is enriched by applying three meta-reaction rules: R1.1, R1.2 and R1.3.

Rule to add a sender: R1.1 This rule consists of nesting a sender (S-node) in each empty sensor (Sr-node depicting a thermometer, a presence sensor or a light sensor) having an outer name x. In fact, a communication group is defined by an hyperedge that links nodes with the same outer names (i.e., outer names are not represented explicitly in the Fig. 5 because they are joined to form hyperedges). Then, we nest in this S-node an x-node to mark its communication group. For lack of space, we present the reaction rules only with algebraic expressions.
   R1.1: $Sr_x.(1) \rightarrow Sr_x.(S.x)$

Rule to add a receiver: R1.2 This rule consists of nesting a receiver (R-node) in each empty actuator (Ac-node depicting a lamp or an air conditioner) having an outer name x. Like with the rule R1.1, we nest in the R-node an x-node.
   R1.2: $Ac_x.(1) \rightarrow Ac_x.(R.x)$

Rule to add a pair of sender and receiver: R1.3 This rule allows to add a pair of sender and receiver in the empty control unit (CU-node) for each communication group (i.e., outer names x and y). We also nest an x-nodes in the first pair and y-nodes in the second one.
   R1.3: $CU_{x,y}.(1) \rightarrow CU_{x,y}.(S.x \mid R.x \mid S.y \mid R.y)$

The meta-reaction rules R1.1, R1.2 and R1.3 are instantiated by changing the name of the control x according to the outer name. In our example, we instantiate R1.1 and R1.2 twice by replacing x with $g0$ then $g1$ for the temperature and the luminosity communication group respectively. These rules are applied several times until there are no more empty devices (Sr and Ac nodes). We instantiate

R1.3 once by replacing x with $g0$ and y with $g1$ and the intantiated rule is applied one time.

The Fig. 6 shows the application effect of the instantiated rules on the bigraph given on the Fig. 5. In this bigraph, there are S-node in sensors, R-node in actuators and both of them in the control unit. The S-nodes and the R-nodes belonging the temperature communication group, contain $g0$-node. Whereas, those belonging the luminosity communication group, contain $g1$-node .

Scale 2: Deployment Scale. This scale represents the middleware components that ensure the communication between the application components. Here, we use the Event-Based Communications (EBC) which provides three types of entities: *event producers (EP)*, *event consumers (EC)* and *channel managers (CM)*. The *EP* and *EC* are connected to *CM*. The *EP* sends data to the *CM* to which they are connected. The *CM* returns a copy of the received data to all the *EC* which are connected to it. Therefore, we enrich the bigraph obtained at the previous scale (defined in Fig. 6) by applying the following meta-reaction rules:

Rule to add a *CM*: R2.1 This rule enables to add a *CM*-node to each communication group (e.g. a set of juxtaposed nodes linked by one hyperedge). The *CM*-node is placed in one node belongs to the communication group. It contains also a nested node to mark its communication group.
   R2.1: $/x \ Y1_x \ || \ Y2_x \ || \ ... \ || \ Yn_x \rightarrow /x \ Y1_x \ || \ Y2_x \ || \ ... \ || \ (Yn_x \ | \ CM.x)$
Rules to add an *EP* and an *EC*: R2.2 and R2.3 These rules enable to add an *EP*-node to each sender and *EC*-node to each receiver. The x-node indicates the communication group to which the receiver or the sender belongs.
   R2.2: $S.x \rightarrow S.EP.x$
   R2.3: $R.x \rightarrow R.EC.x$
Rules to link *EP*s and *EC*s with *CM*: R2.4 and R2.5 The meta-reaction rule R2.4 allows to link an *EP* and a *CM* that belong to the same communication group (i.e, having a nested x-node). whereas R2.5 allows to link an *EC* and a *CM*.
   R2.4: $EP.x \ || \ CM.x \rightarrow /y \ EP_y \ || \ CM_y.x$
   R2.5: $EC.x \ || \ CM.x \rightarrow /y \ EC_y \ || \ CM_y.x$

The above meta-reaction rules are instantiated by replacing x with $g0$ then $g1$ for the temperature and the luminosity communication group respectively. The Fig. 7 shows the application effect of the set of these instantiated rules on the bigraph given on the Fig. 6. For the luminosity communication group, we find *EP*-node nested in each sender and *EC*-node nested in each receiver belonging this group. All of them are connected to the *CM*-node which is nested in the *CU*-node. Also, for the temperature communication group, all the *EP*-nodes and the *EC*-nodes belonging this group are connected to the *CM*-node which is nested in the *Ac*-node. This bigraph is one of a set of possible bigraphs obtained after applying these rules due to the choice of the channel manager placement (i.e., the *CM*-node is deployed on one node belongs to the communication group).

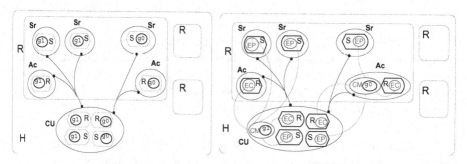

Fig. 6. The communication scale   **Fig. 7.** The deployment scale

4   Related Work

Current research studies on component deployment propose various approaches.

Architecture-Based Approaches. These approaches use Architecture Description Langauge (ADL). The work[4] presents an ADL extension for specifying a context-aware deployment. This deployment is performed in a propagative way and is driven by constraints put on the resources of the target hosts. However, it does not perform the automatic deployment planning and optimization.

MDA-Based Approaches. These approaches use usually OMG D&C specification [5] which offers three models. The *component model* defines descriptors for components and configurations, the *target model* defines descriptors for the target site on which applications can be deployed and the *execution model* defines the *DeploymentPlan*, which describes deployment decisions. It defines an ExecutionManager which executes application according to this deployment plan.

Some frameworks have been developed on the top on this approach to support component deployment like DAnCE [6], Dacar [7] and Deployment factory [8]. DAnCE is a QoS-enabled Component Deployment and Configuration Engine targeted for DRE systems. This framework deals only with CORBA Component Model. Whereas Deployment Factory is an unified environment for deploying component based applications. This framework does not deal with reconfigurable systems. However, Dacar is a model-based framework for deploying autonomic software distributed systems. Some MDA-based approaches use UML including [9]. This work proposes a UML extension named "DM profile" ensuring a high-level description for modeling the deployment and its management in distributed application. All these research activities do not focus on deployment planning and deployment optimization.

5   Conclusion and Future Work

In this paper, we have presented an approach for modeling and formalizing the deployment. We have proposed a multi-scale modeling approach based on bigraphs and bigraphical reactive system. It performs three scales: deployment infrastructure scale, communication scale and deployment scale. The first scale is given by the designer. Whereas the other scales are obtained using a BRS. So, we define a series of meta-reaction rules ensuring the transition between scales. These meta-reaction rules are instantiated according to the bigraphical models specified by the designer.

In future work, we aim to generalize this contribution and alter the enriching rules to generic ones. Besides, we plan to define more scales for modeling and accomplish the third step of our approach (selecting a deployment architecture).

Acknowledgments. This research is supported by the ITEA2's A2NETS (Autonomic Services in M2M Networks) project[1].

References

1. Jensen, O.H., Milner, R.: Bigraphs and mobile processes. Technical Report UCAM-CL-TR-580, University of Cambridge, Computer Laboratory (February 2004)
2. Birkedal, L., Debois, S., Elsborg, E., Hildebrandt, T., Niss, H.: Bigraphical models of context-aware systems. In: Aceto, L., Ingólfsdóttir, A. (eds.) FOSSACS 2006. LNCS, vol. 3921, pp. 187–201. Springer, Heidelberg (2006)
3. Khlif, I., Hadj Kacem, M., Drira, K.: Une approche de description multi-échelles et multi points de vue pour les architectures logicielles dynamiques. In: Conférence Francophone sur les Architectures Logicielles, Montpellier, France (May 2012)
4. Hoareau, D., Mahéo, Y.: Constraint-based deployment of distributed components in a dynamic network. In: Grass, W., Sick, B., Waldschmidt, K. (eds.) ARCS 2006. LNCS, vol. 3894, pp. 450–464. Springer, Heidelberg (2006)
5. Object Management Group, Inc.: Deployment and configuration of component-based distributed applications specification, version 4.0 (April 2006)
6. Deng, G., Balasubramanian, J., Otte, W., Schmidt, D.C., Gokhale, A.: Dance: A qos-enabled component deployment and configuration engine. In: Dearle, A., Savani, R. (eds.) CD 2005. LNCS, vol. 3798, pp. 67–82. Springer, Heidelberg (2005)
7. Dubus, J., Merle, P.: Towards Model-Driven Validation of Autonomic Software Systems in Open Distributed Environments. In: Workshop M-ADAPT, in Conjunction with ECOOP 2007, Berlin, Germany (July 2007)
8. Hnetynka, P.: A model-driven environment for component deployment. In: Proceedings of the Third ACIS Int'l Conference on Software Engineering Research, Management and Applications, SERA 2005, pp. 6–13. IEEE Computer Society, Washington, DC (2005)
9. Miladi, M.N., Krichen, F., Jmaiel, M., Drira, K.: A UML based deployment and management modeling for cooperative and distributed applications. In: Proceedings of the ACIS International Conference on Software Engineering, Management and Applications (SERA 2010), Montreal, Canada, 16 p. (May 2010)

---

[1] https://a2nets.erve.vtt.fi/

Classification of Design Decisions – An Expert Survey in Practice

Cornelia Miesbauer and Rainer Weinreich

Johannes Kepler University Linz, Austria
{cornelia.miesbauer,rainer.weinreich}@jku.at

Abstract. Support for capturing architectural knowledge has been identified as an important research challenge. As the basis for an approach for recovering design decisions and capturing their rationale we have performed an expert survey in practice to gain insights into the different kinds, influence factors, and sources for design decisions and also on how they are currently captured in practice. The survey has been performed with software architects, software team leads, and senior developers from six different companies in Austria with more than 10 years of experience in software development on average. The survey confirms earlier work by other authors on design decision classification and influence factors but also identifies additional kinds of decisions and influence factors not mentioned in this previous work. In addition, we gained insight into the practice of capturing, the relative importance of different decisions and influence factors, and on potential sources for recovering decisions.

Keywords: Software Architecture Knowledge Management, Design Decisions, Design Decision Classification, Capturing Design Decisions.

1 Introduction

Documenting the rationale of architectural choices is at the heart of software architecture knowledge management (SAKM) [1]. During the last years several approaches for capturing design decisions and documenting their rationale have been proposed and also successfully applied in practice [1]. If architectural knowledge has been captured adequately it serves as a means for preserving otherwise tacit knowledge. However, capturing and maintaining design decisions and their rationale raises the same issues as creating and maintaining other kinds of documentation, like the high effort involved in documenting [2][3], the lack of immediate benefits [4], the lack of time and budget [5] and the general difficulty of documenting design decisions during product development [4][6].

Different approaches have been developed to specifically address the problem of efficiently and systematically capturing design decisions. For example, ADDR [7] is an approach that aims at recovering architectural design decisions by comparing architectural views from different releases of a software system. The result is an architectural delta, which provides clues to an architect for recovering decisions. Another example is presented by Eloranta and Koskimies [8], which aim at

K. Drira (Ed.): ECSA 2013, LNCS 7957, pp. 130–145, 2013.

systematically recovering and documenting architectural design decisions during architecture reviews. They specifically use the DCAR [9] review method, which is a decision-oriented review method, though in principle, any other architecture review method could be used. For example, identifying design decisions and rationale as part of *architectural approaches* is also an important aspect of ATAM (see [10], p.48).

We are currently working on an approach combining several strategies for facilitating the capturing of design decisions both on technical and process levels. On the process level we intend to support capturing and maintaining architectural decisions during architectural reviews through context information [11] and through providing a conceptual framework for capturing specific types of architectural decisions and influence factors for such decisions. On a technical level we intend to (automatically) detect design decisions in code and other artifacts and to support the (manual) recapturing of the rationale for the detected decisions. We intend to base this work on already existing work on extracting architectural structures from already implemented software systems [12].

To support these planned (and partly ongoing) research activities we conducted an expert survey in practice to identify the potential kinds of architectural decisions, their drivers, and the sources of their documentation as used in practice. The survey has been performed with software architects, software team leads, and senior developers from six different companies in Austria with more than 10 years of experience in software development on average. It confirms earlier work by other authors on design decision classification and influence factors but also identifies additional kinds of decisions and influence factors not mentioned in this previous work. In addition, we gained insight into the practice of capturing, the relative importance of different decisions and influence factors, and on potential sources for recovering decisions.

The remainder of this paper is structured as follows: In Section 2 we discuss some previous and related work on design decision classification and on potential influence factors for these decisions. In Section 3 we present the research objectives and research questions. In Section 4 we describe the research approach and the study design. In Section 5 we present the results of the survey. The findings are discussed in more detail in Section 6. Validation and limitations are discussed in Section 7. The paper is concluded with the main findings in Section 8.

2   Previous and Related Work

A taxonomy of design decisions is presented by Kruchten [13][14] and Kruchten et al. [15]. In this taxonomy architectural design decisions are classified into existence decisions, nonexistence decisions (bans), property decisions, and executive decisions. An existence decision states that some element/artifact will exist in the systems design or implementation [14]. Existence decisions can affect either the structure or the behavior of systems. Structural decisions lead to the creation of subsystems, layers, and components while behavioral decisions are more related to how elements interact to address some functional or nonfunctional requirement. Kruchten argues that existence decisions are the least important to capture since they are the most visible element in the systems design or implementation. Still they should be captured in order to relate them to other decisions (e.g., to alternatives). We should add that Kruchten implies that the rationale for a decision is documented as part of the design or implementation artifact. The second kind of decisions is nonexistence decisions or bans. Such decisions state that some element will not appear in the design or implementation. It is very important to document such decisions and their rationale since they are not visible from the resulting architecture design or implementation [14]. The third kind of decisions is property decisions. Property decisions state central qualities of a system and include design rules and guidelines as well as constraints on a system (in the sense of a property the system will not exhibit). Finally, executive decisions do not relate to the design or the system qualities and are driven by the business environment. They constrain the other kinds of decisions and affect the development process, the people, the organization, and the choices of technologies and tools.

Influence factors are very important for characterizing a design decision and for providing the rationale for a design decision. Therefore, many authors propose to capture influence factors [5], also called forces [15][9] and drivers [7][16]. In a survey on architectural design rationale Tang et al. [5] identified several factors that influence decision-making using a quantitative survey on design rational with 81 practitioners with more than 3 years of experience. The participants were asked about factors that influence their design choices. Tang et al. proposed a number of generic factors identified in literature including design constraints, design assumptions, weakness of a design, cost and benefit of a design, design complexity, certainty of design, certainty of implementation and tradeoffs between alternative designs. They then collected the relative importance of these factors according to the participants of the study, the frequency of use, and the frequency of documentation. For most of the presented generic factors they observed that the usage frequency is less than the perceived importance, and the documentation frequency is again less than the usage frequency. In terms of usage frequency, constraints on the design, design benefits, and certainty of design were rated highest. In addition to these generic factors, the participants revealed a number of additional influence factors (without commenting on their importance, their frequency of use and their frequency of documentation). Tang et al. classified these additional influence factors into the three broad categories: business-goals-oriented, requirements-oriented, and constraints and concerns.

In the study presented in this paper we also build on the work presented above and contribute to its validation. We mainly asked questions about the kind of architectural design decisions made in practice, how they are documented, and how they can be classified based on examples mentioned by practitioners. We related the results of the study to the classification presented by Kruchten and discussed above. Since we also intend to support capturing of the rationale of decisions in our future work, we additionally wanted to know which factors typically influence design decisions made in practice and how strong this influence is perceived by practitioners.

This relates mainly to the perceived importance and the frequency of use of factors as reported by Tang et al. As an important difference, we related our findings not only to the generic factors mentioned in the work by Tang et al. but included the additional factors they identified during their study on generic factors.

3 Objectives and Research Questions

The main objective of the study is to understand how architects, but also developers, deal with design decisions in practice. As part of this objective we first wanted to know how design decisions are actually made and how they are documented. Therefore, the first research question is

RQ1: How are design decisions made in practice and how are they documented?

In order to further support the automatic detection of design decisions in different artifacts like code and design we wanted to find out which design decisions architects and senior developers think about and how those decisions can be classified.

RQ2: Which kinds of design decisions are typically made in practice and how can they be classified?

The third aim of conducting this survey has been to get more information on factors that usually influence decisions. We wanted to figure out which factors architects and senior developers are aware of and which factors they are not.

RQ3: Which factors usually influence design decisions and how strong is this influence as perceived by architects and senior developers?

We used the factors identified by Tang et al. (and discussed in the previous section) as a basis for rating influence factors and extended these factors with additional factors from the answers given to the previous questions and from our own experience.

4 Research Approach

The study has been performed using expert interviews. Expert interviews are a widely used and integral part of qualitative research [17]. We decided to use qualitative expert interviews since they are typically used when the focus is on generating new knowledge instead of quantifying existing knowledge. We decided on qualitative interviews with a guide that contains open questions to gather as many examples of design decisions as possible. Our decision to use open questions was made in order to get new information about design decisions and to find out, which types of design decisions experts are aware of and which kinds of decisions are made unaware and as a consequence are not documented. We assumed to get more specific information about how architects, but also developers think about design decisions in practice by conducting the interviews in the style of a discussion. To interpret the results we used content analysis with a-priori codification to assign statements to specific research questions.

After defining our research goals and questions, we planned the survey. The study has been performed in four steps. First we defined the criteria for the selection of the experts. This was followed by the definition of the interview guide with questions addressing our research questions. We selected a predefined categorization for codifying the interviews. In the third step we conducted the interviews using the guide and transcribed them word-by-word. Finally, we used codification on the basis of the predefined categories for data analysis. These steps are described in greater detail below.

Sampling. We targeted software engineers, lead developers and software architects from different companies in Austria. We aimed particularly at people who had more than three years of professional experience in software architecting and development. All in all we interviewed 9 experts from six different companies with expertise in industrial and enterprise software system development. All study participants were male and had at least a master degree in computer science. In addition, they had at least 3 years of professional experience in software engineering, the average experience being more than 10 years. Seven of them are actually working as a team lead or software architect. They work in teams of varying size between 2 and 15 developers, but only two teams are larger than 5 team members. 4 participants of the study have gained experiences in more than three companies.

Definition of Interview Guide. We conducted the interviews using an interview guide with open questions according to [18]. The questions have been defined in such a way that the experts were able to talk very openly about their professional experiences, previous projects and teams. We divided the guide into three parts containing 16 main questions. Each of the main questions contained 2 to 4 subquestions, which we asked when the participants were not actually talking about a specific topic. In the first part (2 questions) we wanted to know more about the experts and their background. The second part (10 questions) aimed at collecting examples of design decisions and design decision categories. In this part we asked questions about the decision making and documentation process. We placed the questions without giving any examples. For example, we asked, who would make design decisions, whether they could provide examples of design decisions, when decisions are made, and whether they are documented or not. We aimed at being able to construct decision categories solely from the examples mentioned by the study participants. Again, the questions were asked conversationally to not restrict the participants in their conversation, but to inspire them to talk freely. The last part (4 questions) of the guide focuses on the known categories for design decisions and influence factors we discussed in Section 2. In this case, we confronted them with the specific categories, asked them for examples in the categories and asked them about the role (i.e., the frequency) of such decisions in their work (including previous projects). We also asked them how and where certain types of decisions are documented. The questions in this part strived for completeness, i.e., to get information on types of decisions they had not mentioned previously, but also on the perceived frequency of such decisions.

Conduction of Interviews. All interviews were conducted personally by the same person and recorded on agreements with a Dictaphone. The interviews took between 30 and 60 minutes per expert, 43 minutes on average. The interview guide ensured that all needed questions were answered, but the interviews had the character of a natural conversation. We wanted the participants to talk freely about their experiences.

Data Analysis. We transcribed all interviews literally to make them available for analysis and then analyzed the text using content analysis. This included systematically searching and coding with predefined categories using a-priori coding as suggested by Mayring [19]. This step was performed using the 4-eyes principle to mitigate threats to validity. Based on the research questions from Section 3 we defined the following main categories for analysis:

Background of Experts. Interesting facts about the experts are encoded to get basic information about the background of the experts. We defined *professional experience, functions,* and *project sizes* as the three subcategories to make statements about their experience. The subcategory *interesting facts* should contain additional information of interest about the experts, their experience, and/or personal preferences.

Capturing Design Decisions. This category is used for gathering all information about making and capturing design decisions, but also for getting information about how decisions are documented in the project or company. Information in this category helps us to answer our first research question (see Section 3). We further divide this category into four subcategories: the *decision-making process* subcategory captures information about the decision making process; the *decision maker* subcategory collects information about who makes and/or documents decisions; in the *decision-reasoning* subcategory we gather information on documenting the rationale of decisions; finally, in the *decision documentation* subcategory we collect all information on how decisions are documented, what is actually documented, and where they are documented.

Design Decision Classification. This main category contains subcategories for *examples* on design decisions, *definitions* of the term design decision and mentioned *categories* for classifying design decisions. The information from the subcategories *example* and *categories* is used for determining categories for design decisions classification solely based on the examples mentioned by the participants of the study. A further category, called *categories used,* is used for collecting the opinions of experts on given decision types (according to the classification provided by Kruchten). The information collected in all subcategories is used for answering the second research question (RQ2). Information encoded with subcategory *categories used* is also used for answering the first research question (RQ1).

Influence Factors for Decision Making. All mentioned influence factors for decision-making are collected within this category. The subcategory *influence factors impact* collects influence factors and their perceived impact after having provides examples for influence factors published by Tang et al. [5]. Information from this category is used for answering the third research question (RQ3) mentioned in Section 3.

5   Survey Results

We have structured the results into three different areas addressing the primary research questions. In the following subsection we comment on the different kinds of design decisions that have been mentioned by the survey participants and how they can be related to the taxonomy presented by Kruchten. This is followed by results on how and when design decisions are captured. Finally, we will present results on potential influence factors for design decisions.

5.1   Classification of Design Decisions

When talking about design decisions we asked the experts about the kinds of decisions they are usually confronted with. In addition, we collected the different kinds of decisions when asking about which decisions are usually documented and which not. Overall we collected 22 different categories of architectural design decisions. We then mapped these categories to the taxonomy proposed by Kruchten. This taxonomy includes existence decisions (structural, behavioral, ban), executive decisions (tool, technology, process, organization), and property decisions (guidelines, design rules, constraints). The result is shown on the left side of Figure 1. As shown in the figure 73% of all mentioned categories could be mapped to existence decisions, but no bans were mentioned. 23% could be mapped to executive decisions, though none of them were process or tool decisions. 4% of could be mapped to property decisions. We noted that participants usually classified design decisions using different levels, e.g., personal, project, organizational, module, deployment and architecture level. From the mentioned levels we were able to identify four main levels: implementation, architecture, project, and organization. We will discuss this in more detail in Section 6.

Additionally, we collected categories based on the examples for decisions provided by the participants (contrary to the mentioned decision types or categories as discussed above). In total we collected 120 examples of design decisions. We then mapped the examples to the categories of the Kruchten taxonomy. The result of this analysis is shown in the right side of Figure 1. As shown in the figure, both kinds of analysis provided nearly the same results. About two-thirds of the examples were existence decisions and about a quarter of all examples could be assigned to the executive decision category (most of them technology decisions).

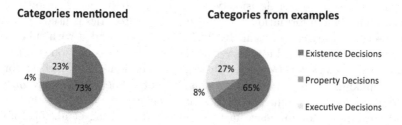

Fig. 1. Categories mentioned based on the Kruchten taxonomy [14]

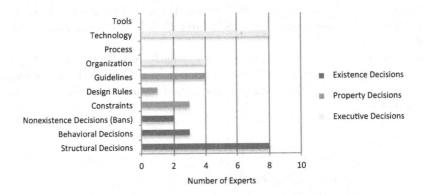

Fig. 2. Categories from examples mentioned by number of experts

Figure 2 provides a more detailed overview of the number of experts that mentioned examples belonging to one of the subcategories in the Kruchten taxonomy. As shown in the figure, most survey participants provided examples for structural (components, interfaces, layering) and technology decisions (middleware, libraries, protocols). Decisions on tools and processes were not mentioned by any of the participants. As shown in the next section, such decisions are actually made, but rarely documented.

5.2 Capturing Design Decisions

The participants provided several examples, where the documentation of central design decisions would be useful, including training of new employees, arguing with customers during development, resolving production problems, impact analysis during product maintenance, and preventing knowledge vaporization. About half of the participants mentioned that they experienced to be personally affected by knowledge vaporization, meaning they forgot decisions they made themselves. All in all, all participants agreed on the usefulness of capturing design decisions.

We also asked them about the decision process and about whether and how decisions are documented. Decisions with a local scope (e.g., within a component) are usually made by developers on their own. Such decisions were usually called low-level decisions during the interviews. Architectural decisions (also high-level or cross-component decisions) are typically a group effort with one person in charge being responsible for making the final decision.

They also named a number of places for documenting design decisions. Examples named were source code (for low-level decisions), meeting minutes (in larger teams), project diaries (in smaller teams), issue tracking systems, and wikis. Especially wikis seemed to work well, which corresponds to experiences reported by other authors [20]. However, the most frequent form of documentation is meeting minutes. Also, most of the participants noted that while important design decisions are usually documented, their rationale is not. One exception seems to be technology decisions, which are made carefully and which are usually documented.

In the second part of the interview we explicitly provided all subcategories to the experts and asked if and how decisions from the different categories are made and documented. The results of this second round of questions are shown in Figure 3.

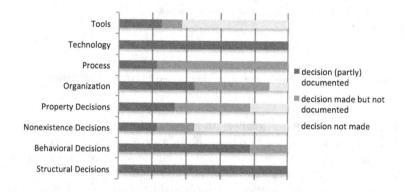

Fig. 3. Decisions made and documented (expert answers)

The results confirm the importance of technology decisions. According to the study participants technology decisions are made at an early stage of the project and hardly change during development. Typically different alternatives are explored and discussed. The results also show that decisions on tools are not important during the design process. It is interesting that process decisions are made by all experts, but were not mentioned when we asked for different kinds of decisions without providing any categories. All experts mentioned that they document structural decisions, at least partially. But after we brought into question what they document exactly, we found that they usually only document the result of the decision, but not the rationale or the alternatives. They also mentioned that the level of abstraction is important for documentation. Decisions on high-level design (i.e., architectural decisions) are usually documented. Decisions with a local scope are either documented in code, in issue tracking systems or they are not documented at all.

The results on tool-related decisions reinforce the previous findings that decisions about tool selection are of low significance. The interviews revealed that the tool suite is either predetermined, or not important.

Contrary to the previous results on process decisions (without providing the Kruchten taxonomy) the experts consider also those decisions. None of the 120 mentioned examples or 22 categories of design decisions (see Section 5.1) could be assigned to this category. According to what is shown in Figure 3 those decisions are important, but rarely documented.

5.3   Influence Factors for Decision Making

We also wanted to know different influence factors on the design decisions taken. For this we asked the study participants for examples of influence factors (without mentioning of any factors) and mapped the provided influence factors to different categories. As the basis for the categories we used the factors identified in a survey conducted by Tang et al. [5], which we extended with additional factors that emerged from the provided answers.

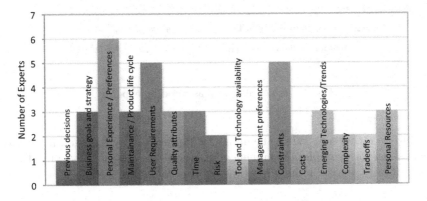

Fig. 4. Influence factor categories based on Tang et al. [5]

The results are shown in Figure 4. The figure shows how many experts mentioned influence factors in these categories. It is interesting that the most frequently mentioned influence factor was personal experience, which was mentioned by two thirds of the participants, followed closely by user requirements and constraints. Business goals, time and quality attributes were mentioned by 30% of the study participants. Further factors that were mentioned include the qualification of employees, available personnel resources, and emerging technologies and trends.

We later asked the participants about the degree of influence of certain influence factors (large, medium, low). In this case we used factors mentioned by Tang et al. and extended them by factors that already emerged when preparing the study, like personal experience and previous decisions. Therefore, some categories that emerged as result of the questioning itself (like emerging technologies and trends) are not included.

The results are shown in Figure 5. Most participants (7 of 9) mentioned that personal experience and preferences have a large influence. It is interesting that 6 of them had already mentioned this before. The influence of quality attributes in general has not been rated as high as we would have expected. Some experts mentioned that quality attributes are considered in principle, but that other factors ultimately have more weight. While business goals and strategies seem to be very important for decision-making, the influence of management preferences

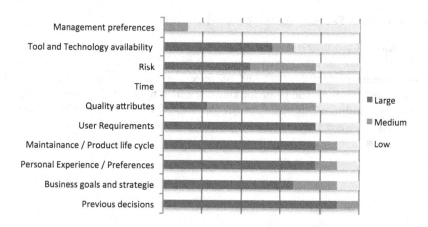

Fig. 5. Influence factors as rated by experts

seems to be rather low. While the influence of previous decisions did not emerge when asking for examples for influences above, it was quite highly ranked when we specifically asked for the importance of this category.

6   Summary and Discussion of Results

We will discuss the results primarily from the perspective of the research questions stated in Section 3.

6.1   On Making and Documenting Decisions

The participants of the study were aware of the importance of documenting design decisions and of documentation in general. They mentioned various reasons in favor of documentation. The problem of knowledge vaporization even on a personal level was mentioned by several of the participants.

In terms of making decisions they mainly distinguished between decisions with a local and a global (cross-component) scope. Local decisions are made by individuals and sometimes discussed in reviews afterwards. Such low-level decisions are documented at various places including source code and issue management systems, or they are not documented at all. Global decisions (e.g., architectural decisions) are usually discussed in team meetings and documented in project diaries, meeting minutes, and wikis. Minutes of meeting seemed to be used most often, wikis were mentioned to be very useful, and project diaries are useful in small teams.

Structural and behavioral decisions as well as technology decisions are usually documented, while decisions on tools, process, organization, properties, and bans are only documented by a few. Decisions on tools and bans seem to be not important for most of the participants. Finally, while most important decisions seem to be documented, their rationale is often not.

We can draw some conclusions from these findings. For example, documenting decisions makes even sense in smaller teams, because knowledge vaporization is also present at the level of individuals. Lightweight approaches like diaries can be used in such a case. In larger teams, support for collaborative decision-making is required, both on a process and on a tool level. Finally, we need to further investigate ways to explicitly support the capturing of rationale with minimal effort.

6.2   On Design Decision Classification

When analyzing the types of decision and possible decision categories from examples provided by the experts, and mapping them to the taxonomy provided by Kruchten, we saw that about 70% of all decisions mentioned are existence decisions (with structural decisions dominating) and about 25% are related to technology decisions. This shows that the participants of the study are still heavily structure- and technology-minded when thinking about architecture. Also nonexistence decisions (bans) were never mentioned and are not documented. This is a problem, since (as pointed out by Kruchten) such decisions would be important to document, because they are not manifested in the documentation of architectural solution structures and also cannot be derived from an implementation. Bans are usually expressed to gradually eliminate possible design alternatives [15].

While the collected types of design decisions could be mapped to the taxonomy provided by Kruchten, we noted that the study participants mostly classified design decisions according to different levels, like personal level, implementation level, project level, etc. By aggregating semantically similar levels we were able to identify four main levels: implementation, architecture, project, and organization. The reason for this could be that we also asked for the process of decision making, i.e., how decisions are made, how they are documented, and by whom (other interpretations have been suggested by the participants of the study when we provided them with the results for validation; see Section 7).

For example, decisions at the organizational level are made by the management in coordination with qualified persons, such as software architects for technical advice. Decisions at this level are usually made once and rarely change. While they are only constrained by other decisions in this level they limit the decision space of the other levels. Decisions made within this level, like programming guidelines or strategic (technical) orientation are often well documented. Project-level decisions are made by project managers, architects, and also customers at the beginning of a project. They include requirements, constraints, and process decisions. They are usually documented (except for process decisions) but their rationale is not captured because it is not considered to be relevant for decisions at lower levels. Decisions at the architecture level are typically made by software architects and team leads. They are discussed in meetings and workshops and they are documented in meeting minutes and wikis. Decisions at this level are constrained by decisions within the same level or by decisions at higher levels. Finally, implementation level decisions (i.e., decisions within a component) are often made ad hoc and independently by developers. Such decisions are documented in the code, in issue tracking systems, or they are not documented at all. Decisions at this level are constrained by decisions at higher levels.

Whether the described levels are adequate for partitioning the decision space needs to be further investigated, but we think they might be useful when thinking about how to support decision capturing, since they provide separation of concerns in terms of stakeholders involved, the process of capturing, and the potential means used for capturing.

6.3   On Influence Factors

Influence factors mentioned by most participants were requirements and constraints. The importance of constraints aligns well with the study on design rationale by Tang et al. [5], who state that "the design constraint rationale is used most frequently ... (because) designers are usually expected to explore the solution space within certain business and technical constraints". They did not investigate the influence of requirements in their study, but it is not surprising that requirements drive design decisions. What is interesting, however, is that personal experience and preferences, and previous decisions have been mentioned multiple times by nearly all participants of our study. This supports another work by Tang [21] where he states that design making is heavily influenced by various kinds of biases, which might potentially lead to unsound design decisions. He proposes various techniques for design reasoning. An important technique is documentation and making all influences and assumptions explicit. This is the basis for self-reflection, which can further reduce biases. We agree with Tang that while documenting design decisions may be costly, wrong decisions are costly, too. But all in all, we still need to further investigate design reasoning to find ways for better supporting the reasoning process of decision-making. Capturing the rationale and making influence factors explicit could be elements of an approach for supporting the decision making process.

7   Validity

The criteria for research rigor and quality in quantitative empirical research methods do not fit with qualitative methods [22]. Gasson [23] discusses and compares quality criteria of quantitative and qualitative methods. In general, the notion of validity is replaced by trustworthiness. Criteria like objectivity, reliability, internal and external validity are replaced by confirmability, dependability/auditability, internal consistency, and transferability [23].

Various techniques for ensuring these criteria have been proposed [23][19]. For example confirmability can be addressed by using reflexivity to reduce subjectivity, making assumptions and frameworks explicit, documenting the rationale underlying the constructs used, and getting feedback on research results. Dependability/auditability can be addressed by establishing clear and repeatable procedures for the research process and making the process explicit (through documentation). Internal consistency can be achieved by comparing different views on the same data and by explaining from which data the constructs discussed are derived. Finally, transferability requires an explicit description of the context of a study like education and background of participants to be able to judge the applicability of the results in other contexts.

We addressed confirmability by performing intermediate steps like the assignment of categories on the basis of the four-eyes-principle. In addition we used communicative validation by summarizing intermediate results and asking the experts for reflection and general feedback on the results. We received feedback from eight out of nine experts. Through this feedback we got additional interesting facts from the experts. Two of them mentioned that they would not include process decisions in the design decisions, so presumably these decisions were not mentioned when we asked for examples and categories of decisions (see Section 5.1). One of them noted that decisions about tools are not directly related to the architecture, as they are already provided indirectly through technology decisions. Quite contrary, another expert mentioned that he would have thought that tool and process decisions are usually documented as, especially in large companies, a lot of time and money is spent on standardization and documentation. Two emphasized again that the personal factor has a very high impact on their decision-making.

In terms of dependability/auditability we followed a standardized research process (documented in Section 4) and used approved methods for data analysis, such as the qualitative content analysis method as described by Mayring [19]. Internal consistency is addressed describing different views on collected data like the generation of decision categories from mentioned categories and from mentioned examples from decisions. Finally, transferability is addressed by capturing and describing the background of the study participants.

Like most surveys our study has several shortcomings. As many qualitative studies, we have a limited number of samples. This is acceptable from our point of view, since our main aim was to get suggestions for new ideas and approaches on supporting the capturing of architectural knowledge and not the evaluation of existing knowledge. There are also shortcomings in terms of transferability. While we were able to question rather experienced people with a master degree in computer science and more than 10 years of professional experience, most of them were educated at two universities in Upper Austria. This means that many of them had a similar school of thought. This has also been pointed out by one of the participants when reflecting on the results concerning the different levels of design decisions. To overcome these shortcomings, we plan to extend the study be including further international experts as part of our future work.

8   Conclusion

Our long-term research objective is to improve the capturing of design decisions in software development processes. We aim specifically at making the process more efficient by detecting decisions in various artifacts and by providing support for capturing decisions and their rationale at the process and tool level.

In this study, we gained important insights in how decisions are currently made and captured in practice, in the kinds of decisions that are made and actually documented, and in the influence factors or drivers for design decisions (which might provide the rationale for decisions). The results of our study confirm results of other work in this area. Architects and designers mainly think of structural and technology decisions. Important decisions are usually documented, though their rationale is often not. Main influence factors are user requirements and other constraints. But the participants also mentioned the high influence of personal experience and preferences. This is not necessarily a problem and can even be beneficial, especially if someone has years of experience in a specific problem domain. However, as Tang [21] points out this may also lead to wrong decisions. Therefore, we also consider it worthwhile to investigate on techniques for reducing such biases and thus supporting an objective and reasoned decision process.

The alternative classification of design decisions based on different abstraction and organizational layers (implementation, architecture, project, business) may be an interesting basis for our planned work on decision detection and capturing. Especially, since stakeholders, techniques used for capturing, kind of information captured on the different levels, and processes for capturing seem to be different on these levels.

References

1. Babar, M.A., Dingsøyr, T., Lago, P., van Vliet, H. (eds.): Software Architecture Knowledge Management: Theory and Practice. Springer (2009)
2. Lee, J.: Design rationale systems: Understanding the issues. IEEE Intelligent Systems 12(3), 78–85 (1997)
3. Capilla, R., Nava, F., Carrillo, C.: Effort estimation in capturing architectural knowledge. In: 23rd IEEE/ACM International Conference on Automated Software Engineering, pp. 208–217 (2008)
4. Lee, L., Kruchten, P.: Capturing software architectural design decisions. In: Canadian Conference on Electrical and Computer Engineering, pp. 686–689 (2007)
5. Tang, A., Babar, M.A., Gorton, I., Han, J.: A survey of architecture design rationale. J. Syst. Softw. 79(12), 1792–1804 (2006)
6. Capilla, R., Dueñas, J.C., Nava, F.: Viability for codifying and documenting architectural design decisions with tool support. J. Softw. Maint. Evol. 22(2), 81–119 (2010)
7. Jansen, A., Bosch, J., Avgeriou, P.: Documenting after the fact: Recovering architectural design decisions. J. Syst. Softw. 81(4), 536–557 (2008)

8. Eloranta, V.P., Koskimies, K.: Agile software architecture knowledge management. In: Babar, M.A., Brown, A.W., Koskimies, K., Mistrik, I. (eds.) Agile Software Architecture: Aligning Agile Processes and Software Architecture. Elsevier (to appear, 2013)

9. van Heesch, U., Eloranta, V.P.P., Avgeriou, P., Koskimies, K., Harrison, N.: DCAR - decision-centric architecture reviews. IEEE Softw. Early Access (2013)

10. Clements, P., Kazman, R., Klein, M.: Evaluating Software Architectures: Methods and Case Studies. Addison-Wesley Professional (2001)

11. Miesbauer, C., Weinreich, R.: Capturing and maintaining architectural knowledge using context information. In: Joint 10th Working Conf. on Software Architecture & 6th European Conf. on Software Architecture. IEEE (2012)

12. Weinreich, R., Miesbauer, C., Buchgeher, G., Kriechbaum, T.: Extracting and facilitating architecture in service-oriented software systems. In: Joint 10th Working Conf. on Software Architecture & 6th European Conf. on Software Architecture. IEEE (2012)

13. Kruchten, P.: An ontology of architectural design decisions in software intensive systems. In: 2nd Groningen Workshop on Software Variability, pp. 54–61 (2004)

14. Kruchten, P.: Documentation of software architecture from a knowledge management perspective design representation. In: Ali Babar, M., Dingsøoyr, T., Lago, P., Vliet, H. (eds.) Software Architecture Knowledge Management, pp. 39–57. Springer, Heidelberg (2009)

15. Kruchten, P., Lago, P., van Vliet, H.: Building up and reasoning about architectural knowledge. In: Hofmeister, C., Crnkovic, I., Reussner, R. (eds.) QoSA 2006. LNCS, vol. 4214, pp. 43–58. Springer, Heidelberg (2006)

16. Zimmermann, O., Koehler, J., Leymann, F., Polley, R., Schuster, N.: Managing architectural decision models with dependency relations, integrity constraints, and production rules. Journal of Systems and Software 82(8), 1249–1267 (2009)

17. Buber, R., Holzmüller, H.H. (eds.): Qualitative Marktforschung. Betriebswirtschaftlicher Verlag Dr. Th. Gabler/GWV Fachverlage GmbH, Wiesbaden (2007)

18. Helfferich, C.: Die Qualität qualitativer Daten Manual für die Durchführung qualitativer Interviews. VS, Verl. für Sozialwiss. Wiesbaden (2011)

19. Mayring, P.: Einführung in die qualitative Sozialforschung: eine Anleitung zu qualitativem Denken. Beltz, Weinheim (2002)

20. de Boer, R.C., van Vliet, H.: Experiences with semantic wikis for architectural knowledge management. In: 2011 Ninth Working IEEE/IFIP Conference on Software Architecture, pp. 32–41 (2011)

21. Tang, A.: Software designers, are you biased? In: Proceedings of the 6th International Workshop on SHAring and Reusing Architectural Knowledge, SHARK 2011, pp. 1–8. ACM, New York (2011)

22. Adolph, S., Hall, W., Kruchten, P.: Using grounded theory to study the experience of software development. Empirical Software Engineering 16(4), 487–513 (2011)

23. Gasson, S.: Rigor in grounded theory research: An interpretive perspective on generating theory from qualitative field studies. In: Whitman, M.E., Woszczynski, A.B. (eds.) The Handbook of Information Systems Research. Idea Group Inc. (IGI) (2004)

Team Situational Awareness and Architectural Decision Making with the Software Architecture Warehouse

Marcin Nowak and Cesare Pautasso

Faculty of Informatics, University of Lugano, Switzerland
marcin.nowak@usi.ch, c.pautasso@ieee.org
http://saw.inf.usi.ch

Abstract. The core of the design of software architecture is all about architectural decision making. A high-quality design outcome sets high requirements, not only on the skills and knowledge of the design team members, but also on the management of the decision making process. We claim that in order to deliver high quality decisions, the design team needs to obtain a high level of situational awareness. To address this, we present an analysis of the problem of team situational awareness in design workshops and propose a model on how stakeholder positions help to build consensus within the argumentation viewpoint of architectural decisions. We show how the Software Architecture Warehouse tool has been extended to support the argumentation viewpoint within its live design document metaphor to provide support for co-located and distributed design workshops.

1 Introduction

As a result of the trend of globalization in the software industry, remote collaboration and decision making within distributed teams is growing in importance. Due to the complex nature of software systems, the design of software architecture holds many qualities specific to so-called wicked problems [6,17] and often cannot be addressed with simple goal-driven optimization methods [7]. To address these problems, the discipline of Software Architecture Knowledge Management (SAKM [3]) was born and a number of systems specialized in architectural decisions management have been proposed (PAKME [4], ADDSS [5], ArchDesigner [2], (e)AREL [19], ADkwik [22]). Whereas a subset of these tools explicitly targets the collaboration needs of distributed or co-located design teams, only limited support is offered for raising the level of situational awareness in the context of design workshops.

This paper makes the following contributions: it proposes a novel argumentation viewpoint for capturing architectural knowledge, in which the positions of multiple stakeholders and design team members can be captured. The positions follow a well defined life cycle and their state can be aggregated to 1) determine the level of consensus around each design issue 2) track the progress

K. Drira (Ed.): ECSA 2013, LNCS 7957, pp. 146–161, 2013.
© Springer-Verlag Berlin Heidelberg 2013

of the design workshop; and 3) facilitate capturing the rationale of each decision made by the team. The argumentation view has been implemented as part of the Software Architecture Warehouse, a collaborative design tool based on the live design document metaphor. Thanks to its real-time synchronization of design spaces, it provides an additional, complementary communication channel that in our experience can enhance the efficiency of both the open, divergent and the closed, convergent phases of design discussions [10].

This paper is structured as follows: in next Section we present an a brief relation over background and related work about collaborative architectural decision management; then we delimit the scope of the problem addressed by our research. In Section three we introduce the concept of argumentation viewpoint. Section four positions situational awareness in the context of architectural decision making. The Software Architecture Warehouse - the collaborative design tool implementing the argumentation viewpoint – is presented in Section five. In Section six we present our preliminary evaluation results and wrap up with conclusions in Section seven.

2   Related Work and Background

The decision making process [13], and in particular the software architectural decision making process have been a subject of many studies [9]. The topic of collaborative design has been less studied and it is only partially supported in the ISO 42010 decision meta-model [1]. Out of the seven architectural decision modeling tools reviewed in [18] only three provide support for collaboration, but none of them is suitable for a low-latency, design workshop environment. Our work is complementary to existing frameworks and meta-models, since it targets dynamic decision making activities within a team.

2.1   The Problem of Collaborative Design

The factors that limit the efficiency of the decision making process within a design team are manifold [10], e.g., the partial overlap of the participants' expertise, the complexity of the domain and the wicked nature of the software architectural design problem [17].

In our experience running design workshops, we have observed that the decision making process can be very chaotic, difficult to control and to organize without a proper reference framework and tool support. A solid framework for organizing the decision making process was proposed in [22].

Another problem is related to the volatility of the decisions. Systematic recording and documentation of the discussion flow is needed to mitigate decision evaporation. An open challenge for the architectural decision management tools is to capture useful content as much as possible during the workshop without hindering the brainstorming or the decision making activities. The goal is to reduce the cognitive load required to record alternatives and decisions, without the need to resort to dedicated minute takers or scribes.

We also see a big potential in groupware support for creating an environment in which awareness of the design is shared between team members. Due to the inherently limited and partially overlapping expertise of each design team member, in order to achieve high decision quality, the efficient reuse of previous decision experience is essential. In other words, before making design decisions, it is essential to elicit and decide what is to be decided out of the available design space. The elicitation of design issues can be done offline as part of the workshop preparation, but the selection of relevant architecture alternatives sometime can only happen during the live brainstorming.

Another major difficulty in efficiently running architectural design workshops is to keep the focus of the entire design team on the same design issue. In a co-located design workshop, thanks to high bandwidth of face to face communication, depending on the size of the team, this requires some good moderation by the lead architect, but still may be time consuming. Due to the more limited communication bandwidth, in distributed workshops it becomes more challenging to keep the collective attention of all remote participants in focus. This is critical when pruning possible alternatives: as the decision making time grows near, all team members need to be aware of which decision is about to be made.

Another fundamental problem concerns the nature of the architectural design solutions. There are many ways how solution can be unsuitable for the stakeholders. The most critical cases are when solution is either internally inconsistent (decisions contradict each other), or unacceptable (due to violation of constraints). These two cases can be relatively easily eliminated when using a systematic decision making process that includes solution validation activities (see [22]). It is often the case that there are multiple valid, acceptable solutions. In such situation the best solution candidate should be chosen by evaluating its value for the stakeholders. Given that only some of the qualities of the solution are easy to assess quantitatively, this process can be automated (see [7]) only to a certain extent. When the alternative solutions lie on the Pareto frontier, it becomes necessary to trade-off different quality attributes against one another. It is particularly challenging to do so without a high level of situational awareness among the design team.

All in all, out these challenges, in this paper we target the need for 1) preparing the discussion by re-using existing architectural knowledge; 2) focusing the attention of the team; 3) recording the individual position of each stakeholder; 4) making the consensus building process transparent.

2.2   From Situational Awareness to Good Decisions

One fundamental assumption that we are making in this paper is that good design decisions are well-informed decisions made by a team with a high level of situational awareness.

Situational awareness is the term used to describe the perception and comprehension of a particular environment, which can vary – as proposed by [8] – across three levels:

- **Perception** (SA_1) – the status, properties, features of relevant elements of the environment are recognized and monitored,
- **Comprehension** (SA_2) – making sense of, recognizing relations, and interpreting the values of the attributes perceived on the previous level (SA_1),
- **Projection** (SA_3) – predictions over the future state of the environment are made based on the knowledge about its current condition (SA_1) and expected dynamics (SA_2).

The original application of the concept of situational awareness was in the applications involving efficient decision making within fast-changing, dynamic environments such as emergency services or battlefield operations. Under such conditions, for the sake of efficiency, decision making is often centralized and authoritative and must happen within strict time limits. Such strategy is often not suitable for the situations when the expertise required to make decisions is distributed among multiple stakeholders.

Although conditions requiring situational awareness of the battlefield are significantly different from the ones within an architecture design workshop, we find a certain number of similarities that lead us to propose to apply the concept of team situational awareness to enhance the efficiency and quality of the collaborative architecture design process. In particular the situational awareness shared among the whole team can help to efficiently argument and build consensus about each decision. A design team sharing a high level of situational awareness can gather relevant information, interpret it from different viewpoints of the involved stakeholders, exchange (well grounded and justified) positions based on assumptions, expectations and predictions over the quality of the resulting architecture, and eventually converge to a single consensus decision.

3   Decision Model and Argumentation Viewpoint

The starting point of our considerations is the decision meta-model proposed in the standard ISO 42010 [1] (see Figure 1). We propose to use the Architectural Decision entity (see Figure 2) to establish a relation between a design issue (representing the problem domain) and multiple design alternatives (from the solution domain). This is similar to what Kruchten proposes in [14] with a relation type named **is an alternative to** which is meant to relate decisions "addressing the same issue". Similarly to [11], we propose to introduce the Design Issue as a first-class entity. An advantage of representing design issues and design alternatives explicitly, is that identification and reuse of design decisions is promoted [15].

The argumentation viewpoint we propose consists of:

Design Issue – A reusable aspect of the system design (from the problem domain) that can can be addressed with one or more design alternative to produce an architectural decision model.

Design Alternative – An action, method, or pattern that can be used to address particular design issues. In some cases, each design alternative can be reused within the context of multiple design decisions.

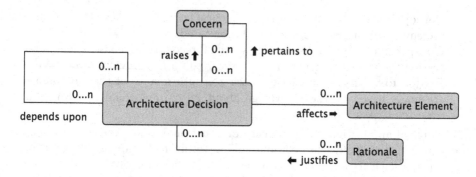

Fig. 1. Elementary architectural decision meta-model after ISO 42010 [1]

Position – A subjective take of a design team member on a design alternative applied in the context of particular design issue. For example, the position can be positive, negative, or neutral. The rationale for the position can also be captured with a natural language description. This can be complemented by a weight associated to the uncertainty or confidence level of the position.

In the simplest case, undecided or open architectural decision would be represented just by the design issue with no alternatives or positions associated to it. Normally, the agenda of a design workshop includes a set of open design issues to be discussed. During the workshop, the design team elicits, generates or captures one or more design alternatives that are related to the design decision under discussion. At this point, positions are used to state the subjective evaluation of each stakeholder or each design workshop participant. Additionally, positions can be justified by relating them to the *decision force* or an *action* (see [21]) that a particular stakeholder recommends to be taken. This provides added value by helping to refine and express the rationale justifying the position. The uncertainty of the position can be explicitly expressed by the stakeholder

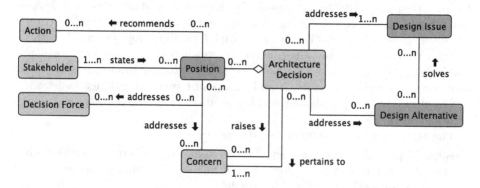

Fig. 2. The argumentation viewpoint meta-model of the architectural decision with Position related to other decision model elements: Action, Stakeholder taken from [20], Decision Force from [21].

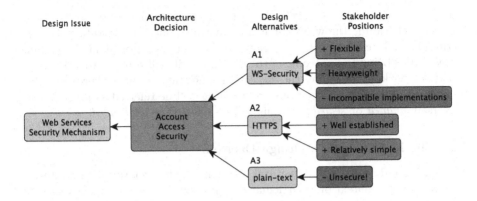

Fig. 3. An example design decision from the service oriented architecture design space together with a number of positions

so that its weight can be taken into account while bringing the decision process to the end. The result is a closed architectural decision which binds the design issue with the chosen alternative.

In Figure 3 we present an example of a design decision from the design space of service oriented architectures. Three design alternatives have been proposed to address the design issue of selecting a Web services security mechanism. Six stakeholders positions have been recorded. Colors and symbols reflect the actions (see [20, Fig. C.3]): green (+) for *validate* and red (-) red for *reject* respectively.

3.1 The Life Cycle of Positions within Alternatives

At the beginning of the workshop, each architectural decision starts with no stakeholders' positions recorded (Figure 4). The *aligned* state is reached when all the positions associated to one alternative refer to the same *action*. For example, in Figure 3 all positions related to HTTPS are positive. This can be interpreted as representing the state of consensus among all stakeholders. The *colliding* set of positions exists when positions refer to more than one different *action*. In the example, both positive and negative positions are associated with WS-Security.

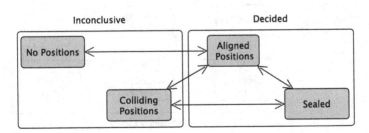

Fig. 4. The state diagram of the life cycle of architectural alternatives. The state of the alternative is aggregated from the actions of its positions.

In this situation, when stakeholders cannot agree on the action to be taken, the architect leading the workshop can solve the conflict by overriding the conflicting positions expressed by the team members. Thus, after manually naming one action as being the outcome of the discussion, it will proceed to seal the alternative, marking the end of the discussion. The state in which there are either *no positions* recorded, or positions are *colliding* will be referred as *inconclusive*; conversely *aligned* or *sealed* positions will be referred to as *decided*.

3.2   The Life Cycle of a Design Decision

The aggregated state of architectural decisions made over the design alternatives within the context of a particular design issue can be conveniently used to monitor the progress of the decision making process (see Figure 5).

Design decisions about a given design issue start their life-cycle with *no alternatives* recorded. As the design progresses, stakeholders elicit (or reuse) one or more relevant design alternative, leaving the design decision in the state with *no decisions*, since no single alternative has yet been selected. Later, stakeholders record their positions and make decisions. In the situation when at least one alternative is in an *inconclusive* state, one can speak about *incomplete* choice. The case when all design alternatives are *decided*, we recognize three types of *complete choice*. To distinguish them we need to check not only whether there is an agreement on the positions about the alternative, but also on whether the agreement is about a positive (i.e., acceptance, validation, approval – see [20]), or negative (i.e., rejection) decision. Rejected alternatives are discarded and based on how many alternatives remain we distinguish: 1) the *conclusive choice* happens when there is exactly one remaining alternative; 2) the *inconclusive choice* happens where there are multiple acceptable alternatives; 3) the *warring choice* represents the case where no alternative is left on the table.

In the example shown in Figure 6, we see a design decision with four alternatives. The first two (BEEP, TCP) have been rejected, while the last two (MQ, HTTPS) have been validated. Therefore the state of decision is inconclusive, since there is more than one alternative left. Assuming that only one alternative is required to settle the issue, another iteration of the discussion will be required

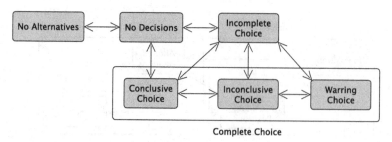

Fig. 5. The state diagram of the life cycle of a design decision. The state of the decision is aggregated from the state of its alternatives.

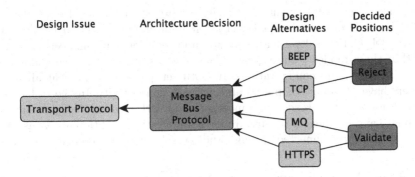

Fig. 6. An example design issue of a transport protocol selection with four design alternatives (protocols) and a complete, inconclusive choice between the alternatives

to refine the choice among the two remaining alternatives, for example, based on additional constraints given by other design issues, concerns or decision forces.

4   Shared Situational Awareness of the Design Space

In the previous sections we have introduced the concept of situational awareness, we scoped the problem of collaborative decision making and finally, we proposed the argumentation viewpoint for modeling architectural decisions. In this section we combine those elements into a mechanism for supporting design teams in the efficient design of software architecture.

First we shall explain that by shared situational awareness, in the context of the architectural decisions, we understand 1) providing decision stakeholders with a customized view over the design space that delivers exactly the information needed for making high quality decisions, 2) providing the means to synchronize the focus of attention of the team, and 3) recording, sharing and analyzing the positions of the design workshop participants. The aim of the first two techniques is to bring the situational awareness of the team to the level of perception (SA_1), whereas the third enables comprehension (SA_2).

Architecture design is a process leading the design team towards the creation of software architecture that has qualities desired by the stakeholders. In general terms, decision making within the design can be principally divided into two modes [12]. The first mode, so-called *open*, happens when the design discussion tends to be divergent and exploratory both in the problem and the solution domains. In this mode, new design alternatives are discovered and new design issues are identified. The *closed* mode, instead, is used to evaluate features and properties of elicited design issues and alternatives. At first, during the fast triage, unfeasible design alternatives are quickly excluded from the scope of the design space. Next, based on the stakeholder's evaluation choices are made within the "closed" project design space. In fact, there is no strict temporal separation between these two modes of operation. Often, transitions between open and closed are needed due to the refinement of the available domain expertise that implies need for readjustment of the choices previously made. In a way, the synergy between open and closed decision making modes is similar to the twin peaks model relating software architecture and requirements engineering [16].

Within these modes we are going to make a distinction between collocated and distributed team configurations. In both setups we assume that all team members have personal computers and network connectivity. In the collocated configuration the team is sharing a meeting room with common facilities such as whiteboard and beamer. In the distributed configuration, additionally we assume that team sites are connected through audio (and video) conferencing systems.

4.1 Open Mode, Divergent Discussion

In the open mode, the design team brainstorms freely over an open design space, creates, edits and destroys design issues, alternatives and decisions. The main needs of the team operating in this mode are related to the efficient capturing of decision model items without getting in the way of the decision making process. The captured information needs to be delivered to the all design team members in a form that stimulates further brainstorming. Not getting in the way is particularly important in the co-located scenario, when the bandwidth of the face to face communication is very high and – for some kind of interactions – a collaboration tool may become an obstacle. The clear benefit of tool-supported collaboration in this phase lies in the efficiency of generating new design alternatives in parallel, since each participant can propose his ideas through the tool interface. The moderator can drive the discussion towards the new contributions in due time, but in any case, the proposed alternatives do not evaporate. Furthermore, thanks to the shared view over the design space and the low-latency with which additions are propagated, everyone on the team is aware about everyone else's contributions (and thus redundant contributions can be culled).

4.2 Closed Mode, Convergent Discussion

In the closed mode, the design team focuses mainly on the evaluation of the elicited design elements in order to find and agreement over a possibly optimal solution. To this end we find it particularly important to build a shared awareness of stakeholders' positions about the design alternatives in question. This can be achieved by sharing each position in real-time within the context of particular design issues and alternatives. For small, co-located teams such awareness can be intuitively built by the design team leader summarizing the current state of the discussion, but in large and/or distributed teams, management of explicit stakeholders' positions is essential.

The efficient capture and reuse of the design discussion comes with the risk of easy derailment in case when it is not moderated appropriately. Discussion moderation of the co-located team can be done by the lead architect by bringing the attention of the group to the particular topic, which can be for example visualized on the beamer. The non-verbal communication bandwidth in the distributed configuration is very limited, so we see a big potential in asynchronous

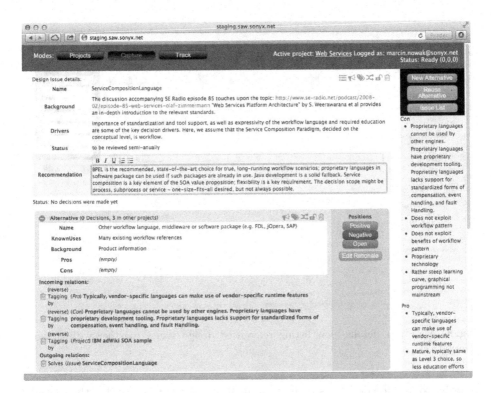

Fig. 7. A detailed view of the design issue during the collaborative editing of one of
its attributes

sharing of design space pointers and view references in a manner similar to instant messaging systems. These pointers identify a design issue, alternative or a
decision and are particularly useful to bring the attention of the design team to
a particular attribute or feature. Being able to efficiently share a precise reference to a view over the design space is very useful to synchronize the focus of
attention quickly and then proceed with the decision making to converge.

5   The Software Architecture Warehouse

In this section we present details of the prototypical functionality that we implemented in the Software Architecture Warehouse (SAW) to address the needs
and requirements introduced in the previous sections.

5.1   Shared Design Space Awareness

SAW is implemented as a tool to help the entire software architecture design
team achieve a high level of situational awareness about architectural decisions
and the corresponding design space being traversed during a design workshop.

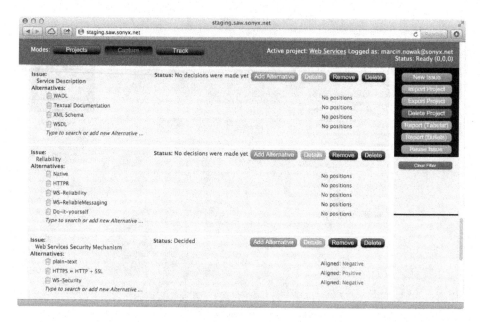

Fig. 8. A project details view listing referenced design issues together with design alternatives

In order to provide designers with an elementary (perception) level of the shared awareness (SA$_1$) we have introduced the live design document metaphor. Any change to the design elements and relations between them are immediately propagated (with low-latency) to all the design team members participating in the workshop (see Figure 7). Due to the connected nature of the architectural decision representation, the live-document paradigm extends beyond content updates within particular views. To this end, SAW propagates design space alterations to all views. For example alterations made to a design alternative are instantly reflected in the project details and project summary views (see Figure 8). To deal with conflicting edits, SAW follows an optimistic strategy whereby users can see which parts of the document are being edited by others and thus can refrain from entering concurrent modifications. The same mechanism also helps users to see where the attention of other users is being directed.

Additionally, in order to ease interpretation of the decision state, and thus bring users to a higher level of situational awareness (comprehension - SA$_2$) we have implemented visual aids indicating the state of particular design space elements. For example the decision status of the design issues and alternatives is color-coded so that stakeholders can get an overview at first glance about the level of consensus (see Figure 9). Also in the case of positions, new contributions can be entered in parallel and updates are immediately propagated to all participants.

Targeting the projection level of situational awareness (SA$_3$), participants may base their positions on the knowledge associated with each design issue alternative (e.g., decision drivers, concerns). Likewise, they may navigate through the

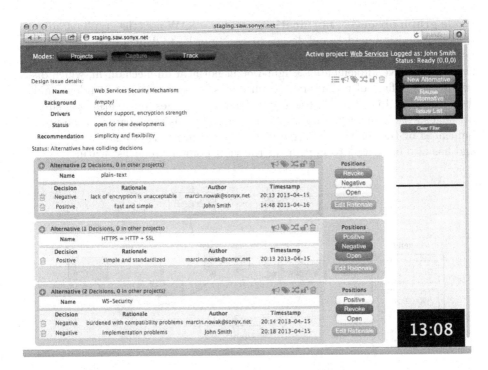

Fig. 9. A view presenting a design issue with three alternatives, two of which have aligned positions (second and third), the other (first) has colliding positions

design space following arbitrary kinds of relationships (influence) between issues and/or alternatives. This way, the impact of decisions can be analyzed from a global perspective.

5.2   System Architecture

Client-Server split – Traditional Web applications rely on the thin-client paradigm. Over time, many server-side Web-frameworks were conceived to cope with the growing complexity of Web applications (RoR, Django, etc.). The traditional Web applications leave all MVC layers to be handled by the server side, leaving only view rendering for the Web browser. This approach has the advantage of containing all application code within a single location, however it is not suitable to support the live document metaphor. Since every user interaction with the system triggered a call to a rather heavy server-side stack, the result was rather limited scalability. In the process of architecting and implementing SAW we have soon realized that the level of interactivity required to realize the desired liveness of the user experience could not be implemented with the use of traditional server-side frameworks. To this end we have implemented server-side SAW as a thin layer wrapping a NoSQL database. The interactive user-interface is implemented following the MVVC pattern in JavaScript (with Backbone http://backbonejs.org/ and Marionette http://marionettejs.com/).

Node graph observer, notification system – SAW uses the graph paradigm to persist decision models and design spaces. In order to deliver high user awareness over the shared design space, a suitable data replication mechanism is needed. We have implemented a light-weight notification mechanism, which distributes identifiers of the altered graph nodes, so that clients can reload node data if needed. In case when the graph structure changes, by creating or removing edges between nodes, a notification of this event is propagated to the nodes influenced by the change (see Figure 10). The notification system is very general and has also been used to implement the view pointer broadcast feature.

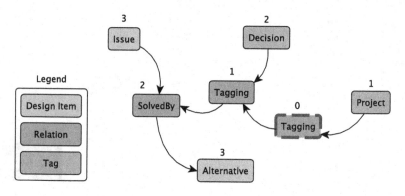

Fig. 10. Event propagation over the shared graph model. Views can subscribe to observe changes within a certain distance of their model elements.

6   Formative Evaluation

The concept of team situational awareness and its support within the Software Architecture Warehouse has been validated through three formative evaluation cycles over the past 2 years. Different releases of SAW has been used in more than 50 co-located design workshops, with groups of 5-10 students attending each session. In some cases, the same participants have repeatedly used the tool, and provided us with feedback about its progress, performance and usability. The participants played the role of software architects (including the lead architect), software developers as well as other stakeholders, such as customers or end-users of the systems being designed. SAW has also used in distributed design workshops over conference calls and in hybrid workshops with some co-located participants and others connecting remotely. For space reasons we focus in analyzing the experience we have gathered in the co-located design workshops. The feedback received has helped to refine the concept of team situational awareness and improve the tool usability and scalability.

We have observed that the usage patterns and load may greatly vary in intensity over a design workshop session (in average 2h), making the real-time performance requirement very challenging to achieve without sufficient resources on the server-side and over an unreliable network. We have tested the performance of the system, and there is no noticeable delay of event propagation with up to 20 participants who are collaboratively editing a design space made of up to 100 issues (with 5 alternatives each). The tool is also ready for a Cloud-based deployment and each tier can be separately distributed for additional performance.

Concerning the impact on the cognitive load of the lead architect, we have found out that only users that have accumulated some experience with the tool's user interface can be effective in capturing the discussion while leading it. In other cases we had to resort to recruiting minute takers (or scribes) that would act as a proxy between the lead architect at the whiteboard and the design decisions tracked by the tool and displayed with the beamer. In general, since all participants have the possibility to contribute their input into the shared knowledge repository, over multiple sessions, we observed that it was no longer necessary to employ a single dedicated scribe as this role was spontaneously shared among all participants, after they realized about the presence of the additional communication channel.

The feature to broadcast pointers over the design space was suggested by one user in order to make it efficient to navigate to a specific design view. The user would copy and paste the URI of the page displaying the relevant information and share it with the rest of the participants with an instant messenger. After observing this behavior we decided to implement explicit support for this feature by taking advantage of the existing notification infrastructure. This way we can guarantee that it is very efficient to ensure that all participants are seeing the same view at the same time.

Concerning the tracking of positions within the argumentation view, we experimented with two levels of detail. The initial lightweight solution was a simple positive or negative vote over each alternative. Then we added the ability to retract positions and recast votes, since people needed to be able to change their mind as the consensus building process was taking place. At a more fine-granular level, users can also enter the rationale and confidence level of their position. This required additional time and effort and has been met with some resistance. In particular, not all users can immediately and independently provide a rationale for their position and prefer to wait for others to express their viewpoints and piggy back their position on the previous ones.

Another feature added based on explicit user feedback, was the ability to seal the state of decisions to explicitly mark the conclusion of the discussion over certain issues. This has also been used to track the progress of the workshop. This way the tool can provide a separate list of open issues, which need to be decided upon - this list keeps shrinking during the closed phase of the discussion, providing all participants with a sense of accomplishment, while the list of sealed and decided issues grows.

We have also observed that SAW added an additional communication channel to the discussion, in a way that workshop participants could contribute to the design space without interrupting the ongoing discussion. Similarly, some participants which were intimidated by the lead architect, felt empowered to make their contributions through SAW, silently and in the background. Once discovered by the rest of the team, these contributions have often proven to be highly relevant for the quality of the final design.

In the feedback surveys we conducted, the majority of workshop participants reported that thanks to the possibility to access shared positions of other designers, they felt more confident about the quality of the decisions being made during the design workshops actively supported with SAW.

7   Conclusion

In this paper we have performed an analysis of the problem of collaborative decision making in the context of software architecture design workshops. Based on the idea of enhancing the situational awareness of the whole design team, we have proposed a novel argumentation viewpoint of the standard software architectural decision model and discussed the life cycle of design decisions within the open and closed phases of a lightweight collaborative design process. The concepts presented in this paper are fully implemented by the Software Architecture Warehouse, a prototype architectural decision management tool targeting real-time support for co-located and distributed design teams. Selected aspects of the tool architecture have been discussed together with the promising results of our preliminary evaluation.

Future work aims on developing metrics and detection strategies to raise further the team situational awareness to the projection level (SA_3). In the near future we plan an extensive evaluation with our industry partners for closely studying the dynamics of collaborative design processes within distributed design teams.

Acknowledgement. This work is partially supported by the Swiss National Science Foundation with the CLAVOS project (Grant Nr. 125337).

References

1. ISO/IEC 42010 – Systems and software engineering – architecture description (2011)
2. Al-Naeem, T., Gorton, I., Babar, M.A., Rabhi, F., Benatallah, B.: A quality-driven systematic approach for architecting distributed software applications. In: Proc. of the 27th International Conference on Software Engineering (2005)
3. Babar, M.A., Dingsøyr, T., Lago, P., van Vliet, H.: Software Architecture Knowledge Management - Theory and Practice. Springer (2009)
4. Babar, M.A., Gorton, I.: A tool for managing software architecture knowledge. In: Proceedings of the Second Workshop on SHAring and Reusing Architectural Knowledge Architecture, Rationale, and Design Intent, SHARK-ADI 2007 (2007)
5. Capilla, R., Nava, F., Pérez, S., Dueñas, J.C.: A web-based tool for managing architectural design decisions. SIGSOFT Softw. Eng. Notes 31(5), 4 (2006)
6. Conklin, J.: Dialogue Mapping. Wiley (2006)

7. de Gooijer, T., Jansen, A., Koziolek, H., Koziolek, A.: An industrial case study of performance and cost design space exploration. In: International Conference on Performance Engineering (2012)
8. Endsley, M.R.: Theoretical underpinnings of situation awareness: a critical review. In: Endsley, M.R., Garland, D.J. (eds.) Situation Awareness Analysis and Measurement. Lawrence Erlbaum Associates, Mahwah (2000)
9. Falessi, D., Cantone, G., Kazman, R., Kruchten, P.: Decision-making techniques for software architecture design: a comparative survey. ACM Computing Surveys 43 (2011)
10. Hirokawa, R.Y., Poole, M.S. (eds.): Communication and Group Decision Making, 2nd edn. SAGE Publications, Inc. (1996)
11. Jansen, A., Bosch, J.: Software architecture as a set of architectural design decisions. In: Proceedings of the 5th Working IEEE/IFIP Conference on Software Architecture, WICSA 2005 (2005)
12. Kerr, D.S., Murthy, U.S.: Divergent and convergent idea generation in teams: A comparison of computer-mediated and face-to-face communication. Group Decision and Negotiation 13, 381–399 (2004)
13. Klein, G.: Sources of Power. MIT Press (1999)
14. Kruchten, P., Lago, P., van Vliet, H.: Building up and reasoning about architectural knowledge. In: Hofmeister, C., Crnković, I., Reussner, R. (eds.) QoSA 2006. LNCS, vol. 4214, pp. 43–58. Springer, Heidelberg (2006)
15. Nowak, M., Pautasso, C., Zimmerman, O.: Architectural decision modeling with reuse: Challenges and opportunities. In: Proceedings of the 5th Workshop on Sharing and Reusing Architectural Knowledge, SHARK 2010 (2010)
16. Nuseibeh, B.: Weaving together requirements and architectures. IEEE Computer, 115–119 (2001)
17. Potts, C., Burns, G.: Recording the reasons for design decisions. In: Proc. of the 10th International Conference on Software Engineering, pp. 418–427 (1988)
18. Shahin, M., Liang, P., Khayyambashi, M.-R.: Architectural design decision: Existing models and tools. In: Joint Working IEEE/IFIP Conference on Software Architecture 2009 and European Conference on Software Architecture 2009, WICSA/ECSA 2009, pp. 293–296 (2009)
19. Tang, A., Jin, Y., Han, J.: A rationale-based architecture model for design traceability and reasoning. Journal of Systems and Software 80(6), 918–934 (2007)
20. van Heesch, U., Avgeriou, P., Hilliard, R.: A documentation framework for architecture decisions. Journal of Systems and Software 85(4), 795–820 (2012)
21. van Heesch, U., Avgeriou, P., Hilliard, R.: Forces on architecture decisions - a viewpoint. In: Joint Working IEEE/IFIP Conference on Software Architecture and European Conference on Software Architecture, WICSA/ECSA, Helsinki, Finland, August 20-24. IEEE (2012)
22. Zimmermann, O., Koehler, J., Leymann, F., Polley, R., Schuster, N.: Managing architectural decision models with dependency relations, integrity constraints, and production rules. Journal of Systems and Software 82(8), 1249–1267 (2009)

Architectural Decision-Making in Enterprises: Preliminary Findings from an Exploratory Study in Norwegian Electricity Industry

Mohsen Anvaari, Reidar Conradi, and Letizia Jaccheri

Norwegian University of Science and Technology, Trondheim, Norway
{mohsena,conradi,letizia}@idi.ntnu.no

Abstract. Motivation: The current literature in the architectural knowledge domain has made a significant contribution related to documenting software architectural decisions. However, not many studies have been conducted to assess the architectural decision-making and decision reuse processes through empirical investigations. Besides, the effect of the relationships among the actors in a software ecosystem on the architectural decisions-making process of each actor is not well studied. **Goal:** The objective of this paper is to identify the main processes and issues on the architectural decision-making in large-scale enterprises by considering the relationships among the enterprises and other actors of the ecosystem. **Method:** We conducted semi-structured interviews with six Norwegian companies in the software ecosystem of electricity industry. **Results:** Regarding the architectural decision-making process, the findings are in line with previous empirical studies, showing that most of the companies are not using well-known academic approaches such as ATAM, they are rather using their own procedures. The study also shows that the relationships among the actors of a software ecosystem could significantly affect the architectural-decision making process in each of the actors, for example, by limiting their alternative solutions. Finally, the results confirm that it is advantageous for the enterprises to reuse the architectural decisions across their various projects or for cooperative companies to reuse the decisions across their similar projects. **Conclusion:** Improving the reusable architectural decision frameworks by considering the relationships among the actors in a software ecosystem would be beneficial for the industry.

Keywords: Architectural decision making, enterprise applications, empirical study, software ecosystem, electricity industry.

1   Introduction

In the current industrial environments, enterprises[1] employ various software applications to automate their daily business processes and activities. They buy the applications from different vendors and use them either separately or as an integrated system based on a high

---

[1] "An enterprise is one or more organizations sharing a definite mission, goals and objectives to offer an output such as a product or a service" (Chen et al., 2008).

K. Drira (Ed.): ECSA 2013, LNCS 7957, pp. 162–175, 2013.

level structure (architecture). Therefore the concepts such as *enterprise application[2]*, *enterprise application development (EAD)*, *enterprise application integration (EAI)*, *enterprise architecture* and similar terms have been developed and used for many years in the both academia and industry.

By evolving and expanding the usage of such systems, the amount of transactional data between different applications have been dramatically increased and as a result many enterprises automate the data transfer between their applications. Therefore a movement from software as an island to software as a systems-of-systems has been emerged for many years (Maier, 1998). A classical challenge in this landscape is integration and interoperability issue (Chen et al., 2008)(Fisher, 2006) because the applications are developed based on different platforms (programming languages, operating systems, network protocols, etc.). Many approaches, trends and standardizations have been introduced to decrease the interoperability challenges (Chen et al., 2008) but still interoperability is one of the main concerns in EAD.

One of the most successful approaches for solving the interoperability issue is service-oriented development and many enterprises are using service-oriented architecture (SOA) as their architectural style. Although SOA is shown to be highly successful to alleviate the interoperability problem, implementing a SOA in an enterprise is not easy and has to meet domain-specific non-functional requirements with explicit software quality criteria (Zimmermann et al., 2007). There are many ways of implementing a SOA and no single SOA fits all purposes and constraints of an organization. Therefore many architectural design issues and tradeoffs arise (ibid), and architects have hard time to make "right" architectural decisions. Such decisions would include strategic concerns about technology and product selection, finding the right service interface granularity, and numerous decisions that deal with non-functional aspects (ibid). Zimmermann et al. have captured 130 such SOA decisions till 2007. This shows how challenging is to choose between different decisions (ibid).

How do enterprises deal with complex integration and how do they make efficient architectural decisions? What are their main challenges (technical and organizational) to make the right decisions? Do the enterprises reuse their architectural decisions in their different but similar projects? What about software consultant companies, do they reuse architectural decisions in different enterprises in the same domain? How the relationships between different companies and organizations in an industrial domain would affect their architectural decisions?

Even though the *architectural decision* concept (and the broader concept, *architectural knowledge[3]*) has gained increasing attention in the software architecture community in the last decade, still there are some deficiencies in answering to the mentioned questions:

- Based on our literature review, existing works in the architectural knowledge are more theoretical frameworks and tools developed in the academia and very few empirical researches exist in the area. Even though the theoretical works have been often evaluated by industrial case studies, the assumptions and claims about architectural decision-making in enterprises are seldom obtained through empirical

---

[2] An enterprise application is a distributed, software-intensive system that automates business processes and activities in an enterprise (Zimmermann, 2009).

[3] Architectural knowledge = architectural decisions + architectural design (Kruchten et al., 2006).

studies. The motivations for developing such frameworks and tools are mostly gained from either previous literature or authors' personal experiences in the industry. There is a lack on getting insights from the industry in a more systematic way.

- Even those few empirical studies in the area (we will try to cover them in the related work section) are mostly focused on the decision documentation and representing. The decision-making process in the industry has not been often studied empirically.
- Despite all these, still there are some empirical studies and surveys to understand the decision-making and reasoning process of architects in the industry. But first of all they are not discussing the reusable architectural decisions in EAD (Zimmermann, 2009). Furthermore they don't consider the effect of companies relationships on the decision-making process.

Considering the above issues, the goal of this paper is to get insights for answering to the mentioned questions by observing the current situation of software development and integration in the Norwegian electricity industry. The remainder of the papers is organized as follows: In the section 2 the related work will be discussed. Section 3 presents the design of the research including the research goal and questions and the research method. Section 4 presents the results of the study and section 5 analysis the resutls. Finally section 6 remarks the conclusions and also discusses the future work.

2   Related Work

To find out the related areas to this research, we consider three dimensions: topic of interest, research method and research context. The topic of our research is generally related to the architectural knowledge and more specifically the architectural decision area. If we divide the works in this dimension to the *making the decisions* and *documenting the decisions*, our work is focused more in the making the decisions. Concerning the research method, if we consider *theoretical-based researches* and *empirical investigations*, this research is related to the empirical investigations. Regarding the context, we split the current work into the research that studies the architectural decisions in a company regardless of its position in the software ecosystem (SECO), and research that considers the company position in SECO. Our work focus is on the latter.

2.1   Making Architectural Decisions

Making architectural decision is the process of selecting one alternative among different alternatives for solving a design issue in a software system (Falessi et al., 2011). As we mentioned earlier, this concept is a part of architectural knowledge and has become increasingly important in the software architecture community since the beginning of 2000s. Many researchers have worked in this area and have discussed the importance of the decisions and the rationale behind the decisions. Many tools and frameworks have been developed by the researchers to support the practitioners in the activities around the architectural decisions. Babar et al. in their book that published in 2009 have reviewed and gathered many of the works that have been done in this area in the last decade (Babar et al., 2009). Tang et al. have also covered some of the existing architectural knowledge management tools (Tang et al., 2010).

Although the existing work in architectural knowledge area focuses more on documenting and representing the decisions, still there is some work that supports the decision-making process. For example Falessi et al. have reviewed and compared the available techniques and tools for making architectural decisions in their comparative survey (Faless et al., 2011). However, most of the existing frameworks and tools have a general approach and are not specified for the enterprise application development and integration (Zimmermann, 2009) that is the interest of this research. Furthermore, seldom they consider reusing the architectural decisions in the similar projects or domains while many issues recur in the enterprise projects and reusing the architectural decisions from previous projects would be helpful (Zimmermann, 2009). Although Falessi et al. have mentioned that reuse can help to simplify the architecting (Falessi et al., 2011) they have not considered it in their analysis. Zimmermann's work (Zimmermann, 2009) is actually a reusable architectural decision model in enterprise application development and integration and therefore is a source of inspiration for our work. Even though, he has not considered the effect of companies relationships on their architectural decisions.

Finally, as discussed earlier, the motivations and insights for developing frameworks, techniques and tools that support the decision making process in the industry have been gained mostly from researchers' personal experiences and not through a systematic empirical observation. Nevertheless, recently some few empirical studies have been conducted in this area that we will discuss them in the next part.

2.2   Empirical Studies

In software engineering research in general, without knowing the fundamental mechanisms that derive the costs and benefits of software tools and methods for a certain application, "we can't say whether we are basing our actions on faulty assumptions, evaluating new methods properly, and inadvertently focusing on low-payoff improvements. In fact, unless we understand the specific factors that cause tools and methods to be more or less cost-effective, the development and use of a particular technology will essentially be a random act. Empirical studies are a key way to get this information and move towards well-founded decisions" (Perry et al., 2000). It is the same situation in the architectural decisions area and conducting empirical studies and observations would be the base for developing effective methods, frameworks and tools.

Till 2005, there were little empirical evidence about architectural decisions and how practitioners treat them in the practice (Tang et al., 2005). Tang et al. conducted a survey on the use and documentation of architecture design rationale in 2005. Even though, their main focus was to understand how practitioners think about decision rationale, how they use and document them, and what factors prevent them from documenting decision rationale (ibid). Making the decisions were not the focus of their investigations. Hoorn et al. were interested in the same direction and did a broad survey to better understand what architects really do and what kind of support they need for sharing architectural knowledge (Hoorn et al., 2011).

Ivanovic and America has conducted a study to gain knowledge on information needed for architecture decisions made by architects and managers (Ivanovic and America, 2010). The reuse aspect of the decisions is not in their work. Also they have conducted their study only in one industrial organization and therefore considering the ecosystem relationships that we are interested in is not in their research.

Finally, van Heesch and Avgeriou in their study have investigated how experienced architects reason in the context of industrial projects, how they prioritize the problem space, how they propose solutions for the problem and how they choose among solutions (van Heesch and Avgeriou, 2011). Their work is relevant to our research topic but still lacks the reuse aspect and also has not considered software ecosystem relationships. In the next part we will explain the software ecosystem concept and what we mean by a software ecosystem relationship and how we want to illustrate the software ecosystem of our research context.

2.3   Software Ecosystem

A software ecosystem (SECO) is "a set of actors functioning as a unit and interacting with a shared market for software and services, together with the relationships among them" (Jansen et al., 2009). The actor type in a SECO could be supplier, independent software vendor, software consulting company or intermediary, and customer (Brinkkemper et al., 2009). Interaction or relationship type could be product flow, service flow, financial flow and content flow (ibid). There are several ways to model and illustrate a software supply network (SSN) within a SECO (Lucassen et al., 2012). In the section 3.2, to illustrate the SSN of our research context that is Norwegian electricity industry, we have created a figure that is based on the model by (Brinkkemper et al., 2009). Since we are interested to see how the SECO relationships would affect the architectural decisions, some customizations have been made to the model to fit to our context and intentions. To our best knowledge there is no empirical study that has considered the effect of SECO relationships on the architectural decision processes.

3   Research Design

Our investigation is an exploratory study (Robson, 2011) which aims to identify the situation in a real world context. Qualitative data is collected by interviews and analyzed using thematic synthesis. In the following sections we explain the research questions, the context of the study, data collection and analysis methods and threats to results validity.

3.1   Goal

The goal of this research is to identify the main processes and issues on making and reusing architectural decisions in large-scale enterprises by considering the relationships among the enterprises and other actors of the ecosystem. To reach to the goal we are interested to find out:

> RQ1. How do industrial companies make architectural decisions for enterprise application development with respect to decision-making methodology?
> RQ2. How do the companies reuse the architectural decisions in various projects?
> RQ3. How do the software ecosystem relationships affect the decision making process?

By RQ1 we aim to explore the general attitude of companies in making their significant architectural decisions. Such decisions would include the high-level blueprint of their software and information systems to the detailed technical decisions such as choice of integration platform. Although the previous research studies had explored this aspect (van Heesch and Avgeriou, 2011), we investigate the answer to RQ1 by the means of qualitative observations to find out the possible uncover aspects of decision-making process in companies.

The aim of RQ2 is to discover whether companies reuse their architectural decisions in different projects and if the answer is no to investigate if it is possible to do so or not.

RQ3 considers the relationships among various actors in the software ecosystem and its possible effect on the process of making and reusing architectural decisions in each actor.

3.2   Context

Since this research is contextualized in a larger research project on *software engineering support for Smart Grid,* our main case of the study is the Norwegian electricity industry.

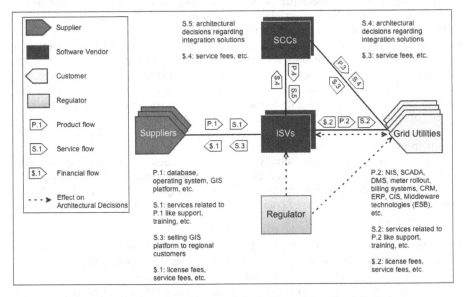

Fig. 1. Current software supply network in the Norwegian electricity industry

The software market in this industry, the same as other domains, has become a software ecosystem including different actors and various relationships between them. The actors make a software supply network to develop and integrate the required software products. Fig. 1. shows the current state of software supply network in the Norwegian electricity industry. It is based on the result of a previous interview that we conducted with an expert in the Norwegian electricity industry and later confirmed by some other experts. The chain of supply network could differ among various customers based on their size and organizational policies, but a typical path can be described as follows: A grid utility (customer) needs different software products to run its daily business activities. The utility negotiates with different national and international independent software vendors (ISV). The ISVs themselves should buy some of their fundamental software components and packages (OS, DB, etc.) from their suppliers and develop their products based on the provided components. Grid utilities later on integrate various software products themselves or ask software consultant companies (SCC) to do it for them. Sometimes ISVs also ask SCCs to help them regarding the software development to produce more interoperable solutions. There is also a national regulator that although doesn't deliver software product or service to the customers but affect the software development in ISVs and software integration in grid utilities by the rules and regulations. So we have added "regulator" as a new actor to the model from (Brinkkemper et al., 2009). Also to show how the SECO relationships would affect the architectural decisions (see sections 4.4 and 5.2), we have added a new object to the model   (the dashed arrow).

3.3   Data Collection and Analysis Methods

To answer to the research questions (see section 3.1) the semi-structured interview has been chosen as the main data collection method of this research. As it was discussed in the context part, our target companies lie in four categories based on their role in the software ecosystem of Norwegian electricity industry: grid utilities, software vendors, software consultant companies and regulator. Our initial plan was to select different samples from each of these categories. Currently there are almost 150 grid utilities in Norway, but the software vendors and also the software consultant companies that are delivering products and service to them are very few and it makes the sample selection challenging. For this stage of our research we conducted interview with 5 grid utilities (all of them have more than 75.000 grid customers) and one software vendor that have 80 percent of market share in Norway. We couldn't convince either the regulator or any software consultant companies that have experiences with software for electricity industry to participate in our study within out time frame.

To prepare the questionnaire, initially we selected 10 questions regarding the decision making process that applies to all categories of companies regardless of their role in the SECO. Some of the questions were inspired by the questionnaire van Heesch and Avgeriou have used in their survey (van Heesch and Avgeriou, 2011). The preliminary set of questions were written as follows:

1. A brief summary of ICT in your organization, your software related activities and roles, your business model, and your software integration approach.
2. What is your typical process for making architectural decisions?
3. What are your challenges (technical and social) in making the decisions?
4. How do you identify architecturally significant requirements from a set of architectural concerns and business context?
5. Who are involved in the analysis process and how do they collaborate?
6. Do you search for alternative solutions for your requirements when you make decisions? Even if you already had a solution in mind?
7. How do you select among alternative solutions? Do you consider and reuse architectural patterns, styles, reference architectures, industrial standards, etc.?
8. Do you reuse the already made decisions between your various projects?
9. How do you validate your final solution? Do you use some approaches like ATAM, CBAM, etc.?
10. Do you validate your architectural solution only in design stage or even later when the whole system is launched?

As it is clear in the above list, the RQ3 is not covered by any of the questions. After doing the first interview, we realized that the effect of SECO relationships is an important influencing factor on the decision-making process and we had not considered it. So we added it to the questionnaire for the next interviews. To this end, we added specific questions for each category to explore the subject from each category aspect. For example we were interested to see whether the decisions in the software vendors are made mainly by them or it is more customer-driven. The similar question was asked from the customers but from the opposite direction to see whether their decisions are affected by vendors or consultant companies.

After finalizing the questionnaire and making appointments with interviewees, the interviews were conducted. Since the data collection method was semi-structured interview, we considered some flexibility in asking the questions based on the answers we got from the interviewees. It means the above set of questions was more an interview guide; some questions would be skipped (for example if the interviewee didn't have any idea about the question) and some new questions would be added during the interview.

To conduct the interview with grid utilities, in some cases the interview had two parts: more general questions were answered by a project manager or head of ICT and the more detailed questions by a software architect or developer. So totally 8 interviews were conducted of which 4 were face-to-face and 4 were through Skype. Among 8 interviewees, 4 were heads of ICT, 2 were software architects, one was software developer and one was project manager. The interviews were captured by a voice recorder and lately were transcribed.

For analyzing the interview data, the step-by-step thematic synthesis proposed by Cruzes and Dybå was applied. It is mainly proposed for a systematic literature review, but is applicable for analyzing the qualitative interview transcripts similar to stage-by-stage method by (Burnard, 1991). The essential aim of these methods is to increase the abstraction level of transcribed texts from the text level to the code and theme level and create taxonomy of higher-order themes (Cruzes and Dybå, 2011). We did the same to reach from the interview results to the answer of our research questions.

4   Results

By thematic synthesis we extracted 18 codes from interview transcripts and those 18 codes were categorized into 4 themes that are described in the following sections. Section 4.1 and 4.2 correspond to RQ1, section 4.3 is related to RQ2 and section 4.4 refers to RQ3.

4.1   Making Architectural Decisions for Enterprise Application Development

In all of the energy companies we interviewed, there is an IT section either as a department (if the organization composes of only one company) or a company within the whole group (if the organization consists of many companies). IT section has a general roadmap or high level strategy for making architectural decisions regarding software enterprise application integration. For instance in some grid utilities the rules from IT sections imply that new products should have proper interfaces or adaptors to be integrated through ESB (enterprise service bus). Or they are emphasizing on reducing information redundancy by engaging SOA-based development. Some of the grid utilities have developed their guidelines based on some international frameworks for developing enterprise architecture. Later on when every department wants to make architectural decisions for their projects, they should make their decisions in alignment with guidelines and principles from IT section of the organization.

The lower level architectural decisions are made at project level in different departments. So each department has either its own software architects or they hire architects from IT department. Then the decisions are made by several meeting among the software architects and project manager (or product owner). If there is a decision about a common solution like ESB, it is rather made at the IT department.

Most of the grid utilities are not familiar with the terms and concepts like ATAM. In practice they are conducting some structured procedure which could be more informal than approaches like ATAM but still they are satisfied with the results. They have several meetings among related stakeholders, define possible alternatives and look at their possible advantages and disadvantage, consider the important non-functional requirements, also look at their organizational limitations and project schedule, and select a solution among alternatives. Some of them do the proof of concept for the selected solution to check whether the solution supports their business requirements.

4.2   Using Standards for Making Architectural Decisions

Although there have been some standards for software integration in Smart Grid for several years (for example IEC 61970 which is also called CIM), almost none of the grid companies have done their integration based on those standards and this makes their architectural decisions more challenging. They are now becoming more aware of the need to apply standards to reduce the interoperability challenges, so they are exploring the standards and are going to use them. Also some of the software vendors are starting to deliver their products based on those standards. So the future of the Smart Grid in Norway would be standard based but currently is not.

4.3   Documenting and Reusing the Architectural Decisions

Some of the companies document important architectural decisions. To this end, they either keep the meeting minutes or use an internal wiki for documentation rather than a specific tool. One of the documentation issues they often have with these approaches is the maintenance of the documentations, especially when it comes to the decisions about software integration, which these days is very dynamic in these companies. So it is hard for them to always update the latest version of the documents.

The situation of reusing the decisions depends on the level of decisions. In high level decisions, 4 out of 6 companies are reusing their high level software integration processes across different projects. The reuse happens in an ad-hoc manner and as it was explained earlier, it is mainly done by setting some high level rules or guidelines by IT departments and different projects should apply them in their integration. One of the companies is composed of both energy and telecommunication parts and is an interesting case in this aspect because overall processes which have been developed in telecommunication is reused in the smart grid initiatives too.

When it comes to the low level architectural decisions almost none of the companies are reusing the decisions across different projects and the decisions are not transferring between different projects in a written sense. The decisions are rather kept in the head of the decision makers even if they are participating in different projects. So some of the companies showed their interest to be familiar with reusable architectural decision frameworks and believe that it would be useful to learn from history and apply the experiences from previous projects in the future projects. One of the companies has a successful experience where for choosing ESB they have reused the requirements and available alternatives from other companies and they were satisfied with the results.

4.4   Effect of Software Ecosystem Relationships on the Architectural Decisions

Most of the grid utilities (customers) believe that the market is vendor driven while the software vendor believes that the market is customer driven. The examples from both sides confirm both claims. So it essentially means that as an actor of an ecosystem each of them affect the other one. From customers point of view they are limited to what vendors deliver and from the vendors side they limit their development to what the customer require. Besides, there are some regulating organizations that also affect the choices of software integration in grid utilities. So in general the interviews showed that the relationship among different actors of the software ecosystem affects the architectural decisions in each actor. The effect of these relationships is described as follows.

Effect of Regulators on the Architectural Decisions of Grid Utilities
One obvious example to show the effect of regulators on the architectural decisions in the grid utilities is SCADA (supervisory control and data acquisition) system. The grid utilities want to have a fully integrated system and therefore desire to add SCADA to their SOA-based integrated system as well, but the security regulations from Norwegian electricity regulator, which in opinion of grid utilities are old-fashion, have limited them. So they should treat SCADA as a silo system and do all the interactions and information exchange manually.

Effect of Vendors on the Architectural Decisions of Grid Utilities
An interesting example that shows the effect of vendors on the architectural decisions is a situation in one of the grid utilities where they wanted to decide choosing between IPv6 and the lower versions. For launching AMS (advanced metering system) project, they will install more than 200,000 IP-based devices in their municipality, so technically they preferred IPv6. But their challenge was that most of current vendors don't deliver products that support IPv6. Now some more professional vendors like Cisco are joining the Smart Grid market and that grid utility has finally decided to use IPv6. Another example by the same grid utility is a decision about separating the database of DMS (distribution management system) from other systems. The reason for the decision also relates to what the vendors deliver. The DMS should use a NIS (network information system) and a NIS itself is based on a GIS (geographical information system). The problem is that the current GIS suppliers don't have a electric schematic layer. What is now on the GIS is a general network of nodes and edges. So the DMS the grid utility has bought should have a separate database to include electric schematic layer.

Effect of Customers on the Architectural Decisions of Vendors
The interviewed software vendor with an example showed how their architectural decisions depend on what the customers require. The vendor has two alternatives for deliver their products based on SOA: WS or REST-based services. Although they are aware of some advantages of REST-based services they are still stick to the WS and the reason is that none of their customers have asked for REST-based services in their request for proposal.

5   Discussion

In this part we discuss our findings in position with the previous findings from related literature. The part is organized based on our three research questions. In addition, section 5.4 discusses the possible threats to validity.

5.1   Architectural Decision-Making for Enterprise Application Development

As we discussed in the related work, the study by van Heesch and Avgeriou is a relevant empirical research about architectural decision-making in industrial companies that is actually the aim of our RQ1 too. One of the results of their study is that the greatest part of architects doesn't follow particular architecture approaches from the literature (such as ATAM, SAAM, goal-oriented paradigm, etc.), they rather adopt architecture activities to define their own customized approach to making architectural decisions (van Heesch and Avgeriou, 2011).   The result of our study also in line with their finding showed that most of the companies are not using systematic approaches such as ATAM to make and evaluate their architectural decisions. Even thought, it doesn't mean that the companies are making their architectural decisions in a totally intuitive way. Both our results and findings from van Heesch and Avgeriou's survey show that the companies identify architecturally significant requirements (architectural analysis), find different candidate solutions for the requirements consider advantages and disadvantages for candidate solutions (architectural synthesis) and validate the chosen solution against the requirements (architectural evaluation) (van Heesch and Avgeriou, 2011). In spite of similarities, different companies of our study have different procedures for each of mentioned processes. For example for architectural evaluation some use proof of concept while some launch real industrial prototype to evaluate the chosen solution.

5.2   Reusing Architectural Decisions

Zimmermann has done a significant work on reusing the architectural decisions for enterprise application development. Before that not many researches have been conducted on this topic (Zimmermann, 2009). One of our aims was to find out whether the interviewed enterprises predict the required architectural decisions in a new project based on experiences from previous projects that have been done in either their department of other departments of the same organization. As results show, some of them reuse high-level architectural decisions in term of architectural guidelines or rules but none of them reuse the low-level architectural decisions across various projects.

Reusable architectural decision model (RADM) developed by Zimmermann has been evaluated by several case studies and the results show how efficient it would be to reuse the architectural decisions in similar projects (Zimmermann, 2009). Zimmermann has employed his model in different industrial cases, from software vendors to software consultant companies and large-scale enterprises like telecommunication companies. But he has mainly applied his model on several projects within each company. What we observed through the interviews was the potential to also reuse the architectural decisions across different companies within a software ecosystem. Some of the companies have had collaboration on either writing requirement specification for an enterprise solution (e.g. ESB) or developing reference architecture for smart grid. Applying reusable architectural decisions frameworks like RADM would be very promising for these collaborations and through that the new requirements and justifications to improve RADM would be gained.

5.3   Effect of Software Ecosystem Relationships on the Architectural Decisions

The results of our study show that the relationships among the actors of a software ecosystem could significantly affect the architectural-decision making process in each of the actors. Some previous studies have also discussed the non-technical influences on the architectural decisions. Van Heesch et al. have defined architectural decision forces as any aspect of an architectural problem arising in the system or its environment to be considered when choosing among the available decision alternatives (van Heesch et al., 2012). The non-technical forces they have talked about are personal preferences or experience of the architects, business goals such as quick-time-to-market, low price, or strategic orientations towards specific technologies (ibid). Their reference for considering the influence factors on software architecture is an empirical study by Mustapic et al. that have been conducted to investigate the possible real world influences of software architecture (Mustapic et al., 2004). What they have gained as the influence factors are relationships of system, computer hardware and software architecture, reuse and legacy in architectural design, business and application domain factors, choice of technologies, organizational factors, process related factors and resources used for architectural design (ibid). The most relevant factors to our results are business and application domain factors and organizational factors. The more specific factors they have investigated for these categories are standards, type of customers, production volume, product lifetime, non-functional requirements, distributed development, outsourcing, size and maturity of organization (ibid). So the SECO relationships have not been explicitly covered by the mentioned studies and the results of our study can be considered as a decision factor in addition to what they have extracted before.

5.4   Threats to Validity

Internal. One potential threat to internal validity of our research is that there were too few interviews to make reliable results. However, all of the companies were the largest enterprises and software vendor in the same software ecosystem. It means that there were few differentiations between the characteristics of the companies (type, size, products, business processes, structure, etc.). Also there is little disagreement among the interviewees from different companies. Therefore we do not assume that interviewing more companies will result to different conclusions. Even though, interviewing with software consultant companies and regulating organizations in the same software ecosystem would increase the reliability of the results. As we mentioned earlier, we couldn't convince them to participate in our study within the time schedule we had.

External. The generalization of the results to all large-scale enterprise based on the enterprises from one industrial domain is arguable. Although large-scale enterprises from other domains like telecommunication, finance or health-care have also challenges on making architectural decisions for enterprise application development, our study shows that the software integration in the electricity industry is more immature than other areas due to lack of standardization and it can affect the architectural decision issues. So we are aware of the threat to external validity and conducting the same interviews with enterprises from other domains would make the results more reliable.

6   Conclusions and Future Work

In this paper we presented the result of interviews with six companies within software ecosystem of Norwegian electricity industry being five grid utilities and one software vendor. Our main goal was to empirically investigate the architectural decision making and reusing situation in the large-scale enterprises to enrich the state of practice in the architectural decisions area. We gained three explicit results:

1- In line with few previous empirical studies, our study show that most of the companies are not using well-known academic approaches such as ATAM, they are rather using their own structured procedures.

2- The relationships among the actors of a software ecosystem could significantly affect their architectural-decision making processes for example by limiting their alternative solutions. This factor should be also considered as an influencing factor on architectural decision making process in addition to the factors previous studies have extracted from the industry.

3- There is a high potential among enterprises to reuse the architectural decisions across their various projects or across different companies within a software ecosystem. The previous reusable architectural decision frameworks have been applied mainly in various projects within one company while our study shows that such frameworks can be applied also in different companies within a software ecosystem that have some kind of collaboration.

In the next step, we are going to apply reusable architectural decision frameworks (such as RADM by Zimmermann or decision forces viewpoint by van Heesch et al.) on some of the large-scale enterprises or software consultant companies in the Norwegian electricity industry. By doing such case studies we are going to investigate how these frameworks can be improved and customized for the electricity industry based on the feedbacks we get from the case studies.

Acknowledgements. The authors would like to thank all interviewees for their participation and their valuable responses.

References

1. Babar, M.A., Dingsøyr, T., Lago, P., van Vliet, H.: Software Architecture Knowledge Management. Springer (2009)
2. Brinkkemper, S., Soest, I.V., Jansen, S.: Modeling of Product Software Businesses: Investigation into Industry Product and Channel Typologies. In: Barry, C., et al. (eds.) Information Systems Development: Challenges in Practice, Theory, and Education, vol. 1, pp. 307–325 (2009)
3. Burnard, P.: A Method of Analysing Interview Transcripts in Qualitative Research. Nurse Education Today 11, 461–466 (1991)
4. Chen, D., Doumeingts, G., Vernadat, F.: Architectures for Enterprise Integration and Interoperability: Past, Present and Future. Computers in Industry 59, 647–659 (2008)
5. Cruzes, D.S., Dybå, T.: Recommended Steps for Thematic Synthesis in Software Engineering. In: The Proceedings of the 5th International Symposium on Empirical Software Engineering and Measurement, ESEM 2011, Banff, AB, Canada (2011)
6. Falessi, D., Cantone, C., Kazman, R., Kruchten, P.: Decision-Making Techniques for Software Architecture Design: a Comparative Survey. ACM Computing Surveys 43(4) (2011)
7. Fisher, D.A.: An Emergent Perspective on Interoperation in Systems of Systems, Software Engineering Institute, Technical Report, CMU (2006)

8. Hoorn, J.F., Farenhorst, R., Lago, P., van Vliet, H.: The Lonesome Architect. The Journal of Systems and Software 84, 1424–1435 (2011)

9. Ivanovic, A., America, P.: Information Needed for Architecture Decision Making. In: Proceedings of the 2010 ICSE Workshop on Product Line Approaches in Software Engineering, pp. 54–57 (2010)

10. Jansen, S., Finkelstein, A., Brinkkemper, S.: Business Network Management as a Survival Strategy: A Tale of Two Software Ecosystems. In: Proceedings of the First Workshop on Software Ecosystems. CEUR–WS, vol. 505 (2009)

11. Kruchten, P., Lago, P., van Vliet, H.: Building up and Reasoning about Architectural Knowledge. In: Hofmeister, C., Crnkovic, I., Reussner, R. (eds.) QoSA 2006. LNCS, vol. 4214, pp. 43–58. Springer, Heidelberg (2006)

12. Lucassen, G., Brinkkemper, S., Jansen, S., Handoyo, E.: Comparison of Visual Business Modeling Techniques for Software Companies. In: Cusumano, M.A., Iyer, B., Venkatraman, N. (eds.) ICSOB 2012. LNBIP, vol. 114, pp. 79–93. Springer, Heidelberg (2012)

13. Maier, M.W.: Architecting Principles for Systems-of-Systems. Systems Engineering 1(4), 267–284 (1998)

14. Mustapic, G., Wall, A., Norstrom, C., Crnkovic, I., Sandstrom, K., Froberg, J., Andersson, J.: Real World Influences on Software Architecture – Interviews with Industrial System Experts. In: Proceedings of the Fourth Working IEEE/IFIP Conference on Software Architecture, WICSA (2004)

15. Perry, D.E., Porter, A.A., Votta, L.G.: Empirical Studies of Software Engineering: A Roadmap. In: Proceedings of the Conference on The Future of Software Engineering, Limerick, Ireland, pp. 345–355 (2000)

16. Robson, C.: Real World Research: A Resource for Users of Social Research Methods in Applied Settings, 3rd edn. Wiley, Chichester (2011)

17. Tang, A., Babar, M.A., Gorton, I., Han, J.: A Survey of the Use and Documentation of Architecture Design Rationale. In: 5th Working IEEE/IFIP Conference on Software Architecture (WICSA), pp. 89–98 (2005)

18. Tang, A., Avgeriou, P., Jansen, A., Capilla, R., Babar, M.A.: A Comparative Study of Architecture Knowledge Management Tools. Journal of Systems and Software 83(3), 352–370 (2010)

19. van Heesch, U., Avgeriou, P.: Mature Architecting – A Survey about the Reasoning Process of Professional Architects. In: 9th Working IEEE/IFIP Conference on Software Architecture (WICSA), pp. 260–269 (2011)

20. van Heesch, U., Avgeriou, P., Hilliard, R.: Forces on Architecture Decisions – A Viewpoint. In: Proceeding of Joint Working Conference on Software Architecture and 6th European Conference on Software Architecture, pp. 101–110 (2012)

21. Zimmermann, O., Koehler, J., Leymann, F.: Architectural Decision Models as Micro-Methodology for Service-Oriented Analysis and Design. In: SEMSOA Workshop, Hannover, Germany (2007)

22. Zimmermann, O.: An Architectural Decision Modeling Framework for Service-Oriented Architecture Design. PhD Dissertation, University of Stuttgart (2009)

Making the Right Decision:
Supporting Architects with Design Decision Data

Jan Salvador van der Ven[1] and Jan Bosch[2]

[1] University of Groningen, Groningen, The Netherlands
[2] Chalmers University of Technology Gothenborg, Sweden
mail@jansalvador.nl, jan.bosch@chalmers.se

Abstract. Software architects are often forced to make design decisions based on limited information. In this paper, we present an approach that allows software architects to study information about design decisions made by hundreds or more software architects by automatically analyzing the version management data of large open-source repositories. The contribution is, first, that it develops a conceptual model to reason about the automatic derivation of specifically medium level architectural design decisions. Second, we show that it is indeed possible to derive these design decisions automatically from open source projects. This provides a basis for statistical and quantitative reasoning about software architecture design decisions that allows software architects to make better-informed decisions.

Keywords: Architecture, Design Decisions, Architectural Knowledge, Components, Open Source Projects.

1   Introduction

Architects are lonely [1] because they often are the only ones with a system-wide overview and have no peers within the organization. These architects are responsible for making design decisions concerning the system or systems that they are responsible for. A significant portion of these design decisions involves the selection of 3rd party open source or commercial components. In our experience with architects at dozens of companies, this selection is done based on descriptions on websites, anecdotal experiences or sometimes proof of concept implementations [2]. Consequently, despite the best intentions and efforts of the software architect, the design decisions often are guesses based on circumstantial evidence that are only validated once the system has been built or changed and it is, once again, in operation. The vast majority of decisions that software architects are faced with have been made earlier software architects in other organizations working on similar systems. Wouldn't it be great if software architects could get access to the decisions made by other architects, that would allow them to determine what selections were made from a set of alternatives and with what frequency? That would give software architects hard, quantified data to base their own decisions on. The question of course is: how we can access these decisions? Interestingly, over the last decade or more, several

K. Drira (Ed.): ECSA 2013, LNCS 7957, pp. 176–183, 2013.

open-source software repositories have achieved broad adoption and host thousands of projects in virtually any programming language and application domain imaginable. Examples include SourceForge[1] and GitHub[2] with millions of repositories millions of developers. As many of the projects in these repositories are public, there is a large amount of data available about the structure of these projects as well as the evolution of these structures over time. In order to provide the lone software architects with objective, quantified and statistical information about the design decisions that other architects have made, version management systems provide an excellent source of data. However, considering the sheer volume of data, this requires an automated, rather than manual, approach to derive the information that software architects require. In order to achieve that, the first question, which is the research question of this paper, is whether it is feasible to automatically identify design decisions from commit data.

The contribution of this paper is twofold. First, it develops a conceptual model to reason about the automatic derivation of architectural decisions. Second, it shows that it is indeed possible to derive these design decisions automatically. This paper is organized as follows. First, the concept of architectural decision is introduced. Then, our hypotheses are presented. Sequentially, a description of how we acquired and processed the data is given, followed by the analysis or our results. This paper ends with the discussion and future work, related work and some concluding words.

2   Architectural Design Decisions

In research about architectural design decisions [3, 4], typically four aspects of decisions are considered: the *decision topic,* the *choice*, the *alternatives* that are considered and the *rationale* (sometimes formalized as ranking) of the decision. We use these four aspects of architectural decisions to identify decisions in repository data of open source projects. There are different abstraction levels of architectural decisions. As described by de Boer et al. [3], decisions are often related to each other, and this relationship typically forms a tree structure down from more abstract to more concrete (decisions cause new decision topics). Fig. 1. symbolically visualizes such a graph. Generally speaking three levels of decisions can be distinguished:

– **High-Level Decisions.** High-level architecture decisions affect the whole product, although they are not necessarily always the decisions that are debated or thought through the most. Often, people that are not involved in the realization of the project (e.g. management or enterprise architects) heavily affect these decisions. Typical examples of high-level decisions are the choice to adopt an architectural style, use a programming language, application server, or specific large (COTS) components. Changing these decisions typically has a huge impact.
– **Medium Level Decisions.** Medium level decisions involve the selection of specific components or frameworks, or describe how specific components map to each other

---

[1] http://sourceforge.net/
[2] https://github.com/

according to specific architectural patterns. These decisions are often debated in the architecture and development teams and are evaluated, changed and discarded as needed. They have a high impact on the (nonfunctional) properties of the product and are relatively expensive to change.

- **Realization Level Decisions.** Realization level decisions involve the structure of the code, the location of specific responsibilities (e.g. design patterns), or the usage of specific APIs. These decisions are relatively easy to change, and have relative low impact on the properties of the system.

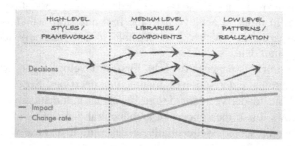

Fig. 1. Relationships between Design Decisions

As we have experienced in our industrial cases [5], the architectural decisions that are hardest to make are the medium level decisions, for the following reasons: a) these decisions have a *high impact* on the functional and non-functional properties of the system; b) they *change constantly*, especially compared to high-level decisions that only change when remaking the system; c) they are *costly to change* because of the impact on the system; d) because new components and version are created constantly, it is *hard to stay knowledgeable* about all relevant alternatives, and; e) they have *unpredictable results* until they are implemented in the system.

The focus of this paper is on medium level design decisions that change during development or maintenance. These decisions express themselves through changes in the version management system, i.e. commits of new and changed code. All of the previously mentioned aspects of a design decision have a reflection in the version history or implementation of the system. The decision topic and the choice have a reflection in the (architecturally relevant) commits. The rationale for the decision can be reflected in the commit message, and the author of the commit can be contacted for additional rationale. Alternatives have reflection in the history of the architecturally relevant commits.

3   Hypotheses

The research approach we utilize consists of the following steps. First, we formed hypotheses about how design decisions are potentially represented in the version history of projects. Second, we selected a set of projects to test our hypotheses on. From these projects, we generated the data that potentially contained architectural design decisions, rationale and information about alternatives. This data was used to validate our hypotheses in a quantitative and qualitative way. The following three hypotheses are used in the remainder of this paper:

- *Hypothesis 1: Medium level design decisions can be identified in the version history of projects.*
- *Hypothesis 2: Commits in version management systems contain rationale of the made architectural decisions.*
- *Hypothesis 3: Alternatives can be found in the structure of commits in version management systems.*

4   Mining Git Repositories

This section describes how the data from the git repositories was processed to usable data in the Gitminer tool. We have looked at projects that contained a Gemfile, that were used by the community (>1 watcher, >1 fork), were active (change in last month) and were of moderate size (between 0,3 and 10Mb). From Google's BigQuery API[3] we have searched project urls that satisfied these criteria, resulting in 710 projects.

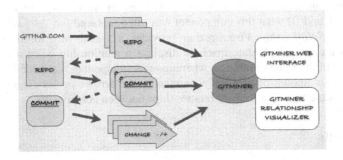

Fig. 2. Processing of Repos to Gitminer

For the processing of the data from the repos, we used git[4] tooling. We only looked at the history of the Gemfile, as this file contained information about used components. In Fig. 2. this processing is visualized. First, a set of repos is selected and cloned to a local computer. Then, every commit on the Gemfile is taken, and every line that changed in the Gemfile within the commit is processed to a database insert query. To do this, we have automatically processed the output from the *git log* command, which outputs the history of a file. At last we inserted the queries to the database.

---

[3] https://developers.google.com/bigquery/
[4] http://git-scm.com/

Table 1. Acquired Repo Data

Parameter	Total #
Projects involved	710
Total commits	12600
Total commit messages > 30 characters	7527
Total changed lines	40464

In our processing, we removed lines that were added and removed in the same commit (typically a copy-paste of lines to a different location in the same file) and lines that did not concern gems (but, for example comments). A summary of the resulting amounts after the above-mentioned steps is presented in Table 1.

4.1 Analyses Tool: Gitminer

In order to proof or disprove the hypotheses posed in this paper, we created two different 'views' on the data in the Gitminer database. The *Gitminer Web Interface* is a web interface that enables users to browse thought commits. This tool shows the commits that *removed* the component you are looking for, as this indicates that a specific decision was made to remove (or replace) a component. The view includes the commit messages, the date of the commit and the contact details of the authors. In this view you can see for every component: A) what replacements of this component are often used, and B) what this component was often replaced for. As a second view, the *Gitminer Relationship Visualization* provides a visual way to identify what components are related. A state machine displays a relationship when a component was removed in the same commit as where another component was added. A number representing the amount of projects accompanies the arrows in the diagram. In this view it is possible to see patterns of relationships between components.

5 Results

For our *quantitative* results, we have presented 100 different commits to six subject matter experts. We randomly picked 100 commits from the Gitminer database that had commit messages of more then 30 characters (therefore, had a solid chance of containing rationale). We distributed the commits among our subject matter experts. The participants that conducted the research were experienced Ruby software developers, experienced software architects, and researchers with software engineering background and experience. We asked them to answer if the presented commit involved a design decision, rationale for a decision and relevant information about alternatives for a decision.

Table 2. Quantitative Results

%	Decision?	Rationale?	Alternatives?
% Yes	61,75 %	25,50 %	4,75 %
% No	38,00 %	68,75 %	84,00 %
% Empty	0,25 %	5,75 %	11,25 %

During our analysis of the data collected with the Gitminer tool, we found additional *qualitative* results in addition to the quantitative results. We identified different aspects related to design decisions, that we used as expert validation:

- There were commit messages that indicated changes of components and rationale about them. E.g. "use mysql2 instead of mysql because of shit encoding".
- Commit messages where a decision is made, but the rationale was clearly missing: "Changed to jeweler2", or "remove thin"
- Many messages described configuration issues: "Unfortunately, we can't put ruby-debug in the gemfile because it breaks 1.9.2 compatibility ...".

6   Analysis

As shown in Table 2, roughly 60% of the commits on Gemfiles were considered as concerning a design decision. For our whole dataset, this would mean that 60% of the 7527 commit messages contains decisions (~4500). Of course, the other commit messages (with < 30 characters) could also contain decision information, so this number could very well be higher. Calculated in the same way, about 1900 commit messages contain rationale about made decisions. When relating this to the number of projects, on average every open source project we used contained ~ 6 decisions in commits and ~3 commit messages with relevant rationale. Following, we will discuss our hypotheses and related results.

Hypothesis 1: Medium level design decisions can be identified in the version history of projects. The subject matter experts have identified architecture design decisions in the commit messages. This is a clear quantitative indication that decisions exist in the commit messages of open source projects. Qualitatively, the researchers found several interesting design decisions. This qualitatively strengthens the validity of this hypothesis. Concluding, hypothesis 1 is confirmed by our data.

Hypothesis 2: Commits in version management systems contain rationale of the made architectural decisions. Rationale was found in 25,5% of the commits that were inspected by the subject matter experts. Qualitatively the researchers found rationale in many cases. This qualitatively strengthens the validity of this hypothesis. Concluding, hypothesis 2 is also confirmed by our data.

Hypothesis 3: Alternatives can be found in the structure of commits in version management systems. Our subject matter experts have not found many alternatives in the commit messages from the version management system (< 5%). So, quantitatively we have no evidence that alternatives can be found. So, hypothesis 3 is *not* confirmed by our data. However, alternatives were clearly identified by the researchers in the Relationship Visualization. So, based on the qualitative data we still think we could be able to find information about alternatives, but not solely in the commit messages.

7   Discussion and Future Work

In order to be able to discuss the architectural design decisions we discovered in this paper, we had to scope the definition of these decisions. We selected medium level design decisions that concerned component selection. For the validation we have taken only the commit messages that contained more then 30 characters. Based just on this research, it is tough to generalize to other kinds of architectural decisions.

We assumed that every added or removed line in the Gemfile was a potential decision. However, in Gemfiles there are non-gem lines too. For example, there can be conditional lines or groups that are only called in specific situations. We have chosen to remove those lines. Hence, dependent on how often this happens, it could be that some of our found decisions are conditional.

As a reflection on our research, we considered the commit messages to be very useful in understanding what happened in a project. However, the messages were sometimes cryptic and short. In that case, data from multiple projects needed to be used for making similar decisions. The component relationships were interesting from a research point of view as an indication for dependencies and alternatives.

We are investigating ways to increase the number of repositories in the database, to be able to base the advice on a larger data set. In addition to this, we are planning to experiment with our approach on other programming languages. For example, the pom file of Maven (Java) projects could be used similar to Gemfiles. Also, we are working on making the results accessible to the public. As noted by several people that studied our results, the results could be used to statistically advice people about their architecture.

8   Related Work

There has been much attention to documenting software architectures [6], as well as documentation templates [7] and computational modeling [8]. A topic that is being discussed heavily is the role of the architect [1] and the role of 'the architecture document' in the design process [5]. Here, often the architect is responsible for creating and maintaining the architecture documentation. However, the architect is never supported in making these decisions in any way.

In the architecture design decision research hierarchical structures are used to model architectural knowledge [3] or design decisions [9, 10]. This research often emphasizes the recording of decisions, and the extraction of decisions later in the development process. However, we have not find any work where statistical data is used to help architects make better decisions. Dagenais and Robillard [11] investigated open source development for finding decisions based on surveys and documentation. Another mining initiative involves searching open source java frameworks [12], that focuses on code fragments instead of architectural decisions.

On the web, there are several initiatives that provide statistical data about software projects. For example, there are tools that help developers increase code quality by providing statistics about the code [13]. However, to the best of our knowledge no research or practical solution exists that actually searches for design decisions in the version history of software projects.

9   Conclusions

In this paper, we have given architects the first step to a wider knowledgebase for relying their architecture decisions on. We have shown that it is possible to extract architectural design decision information from the version management of open source projects, by automating the process of extracting the decisions, and validated that architectural decisions can be derived from commits on the system.

Architects that are facing problems related to selecting components can benefit from this, by seeing what happened in similar situations in other software projects. The information presented in this research is based on real world projects, which are actually used, build and maintained around the world. By using this information, architects can be supported statistically for making their decisions.

Acknowledgements. We would like to thank the subject matter experts for helping us with the research. Also, we would like to thank the people of Factlink for the help during the development of our theory and tooling.

References

[1] Farenhorst, R., Hoorn, J.F., Lago, P., van Vliet, H.: The Lonesome Architect. J. Syst. Softw. 84(9), 1424–1435 (2011)

[2] Gorton, I., Liu, A., Brebner, P.: Rigorous Evaluation of COTS Middleware Technology. IEEE Computer 36(3), 50–55 (2003)

[3] de Boer, R.C., Farenhorst, R., Lago, P., van Vliet, H., Clerc, V., Jansen, A.: Architectural knowledge: getting to the core. In: Overhage, S., Ren, X.-M., Reussner, R., Stafford, J.A. (eds.) QoSA 2007. LNCS, vol. 4880, pp. 197–214. Springer, Heidelberg (2008)

[4] Tyree, J., Akerman, A.: Architecture Decisions: Demystifying Architecture. IEEE Softw. 22(2), 19–27 (2005)

[5] van der Ven, J.S., Bosch, J.: Architecture Decisions: Who, How and When? To be Published in: ASA. Agile Software Architectures (2013)

[6] Clements, P., Garlan, D., Bass, L., Stafford, J., Nord, R., Ivers, J., Little, R.: Documenting Software Architectures: Views and Beyond. Pearson Education (2002)

[7] Kruchten, P.: The Rational Unified Process: An Introduction. Addison-Wesley (2003)

[8] OMG. UML Specification, Version 2.0 (2012), http://www.omg.org/spec/UML/

[9] Jansen, A.G.J., Bosch, J.: Software Architecture as a Set of Architectural Design Decisions. In: Proceedings of the 5th IEEE/IFIP Working Conference on Software Architecture, WICSA 2005 (2005)

[10] van der Ven, J.S., Jansen, A., Nijhuis, J., Bosch, J.: Design Decisions: The Bridge between Rationale and Architecture. In: Rationale Management in Software Engineering, pp. 329–348. Springer (2006)

[11] Dagenais, B., Robillard, M.P.: Creating and evolving developer documentation: understanding the decisions of open source contributors. In: Proceedings of the Eighteenth ACM SIGSOFT International Symposium on Foundations of Software Engineering (2010)

[12] Thummalapenta, S.: SpotWeb: Detecting Framework Hotspots via Mining Open Source Repositories on the Web. In: Proceedings of the 2008 International Workshop on Mining Software Repositories, MSR (2008)

[13] Bluebox, Code Climate (2013), https://codeclimate.com/

Architecture-Centric Modeling of Design Decisions for Validation and Traceability

Martin Küster

FZI Research Center for Information Technologies, Software Engineering,
Haid-und-Neu-Str. 10-14, 76131 Karlsruhe, Germany
kuester@fzi.de
http://www.fzi.de/se

Abstract. Access to previously made architectural design decisions allows for faster understanding and more educated decisions during software evolution. Templates and ontologies have been proposed to document such decisions. In this paper we argue that documenting the architectural design decisions can be intertwined with a standard architecture documentation process. For that, we propose architecture-specific decision types equipped with OCL constraints capable for decision conformance checks. We present an initial evaluation based on a preliminary case study with a typical three-tier web-application and the decisions associated with its implementation.

Keywords: design decision, architectural model, traceability, constraint checking.

1 Introduction

Documented design decisions on an architectural level are beneficial for many reasons. For example, while modifying an architecture, explicit statements about the intention and rationale of architectural elements help the architect to make better decisions, without repeating himself or invalidating decisions taken before (cf. [1]).

In [2], based on a case study, we identified requirements for beneficial decision documentation. One central element was the connection of the specification of the software (such as use case diagrams, or textual requirements documents or models) to design artifacts, especially on the architecture level to avoid context switches. This work proposes a solution for the linkage between decision- and architectural elements to ease architecture evolution.

In this paper, we build on existing decision models, and focus on semantic linkage to architecture elements for automatic validation of existing decisions. Links to drivers of a decision enable traceability and system understanding. We propose to combine the two prime use cases of decision models (validation and traceability) with an integration into architectural decscription langauges (ADLs).

K. Drira (Ed.): ECSA 2013, LNCS 7957, pp. 184–191, 2013.

Instead of providing a generic linking or tracing mechanism we propose a compact domain-specific language (DSL) for recording architectural decisions. The proposed decision types are supplied with OCL constraints that can check whether the decision is still valid. This is especially useful when the architectural model changes over time and the decisions made have to be reconsidered.

The approach and the elements of the decision types are evaluated using a simple real-world implementation of a three-tier web application and its architectural model. Typical evolution scenarios show how the modeled decisions can improve evolutions steps and changes made to the architecture.

2   Motivating Example

Virtualization techniques in software architectures bring many benefits. However, the work of an architect managing such virtualized environments got more difficult as a result of more degrees of freedom. Here, the explicit consideration of decisions taken while designing the different virtualized layers is more important than before to support system understanding and longevity of the software- and hardware architecture.

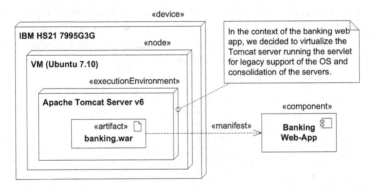

Fig. 1. Example of a virtualization decision following the Y-template as described in [3]. Architecture model following the UML 2.4.1 standard [4].

Introducing virtualization is a typical decision taken by an architect. Fig. 1 examplifies the situation. The decision attached to the deployed web app states that the Banking web application is deployed in a Tomcat server that runs in a virtualized Linux box. The basic problem with such an annotation-based mechanism is that the additional information is not linked semantically to the architecture model. When the architecture changes, or when a driver of the decision (e.g. a consolidation issue) is reverted or reconsidered, the necessary information which elements could be affected cannot be achieved easily. Validation of a changed architecture is only possible if all decisions are reviewed.

We propose to introduce a designated decision model element *(virtualization)* that can be linked to the relevant artefacts and which can be automatically checked by an OCL constraint.

3   Modeling of Architectural Design Decisions

The key idea of the proposed architectural design decision model to express architectural design decisions with special constructs that reference the architectural model. These links allow for validation of the decisions with pre-defined OCL constraints.

The metamodel builds on existing work by Capilla et al. [5] and extends it by adding direct links to elements as found important by Falessi [6].

3.1   Constraint Checking with OCL

Consider the example ADD (replication) given in Fig. 2. The element Replication is a subclass of Decision and inherits all attributes. It brings (by the additional references and by the OCL constraint) semantics that cannot be expressed without explicit type-safe modeling of the respective design decision. In the case of replication, we reference a UML Class and a UML Component. The semantics that are expressed by the OCL constraint in the grey box states that the referenced component should be instantiated multiple times (given by the attribute *numberReplicas*). The element that contains the replicas is referenced by *clazz*. This class contains the replicated component instances as UML Properties referenced by *ownedAttribute*. Therefore, we get the constraint counting the number of owned attributes (contained elements) that conform to the referenced component. It must be equal to the stated number of replicas.

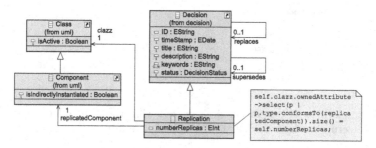

Fig. 2. Replication decision with OCL constraint and links to UML

We can easily see that given a reasonable set of semantically rich decision types, we can specify a lot of typical architectural decisions and ensure the validity of the decision in the architectural model by the OCL constraints that the decision types bring along.

3.2   Decision Types

The different types of decisions that we consider most relevant for architecture evolution is listed in Table 1. We do not claim that the list is complete. It is based on the two main viewpoints for architecture modeling, which is the structural and deployment viewpoint. We introduced a decision type for each architectural element that should (and can) be validated or linked to issues or requirements. The table gives, for each decision type, the set of linked architectural elements on which the OCL constraint can be evaluated. The constraint itself is described textually. The OCL constraints are stored directly in the Ecore model as annotations.

Table 1. Table summarizing the decision types including a textual description of the semantics of the constraint that is attached to the architectural design decision

Decision Type	Constraint
Virtualization	ExecutionEnvironments are not put directly to devices (deployment via Nodes).
AllocateSeparately	Components are deployed separately (on different Nodes).
AllocateToghether	Components are explicitly deployed on the same Nodes.
NeverAllocateTo	The Component is not deployed to the referenced Nodes.
AllocateTo	The Component shall only be deployed to the referenced Nodes.
InterfaceDesign	Method (must be part of an interface) is introduced as a result of an issue.
Replication	The Component is replicated (multiple instantiation) within the referenced Class.
SingleInstatiation	The Component is instantiated only once (explicit exclusion of replicas).
IntroduceComponent	The Component is introduced as a result of an issue. Do not remove without considering the decision.
ReuseComponent	An existing Component (e.g. third-party lib) is added to the architecture. Do not remove without considering the decision.
SplitComponents	The realized functionality (given by a functional requirement) is split between the referenced Components.
Decision	Arbitrary OCL constraints.

Most of the elements listed under the deployment and structure viewpoint are hoped to be self-explanatory. The user-defined decision type can be used to specify technical decisions such as project guidelines, programming languages etc., or non-technical consideration such as teams, deadlines, etc.

4   Case Study

For the case study outlined in the following, we implemented a typical three-tier web application. The application offers services for storing and retrieving user data. A servlet serves the http requests and accesses a relational user database via an object-relational mapper.

By giving the architectural design decisions of a real-world example, we want to show that the decision types that we proposed in Sec. 3 are sufficient for modeling typical decisions in a component-based system. The list can be extended

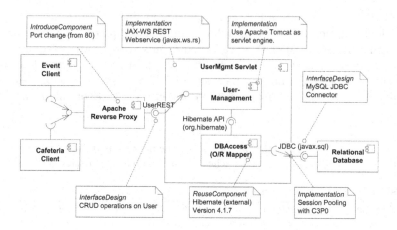

Fig. 3. Case study architecture: a web application for user management

whenever finding a recurring decision type that is used in a real-world example and that is necessary for validation or traceability.

The overall complexity of the application is fairly low. But still, the number of decisions taken while designing the system is significant (seven decisions for only four server components and additional three decisions for three assembled components).

4.1   Initial Architecture and Design Decisions

The initial component architecture of the case study is depicted in Fig. 3. The initial deployment of the components on a local machine is shown in Fig. 4. The decisions are attached as notes for better readability. In the model, all design decisions are linked with the architectural element and an issue that was the driver of the decision (not part of the diagram).

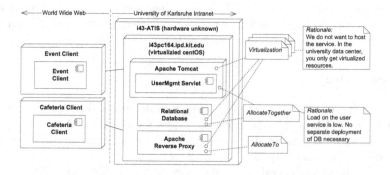

Fig. 4. Case study architecture: Deployment of the web application

4.2 Change Scenarios for Validation

Validation of documented design decision is a key concept of the outlined model-based approach. In this section, we show what kind of changes to the architecture can be supported with the built-in OCL constraints. In a larger architecture, the effect of the automation that comes with the incorporated constraints is more visible since not all decisions can be kept in mind. However, the change scenarios we show are examples of changes that are protected against architectural drift.

System Structure. Any existence decision (such as *Introduce-* or *ReuseComponent*) is protected against removal of its element. Deletion of the element violates the existence constraint leading to an invalidated design decision. In case of the reuse of a component (O/R mapper library), the interface is external and cannot be modified. Changing the interface of a reused component leads to a violation. Changes to interfaces that are guarded by an *InterfaceDesign* lead to violations only if a method that has been added intentionally is removed. For example, the CRUD-operations in the UserREST interface are marked by a design decision. If either of them is removed, the decision is invalidated.

The violations are marked as icons in the architecture model as well as in the problem view of the integrated development environment (IDE).

Deployment. Two decisions in Fig. 4 are intentional allocations of components to a specific node (*AllocateTogether* and *AllocateTo*). Moving one of the components to a different node will lead to a violation. The *Virtualization* decision checks whether there is (at least one) virtual Node between the Device and the allocated component. Deploying the component directly to a device invalidates the decision.

4.3 Change Scenarios for Understanding and Traceability

For traceability, the issues and requirements linked to design decisions are of importance. For better readability, they are not included in the figures (Fig. 3 and Fig. 4). To illustrate the benefit of the upstream traceability included in the

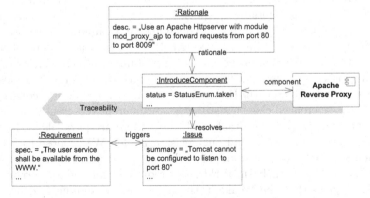

Fig. 5. Evolution context of the *Apache Reverse Proxy* component

decision model, we give the full decision model with linked issues as a separate object graph (Fig. 5). As we identified in our previous work [2], it is crucial for good system understanding to avoid switches between the different artifacts (requirements, issues, architectural elements).

The graph shows that the elements that represent the *evolution context* of the component are navigable from the architectural element. The related elements, especially the issues that triggered the existence of the element or its modification, can be displayed around the architectural element in one view. By that, we can support the architect with additional information that is needed for the deliberate evolution of the software architecture.

In the example, the reverse proxy was introduced because of a technical limitation, which was the inability to configure reserved ports (0..1023) in the servlet engine. The problem was raised to an architectural issue, which could be solved by introducing an additional component delegating to a different port.

From our experience, this is a common pattern. The architecture is initially designed based on functional or non-functional requirements. But after a while, modifications or additions are made that are hard to understand without explicit knowledge management support. Instead of browsing a (possible large) document of architectural decisions, the architect can simply navigate to the element about which she needs additional information.

With the proposed approach, the architecture understanding can be improved especially for architects new to the system or parts of it.

5   Related Work

Decision templates as given by Tyree et al. [7] have been the earliest forms of architecture knowledge management. They are complete, but do not link into the solution space, which is the architecture. Early work on decision views were presented by Dueñas and Capilla [8]. They outlined the idea of additions to UML for decision support, but did not provide any implementation. The idea was refined in Tang's work [9] on AREL (Architecture Rationale and Elements Linkage). The architectural elements (AE) are not differentiated, making it impossible to check constraints in a type-safe manner as outlined in this paper. Validation is the key contribution of Könemann and Zimmermann's work [10] on combining design decisions with design documents. The concept of having constraints that check whether a decision is still fulfilled is very similar to ours. By introducing special decision types, we can make checks or validations that are impossible with the ones in Könemann's work, which is mostly conservative checking if the referenced elements still exist. A different representation, semantic wikis, are proposed by DeGraaf et al. [11]. There are parallels between the ontology that they presented and our decision model. We propose to keep the requirements model separate from the architecture model. Our decision model is in the middle knowing both worlds, the requirements and the architecture world. The finding that they make in the paper can be summarized by saying that the expressive links between wiki pages lead to a higher effectiveness of software architects and developers. We follow this line of argument, but use a different representation (model instead of ontology). Lastly, a recent publication by van Heesch et al. [12] showed that decision making support is suited explicitly for young developers lacking years of experience. The findings suggest that the different decision viewpoints help in exploring and evaluating solution options.

Acknowledgments. The authors thank Zoya Durdik from FZI and Anne Koziolek from KIT for fruitful discussions of the decision model. We thank Armağan Kilic for supporting us as part of his Master's thesis. We thank Emre Taşpolatoğlu for implementing the user management system. The work has been funded by BMBF project grant no. 01IS12012B (MOHITO).

References

1. Farenhorst, R., de Boer, R.: Knowledge management in software architecture: State of the art. In: Babar, M.A., Dingsøyr, T., Lago, P., van Vliet, H. (eds.) Software Architecture Knowledge Management, pp. 21–38. Springer, Heidelberg (2009)
2. Küster, M., Trifu, M.: A Case Study on Co-Evolution of Software Artifacts Using Integrated Views. In: Proceedings of the WICSA/ECSA 2012 Companion Volume - WICSA/ECSA 2012, p. 124 (2012)
3. Zimmermann, O.: Making Architectural Knowledge Sustainable The Y-Approach. In: SATURN Conference. Software Engineering Institute, CMU (2012)
4. Object Management Group (OMG): UML Infrastructure (2011)
5. Capilla, R., Zimmermann, O., Zdun, U., Avgeriou, P., Küster, J.M.: An enhanced architectural knowledge metamodel linking architectural design decisions to other artifacts in the software engineering lifecycle. In: Crnkovic, I., Gruhn, V., Book, M. (eds.) ECSA 2011. LNCS, vol. 6903, pp. 303–318. Springer, Heidelberg (2011)
6. Falessi, D., et al.: A Value-Based Approach for Documenting Design Decisions Rationale: A Replicated Experiment, pp. 63–69 (2008)
7. Tyree, J., Akerman, A.: Architecture Decisions: Demystifying Architecture. IEEE Software 22, 19–27 (2005)
8. Dueñas, J.C., Capilla, R.: The decision view of software architecture. In: Morrison, R., Oquendo, F. (eds.) EWSA 2005. LNCS, vol. 3527, pp. 222–230. Springer, Heidelberg (2005)
9. Tang, A., Jin, Y., Han, J.: A rationale-based architecture model for design traceability and reasoning. Journal of Systems and Software 80, 918–934 (2007)
10. Könemann, P., Zimmermann, O.: Linking design decisions to design models in model-based software development. In: Babar, M.A., Gorton, I. (eds.) ECSA 2010. LNCS, vol. 6285, pp. 246–262. Springer, Heidelberg (2010)
11. de Graaf, K.A., et al.: Ontology-based Software Architecture Documentation. In: 2012 Joint Working IEEE/IFIP Conference on Software Architecture and European Conference on Software Architecture, pp. 121–130. IEEE Computer Society (2012)
12. van Heesch, U., Avgeriou, P., Tang, A.: Does decision documentation help junior designers rationalize their decisions? - A comparative multiple-case study. Journal of Systems and Software (2013)

Difficulty of Architectural Decisions –
A Survey with Professional Architects

Dan Tofan[1], Matthias Galster[2], and Paris Avgeriou[1]

[1] University of Groningen, The Netherlands
d.c.tofan@rug.nl, paris@cs.rug.nl
[2] University of Canterbury, New Zealand
mgalster@ieee.org

Abstract. Much research exists on architectural decisions, but little work describes architectural decisions in the real-world. In this paper, we present the results of a survey with 43 architects from industry. We study characteristics of 86 real-world architectural decisions and factors that contribute to their difficulty. Also, we compare decisions made by junior architects and senior architects. Finally, we compare good and bad architectural decisions. Survey results indicate that architectural decisions take an average time of eight working days. Dependencies between decisions and the effort required to analyze decisions are major factors that contribute to their difficulty. Compared to senior architects, junior architects spend a quarter of the time on making a decision. Good architectural decisions tend to include more decision alternatives than bad decisions. Finally, we found that 86% of architectural decisions are group decisions.

1   Introduction

The architecture of a software system is the result of a set of architectural design decisions [1]. Architectural decisions have a key influence on the functional and quality characteristics of software systems [2]. Examples of architectural decisions are choosing development frameworks or architectural patterns. Given the importance of architectural decisions and their significant impact on system development, much interest exists for research on architectural decisions. However, characteristics of architectural decisions and factors that contribute to their difficulty have not yet been studied in industrial practice. An in-depth understanding of the characteristics and difficulty of architectural decisions would enable researchers to propose approaches that help practitioners in their decision making activities. Thus, we conducted a survey to answer the following research questions:

RQ1. What Are the Characteristics of Architectural Decisions?
To answer RQ1, we define measurable characteristics (Table 1) of architectural decisions. Previous research has shown that the concept of architectural decisions gained importance among practitioners, despite the fact that the definition of software architecture in terms of architectural decisions was not completely adopted in practice

K. Drira (Ed.): ECSA 2013, LNCS 7957, pp. 192–199, 2013.

[3]. Another survey with practitioners provides insights on knowledge sharing for architectural decisions [4]. However, we could not find any study that investigates the characteristics of architectural decisions.

RQ2. What Factors Make Architectural Decisions Difficult?
To answer RQ2, we defined a list of factors derived from literature and discussions with experts. The resulting metrics were 22 factors (Table 2) that survey participants rated. Once we know what makes architectural decisions difficult, we can devise approaches that focus on mitigating the difficulty of making decisions.

RQ3. What Are the Differences between Junior and Senior Software Architects?
The experience of architects influences their decision making [5,6]. Thus, we propose RQ3 to investigate how difficulty and characteristics of decisions vary with the level of experience. This helps researchers propose targeted solutions to address the difficulties perceived by either junior architects or experienced architects. Previous research showed that naïve architects (i.e. undergraduate students) do not make trade-off between requirements, and do not evaluate critically their decisions [5]. Furthermore, professional architects very often search for many design alternatives in their decision making [6]. Additionally, professional architects do not consider risk assessment as very important [6].

RQ4. What Are the Differences between Good and Bad Architectural Decisions?
We propose RQ4 for studying the differences between decisions with a more preferable outcome (i.e. *good* decisions) and decisions with a less preferable outcome (i.e. *bad* decisions). Answering RQ4 highlights characteristics and difficulty factors linked to good and bad outcomes of architectural decisions.

2   Survey Design and Results

2.1   Survey Design

To develop the survey, we reviewed existing literature on architectural decisions (e.g. [2,5,6]). From the literature, we identified factors that contribute to the difficulty of architectural decisions. Next, we interviewed four senior architects, each with at least ten years of experience as an architect. We asked each architect to identify two architectural decisions they had been involved in, and discussed the difficulty factors for both decisions. Afterwards, we asked the architects to propose other items that contribute to the difficulty of a decision to be included in the questionnaire used to collect the survey data. The architects also provided thoughtful feedback on the structure of the questionnaire. We piloted the questionnaire with other practitioners, and improved it by rephrasing some questions to increase clarity.

After a welcome message, participants had to confirm that they were directly involved in making architectural decisions during the last two years. The survey continued with a few questions about the background of participants. Next, participants were asked to indicate a good architectural decision (i.e. *good* or *bad* outcome, according to their judgment), and described its characteristics (Table 1). Next, participants were asked to rate the 22 statements in Table 2 about the difficulty of their good architectural decision on a Likert scale. Similar steps had to be performed for the bad architectural decision.

Our target population was software architects who were directly involved in making software architectural decisions during the last two years. To reach our target population, we sent survey invitations to architects in our personal networks. Furthermore, we posted survey invitations on LinkedIn groups and ran paid ad campaigns using LinkedIn and Google. We received 43 valid responses from 23 countries on five continents. Twelve participants had up to two years of experience as architects, ten participants had three to five years of experience, thirteen participants had six to ten years of experience, seven participants had eleven to fifteen years of experience, and one participant had more than fifteen years of architecting experience.

2.2   Results for RQ1 - Characteristics of Architectural Decisions

Participants indicated the actual and the elapsed time (i.e. actual time is spread over the elapsed time, as architects are also involved in other activities) they spent for making the 86 architectural decisions (Table 1). On average, architectural decisions took about eight working days, and elapsed over around 35 working days. Participants indicated how many people were involved directly and indirectly in making the architectural decisions. The number of indirectly involved persons excludes the directly involved persons. The results are shown in Table 1. On average, each architectural decision involved three persons that were directly involved. When making an architectural decision, more alternatives are considered. We asked participants to indicate the number of alternatives they considered at the beginning of their decision making process, and the number of alternatives they studied for an extended period of time. Results are shown in Table 1. Architects consider quality attributes in their decisions. However, it is not clear how many quality attributes they consider in practice, so we asked them to indicate this number for their decisions (Table 1).

Table 1. Metrics for actual/elapsed time (in working days), number of directly and indirectly involved persons, number of alternatives considered in the beginning/extended time, and number of quality attributes considered when making the architectural decisions

Metric	Actual	Elapsed	Direct	Indirect	Begin	Extend	#QA
Average	7.85	34.74	3.12	7.05	2.91	1.96	4.74
Std. dev.	9.22	70.59	1.54	8.91	1.43	0.84	4.19
Min.	0.50	0.63	1	0	1	0	0
Max.	44	600	8	50	8	4	30
Mode	1	5	3	3	3	2	3

2.3   Results for RQ2 - Difficulty of Decisions

Participants rated 22 factors (Table 2) on the difficulty of their architectural decisions, indicating their level of agreement with the statements, using the following values: *(strongly) disagree, neutral, (strongly) agree*, and *not applicable*.

Results for each factor are summarized in Fig. 1 (left). From the bar charts, we notice the following. Participants indicated **most agreements** (including strong agreements) with statements on *dependencies with other decisions* (F13 for 69 decisions), *major business impact* (F14 for 60 decisions) and *serious negative consequences* (F16 for 59 decisions). Participants indicated **most disagreements** (including strong disagreements) with statements on *having too many alternatives* (F8 for 57 decisions), *too many people involved in decision making* (F12 for 49 decisions), *lack of domain-specific knowledge* (F21 for 46 decisions), and *having too few alternatives* (F9 for 45 decisions). Participants indicated **most neutral** standpoints with statements *on respecting existing architectural principles* (F15 for 24 decisions), *needing lot of effort for analyzing decision alternatives* (F10 for 21 decisions), and *having much peer pressure* (F18 for 21 decisions).

Table 2. List of 22 factors that contribute to the difficulty of architectural decisions

ID	The decision was difficult because...
F1	you received conflicting recommendations from various sources about which decision alternative to choose
F2	there were no previous similar decisions to compare this decision against
F3	it was hard to identify a superior decision alternative from the alternatives under consideration
F4	the decision required a lot of thinking from you
F5	it was hard to convince stakeholders to accept a certain decision alternative
F6	stakeholders had strongly diverging perspectives about the decision
F7	you needed to influence some stakeholders without having formal authority over them
F8	the decision had too many alternatives
F9	the decision had too few alternatives
F10	analyzing alternatives for this decision took a lot of effort
F11	some quality attributes were considered too late in the decision making process
F12	too many people were involved in making the decision
F13	dependencies with other decisions had to be taken into account
F14	the decision had a major business impact
F15	you had to respect existing architectural principles
F16	serious negative consequences could result from the decision
F17	too little time was available to make the decision
F18	you had a lot of peer pressure
F19	of the trade-offs between quality attributes
F20	you lacked experience as an architect
F21	you lacked domain-specific knowledge (e.g. new customer)
F22	more information was needed to reduce uncertainty when making the decision

Fig. 1 (right) shows average values for all factors, calculated as follows. We assign numerical values to the Likert scale: *strongly disagree* (1), *disagree* (2), *neutral* (3), *agree* (4), and *strongly agree* (5). *Not applicable* values are ignored. We acknowledge challenges with treating a Likert scale as either an interval or categorical data. Still, we use averages because they are easy to understand for a large audience.

From Fig. 1 (right), we notice that *dependencies with other decisions* (F13) and *major business impact* (F14) have highest average agreements across participants. *Negative consequences* (F16) received second highest average. *Effort for analyzing alternatives* (F10), *lack of similar decisions* (F2) and *requiring a lot of thinking* (F4) received high agreements from participants.

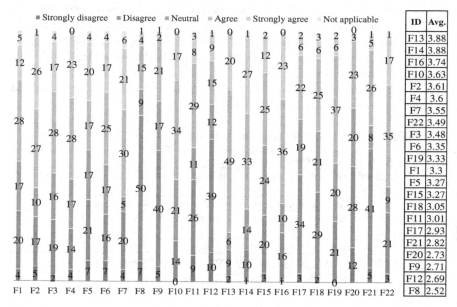

Fig. 1. Survey results for each factor (left), and sorted average values for factors (right) - a higher average indicates stronger agreement with the difficulty of a factor

We notice that some factors have averages that suggest disagreement that they contribute to the difficulty of architectural decisions, i.e. have averages smaller than three (neutral). For example, *too many* (F8) or *too few* (F9) alternatives contribute little to difficulty, similar to *lack of experience* (F20) and *domain-specific knowledge* (F21). However, the last two factors need to be considered in the context that many participants were senior architects, who might have enough experience and knowledge.

2.4   Results for RQ3 - Differences between Junior and Senior Architects

We divide survey participants in junior and senior architects as follows. Junior architects have up to five years of experience as architects, and senior architects have six or more years of experience as architects. Based on this criterion, 22 junior and 21 senior architects answered the survey.

To compare the answers from junior and senior architects, we use the Mann-Whitney U test, a non-parametric test. We investigate the differences between junior and senior architects with regard to the 22 factors in Table 2, and the metrics in Table 1. We obtain significant statistical differences (*p*-values less than 0.05) between junior and senior architects for five difficulty factors and one characteristic. Junior architects considered *conflicting recommendations on what to consider for a decision* (F1) as more significant to making a decision difficult. Also, in contrast to senior architects, junior architects found that if *lots of thinking is required* (F4), decisions become more difficult. In turn, senior architects found that decisions become more difficult if they *have a major business impact* (F14). There are differences between junior and senior architects on *experience* (F20) and *domain-specific knowledge* (F21); these differences can be expected to some extent, because senior architects have more experience and domain-specific knowledge. Additionally, senior architects spend four times more actual time on their decisions than junior architects.

2.5   Results for RQ4 - Differences between Good and Bad Decisions

Comparing participants' answers on their good and bad architectural decisions increases our understanding on the quality of architectural decisions, by analyzing the link between the two aspects of quality: difficulty (the 22 factors in Table 2) and outcome (good and bad decisions). Furthermore, we analyze the link between the characteristics of architectural decisions and their outcome (e.g. are there differences between the time spent on good or bad decisions?).

We compare differences between the 43 good and 43 bad decisions using the Wilcoxon signed ranks test, a non-parametric statistical test for comparing groups of two related samples. We treat *'not applicable'* answers as missing values. Similar to the analysis in Section 2.4, we investigate the differences between good and bad decisions related to the data in Table 1 and Table 2.

We found statistically significant differences on *having too few alternatives* (F9), with a tendency for disagreement with F9 on good decisions, and for neutral with F9 on bad decisions. For bad decisions, participants indicated that *some quality attributes were considered too late* (F11), in contrast with good decisions. Also, *dependencies with other decisions* (F13) are more difficult for good than bad decisions. Participants disagreed on *too little available time* (F17), *much peer pressure* (F18), and *lack of experience* (F20) for the good decisions, in contrast with the bad decisions.

Regarding the decisions characteristics, we found statistically significant differences between the number of alternatives considered at the beginning of the decision making process, number of alternatives studied for an extended period of time, and the number of quality attributes. For all these, the good decisions had higher numbers.

3   Discussion

An architectural decision takes an average actual time of around eight working days, over an average elapsed time of 35 working days (Table 1). The survey results indicate no significant differences between good and bad decisions regarding actual and elapsed time. However, participants considered they had enough time for the good decisions, and not enough time for the bad decisions.

The actual time junior architects spend on making a decision is one quarter of that spent by senior architects. We expected senior architects to spend less or similar amounts of time to junior architects, because of their extra experience. A possible explanation is that senior architects might deal with higher impact, time consuming decisions than juniors. A future comparison should use a ratio of time per decision impact, which can be quantified as the estimated cost of reversing the decision.

Another insight from this survey concerns the number of people involved in architectural decisions. The importance of stakeholders in architectural decisions is widely recognized in the literature. Stakeholders are always involved indirectly in decision making. However, no studies mention the direct involvement of stakeholders in decisions, as decision makers, rather than decision influencers. Researchers need to know if architectural decisions are typically made by one person (i.e. the architect) or by groups of persons (i.e. one or more architects, and other stakeholders). For example, researchers can propose group decision making approaches, if a relevant proportion of architectural decisions are made in groups. A surprising result is that only 14% of the decisions in the survey were made by individuals. The typical architectural decision has three decision makers (Table 1). We consider that group architectural decision making is a much needed research direction.

Regarding difficulty of decisions, we notice that dependencies with other decisions contribute much to difficulty of decisions. Results from a related survey [6] indicate that architects often come across such dependencies. Moreover, researchers proposed various approaches for handling decisions dependencies (e.g. [7]). Our survey confirms the relevance of the topic, and the need for disseminating research results to practitioners. We also found that analysis effort and lack of similar (or previously made) decisions increase difficulty of decision making. This suggests that practitioners welcome approaches that help them analyze decisions, and appreciate examples of similar decisions as opportunities to reuse architectural knowledge.

Regarding differences between junior and senior architects, we found that junior architects need help to address the difficulties of analyzing decisions, such as handling conflicting recommendations. This is not relevant for senior architects. We consider that existing documentation approaches help junior architects. However, documentation could be improved by adding capabilities for analyzing decisions.

Regarding differences between good and bad decisions, the survey results indicate that good decisions have more alternatives than bad decisions. Therefore, as a rule of thumb, we recommend practitioners to identify three or more alternatives. Also, this study confirms that practitioners should pay attention to quality attributes and decisions dependencies while making architectural decisions.

To increase **internal validity**, we piloted and refined the questionnaire to ensure that participants could understand it. Also, we added explanatory text with small examples to the questions, so that participants could easily interpret the questions. To address **construct validity**, we discussed our conceptualization of decision difficulty with experienced architects, who helped us refine it. The very low numbers of 'not applicable' answers to survey items indicates that the survey items indeed measure difficulty of decisions. We increased the **external validity** of this survey by recruiting participants from multiple venues.

4   Conclusion and Future Work

We have two take-away messages for practitioners. First, since architects make decisions that have major business impact, it is important (especially for junior architects) to use decision making tools and processes that help them analyze alternatives and dependencies with other decisions. For example, based on our previous work [8,9], we are developing an open-source tool [10] that will include support for group decision making, analyzing alternatives and dependencies with other decisions. Second, during architectural decision making, considering more alternatives and more quality attributes leads to better decisions.

This paper encourages researchers to conduct future descriptive work on real-world architectural decision making (e.g. provide more data about decisions). Also, researchers can propose decision making support for architects based on their experience levels, and the actual difficulties faced by architects. Finally, this paper provides evidence for the need of future research on group architectural decision making.

References

1. Jansen, A., Bosch, J.: Software Architecture as a Set of Architectural Design Decisions. In: 5th Working IEEE/IFIP Conference on Software Architecture, pp. 109–120. IEEE (2005), doi:10.1109/WICSA.2005.61
2. Zimmermann, O.: Architectural Decisions as Reusable Design Assets. IEEE Software 28(1), 64–69 (2011), doi:10.1109/MS.2011.3
3. Clerc, V., Lago, P., van Vliet, H.: The Architect's Mindset. In: Overhage, S., Ren, X.-M., Reussner, R., Stafford, J.A. (eds.) QoSA 2007. LNCS, vol. 4880, pp. 231–249. Springer, Heidelberg (2008)
4. Farenhorst, R., Hoorn, J., Lago, P., van Vliet, H.: The Lonesome Architect. In: Joint Working IEEE/IFIP Conference on Software Architecture & European Conference on Software Architecture, pp. 61–70. IEEE (2009), doi:10.1109/WICSA.2009.5290792
5. van Heesch, U., Avgeriou, P.: Naive Architecting - Understanding the Reasoning Process of Students. In: Babar, M.A., Gorton, I. (eds.) ECSA 2010. LNCS, vol. 6285, pp. 24–37. Springer, Heidelberg (2010)
6. van Heesch, U., Avgeriou, P.: Mature Architecting - A Survey about the Reasoning Process of Professional Architects. In: 9th Working IEEE/IFIP Conference on Software Architecture, pp. 260–269. IEEE (2011), doi:10.1109/wicsa.2011.42
7. Jansen, A., Avgeriou, P., van der Ven, J.S.: Enriching Software Architecture Documentation. Journal of Systems and Software 82(8), 1232–1248 (2009), doi:10.1016/j.jss.2009.04.052
8. Tofan, D., Galster, M., Avgeriou, P.: Capturing Tacit Architectural Knowledge Using the Repertory Grid Technique (NIER Track). In: 33rd International Conference on Software Engineering, pp. 916–919 (2011), doi:10.1145/1985793.1985944
9. Tofan, D., Galster, M., Avgeriou, P.: Reducing Architectural Knowledge Vaporization by Applying the Repertory Grid Technique. In: Crnkovic, I., Gruhn, V., Book, M. (eds.) ECSA 2011. LNCS, vol. 6903, pp. 244–251. Springer, Heidelberg (2011)
10. Tool for Repertory Grid Technique, https://github.com/danrg/RGT-tool (accessed April 2013)

The Role of Quality Attributes
in Service-Based Systems Architecting: A Survey

David Ameller[1], Matthias Galster[2], Paris Avgeriou[3], and Xavier Franch[1]

[1] Universitat Politècnica de Catalunya (UPC), Barcelona, Spain
{dameller,franch}@essi.upc.edu
[2] University of Canterbury, Christchurch, New Zealand
mgalster@ieee.org
[3] University of Groningen, The Netherlands
paris@cs.rug.nl

Abstract. Quality attributes (QA) play a fundamental role when architecting software systems. However, in contrast to QA in traditional software systems, the role of QA when architecting service-based systems (SBS) has not yet been studied in depth. Thus, we conducted a descriptive survey to explore how QA are treated during the architecting of SBS. Data were collected using an online questionnaire targeted at participants with architecting experience. Our survey shows that QA and functional requirements of SBS are mostly considered equally important. Also, QA are usually treated explicitly rather than implicitly. Furthermore, dependability and performance appear to be the most important QA in the context of SBS. Our results partially show that general findings on QA also apply to the domain of SBS. On the other hand, we did not find a confirmation that QA are primary drivers for the architecting of SBS, or that certain application domains would focus on particular QA.

Keywords: quality attributes, service-based systems, survey, architecting.

1 Introduction

Quality attributes (QA) are characteristics that affect the quality of software systems [1]. Quality attribute requirements are requirements that refer to these quality attributes. For example, demanding a response time of 1 millisecond for a particular function of a system is a quality attribute requirement referring to performance (the QA). QA tend to be more difficult to achieve because they are often not explicitly described by stakeholders, exhibit trade-offs, or are subjective. It has been acknowledged that QA affect the architecting of software systems and thus should be considered from the very start of a software project [2, 3]. One type of software system that has become popular in industry is that of service-based systems (SBS) [4]. In contrast to conventional software systems, the role of QA in the context of SBS has not yet been studied extensively. However, quality is a top challenge in SBS engineering [2, 5]. Even though proposals for quality attributes in SBS exist, there is a lack of empirical studies that investigate QA in practice [6]. To contribute to the

K. Drira (Ed.): ECSA 2013, LNCS 7957, pp. 200–207, 2013.
© Springer-Verlag Berlin Heidelberg 2013

understanding of the role of QA in SBS by providing insights into how QA are treated in practice, we present a descriptive survey. Using the GQM approach [7], the goal of our survey is defined as to *analyse and characterise* (purpose) the *role of QA* (issue) in *SBS architecting* (object) from the perspective of *practitioners and researchers with practical architecting experience* (viewpoint). Section 2 summarizes our research method. Section 3 presents the results of our study. In Section 4 discuss our results. We conclude the paper in Section 5.

2   Research Method

Surveys collect qualitative and quantitative information to provide a "snapshot" of the current status related to a phenomenon [8]. To ensure rigor, repeatability and to reduce researcher bias, we designed a survey protocol following the template proposed for evidence-based software engineering[1]. We defined three research questions:

- RQ1: *How important are QA compared to functionality when architecting SBS?*
- RQ2: *To what extent are QA specific to application domains of SBS?*
- RQ3: *What kind of architectural decisions are used to address QA in SBS?*

Current literature, such as [9, 10, 11], suggests that QA drive the design of software architectures. RQ1 investigates if this is also the case for SBS, or if QA are treated as factors that suggest the use of a service-based solution in the first place but are not considered architecture drivers (service-orientation claims to achieve "qualities", such as interoperability, flexibility, reusability [12]). For RQ2, we aim at providing guidance for software architects by focusing on the QA that are most important for a certain application domain (e.g., healthcare, telecommunication). Finally, RQ3 investigates the transition from QA to architectural decisions by relating QA to the architecture decision types and categories proposed by Kruchten [13].

Survey Design. We conducted a descriptive survey. We required participants to have practical experience in architecting SBS. This included practitioners from industry, researchers, and participants with mixed background (e.g., participants that moved to academy after working in industry, practitioners with part-time academic positions). Participants were recruited through several cycles of advertising (e.g., LinkedIn groups, conferences, and online communities), between May and September 2011.

Data Preparation and Collection. All survey questions[2] on the online questionnaire referred to one particular project that participants had worked on in the past. For most questions, participants could provide comments to complement their answer.

Data Analysis. To ensure the quality of the data obtained from the questionnaire, we applied sanity checks to find obvious errors in data. We used descriptive statistics to analyze the data [14]. Free text answers were coded [15] and underwent content analysis [16] involving all four authors.

---

[1] http://www.dur.ac.uk/ebse/resources/templates/SurveyTemplate.pdf
[2] All questions can be found at
www.essi.upc.edu/~dameller/publications/ecsa13-ap.pdf

Internal Validity. Confounding variables could bias our results [17]. Thus, we applied exclusion and randomization [9]. Exclusion means that participants who are not sufficiently experienced were excluded from the study. Randomization means that we used a sampling technique which led to random participants. Furthermore, to mitigate the risk of ambiguous and poorly phrased questions, we piloted the questionnaire in multiple iterations. Another limitation is that participants might not have answered truthfully to the questions [9]. Thus, we made participation voluntary and anonymous. Finally, the protocol was reviewed by external reviewers.

External Validity. External validity is concerned with generalizing the results to the target population. We assume that our results are applicable to a population that meets the sampling criteria of our survey (i.e., architects with experience in SBS).

3   Results

We obtained 31 valid responses. From these, 18 participants (58%) had experience in both academia and industry. 10 participants (32%) had only experience in industry, whilst 3 (10%) were participants from academia.

3.1   RQ1: How Important Are QA Compared to Functionality When Architecting SBS?

Importance and Explicitness of QA. Functionality and QA were considered equally important by most respondents (Figure 1). When asked whether QA were considered implicitly or explicitly, most respondents (71%) answered "explicitly" (see Figure 2). To identify dependencies between the importance of QA and their implicit or explicit nature, we created a cross-tabulation (Table 1). Eighteen respondents (58%) considered QA and functionality equally important and at the same time made QA explicit. In 6 cases (20%), QA were not made explicit and QA were considered less important than functionality. In all 4 answers (12%) where QA were more important than functionality, QA were made explicit. Fisher's exact test led to $p < 0.001$ which means that there is a statistically significant relationship between the importance of QA and their implicit or explicit nature. Thus, there is a high probability that projects which treat functionality and QA equally important also make QA explicit.

Table 1. Cross-tabulation of the importance of QA and their implicit or explicit nature

	QA explicit	QA implicit	Total
QA were AS important AS functionality	18 (58%)	3 (10%)	21 (68%)
QA were LESS important THAN functionality	0 (0%)	6 (20%)	6 (19%)
QA were MORE important THAN functionality	4 (12%)	0 (0%)	4 (13%)
Total	22 (71%)	9 (29%)	31 (100%)

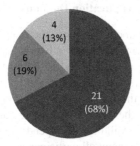

QA and functionality were equally important
QA were less important than functionality
QA were more important than functionality

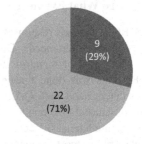

QA were addressed implicitly
QA were addressed explicitly

Fig. 1. QA compared to functionality   **Fig. 2.** Implicit / explicit nature of QA

Impact of Role on How QA Are Perceived. Even though all participants had architecting responsibilities in the project for which they answered the questions, they had different roles. Architects and designers were the majority (17 participants or 55% of all participants). Additional roles included 3 project managers (10%), 2 developers (7%), and 1 participant of each of the following roles: consultant, quality engineer, analyst, industrial researcher, unit manager and standards developer. Cross-tabulations are shown in Table 2 and Table 3. Three participants did not provide any role. Thus, the total number in Table 2 and Table 3 is 28. Fisher's exact test indicated a dependency between the role of participants and the importance of QA ($p = 0.078$). Given the number of architects that considered QA as equally important compared to functionality, this dependency means that architects and designers tend to treat QA and functionality equally important. Furthermore, 71% of architects and designers treated QA explicitly (not statistically significant; Fisher's exact test led to $p = 0.151$).

Table 2. Cross-tabulation of the importance of QA and the role of participants

	Architect	Other	Total
QA were AS important AS functionality	14 (82%)	6 (55%)	20 (71%)
QA were LESS important THAN functionality	2 (12%)	3 (27%)	5 (18%)
QA were MORE important THAN functionality	1 (6%)	2 (18%)	3 (11%)
Total	17 (100%)	11 (100%)	28 (100%)

Table 3. Cross-tabulation of the nature of QA and the role of participants

	Architect	Other	Total
QA explicit	12 (71%)	8 (73%)	20 (71%)
QA implicit	5 (29%)	3 (27%)	8 (29%)
Total	17 (100%)	11 (100%)	28 (100%)

3.2   RQ2: To What Extent Are QA Specific to Application Domains of SBS?

To answer RQ2, we used responses to the question about the most important QA that participants had experienced. During analysis we mapped all QA stated by participants in terms of scenarios to QA for SBS as defined by the S-Cube quality model [18]. This was done through content analysis where combinations of three researchers categorized each QA. Figure 3 shows the frequency distribution of QA. We grouped data-related quality attributes from the S-Cube quality model (data reliability, completeness, accuracy, integrity, validity). Dependability and performance are the most frequently addressed QA. As not all participants provided a complete scenario, the total number in Figure 3 is 28.

Fisher's exact test did not reveal any correlation between QA and domains ($p = 0.456$). We analyzed the correlation between the QA and their importance, and we found that except for dependability and performance which tend to be considered more important than functionality, there is no correlation between other QA and their importance ($p = 0.983$).

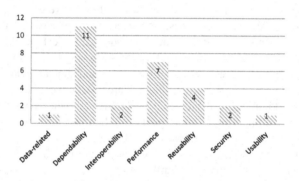

Fig. 3. Frequency distribution of QA

3.3   RQ3: What Kind of Architectural Decisions Are Used to Address QA in SBS?

We used two classifications to differentiate the kinds of decisions. First, we used Kruchten's taxonomy of decision types [13]. Second, we classified decisions based on decision categories: *Ad-hoc*: Solution that is specific to a concrete problem of the project (e.g., the architect decides to create a separate service to store sensitive information about the users to improve the security of the system). *Pattern*: Reusable and widely-known architectural solution (e.g., the decision to use of the Model-View-Controller pattern). *Technology*: A piece of implemented software that fulfills some required functionality (e.g., the use PostgreSQL instead of other DBMS).

Assigning decisions made to accommodate QA to types and categories of decisions was made based on a content analysis involving all authors. Figures 4 and 5 show the results. One decision was not classified because the participant did not provide a description for it. We found a correlation between decision types and decision categories (Fisher's exact test: $p = 0.018$): 83.3% of technology decisions are existence decisions, 69.2% of the ad-hoc decisions are property decisions, and 54.5% of pattern decisions are also property decisions.

QA and Decision Classification. We tried to find correlations between the decision classifications and the QA mentioned by the participants. The results were not significant. We obtained $p = 0.835$ (for types) and $p = 0.741$ (for categories).

QA Treatment and Decision Documentation. As part of analysing the types of decisions made to accommodate QA, we studied if these decisions were actually documented or treated implicitly. There is a correlation between treating QA explicitly and documenting decisions (Fisher's exact test: $p = 0.022$, Table 4). All participants that treated QA explicitly also documented the decisions to accommodate this QA. Also, all participants that did not document decisions treated QA implicitly. We also found a relationship between the importance of a QA and if decisions have been documented ($p = 0.112$, Table 5). Note that only 26 participants provided information about the degree of documentation of their architecture decisions.

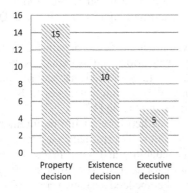

Fig. 4. Decision types

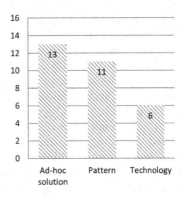

Fig. 5. Decisions categories

Table 4. Cross-tabulation of the nature of QA and documentation

	Not documented	Documented	Total
QA explicit	0 (0%)	18 (78.3%)	18 (69.2%)
QA implicit	3 (100%)	5 (21.7%)	8 (30.8%)
Total	3 (100%)	23 (100%)	26 (100%)

Table 5. Cross-tabulation of the importance QA and documentation

	Not doc.	Documented	Total
QA were AS important AS functionality	1 (33.3%)	17 (73.9%)	18 (69.2%)
QA were LESS important THAN functionality	2 (66.7%)	3 (13.0%)	5 (19.2%)
QA were MORE important THAN functionality	0 (0%)	3 (13.0%)	3 (11.5%)
Total	3 (100%)	23 (100%)	26 (100%)

4   Discussions of Results

Literature argues that QA are important and a major challenge when architecting SBS [2]. Our study showed that 71% of the participants indicated that QA were treated explicitly. This could be an indicator that special attention is paid to QA because they pose a major challenge. On the other hand, general literature about software architecting and design claims that QA drive the architecture [3]. We found that QA were rarely more important than functionality. However, stating that QA drive the architecture is different from stating that QA are more important than functionality. Also, we had indicators that QA were treated as global influence factors or architectural drivers for high-level architectural decisions. This also indicates that using a service-based solution is not only a technology-driven decision but has sound rationale based on QA.

We found that the majority of participants treated QA and functionality as equally important in the context of SBS, in contrast to [9] who argued that QA are more important than functional requirements. In another study, van Heesch and Avgeriou [10] said that more than 80% of participants indicated that quality requirements play a prominent role during architecting. A similar result can be found in our study with practitioners in the context of SBS as only 19% of our participants indicated that QA were less important than functionality.

In [19] the authors conducted a survey to evaluate a catalogue of non-functional properties for SOA. The study found that security was prioritized as being absolutely essential in a quality model for SOA. However, our study showed that security only occurred in two projects. Reusability or dependability, two main features of SBS were not found to be relevant non-functional characteristic in SOA in [19].

A study in the embedded systems industry [20] studied how quality requirements are handled in practice. The study found that usability and performance are the most important quality aspects. While in our study dependability and performance are the most important QA, with usability being the least important QA. The difference in the importance of usability could be due to the nature of embedded systems versus SBS.

Non-functional requirements as seen by architects were studied by Poort et al. [21]. The study found that if architects are aware of non-functional requirements, they do not adversely affect project success. This is in line with our results that most participants consider quality attributes explicitly and at least equally important as functionality.

5   Conclusions and Future Work

We presented the results of a survey to study the role of QA in the context of SBS architecting. Our study provides empirical evidence of the current state of practice. Future work includes the extension of this study by gathering more responses, and a more detailed analysis of QA in industry, for example, by using case studies rather than broad surveys can be used to confirm or refute the findings of our study.

Acknowledgments. This work has been supported by the Spanish project TIN2010-19130-c02-01 and NWO SaS-LeG, contract no. 638.000.000.07N07.

References

1. IEEE Computer Society Software Engineering Standards Committee, IEEE Standard Glossary of Software Engineering Terminology (1990)
2. Gu, Q., Lago, P.: Exploring Service-oriented System Engineering Challenges: A Systematic Literature Review. Service Oriented Computing and Applications 3, 171–188 (2009)
3. Ozkaya, I., Bass, L., Sangwan, R., Nord, R.: Making Practical Use of Quality Attribute Information. IEEE Software 25(2) (2008)
4. O'Brien, L., Bass, L., Merson, P.: Quality Attributes and Service-Oriented Architectures, Technical Report, SEI CMU, Pittsburgh, PA (2005)
5. O'Brien, L., Merson, P., Bass, L.: Quality Attributes for Service-oriented Architectures. In: International Workshop on Systems Development in SOA Environments, pp. 1–7. IEEE Computer Society, Minneapolis (2007)
6. Mahdavi-Hezavehi, S., Galster, M., Avgeriou, P.: Variability in Quality Attributes of Service-based Software Systems: A Systematic Literature Review. Information and Software Technology 55(2), 320–343 (2013)
7. Basili, V., Caldiera, G., Rombach, D.: The Goal Question Metric Approach. In: Marciniak, J.J. (ed.) Encyclopedia of Software Engineering, pp. 528–532. John Wiley & Sons, New York (1994)
8. Wohlin, C., Hoest, M., Henningsson, K.: Empirical Research Methods in Software Engineering. In: Conradi, R., Wang, A.I. (eds.) ESERNET 2001. LNCS, vol. 2765, pp. 7–23. Springer, Heidelberg (2003)
9. van Heesch, U., Avgeriou, P.: Mature Architecting - A Survey about the Reasoning Process of Professional Architects. In: WICSA, 2011, pp. 260–269 (2011)
10. van Heesch, U., Avgeriou, P.: Naive Architecting - Understanding the Reasoning Process of Students - A Descriptive Survey. In: Babar, M.A., Gorton, I. (eds.) ECSA 2010. LNCS, vol. 6285, pp. 24–37. Springer, Heidelberg (2010)
11. Bachmann, F., Bass, L.: Introduction to the Attribute Driven Design Method. In: ICSE 2001, pp. 745–746.
12. Erl, T.: Service-Oriented Architecture (SOA): Concepts, Technology, and Design. Prentice Hall, Upper Saddle River (2005)
13. Kruchten, P.: An Ontology of Architectural Design Decisions in Software-intensive Systems. In: 2nd Groningen Workshop on Software Variability, Groningen, The Netherlands, pp. 54–61 (2004)
14. Kitchenham, B., Pfleeger, S.L.: Principles of Survey Research - Part 6: Data Analysis. ACM SIGSOFT Software Engineering Notes 28, 24–27 (2003)
15. Miles, M.B., Huberman, A.M.: Qualitative Data Analysis, 2nd edn. Sage Publications, Thousand Oaks (1994)
16. Krippendorff, K.: Content Analysis: An Introduction to its Methodology, 2nd edn. Sage Publications, Thousand Oaks (2003)
17. Ciolkowski, M., Laitenberger, O., Vegas, S., Biffl, S.: Practical Experiences in the Design and Conduct of Surveys in Empirical Software Engineering. In: Conradi, R., Wang, A.I. (eds.) ESERNET 2001. LNCS, vol. 2765, pp. 104–128. Springer, Heidelberg (2003)
18. Gehlert, A., Metzger, A.: Quality Reference Model for SBA, Deliverable #CD-JRA-1.3.2, S-Cube, p. 64 (2009)
19. Becha, H., Amyot, D.: Non-functional Properties in Service Oriented Architecture – A Consumer's Perspective. Journal of Software 7(3), 575–587 (2012)
20. Svensson, R.B., Gorschek, T., Regnell, B.: Quality requirements in practice: An interview study in requirements engineering for embedded systems. In: Glinz, M., Heymans, P. (eds.) REFSQ 2009 Amsterdam. LNCS, vol. 5512, pp. 218–232. Springer, Heidelberg (2009)
21. Poort, E.R., Martens, N., van de Weerd, I., van Vliet, H.: How Architects see Non-Functional Requirements: Beware of Modifiability. In: Regnell, B., Damian, D. (eds.) REFSQ 2011. LNCS, vol. 7195, pp. 37–51. Springer, Heidelberg (2012)

Maintaining Architectural Conformance during Software Development: A Practical Approach

Claire Dimech and Dharini Balasubramaniam

School of Computer Science, University of St Andrews,
St Andrews KY16 9SX, UK
cl.dimech@gmail.com, dharini@st-andrews.ac.uk

Abstract. Software architecture provides a high-level design that serves as the basis for system implementation and communication among stakeholders. However, changes in requirements and lack of conformance checks during development can cause the implemented architecture to deviate from the intended one. Such architecture degradation can cause rapid software aging and high maintenance costs. Conformance checking to detect inconsistencies between a model and its corresponding implementation is one of the strategies used to minimise architecture degradation. Existing conformance checking tools often require formal architecture specifications, which are not usually available outwith academic settings, or manual intervention in the process, which affects their viability. This paper describes an automated approach that uses mappings between architecture models in UML and corresponding implementations in Java to check conformance. These notations have been chosen for their adoption in industry. A customisable tool called Card, which implements this approach, is also introduced and evaluated.

Keywords: conformance checking, software architecture, architecture degradation.

1 Introduction

Software Architecture [1] defines the structure of a system in terms of its components and their interactions. It is a key tool for the software industry because it improves communication between stakeholders, facilitates early design decisions, promotes transferable abstractions of a system and can be used as the basis for system implementation [2].

One of the current challenges facing software industry is architecture erosion [3], which refers to the deviation of the descriptive architecture (reflecting the implementation) from the prescriptive architecture (as defined by the software architect) [2]. Such architectural degradation may arise due to several factors, including: (i) unawareness by software developers; (ii) possibly conflicting requirements that are unforeseen in the early stages; (iii) technical difficulties that arise during implementation; and (iv) the pressure of deadlines that are not uncommon in software development.

K. Drira (Ed.): ECSA 2013, LNCS 7957, pp. 208–223, 2013.

Potential consequences of architecture erosion include failure to meet functional or quality requirements, brittle systems, high maintenance costs and ultimately rapid software aging [4] and obsolescence. Architecture erosion is a well-recognised problem and a number of approaches have been proposed to prevent, minimise or repair erosion [5], mainly based on the concept of *conformance*. However most of these approaches require a formal and rigorous specification of software architecture as well as one or more conformance tools. The former is not typically available in industrial practice except in a few specialised domains, while the latter are not necessarily integrated into a standard software development environment. They may also require a degree of manual intervention in the checking process, which limits their viability in industry.

The aim of the work presented in this paper is to develop a widely accessible and automated means to identify architecture erosion without the need for formal specifications, architecture description languages (ADLs) and stand-alone conformance checking tools. This work resulted in a tool called Card (**C**ontrolling **A**rchitectural **D**egradation), which uses the Unified Modeling Language (UML) 2.0 for software architecture representations and Java as the implementation language.

Some of the novel features of this work include:

- A set of rules defining conformance between UML 2.0 class and sequence diagrams and Java constructs,
- The concept of a master specification, which can be either the model or implementation, to cater for different software development methodologies, and
- An Eclipse plug-in, implementing conformance checking as defined by the above rules with a variety of customisation features.

The combination of a flexible model, an implementation using industrially relevant languages and the ability granted to users to select only required features is a significant contribution to the state of the art.

The paper is structured as follows. Section 2 introduces a case study that is used to illustrate relevant concepts and implementation details. The notion of architectural conformance in software development is discussed in Section 3 and the design and implementation of our tool is presented in Section 4. Section 5 contains details of the evaluation carried out while Section 6 compares the framework with some related work. Finally, we provide some conclusions and thoughts on future work in Section 7.

2   Example

In order to illustrate our approach, we introduce a simple case study using part of an application that sends requests to music servers in the form of query strings, and collects and stores the responses in appropriate data structures for further processing. The UML 2.0 package diagram representing the relevant overall architecture is shown in Fig. 1.

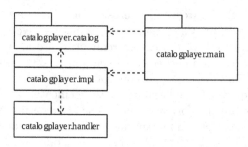

Fig. 1. High-level Package Structure of the Application

Thus, the application contains components that model the relevant logical concepts, handle responses from servers and implement the concepts.

Two architecture representations of the same system are presented: the original design as intended by the architect (Fig. 2), which serves as the master, and a possibly deviated architecture extracted from the implementation (Fig. 3 overleaf), which acts as the slave that must conform to the master specification.

The *catalog* package defines all the interfaces that are used in the application, such as *Query, Resource,* and *SearchResult. Album* and *Track* inherit from the superclass *Resource.* The *CatalogFactory* class is a factory for *Catalog* implementations.

The *impl* package consists of all the classes that implement the above interfaces. Therefore, the same relations must be maintained between classes, especially among *Album, Track* and *Resource.* The *impl* package communicates with the *handler* package, and specifically with a class called *CatalogPlayerResponseHandler. CatalogImpl* has to receive music details from external servers and the handler is used to process responses received from these services. The main class resides in the *main* package.

We will use these designs in later sections to illustrate our approach and tool.

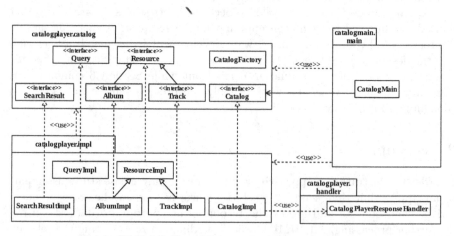

Fig. 2. UML 2.0 Class Diagram for Master Architecture

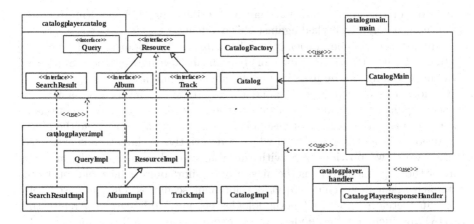

Fig. 3. UML 2.0 Class Diagram for Slave Architecture

3   Architecture Conformance for Software Development

Three main strategies are used to control architecture erosion: minimise, prevent and repair [5]. The strategy to minimise erosion, which is arguably the most useful in practice, can be implemented by several techniques including architecture design documentation, architecture analysis and architecture compliance (or conformance) monitoring. The last technique is used to establish whether an implementation conforms to its intended architecture according to some rules defined to capture the notion of conformance between the two artefacts.

3.1   Conformance Model

Fig. 4 below illustrates our vision of conformance checking in the broader context of the software development lifecycle and shows the possible evolutions of interactions between a model and its implementation.

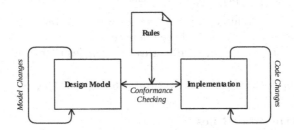

Fig. 4. Overview of Conformance between Model and Implementation

The model and the code can change independently. The *conformance checking* operation detects any incompatibilities between the two descriptions as violations of the *conformance rules*. A novel feature of our approach is that either the model or the implementation may be the initiator of change (master) and conformance may be checked against this artefact.

Conformance can be statically checked during development and when the system is off-line for maintenance, or dynamically during execution. Static and dynamic checking can be used in a complementary manner.

Conformance checking requires one artefact to act as the correct version (the master) against which another artefact (the slave) is compared. Traditionally, the prescriptive architecture or design is considered the master, while the implementation acts as the slave, from which a descriptive architecture is extracted. In this work, we provide users with the ability to choose either the architecture or the implementation as the master and tailor conformance analysis to the approach taken in specific project development scenarios. Our proposed solution can therefore extend to methodologies beyond Model-Driven Architecture (MDA) and include more modern approaches such as Agile Development.

Given two small UML diagrams of a system, a human can detect any violations by visually comparing the models. However, this is time consuming, difficult and error-prone for non-trivial systems, which may have multiple views of the architecture and complex diagrams representing them. Automated conformance checking is preferable in such cases, and requires suitable architecture representations of the master and the slave as well as a set of rules that define conformance between the two. Data structures for architecture representations are discussed in Section 4.2.

We divide conformance rules into two categories: *structural* and *interaction* rules. The former is concerned with the architecture's static structure, such as existence of certain elements and inheritance, while the latter is concerned with aspects such as the order of method invocation and communication integrity. In Card, structural rules are mainly derived from UML 2.0 class diagrams while interaction rules are derived from both class and sequence diagrams. Some of the rules were inspired by the work carried out by [6]. Examples of conformance rules used in our framework are introduced in subsections 3.2 and 3.3. A description of all 19 conformance rules currently used in Card is available from [7].

In the following examples, we assume that:

- the Prescriptive Architecture (PA) refers to the *master*,
- the Descriptive Architecture (DA) refers to the *slave*,
- P(DA) refers to the set of architectural properties extracted from the DA, and
- P(PA) refers to the set of architectural properties extracted from the PA.

3.2 Some Structural Rules

Definition 1. (Element Existence Rule). *DA conforms to PA only if every element that exists in PA, exists also in DA.*

Definition 2. (Inheritance Relationship Rule). *DA conforms to PA only if for every inheritance relationship in PA, there is a corresponding relationship in DA.*

Considering the examples in Figs. 2 and 3, it can be observed that *TrackImpl* does not inherit the class *ResourceImpl*, and therefore this rule is violated.

3.3   Some Interaction Rules

Definition 3. (Communication Integrity - Absent Link Rule). *DA conforms to PA only if every entity that communicates with another entity in PA has the same association in DA.*

In the example shown earlier, there is a communication link missing between the packages *impl* and *handler*, thus resulting in a violation of this rule.

Definition 4. (Temporal Rule). DA *conforms to* PA *only if the same sequence of method calls is maintained in both* PA *and* DA.

This rule can be expressed using UML 2.0 sequence diagrams, such as the one below:

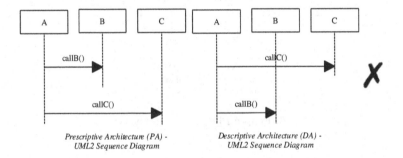

Prescriptive Architecture (PA) -   Descriptive Architecture (DA) -
UML2 Sequence Diagram   UML2 Sequence Diagram

Fig. 5. Sequence Rule Example

In the example shown above, it can be observed that in PA, method *callB* is called before method *callC*. On the other hand, in DA, *callC* is called before *callB*, and therefore, the sequence is violated.

Currently Card only checks simple interactions. Choices and iterations are part of our plans for future work.

4   Card: An Eclipse Plug-in to Support Conformance Checking

In this section, we describe the design and implementation of an Eclipse plug-in to support static conformance checking between UML and Java according to the rules described in Section 3. A release of Card and associated documentation can be found at https://code.google.com/p/card-plugin/downloads/list.

4.1   The Design of Card

The overall architecture of Card is depicted in Fig. 6 below:

The framework contains two pre-processing modules: one for UML 2.0 diagrams and the other for Java source code. The Card Engine accepts users' preferences and the output from the pre-processing phases as input, checks their conformance and displays any violations to users. In this case, typical users are likely to be *Software Developers* and *Software Architects*. The following list explains in more detail the purpose of each of these modules.

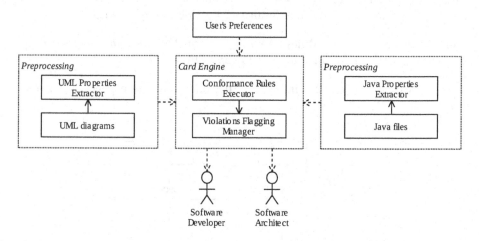

Fig. 6. Eclipse Plug-in Design Overview

- **Pre-processing.** Card searches for UML and Java files in the chosen Eclipse project and uses the pre-processors to extract architecturally relevant properties. These properties are stored in customised data structures for later conformance analysis. Existing APIs and frameworks such as the Eclipse Java Development Tools (JDT) API [8] and Eclipse Modeling Framework (EMF) [9] are used to extract relevant properties.
  - *Java Code Extraction Tool.* This tool is able to access Java projects by requesting a handle to the current instance of *IJavaProject.* This object, which is accessible through the JDT API, provides a pointer to the project's resources such as Java package fragments, classes, interfaces, methods and fields. The packages and classes of the chosen project are navigated to extract architectural properties and store them in a Map data structure (Section 4.2).
  - *UML Extraction Tool.* Card supports UML 2.0 diagrams constructed using the Papyrus[1] plug-in. Papyrus generates a standardised underlying XML format for representing UML diagrams that is recognised by the

---
[1] `www.eclipse.org/papyrus`

EMF. The XML files are then parsed into a data structure where each node represents a possible architectural property. Relevant properties are then stored in a map structure (Fig. 9).

- **User Preferences.** Users' preferences, which define the settings chosen by users through a wizard, are also among the inputs to the Card engine. Users can select (i) all or a subset of the conformance rules, (ii) the importance / severity level of these rules (HIGH, MEDIUM or LOW), (iii) whether conformance should be checked automatically on each update or on user request (iv) the master artefact and (v) whether UML files should be automatically or manually selected. Fig. 7 shows a screenshot of the wizard that provides these customisation features.

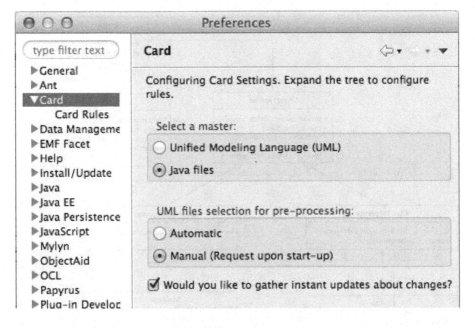

Fig. 7. Card Preferences

- **Card Engine.** This module is the core of our conformance checking framework and can be further decomposed into the following modules.
  - The *Conformance Rules Executor* executes conformance rules on the properties that were extracted from UML and Java files according to the users' preferences. Rules are implemented as Java methods which are invoked over the stored architectural properties.
  - The *Violations Manager* displays appropriate messages to the user showing details of any violations detected. Violations are displayed in the form of compilation errors. If Java is the slave, each error message contains a line number corresponding to the mismatch; otherwise the violation refers to the relevant .uml file.

4.2   Representation of Architectural Properties

Fig. 8 below shows the class diagram for the metadata structure that holds the architecturally relevant properties captured by Card. *EntityProperties* is an abstract class from which two other classes, *ClassProperties* and *Interface Properties*, inherit. They represent class and interface details. In addition to the inherited elements, *ClassProperties* contains a list of *InterfaceProperties* and an instance of itself. The former holds the list of interfaces that a class may implement, while the latter is used to refer to the class from which it may inherit. Thus a class can implement multiple interfaces, but extend only one class. On the other hand, *InterfaceProperties* can only extend a list of interfaces. This design conforms to the definition of UML [10].

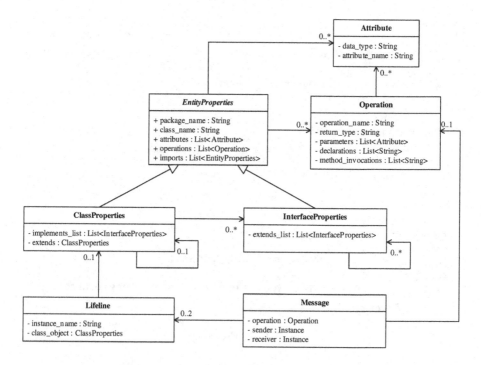

Fig. 8. Representing Architectural Properties

The *Attribute* class holds properties related to an attribute, such as attribute name and its data type, while *Operations* holds properties related to methods, such as method name, its return type and a list of *Attribute* parameters.

Properties that can be expressed in UML 2.0 sequence diagram are also fundamental to Card. These include *Lifeline* and *Message*. The Lifeline can be represented as a combination of the instance name together with the class name [11]. The class name will be a reference to the previously introduced *ClassProperties*. *Message* refers to the operation name and the interaction between two lifelines: *sender* and *receiver*.

Card currently assumes that naming conventions are maintained between UML and Java code. The following design decisions were also made regarding UML 2.0 sequence diagrams:

1. Lifeline name will have the following format: *Instance name : Class name* [11].
2. Iterations and conditions are not taken into account during conformance checking for the initial implementation.
3. Two levels of nesting will be considered.
4. Card will always choose the first object encountered in the map that matches both Lifeline and Message.
5. The application is single-threaded.

A hash map data structure, shown in Fig. 9, is used to hold properties from both UML and Java code. Rules are executed over this data structure to detect any violations between the master and the slave.

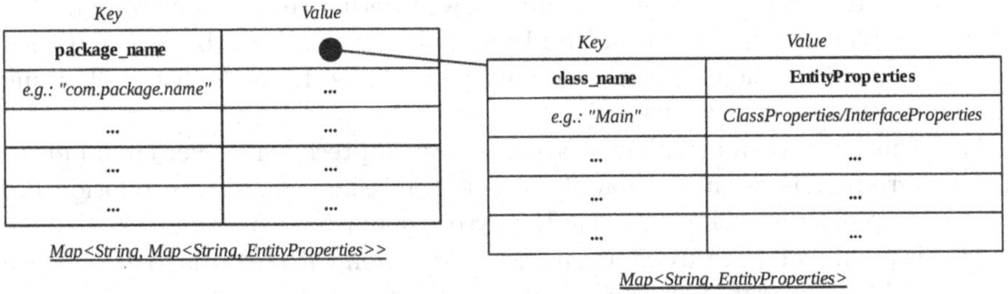

Fig. 9. Map Structure for Storing Properties

A generic map is used to store the package name as the key and a pointer to another map as the value. The package name refers to the package that the entity resides in. *Entity* refers to either a *Class* or an *Interface*. A unique package name is strongly recommended. However, Sun's[2] convention ensures that identical package names are not allowed in a single Java project [12].

The second map stores the entity name as the key and an instance of type EntityProperties as the corresponding value. The EntityProperties will hold all the properties extracted from that specific entity. As mentioned in the previous section, an EntityProperties object can either be of type ClassProperties or InterfaceProperties, depending on the type of entity.

To eliminate the second map, it was initially planned to concatenate the package name and the class name together as the key. However, due to efficiency issues involved in processing strings every time, the chosen approach was preferred.

---

[2] http://www.java.com/en

4.3   Some Highlights of Card Implementation

This section introduces some of the interesting features of Card implementation.

Extensibility and Flexibility. Card has been implemented with extensibility and flexibility as guiding principles. For instance, if new rules are required, they can be easily implemented in separate classes and registered with Card. Since rules are developed in the form of Java methods, researchers and practitioners can build their own rules and embed them in the tool. As shown before, users will also have the option of customising the plug-in as desired.

Precedence of Rules. Some of the conformance rules have to be given precedence over others because there is an implicit ordering imposed by model and language semantics. For instance, the rules concerned with inheritance should not be executed before the confirmation that the class or interface exists.

Whenever a class or interface extends or implements some other entity, the communication integrity rule should exclude these entities. This is because by the time that the system checks whether there is a violation in communication integrity, the implementation and inheritance rules will have already been executed, and therefore the user already knows whether there is a missing inheritance or implementation relationship. Hence, all those entities that are extended or implemented by the entity itself should be excluded from the list of checking communication integrity rules.

Thus inheritance and implementation are given precedence over communication integrity. It is assumed that if there is a missing inheritance relationship between two entities, then only the first error should be displayed.

At this point, software architects have no discretion with regards to precedence of rules. This is determined a priori by the tool itself.

Code Changes Listener. One of the features offered by the Card plug-in is to perform conformance analysis whenever there is a significant change in the code. This functionality can be enabled or disabled from the users' preferences. Code change listeners are built on top of existing listeners. These take the form of an event listener in the Eclipse Plug-in Framework. Whenever a listener is triggered, the rules that have been selected prior to execution are applied.

4.4   Example: Violations Detected

The violations detected by Card between the representations in Figs. 2 and 3 are shown in a partial screenshot in Fig. 10. Violations detected by Card are shown as Eclipse compilation errors. A customised marker was introduced by Card in order to cater for architecture violations. Each violation has an associated code to identify exactly which rule has been violated. For instance, *COMEXTR* refers to Communication Extra, where an extra link between two entities, which violates the architecture, has been noted. In this case, an extra communication link is detected in class *CatalogPlayerResponseHandler*. This violation can be observed in the class diagrams in Figs. 2 and 3. Another rule called *COMMISS* refers to Communication

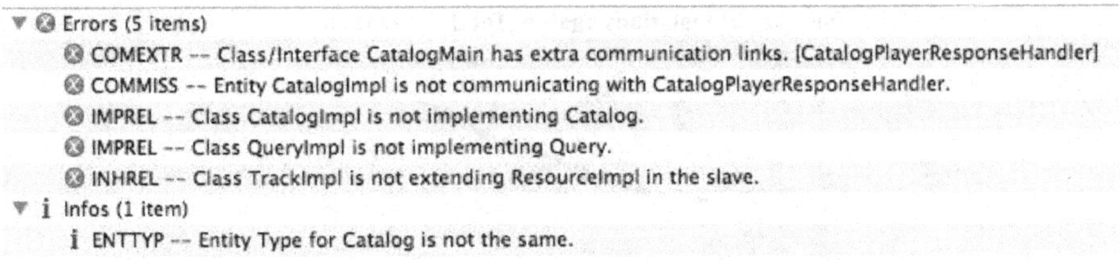

▼ ⊗ Errors (5 items)
  ⊗ COMEXTR -- Class/Interface CatalogMain has extra communication links. [CatalogPlayerResponseHandler]
  ⊗ COMMISS -- Entity CatalogImpl is not communicating with CatalogPlayerResponseHandler.
  ⊗ IMPREL -- Class CatalogImpl is not implementing Catalog.
  ⊗ IMPREL -- Class QueryImpl is not implementing Query.
  ⊗ INHREL -- Class TrackImpl is not extending ResourceImpl in the slave.
▼ i Infos (1 item)
    i ENTTYP -- Entity Type for Catalog is not the same.

Fig. 10. List of Violations Detected by Card

Missing, which indicates that a missing communication link is identified. In the example, *CatalogImpl* does not communicate with *CatalogPlayerResponseHandler* as the architecture demands. The third violation refers to a missing Implementation Relationship (*IMPREL*), where *CatalogImpl* does not implement the interface *Catalog*. The same applies to the fourth violation, but with a different class and interface. The fifth error refers to an absent Inheritance Relationship (*INHREL*), where *TrackImpl* does not inherit from class *ResourceImpl*. The last violation is for information and not an error because the severity level is set as LOW. Each rule can be customised independently, based on the users' preferences. This violation refers to the type of entity, where *Catalog* has a different entity type (interface/class) in the slave when compared to its master.

5   Evaluation

5.1   Soundness and Completeness

The plug-in was tested with Eclipse projects of different sizes, with different number of violations. We verified that the correct number of violations was detected in all cases, as defined by our rules. All the violations that existed in the slave were noted down a priori in each case. A manual comparison was carried out to confirm that the plug-in flagged up all these errors. Thus, while we can not guarantee soundness and completeness without formal proofs, extensive testing so far has not identified any false positives or missed violations.

5.2   Usability

Usability is a crucial attribute for this work. Our aim was to develop a tool that is user-friendly, flexible and offers suitable options for software developers while integrated well within the Eclipse IDE. All system features were designed and implemented with this goal. An evaluation of usability with a user study is envisaged for the future.

5.3   Performance

A project with approximately 8KLoC excluding comments is used for the initial evaluation of the performance of the tool. This project consisted of 9 packages, with a total of 42 classes and interfaces.

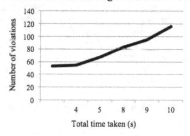

Fig. 11. Number of Violations against Total Time Taken(s) Graph

The time taken to execute this project with different number of violations was recorded. The experiment was repeated three times per execution run, having the same number and type of violations in the same project, to ensure that the results are consistent across different runs. The average value was then taken from all the repetitions. These readings were taken on a Mac OSX computer with 1.8GHz Intel Core i7 and 4GB RAM. The results are plotted in the graph shown in Fig. 11.

As might be expected, the time taken to check conformance increases with the number of violations detected. The time taken is also proportional to lines of code and complexity of the rules selected (not shown). A more extensive evaluation including scalability and impact of dependencies is planned as part of future work.

6   Related Work

Several research projects such as ArchJava [13], DiscoTect [14] and Rainbow [15] provide mechanisms and frameworks to control architectural degradation by using different approaches. ArchJava aims to bridge the gap between the architecture represented in an ADL and the implementation in Java. However, it requires users to learn and use a new language, which is likely to prove a drawback for real world applications. Both Rainbow and DiscoTect deal with runtime conformance, which is outwith the scope of this work.

MagicDraw [16] and IBM[3] Rational Rose [17] are commercial products. MagicDraw allows users to draw UML diagrams and generate code from them to different languages such as Java and C#. RationalRose provides support for model-driven development projects in order to improve the delivery of software product on the market. However, neither product provides support for detecting changes and therefore conformance violations between UML and code.

In [18], the authors present three different techniques for static architecture conformance checking: Reflexion models, Relation Conformance Rules, and Component Access Rules. Reflexion models require a human expert to manually map

---

[3] www.ibm.com

high-level components onto source code elements. This method may be tedious and inaccurate, especially for large-scale systems. Relation Conformance Rules make use of regular expressions to map component names. It focuses on the communication between components. Component Access Rules focus on public methods as the means of how a component is exposed to others.

The tool presented by [19] focuses on test cases for evaluating a UML modelling tool for standard compliance. It processes OCL statements, and by using several other intermediary tools, generates a set of test programs.

The work in [20] also aims to detect mismatches between an architecture and its implementation. It uses Common Off The Shelf products, such as Xlinkit [21], to generate a conformance checking framework. It generates an XMI description from the model and an XML representation of the abstract syntax tree from the source code, which are then used for testing conformance. However, this work lacks the flexibility and customisability of the solution presented in this paper.

The research carried out in [22] provides a method to check and measure static conformance in object-oriented systems. However, its approach requires the developer to inject and annotate Java code to refer to the ownership domain. These annotations are then extracted as architectural structures. The developer has to make a significant contribution here and the approach cannot work without manual annotations. It makes use of ACME ADL to provide a mapping between implementation and design model. This is also different from our work as we use the more accessible UML 2.0 notations.

In [23], a formal approach is used to check architectural compliance in component-based systems. An Eclipse plug-in is provided as a prototypical tool of this conceptual framework. The plug-in works by defining structures as fact-bases, and queries are defined as first order logic statements. This approach requires fundamental user involvement, and queries and structures have to be maintained manually as the project evolves, which can lead to errors. In contrast, our approach automatically identifies the structure of the system without user intervention.

The approach from [24] uses event-notifications to capture traceability between different artefacts in a system, with the advantage that it can be applicable in heterogeneous and globally distributed development environments. However, conformance checking is only applied between requirements and other software artefacts. Whenever a change is detected, a notification is sent to the event server, and messages are then sent to relevant subscribers. This approach focuses on maintaining software systems as their requirements change and evolve.

Structure101 [25] offers a family of products to extract and enforce architectures and remove code tangles. However, their work does not offer the flexibility of choosing a master and a slave between architecture and code and the graphical notation used in not a standard one.

7   Conclusions and Future Work

This paper outlines a practical approach for controlling software architecture degradation, from the conceptual framework that uses a set of rules to define architectural conformance between a model and an implementation, to a functional Eclipse plug-in. It provides a round-trip method to support conformance and evolution that can be applied to different development methodologies.

A more comprehensive evaluation and addressing some of the current limitations (such as lack of support for choice and iteration in sequence diagrams) are two of the immediate plans for further work. Relaxing the need for names to be maintained in the implementation will improve the usability of the tool. The addition of traceability features to provide a link between design and implementation may significantly reduce the impact of conformance analysis, since filtering out rules that are not applicable will improve the overall performance of the tool. The Eclipse plug-in may be extended to suggest corrections for any violations in the slave with respect to the master architecture. Further enhancements will be the addition of rules for more abstract UML 2.0 diagrams, such as Component Diagrams, and the ability to check consistency between UML diagrams as well as against Java implementations.

References

1. Perry, D.E., Wolf, A.L.: Foundations for the Study of Software Architecture. ACM SIGSOFT Software Engineering Notes 17, 40–52 (1992)
2. Taylor, R.N., Medvidovic, N., Dashofy, E.M.: Software Architecture: Foundations, Theory, and Practice, 1st edn. Wiley (2009)
3. van Gurp, J., Bosch, J.: Design erosion: problems and causes. Journal of Systems and Software 61, 105–119 (2002)
4. Parnas, D.L.: Software aging. In: Proceedings of the 16th International Conference on Software Engineering, ICSE 1994, pp. 279–287. IEEE Computer Society Press, Los Alamitos (1994)
5. de Silva, L., Balasubramaniam, D.: Controlling software architecture erosion: A survey. Journal of Systems and Software 85, 132–151 (2012)
6. Tsiolakis, A.: Consistency Analysis of UML Class and Sequence Diagrams based on Attributed Typed Graphs and their Transformation. In: ETAPS 2000 Workshop on Graph Transformation Systems, pp. 77–86 (2000)
7. Dimech, C.: CARD: Controlling Architectural Degradation in Real-life Applications. Master's thesis, University of St Andrews, Scotland, UK (2012)
8. Eclipse: Eclipse Java Development Tools (JDT) Overview, www.eclipse.org/jdt
9. Steinberg, D., Budinsky, F., Paternostro, M., Merks, E.: EMF: Eclipse Modeling Framework, 2nd edn. Addison-Wesley, Boston (2009)
10. OMG Unified Modeling Language (OMG UML), Infrastructure, V2.1.2. Technical report (2007)
11. Bell, D.: UML basics: The Sequence Diagram (2004),
   http://www.ibm.com/developerworks/rational/library/3101.html
12. Friesen, J., Friesen, G.: Java 2 by Example. By Example Series. Que (2002)
13. Aldrich, J., Chambers, C., Notkin, D.: ArchJava: Connecting Software Architecture to Implementation, pp. 187–197. ACM Press (2002)
14. Yan, H., Garlan, D., Schmerl, B., Aldrich, J., Kazman, R.: DiscoTect: A System for Discovering Architectures from Running Systems. In: Proc. Int'l Conf. Software Engineering (ICSE), Edinburgh, Scotland (2006)

15. Cheng, S.W., Huang, A.C., Garlan, D., Schmerl, B., Steenkiste, P.: Rainbow: Architecture-based self-adaptation with reusable infrastructure. IEEE Computer 37, 46–54 (2004)
16. Magicdraw open api user guide, http://www.nomagic.com/files/manuals/ MagicDraw%20OpenAPI%20UserGuide.pdf
17. IBM: Rational rose, http://www-01.ibm.com/software/awdtools/developer/rose
18. Knodel, J., Popescu, D.: A Comparison of Static Architecture Compliance Checking Approaches. In: Proceedings of the Sixth Working IEEE/IFIP Conference on Software Architecture, WICSA 2007, pp. 12–21. IEEE Computer Society, Washington, DC (2007)
19. Bunyakiati, P., Finkelstein, A.: The Compliance Testing of Software Tools with Respect to the UML Standards Specification - The ArgoUML Case Study. In: Dranidis, D., Masticola, S.P., Strooper, P.A. (eds.) AST, pp. 138–143. IEEE (2009)
20. Boerman, R.: On Software Architecture Conformance in the Context of Evolving Systems. Master's thesis, Department of Software Engineering, The Faculty of Electrical Engineering, Mathematics and Computer Science Delft University of Technology (2004)
21. Nentwich, C., Capra, L., Emmerich, W., Finkelstein, A.: xlinkit: A Consistency Checking and Smart Link Generation Service. ACM Trans. Internet Technol. 2, 151–185 (2002)
22. Abi-Antoun, M., Aldrich, J.: Checking and Measuring the Architectural Structural Conformance of Object-Oriented Systems. Technical Report CMU-ISRI-07-119, Carnegie Mellon University, Pittsburgh, PA 15213 (2007)
23. Herold, S.: Checking architectural compliance in component-based systems. In: Proceedings of the 2010 ACM Symposium on Applied Computing, SAC 2010, pp. 2244–2251. ACM, New York (2010)
24. Cleland-Huang, J., Chang, C.K., Christensen, M.: Event-Based Traceability for Managing Evolutionary Change. IEEE Trans. Softw. Eng. 29, 796–810 (2003)
25. Chedgey, C., Hickey, P., O'Reilly, P.: Structure 101, http://www.headwaysoftware.com/index.php

Supporting Consistency between Architectural Design Decisions and Component Models through Reusable Architectural Knowledge Transformations

Ioanna Lytra, Huy Tran, and Uwe Zdun

Faculty of Computer Science
Software Architecture Group
University of Vienna, Austria
{ioanna.lytra,huy.tran,uwe.zdun}@univie.ac.at

Abstract. In recent years, the software architecture community has proposed to use architectural design decisions (ADDs) for capturing the design rationale and the architectural knowledge (AK). As software systems evolve both ADDs and architectural designs need to be documented and maintained. This is a tedious and time-consuming task because of the lack of systematic and automated support for bridging between ADDs and designs. As a result, decisions and designs become inconsistent over time. We propose to alleviate this problem by introducing an AK transformation language supporting reusable AK transformations from pattern-based ADDs to component-and-connector models. In addition, we devise reusable consistency checking rules for verifying the consistency between decisions and designs. Through the use of model-driven transformations, as well as reusable, pattern-based decision models, we ensure the reusability of our approach. We apply our approach in an industrial case study and show that it offers high reusability, is largely automated and scalable, and can deal with the complexity of large numbers of recurring decisions.

1   Introduction

Today, software architectures are usually described in various architectural views [7,3]. The component-and-connector (C&C) model of an architecture is a view that is often considered to contain the most significant architectural information [3]. Although C&C models offer a natural representation of software systems to software architects and designers, they fail to model the design rationale of the architecture and support the sharing of this knowledge among stakeholders. In recent years, software architecture is no longer solely regarded as the solution structure, but also as the set of architectural design decisions (ADDs) that led to that structure [8]. The actual solution structure, or architectural design, is merely a reflection of those design decisions. Architectural design views [11] document the design rationale of the architecture and contribute to the gathering of Architectural Knowledge (AK) and its sharing among different stakeholders. For organizing and documenting AK, various tools and methods that use AK templates [23], ontologies [13] or meta-models [25] have been proposed in the literature. To minimize the effort of documenting architectural decisions, approaches for reusable architectural decision modeling [25] and using design patterns as a basis for documenting reusable ADDs (as [6]) have been proposed.

K. Drira (Ed.): ECSA 2013, LNCS 7957, pp. 224–239, 2013.

Unfortunately, in practice, the ADDs frequently are neither maintained nor synchronized over time with the corresponding C&C diagrams (or other design views) [11]. Thus, ADDs and design views drift apart as software systems evolve. This leads to a potential loss of architectural knowledge, a phenomenon which is known as architectural knowledge vaporization [8,6]. The main reason for the resulting inconsistency and lack of traceability between ADDs and design views is that there is no formal mapping between them. As a consequence, there is no automation for the translation between ADDs and design views, and in practice keeping them synchronized is a tedious manual task that depends highly on the architects' experience and interpretation. Making matters worse, the actual documentation of ADDs is also a tedious and time-consuming task, especially for similar ADDs that occur repeatedly throughout a design.

Our previous work [16] has partially solved this problem by addressing the bridging between the ADDs and designs. It introduced a formal mapping model between different ADD types, on the one hand, and elements and properties of C&C models, on the other hand. Based on this formal mapping model, preliminary component models and OCL-like constraints for consistency checking can be derived. Yet, so far this mapping model had to be manually created and modified. Therefore, the approach is not efficient for handling large numbers of ADDs and/or complex design models. Moreover, in reality there are often several recurring ADDs which can be applied in different contexts and for different elements or properties of the ADDs and designs. As a result, maximizing the reusability of such recurring decisions would significantly enhance the productivity in creating and maintaining the formal mappings between the decisions and the designs. This has not been addressed in our previous work [16] as the formal mapping and the derived constraints can not directly be reused because they are bound to specific elements or properties of the ADDs and designs.

We present in this paper a novel approach aiming to address the aforementioned challenges. In particular, our approach introduces an architectural knowledge transformation language that supports the specification of primitive and complex actions whose enactment leads to automatic updating of design models (i.e., C&C diagrams) based on changes in the ADD view. The transformation languages can be used to formulate the expected outcomes of a certain decision ranging from individual actions, such as creating new elements, grouping a number of elements, and deleting or updating existing elements in the C&C diagrams, to composite actions (e.g., for capturing reusable pattern-based ADDs) that might contain many primitive and/or other composite actions. These actions are designed to support the reusability of specifications in our AK transformation language, as existing actions can be efficiently reused and adapted for different designs where similar architectural decisions are taken. Each action also triggers the instantiation of corresponding constraint checking rule(s).

After the instantiation of the actions for concrete ADDs, we exploit template-based generation rules and model-driven techniques for automatically enacting the actions and generating consistency checking rules automatically. The linking of reusable ADDs to reusable actions and consistency rules (templates) offers higher reusability and automation and results in less complexity and modeling effort for the software architect. The reusability is achieved here (1) through the automatic derivation of parts of the C&C diagrams and consistency checking rules using model-driven templates and (2) by reusing common abstractions shared between common design patterns (see [24]).

To demonstrate our approach, we have implemented a prototype based on two existing tools from our previous work: ADvISE[1] – a tool for assisting architectural decision
making for reusable ADDs, and VbMF[2] – a tool for describing architectural view models and performing model-driven code generation. Our approach presented in this paper
will act as a bridge between ADvISE and VbMF. The prototypical implementation of
our approach has been evaluated in scenarios extracted from an industrial case study to
show that it is feasible and scalable for large numbers of ADDs.

The remainder of the paper is structured as follows. First, in Section 2 we explain
the background for ADvISE and VbMF. In Section 3 we give an overview of our approach and describe the details about the reusable AK transformations and consistency
checking rules. The application of our approach in the industrial case study and the
evaluation of the reusability, complexity and modeling effort are presented in Section 4.
We compare to related work in Section 5 and summarize key contributions in Section 6.

2   Background

In this section we briefly present ADvISE and VbMF, the two tools we integrate for
demonstrating our approach.

2.1   Architectural Design Decision Support Framework

The Architectural Design Decision Support Framework (ADvISE) is an Eclipse-based
tool that supports the modeling of reusable ADDs using Questions, Options and Criteria (QOC) [17] and the decision making under uncertainty. In particular, it assists
the architectural decision making process by introducing for each design issue a set of
questions along with potential options, answers and pattern-based solutions, as well as
dependencies and constraints between them.

The advantage of the reusable ADD models is that they need to be created only once
for a recurring design situation. In similar application contexts, corresponding questionnaires can be automatically instantiated and used for making concrete decisions.
Based on the outcomes of the questionnaires answered by software architects through
the decision making process, ADvISE can automatically generate architectural decision
documentations. Our approach in this paper additionally introduces an architectural
knowledge transformation framework (see Section 3) that supports the specification of
reusable actions and the association of these actions with the elements of the aforementioned ADD models for automatically transforming ADDs into the underlying design
models and generating constraints for consistency checking between them.

2.2   View-Based Modeling Framework

The View-based Modeling Framework (VbMF) is also an Eclipse-based tool that implements a model-driven, architectural view model. That is, it leverages the notion of view

---

[1] http://swa.univie.ac.at/Architectural_Design_Decision_Support_
Framework_(ADvISE)

[2] http://swa.univie.ac.at/View-based_Modeling_Framework

models for describing various concerns of the software systems at different abstraction levels and model-driven development techniques for generating code and configurations from those view models [22]. Among other views, VbMF provides a high-level service component view model –similar to a typical C&C model such as UML component model– for representing essential architectural design elements such as components, ports, connectors, and properties that are independent from the underlying platforms and technologies. Technology- and platform-specific information will be described separately in the low-level view models that refine and enrich the high-level counterparts.

In this paper, we mainly use the high-level service component view model of VbMF (or in short form, the VbMF C&C view) for describing the architectural design of a software system. The advantage of using VbMF is that we can leverage the existing view model integration and transformation mechanisms of VbMF which are based on Eclipse technologies and therefore can be integrated well with ADvISE.

3   Reusable AK Transformations and Consistency Checking Rules

To illustrate the "big picture" of our approach we depict in Fig. 1 an overview of the tools and artifacts along with their interconnections. The artifacts that are automatically derived using model-driven techniques are indicated with dark-gray color.

The *ADD Model Editor* in ADvISE is a tool that is used to create the reusable ADD models (i.e., the artifact *Reusable ADDs* in the figure). It is created only once per application domain. From it, ADvISE can automatically generate *Questionnaires* for making *Actual ADDs*. They are made, possibly multiple times if multiple ADDs are derived from the same reusable ADD model, using the *Questionnaire Editor* tool. For using and manipulating *C&C Diagrams* VbMF provides the *C&C View Editor*. Our approach supports generating the first instance of the C&C Diagrams automatically from the ADD model using *Transformation Actions*. It can further execute automatic *Transformation Actions* on existing view models. In VbMF *C&C Diagrams* can be manually manipulated. To ensure that changes in the C&C models do not violate the ADDs, *Consistency Checking Rules* are generated from the *Transformation Actions*, which are automatically enacted on the *C&C Diagrams* upon changes.

To achieve this in a reusable fashion, the *Reusable ADDs* are formally mapped to *AK Transformation Language Templates*, which are edited with the *AK Transformation Language Editor*. This way, for *Actual ADDs* we can instantiate the corresponding *Transformation Actions* and *Consistency Checking Rules*. Using model-driven techniques they are automatically enacted on the corresponding VbMF *C&C Diagram*.

The binding of templates is realized using Apache Velocity Engine[3]. The parsing and execution of the transformation actions are implemented using Xtend[4], a statically-typed language built on top of Java.

The AK transformation language and its enactment engine play an important role in our approach for enabling the automated and reusable transformation of ADDs into the design models. In the subsequent parts of this section, we explain the language in detail and its illustrative usage in realistic development circumstances.

---

[3] http://velocity.apache.org
[4] http://www.eclipse.org/xtend

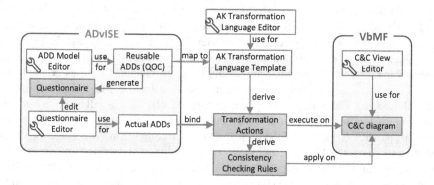

Fig. 1. Approach Overview

3.1 Architectural Knowledge Transformation Language

Essentially, the goal of the AK transformation language is to express the actions that create or update the underlying architectural models (e.g., C&C models) according to the intentions of the software architects reflected by the design decisions. Unlike general model transformation languages (as ATL) our domain-specific language (DSL) is intended to provide simple and comprehensible architecture-specific transformation actions, as well as the structures for grouping, extending and inheriting these actions. Listing 1 presents a formal definition of the AK transformation language in terms of a EBNF like syntax developed using the Xtext DSL framework[5]. Please note that the square brackets in Xtext enable cross-references to other models, in our case, to the elements of the VbMF C&C view. We also use Xtext to generate an Eclipse-based textual editor that can support several useful features such as syntax highlighting, content assist and auto-completion, validation and quick fixes, automated external cross-references resolutions, and so on.

The core of the language consists of basic actions that can be used to create or alter individual elements of the architectural models, for instance, creating a new component, deleting an existing connector, or updating a port. In addition, we introduce special structures, such as Group, Loop, and Compound to support the compositions and extensions of the predefined actions. A Group (defined by the grammar rules in lines 41–42) indicates the grouping of a finite set of components that are sub-components of a particular component. For efficiently handling the iteration and application of similar actions to a finite set of elements of the design model, a Loop (see line 43–44) can be used. A Compound (see line 45–46) represents a structure that embraces multiple actions and even other Compounds. Through an extension, a Compound can inherit the definition of existing Compounds and extend the inherited behavior with additional actions. The semantics of a Compound is an atomic (i.e., all-or-nothing) sequential execution of its inherited compounds and constituting actions.

---

[5] http://www.eclipse.org/Xtext/

```
1  Action:
2    Add | Delete | Update | Group | Loop;
3  Add:
4    AddComponent | AddConnector | AddPort | AddProperty | AddStereotype | AddPrimitive;
5  AddComponent:
6    "add component" name=STRING;
7  AddConnector:
8    "add connector" name=STRING "from" source=[component::Port|FQN] "to" target=[component::
         Port|FQN];
9  AddPort:
10   "add port" name=STRING "kind=" kind=PortKind "to" component=[component::Component|FQN];
11 AddStereotype:
12   "add stereotype" "<<" text=STRING ">>" "to" target=[core::Element|FQN];
13 AddProperty:
14   "add property" name=STRING "type=" type=STRING "value=" value=STRING "to" target=[core::
         Element|FQN];
15 AddPrimitive:
16   "add compound" primitive=[Compound|FQN] name=STRING "("(args+=ID|LIST)+")";
17 Delete:
18   DeleteComponent | DeleteConnector | DeletePort | DeleteProperty | DeleteStereotype;
19 DeleteComponent:
20   "delete component" component=[component::Component|FQN];
21 DeleteConnector:
22   "delete connector" conn=[component::Connector|FQN];
23 DeletePort:
24   "delete port" port=[component::Port|FQN];
25 DeleteProperty:
26   "delete property" property=[component::Property|FQN];
27 DeleteStereotype:
28   "delete stereotype" stereotype=[component::Stereotype|FQN];
29 Update:
30   UpdateComponent | UpdateConnector | UpdatePort | UpdateProperty | UpdateStereotype;
31 UpdateComponent:
32   "update component" component=[component::Component|FQN] "name=" newName=STRING;
33 UpdateConnector:
34   "update connector" conn=[component::Connector|FQN] "name=" newName=STRING;
35 UpdatePort:
36   "update port" port=[component::Port|FQN] ("name=" newName=STRING)? ("kind=" newKind=
         PortKind)?;
37 UpdateProperty:
38   "update property" prop=[component::Property|FQN] ("name=" newName=STRING)? ("type=" newType
         =STRING "value=" newValue=STRING)?;
39 UpdateStereotype:
40   "update stereotype" stereotype=[component::Stereotype|FQN] "text=" newText=STRING;
41 Group:
42   "group" component=[component::Component|FQN] "container" container=[component::Component|
         FQN];
43 Loop:
44   "for" "(" element=ID ":" (params+=FQN)+")" (actions+=Action)+ "end";
45 Compound:
46   "compound" name=ID ("extends" (parent+=[Compound|FQN])*)? spec=Spec;
47 Spec: "("(args+=ID)+")" "{" (actions+=Action)* "}";
48 Import: "import" importedNamespace=FqnWildcard;

50 enum PortKind: provided="PROVIDED"|required="REQUIRED";
51 FQN returns ecore::EString: ID ("." ID)*;
52 FqnWildcard: FQN ".*"?;
53 LIST: ID","ID(","ID)*;
```

Listing 1. Grammar of the AK transformation language

The core actions of the AK transformation language presented in Listing 1 mainly aim at expressing particular changes to individual elements of the corresponding VbMF C&C view. Using the ADvISE tooling, we can associate the options and answers of a certain ADD model with one or many transformation actions in template form, in order to enable the automation of creating and/or updating of the architectural C&C models. Once the generated questionnaires from the ADD model are answered resulting in concrete decisions, the related actions will be bound to concrete elements of the underlying architectural models.

For instance, suppose in a simple case that a selection of an option in an ADD model leads to the definition of the type of a component which will be indicated by introducing a stereotype. In the example in Listing 2 a new stereotype with the value of the template variability `TypeOfComponent` as its name is created and attached to the component denoted by the template variability `A`.

```
add stereotype <<"${TypeOfComponent}">> to ${A}
```

Listing 2. Example of a parametrized transformation action for adding a stereotype

The binding of the template variables during decision making will result in an executable transformation action, such as the one in the example in Listing 3.

```
add stereotype <<"Remote Proxy">> to example.ServiceProxy
```

Listing 3. Example of a transformation action for adding a stereotype

The execution of the transformation action updates the corresponding C&C diagram as it can be seen in Fig. 2.

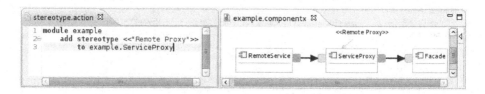

Fig. 2. AK Transformation Language Editor and C&C View Editor

3.2 Recurring Pattern Primitives as Reusable AK Transformations

In the course of decision making, software architects often leverage several recurring architectural elements and structures such as proxies, adapters, gateways, layers, and so forth. The idea of proposing primitives as fundamental elements for describing such recurring design patterns and architectural styles has been investigated by various studies. For example, Zdun and Avgeriou described architectural patterns through a number of recurring architectural primitives in the component-and-connector view using UML profiles [24]. Mehta and Medvidovic developed a framework for defining abstract primitives shared by all architectural styles for composing their elements [18]. In this section, we will describe how to define recurring architectural primitives for modeling certain patterns or styles as action sets, as an example of how to realize reusable AK transformations with our language.

In particular, the expressiveness of our AK transformation language and the support for compositions and extensions through the composite structures mentioned above enable us to define such *recurring architectural primitives* in a reusable and extensible way. In our approach, we specify such recurring primitives using parameterized *action sets* that are based on compounds and can be inherited and extended further. Each action set represents one primitive abstraction that can be used to realize a number of patterns that use this particular primitive as part of their solution (as defined in [24]). The action sets are used via their name and appropriate parameters. In the action set specifications we use variable access in the form ${p-name} to refer to the parameter *p-name*. When actual ADDs are made, the compound parameters are replaced, which also leads to the variable binding of their primitive actions.

In Listing 4, we present the *indirection* compound. Indirection happens when one or more related "proxy" components receive a message on behalf of one or more "target" components, forward the message to these "targets" and receive results from these "targets" also through the "proxy" components [24]. Proxies and adapters are examples of indirection. The parameters cv, A, and B refer to the target component view, the target component, and the client respectively. The variable n will be bounded to the name of the compound "instance" (e.g., Proxy, Adapter, etc.).

```
compound indirection (cv A B) {
  add component "${A}${n}"
  add port "${A}${n}_I1" kind=PROVIDED to ${cv}.${A}${n}
  add port "${A}${n}_I2" kind=REQUIRED to ${cv}.${A}${n}
  add port "${A}_I" kind=REQUIRED to ${cv}.${A}
  add port "${B}_I" kind=PROVIDED to ${cv}.${B}
  add connector "${A}_I_${A}${n}_I1" from ${cv}.${A}.${A}_I to ${cv}.${A}${n}.${A}${n}_I1
  add connector "${A}${n}_I2_${B}_I" from ${cv}.${A}${n}.${A}${n}_I2 to ${cv}.${B}.${B}_I
  add stereotype <<"${n}">> to ${cv}.${A}${n}
}
```

Listing 4. Indirection compound action specification

An example of using the indirection compound is presented in Listing 5.

```
add compound indirection "Proxy" (example Facade Service)
```

Listing 5. Usage example of indirection compound action

This compound action will create a proxy for invoking the component "Service" from the component "Facade". This will happen by replacing the variables n, cv, A and B with "Proxy", the C&C view name "example" and the components "Service" and "Facade", respectively. The transformation of the C&C view includes the creation of a component, two connectors, the corresponding ports and a stereotype. The execution of the compound transformation action triggers the execution of its containing actions. In our example, the enactment of Listing 5 will trigger the execution of the primitive actions in Listing 6.

```
add component "ServiceProxy"
add port "ServiceProxy_I1" kind=PROVIDED to example.ServiceProxy
add port "ServiceProxy_I2" kind=REQUIRED to example.ServiceProxy
...
```

Listing 6. Binding of primitive actions of indirection compound action

A compound can extend other compounds, and therefore, inherits the corresponding action sets of these compounds, thus increasing reusability of the AK transformations.

3.3 Generation of Consistency Checking Rules

Consistency checking is an important mechanism to ensure the integrity of the design models under consideration. For this, we developed a set of predefined parameterized constraint templates that are related to the basic actions of the AK transformation language shown in Listing 1. As a result, the instantiation and binding of the parameterized constraint templates for each action are performed automatically at the same time and in the same manner as the actions, without requiring any additional effort from the developers and architects. In addition, further constraint templates can be easily formulated in an OCL-like syntax supported by the Eclipse Xpand model validation library [6] and connected to the relevant actions. Again, constraint templates need to be defined only once at the model-level and can then be reused for concrete instantiations of the ADD model. For instance, the following parameterized transformation action of Listing 7 will create a component with name A.

```
add component "${A}"
```

Listing 7. Example of a parametrized transformation action to add a component

The resulting C&C model can be checked for its consistency against the related decision ADD by the predefined constraint template of Listing 8, which checks that the added component is present in the C&C model.

```
context component::ComponentView ERROR "ADD ${ADD}: Component ${A} does not exist":
  element.typeSelect(component::Component).exists(c|c.name == "${A}");
```

Listing 8. Example of a parametrized consistency checking rule

We have designed and developed respective constraint templates for each AK transformation language element and each architectural primitive defined above. Similar to the AK transformation language, the ${...} syntax in the constraint rule templates allows to access a variable that is instantiated and bound to particular values of the related actions and models. The outcomes of the instantiation and binding of the parameterized constraint templates are concrete constraints that can be enacted by our model-driven tools. The combination of transformation actions with automatically generated constraints that check that the transformation's semantics are not violated in the C&C diagram, enables us to allow developers and architects to manually change the C&C model. If a manual change violates an architectural decision that has triggered transformation actions, the corresponding constraint checking will signal an error.

4 Case Study and Evaluation

4.1 Case Study

We illustrate the applicability of our approach in the context of an industrial case study on service-based platform integration in the area of industry automation. In our case study, three heterogeneous platforms, a Warehouse Management System—WMS (storage of goods or storage bins into racks via conveyor systems), a Yard Management

---

[6] http://www.eclipse.org/modeling/m2t/?project=xpand

System—YMS (scheduling, coordination, loading and unloading of trucks), and an Enterprise Resource Planning System—ERP (overall commissioning and handling of goods on an abstract level beyond real storage places) need to provide domain-specific services in an integrated manner. For this, an intermediate integration layer will provide services to operator applications developed on top of it. The integration layer must handle various integration aspects including interface adaptation between the platforms, integration of service-based and non-service-based solutions, routing, enriching, aggregation, splitting, etc. of messages and events, synchronization and concurrency issues, adaptation, and monitoring of events.

Table 1. An excerpt of the service-based platform integration ADD model and its corresponding AK transformation actions

ADD Options	AK Transformation Actions

Type of Integrating Component
- None
- Same Interface
- Different Interface
	`add port "${PS}_p1" kind=PROVIDED to ${cv}.${PS}`
	`add port "${IC}_p1" kind=REQUIRED to ${cv}.${IC}`
	
	`#if(${TypeOfComponent} == "None")`
	`    add connector "${IC}_${PS}" from ${cv}.${IC}.${IC}_p1 to ${cv}.${PS`
	`        }.${PS}_p1`
	`    add stereotype <<"Direct call">> to ${cv}.${IC}_${PS}`
	`#elseif(${TypeOfComponent} == "Same Interface")`
	`    add compound indirection "Proxy" (${PS} ${IC})`
	`#elseif(${TypeOfComponent} == "Different Interface")`
	`    add compound indirection "Adapter" (${PS} ${IC})`
	`#end`

Type of Proxy - Local - Remote	`add stereotype <<"${TypeOfProxy} Proxy">> to ${cv}.${PS}Proxy`
Type of Adapter - Local - Remote	`add stereotype <<"${TypeOfAdapter} Adapter">> to ${cv}.${PS}Adapter`

Heterogeneous systems
- No
- Yes
	`#if(${HeterogeneousSystems} == "Yes")`
	`    add compound integrationAdapter "Integration Adapter" (${PS} ${IC})`
	`#end`

Interchangeability
- No
- Yes
	`add property "${PS}Adapter_Interchangeability" type="`
	`    Interchangeability" value="${Interchangeability}" to ${cv}.${PS}`
	`    Adapter`

Adaptation Parameters (String)	`add property "${PS}Adapter_params" type="Parameters" value="${` `    Parameters}" to ${cv}.${PS}Adapter`

To handle these integration aspects in the platform integration domain, in our previous work, we have introduced an ADD model for resolving architectural design issues related to integration and adaptation, interface design, communication style, and communication flow [15]. We present in Table 1 an excerpt of the ADD model of the platform integration scenario consisting of questions and different alternative options (or answers). This would be normally modeled using ADvISE. Note that the dependencies and constraints between the questions, decisions and options are not present in Table 1 for simplicity reasons. This example assists the decision making on the type of integrating component between a platform service PS of one of the three platforms in our case study (WMS, YMS and ERP) and a component of the integration layer IC (cv refers to the target C&C view). Along with the ADD model excerpt we present its associated primitive actions and compound actions based on pattern primitives in pattern form, as defined in Section 3. It consists of 6 questions, uses 8 primitive actions and 2 compound actions (`integrationAdapter` once and `indirection` twice) and is related to 3 patterns: Proxy (local or remote), Adapter (local or remote) and Integration Adapter. We defined in total 6 basic compounds (indirection, shield, grouping, callback, transformer and router) that are used to describe 21 design patterns in our decision model [15]. The definitions of the compounds are omitted because of the space limitation.

The integration of the Velocity template language with our AK transformation language allows us not only to use placeholders (${...}) but also statements (if, foreach, etc.) which begin with the # character and are parsed by the template engine, but ignored by the AK transformation language editor.

To give an example of the binding of the transformation actions, suppose that the architect opts for a remote proxy as an integrating component between the YMS service *TruckMgmnt* and the integration layer component *OperatorFacade*. The actual ADDs will be reflected in the corresponding C&C view by executing the transformation actions of Listing 9.

```
add port "TruckMgmnt_p1" kind=PROVIDED to example.TruckMgmnt
add port "OperatorFacade_p1" kind=REQUIRED to example.OperatorFacade
add compound indirection "Proxy" (TruckMgmnt OperatorFacade)
add stereotype <<"Remote Proxy">> to example.TruckMgmntProxy
```

Listing 9. Transformation actions example from case study

4.2   Generalizability

Our approach is generic to a large extent. The transformation actions and constraint templates constitute reusable AK assets that can be customized and re-used in various reusable decisions. These templates can be applied for any existing ADD model or ADD documentation because the essential concepts and elements of these models and those in the ADvISE ADD model are almost equivalent. In most cases, the binding between the template variables and the elements of ADD models might need human intervention. That is, in order to properly associate a reusable parameterized action template containing some input parameters with a certain ADD, we need to align the parameters with the corresponding values in the ADD.

The C&C view that is created or updated by enacting the transformation actions contains all the information captured by the corresponding ADDs derived from the ADD meta-model. Nevertheless, the AK transformation language is generic and can be applied to similar C&C models or architectural views on different scenarios as well. Please note that the VbMF C&C view contains very similar elements as other typical C&C views. Therefore, our approach is also applicable for most of existing component models such as UML component diagram with marginal effort for adapting the actions to accommodate new elements. This effort will be added to the effort for editing the AK transformation language templates and constraint templates.

4.3   Reusability

Regardless of the initial efforts for creating the reusable AK transformations, architects will benefit from reduced total efforts in case of recurring ADDs and AK transformations. In our approach, reusability is achieved at various levels. First of all, the AK transformations are edited only once for each ADD model and are afterwards instantiated when actual ADDs are made. This kind of reuse is possible by taking advantage of the benefits of model-driven techniques and template engines. In addition, the use of compound actions that can be extended and inherited increases reusability. Finally, the use of the AK transformation language hides the complex model actions which are embedded in its enactment engine.

4.4   Modeling Effort and Scalability

We present in this section a quantitative evaluation on the modeling effort of using our approach. In particular, we document the number of actions (primitive and compound), primitive actions and model actions that are needed per number of recurring ADDs and for four different ADDs that have been already documented in Section 4.1. For the definition of the action templates 4, 4, 6 and 5 actions had to be edited manually for the reusable decisions Direct Calls, Proxy, Adapter and Integration Adapter respectively. With the use of compound actions we reduced the number of required actions in the last three cases, where 7, 6 and 12 actions were contained in the compound actions *add compound indirection* and *add compound integrationAdapter (extends indirection)*. The number of the actions that are directly applied on the C&C model are 13, 35, 32 and 42 respectively for the four ADDs, which means that without the use of the Action Transformation Language the modeling effort would increase significantly.

This benefit is dramatically increased in case ADDs can be reused. For example, in our case study, the integration of the WMS system currently requires some 35 proxies and adapters, meaning that very similar decisions need to be taken over and over again and, as a consequence, they need to be modeled in C&C diagrams over and over again. Table 2 shows this dramatic increase for the aforementioned decisions, in case of a specific decision outcome being selected 1, 5, 10, 20, 50, and 100 times. Clearly, primitive actions already scale much better in terms of modeling effort than manual change actions in models; reusable actions with compounds offer an additional level of support. In particular, in the cases we study, the modeling effort would increase up to 240% if the compound actions would be replaced by primitive actions and up to 740% if instead of the AK Transformation Language single model actions would be used.

We estimated the scalability of our approach by measuring the performance for binding the action templates variables and transforming the actions into C&C views. We opted to conduct our measurements on a normal desktop machine, as our approach will usually need to run on the local machines of the software architects and designers. The machine for testing had an Intel Quad Core i5 2.53GHz with 8GB of memory running Java VM 1.6 and Eclipse Indigo on Debian Linux. Each measurement is performed 100 times and the resulting time, in milliseconds, is calculated on average. We report only the average, as the deviations calculated were small. Table 3 presents the time needed for the binding of the action template variables and for the transformation of the actions into the C&C views per number of actions, respectively.

Table 2. Modeling Effort for Reusable ADDs

		Reusability of ADDs						Average increase of modeling effort
		1	5	10	20	50	100	
Direct Calls	Actions (with compounds)	4	20	40	80	200	400	-
	Primitive Actions	4	20	40	80	200	400	0%
	Model Actions	13	65	130	260	650	1300	225%
Proxy	Actions (with compounds)	4	20	40	80	200	400	-
	Primitive Actions	11	55	110	220	550	1100	175%
	Model Actions	35	175	350	700	1750	3500	775%
Adapter	Actions (with compounds)	6	30	60	120	300	600	-
	Primitive Actions	13	65	130	260	650	1300	117%
	Model Actions	32	160	320	640	1600	3200	433%
Integration Adapter	Actions (with compounds)	5	25	50	100	250	500	-
	Primitive Actions	17	85	170	340	850	1700	240%
	Model Actions	42	210	420	840	2100	4200	740%

Table 3. Performance Measurement

Primitive Actions	5	10	20	50	100	200	500	1000	5000
Binding Time (in msec)	2	3	4	5	6	8	13	21	77
Transformation Time (in msec)	96	102	111	125	147	210	331	671	2748

We can see that the binding and the transformation time increase in a linear manner with respect to the number of actions and remain considerably low even for a big number of actions. In particular, the binding and transformation for 100 actions are accomplished in roughly 6 and 150 ms, for 1000 actions in approximately 20 and 670 ms, and for 5000 actions in about 80 and 2700 ms, respectively. Thus, our approach scales well enough for being integrated in the typical development flow of developers and architects on a typical work station, even for ADDs that create or update large C&C models.

5   Related Work

The documentation of the design rationale, as well as the gathering of Architectural Knowledge (AK) have promoted ADDs to first class citizens in software architecture. For this, many approaches based on decision-capturing templates [23], on ontologies for architectural decisions [13] and decision meta-models [25] have been proposed in the literature. Also, a considerable amount of tools have been developed to ease capturing, managing and sharing of ADDs [21]. These approaches mainly target reasoning on software architectures, capturing and reusing of AK and do not tackle the maintenance and consistency of ADDs with architectural views.

The generation of architectural design views from specifications or other architectural views has been studied extensively in the literature. Pérez-Martínez and Sierra-Alonso [20] use model-to-model transformations to generate component-and-connector architecture models from classes and packages analysis models by using OCL mapping rules. In a different approach [14] variability elements from the problem space are connected to architecture elements in the solution space using a Variability Modeling Language (VML) that provides primitives for referencing and invoking decisions which result in fine-grained or coarse-grained compositions of variable and common core architectural elements. This approach supports rather the composition than the generation of software architectures as it requires that all architectural elements are predefined. Consistency checking between the different models or the documentation of design rationale are not considered in any of the approaches.

A considerable amount of research has been conducted in relating requirements with software architectures. For example, Kaindl et al. [9] suggest that with the use of model-driven approaches we can map requirements to architectural design and Grunbacher et al. [5] introduce the mapping from requirements to intermediate models that are closer to software architecture. A different approach by van Lamsweerde et al. [12] derives software architectures from the formal specifications of a system goal model (KAOS) using transformation rules and refines the architectures incrementally using patterns that satisfy quality of service goals like availability and fault tolerance. In the aforementioned approaches, although the transformations are done automatically, the mapping has to be done manually and is not reusable. Another disadvantage compared to our approach is that the rationale that led from the requirements to the architectural views is not documented. In our work we assume that architectural decision making follows the collection of requirements and precedes the design of software architectures and set our focus on the linking of reusable ADDs to C&C models.

Our approach is not the first one to relate ADDs to software architectures. The problem of inconsistencies between ADDs and software architectures that cause design knowledge vaporization has been discussed before by Choi et al. [2]. For this, they propose to make ADDs more explicit by introducing a meta-model for relating decisions with architectural elements and a decision constraint graph for representing decision relationships and studying decision change impact analysis. Compared to our approach, this approach demands that most of the work is done manually: decision making, architectural design and change propagation during software evolution. STREAM-ADD [4] also relates architectural decisions documented in decision templates with requirements and architectural models generated from these requirements. This approach focusses rather on the integration of systematic documentation of structural and technological decisions with requirements and architectural models than on the consistency checking between decisions and designs.

Traceability links between decision models and architecture models have been used extensively in the literature. Capilla et al. [1] introduce fine-grained traceability links between design decisions and other software artifacts. Knemann and Zimmermann [10] establish links between design decisions and design models in model-based software development in order to support architectural knowledge documentation and reuse, as well as to check consistency. Mirakhorli and Cleland-Huang [19] introduce the TTIM approach that provides a reusable infrastructure for tracing architecture tactics to designs used to trace from tactic-related design decisions to architecture components in which a decision is realized. Also, most of the approaches require significant amount of manual work for the establishment of the traceability links, which can be in our approach automated for recurring ADDs from the mapping of the ADDs to transformation actions and to constraints at template level. Apart from that, none of these approaches target the reusability of these links between ADDs and architectural views, nor do they tackle the complexity of big numbers of reusable ADDs.

6   Conclusions

We present a novel approach that provides reusable and extensible transformation actions and consistency checking rules for (semi-)automatically mapping of the design rationale and knowledge reflected by ADDs onto architectural component models. In particular, our approach introduces an AK transformation language for specifying reusable actions that need to be enacted to automatically create or update the underlying architectural models with respect to particular ADDs. The transformation language provides basic actions for updating individual model elements, as well as expressive composite structures for describing actions applied in a set of elements such as compounds and loops. This enables us, for instance, to define recurring architectural primitives, e.g., to realize reusable specifications for architectural patterns or styles in the transformation language. In addition, our approach supports the specification and automatic generation of consistency checking rules to make sure no manual changes of the component models violate the ADDs. The application of our approach in an industrial case study shows that our approach is applicable in a realistic scenario. Our evaluation illustrates the benefits of our approach in terms of potential modeling effort reduction, as well as its scalability in a typical work environment, even for large model sizes. As discussed, the use of a template engine and model-driven techniques, as well as the support for inheritance and extension in the transformation language significantly enhance its reusability and extensibility. In our future work, we plan to study repair actions for resolving inconsistencies between reusable ADDs and component views, as well as the possibility for bidirectional transformations, i.e., also from component views onto decisions.

Acknowledgment. This work was partially supported by the European Union FP7 project INDENICA (http://www.indenica.eu), grant no. 257483.

References

1. Capilla, R., Zimmermann, O., Zdun, U., Avgeriou, P., Küster, J.M.: An Enhanced Architectural Knowledge Metamodel Linking Architectural Design Decisions to other Artifacts in the Software Engineering Lifecycle. In: Crnkovic, I., Gruhn, V., Book, M. (eds.) ECSA 2011. LNCS, vol. 6903, pp. 303–318. Springer, Heidelberg (2011)
2. Choi, Y., Choi, H., Oh, M.: An architectural design decision-centric approach to architectural evolution. In: 11th Int'l Conf. on Advanced Communication Technology (ICACT), Gangwon-Do, South Korea, pp. 417–422. IEEE Press (2009)
3. Clements, P., Garlan, D., Bass, L., Stafford, J., Nord, R., Ivers, J., Little, R.: Documenting Software Architectures: Views and Beyond. Pearson Education (2002)
4. Dermeval, D., Pimentel, J., Silva, C.T.L.L., Castro, J., Santos, E., Guedes, G., Lucena, M., Finkelstein, A.: STREAM-ADD - Supporting the Documentation of Architectural Design Decisions in an Architecture Derivation Process. In: 36th Annual IEEE Computer Software and Applications Conf. (COMPSAC), Izmir, Turkey, pp. 602–611. IEEE Comp. Soc. (2012)
5. Grunbacher, P., Egyed, A., Medvidovic, N.: Reconciling Software Requirements and Architectures with Intermediate Models. Softw. Syst. Model. 3(3), 235–253 (2003)
6. Harrison, N.B., Avgeriou, P., Zdun, U.: Using Patterns to Capture Architectural Decisions. IEEE Softw. 24(4), 38–45 (2007)
7. ISO: ISO/IEC CD1 42010, Systems and software engineering — Architecture description (2010)

8. Jansen, A., Bosch, J.: Software Architecture as a Set of Architectural Design Decisions. In: 5th Working IEEE/IFIP Conf. on Software Architecture (WICSA), Pittsburgh, PA, USA, pp. 109–120. IEEE Comp. Soc. (2005)
9. Kaindl, H., Falb, J.: Can We Transform Requirements into Architecture? In: 3rd Int'l Conf. on Software Engineering Advances (ICSEA), Sliema, Malta, pp. 91–96. IEEE (2008)
10. Könemann, P., Zimmermann, O.: Linking Design Decisions to Design Models in Model-Based Software Development. In: Babar, M.A., Gorton, I. (eds.) ECSA 2010. LNCS, vol. 6285, pp. 246–262. Springer, Heidelberg (2010)
11. Kruchten, P., Capilla, R., Dueñas, J.C.: The Decision View's Role in Software Architecture Practice. IEEE Softw. 26(2), 36–42 (2009)
12. van Lamsweerde, A.: From System Goals to Software Architecture. In: Bernardo, M., Inverardi, P. (eds.) SFM 2003. LNCS, vol. 2804, pp. 25–43. Springer, Heidelberg (2003)
13. Lee, L., Kruchten, P.: Capturing Software Architectural Design Decisions. In: 2007 Canadian Conf. on Electrical and Computer Engineering, pp. 686–689. IEEE Comp. Soc. (2007)
14. Loughran, N., Sánchez, P., Garcia, A., Fuentes, L.: Language Support for Managing Variability in Architectural Models. In: Pautasso, C., Tanter, É. (eds.) SC 2008. LNCS, vol. 4954, pp. 36–51. Springer, Heidelberg (2008)
15. Lytra, I., Sobernig, S., Zdun, U.: Architectural Decision Making for Service-Based Platform Integration: A Qualitative Multi-Method Study. In: Joint 10th Working IEEE/IFIP Conf. on Software Architecture & 6th European Conf. on Software Architecture (WICSA/ECSA), IEEE Comp. Soc., Helsinki (2012)
16. Lytra, I., Tran, H., Zdun, U.: Constraint-based consistency checking between design decisions and component models for supporting software architecture evolution. In: 16th European Conf. on Software Maintenance and Reengineering (CSMR), Szeged, Hungary, pp. 287–296. Springer (2012)
17. MacLean, A., Young, R., Bellotti, V., Moran, T.: Questions, Options, and Criteria: Elements of Design Space Analysis. Human-Computer Interaction 6, 201–2502 (1991)
18. Mehta, N.R., Medvidovic, N.: Composing architectural styles from architectural primitives. In: 9th European Software Engineering Conf. held jointly with 11th ACM SIGSOFT Int'l Symposium on Foundations of Software Engineering (ESEC/FSE-11), Helsinki, Finland, pp. 347–350. ACM (2003)
19. Mirakhorli, M., Cleland-Huang, J.: Using tactic traceability information models to reduce the risk of architectural degradation during system maintenance. In: 27th IEEE Int'l Conf. on Software Maintenance (ICSM), Williamsburg, VA, USA, pp. 123–132. IEEE (2011)
20. Pérez-Martínez, J.E., Sierra-Alonso, A.: From Analysis Model to Software Architecture: A PIM2PIM Mapping. In: Rensink, A., Warmer, J. (eds.) ECMDA-FA 2006. LNCS, vol. 4066, pp. 25–39. Springer, Heidelberg (2006)
21. Shahin, M., Liang, P., Khayyambashi, M.R.: Architectural design decision: Existing models and tools. In: Joint Working IEEE/IFIP Conf. on Software Architecture and European Conf. on Software Architecture (WICSA/ECSA), Cambridge, UK, pp. 293–296. IEEE (2009)
22. Tran, H., Zdun, U., Dustdar, S.: View-based and Model-driven Approach for Reducing the Development Complexity in Process-Driven SOA. In: Int'l Conf. Business Process and Services Computing (BPSC). LNI, pp. 105–124 (2007)
23. Tyree, J., Akerman, A.: Architecture Decisions: Demystifying Architecture. IEEE Softw. 22(2), 19–27 (2005)
24. Zdun, U., Avgeriou, P.: Modeling Architectural Patterns Using Architectural Primitives. In: 20th ACM Conf. on Object-Oriented Programming, Systems, Languages & Applications (OOPSLA), pp. 133–146. ACM Press (2005)
25. Zimmermann, O., Gschwind, T., Küster, J., Leymann, F., Schuster, N.: Reusable architectural decision models for enterprise application development. In: Overhage, S., Ren, X.-M., Reussner, R., Stafford, J.A. (eds.) QoSA 2007. LNCS, vol. 4880, pp. 15–32. Springer, Heidelberg (2008)

PANDArch: A Pluggable Automated Non-intrusive Dynamic Architecture Conformance Checker

Lakshitha de Silva and Dharini Balasubramaniam

School of Computer Science, University of St Andrews, St Andrews, KY16 9SX, UK
lakshitha.desilva@acm.org, dharini@st-andrews.ac.uk

Abstract. The software architecture of a system is often used to guide and constrain its implementation. While the code structure of an initial implementation is likely to conform to its intended architecture, its dynamic properties cannot be fully checked until deployment. Routine maintenance and changing requirements can also lead to a deployed system deviating from this architecture over time. Both static and dynamic checks are thus required to ensure that an implementation conforms to its prescriptive architecture throughout its lifespan. However, runtime conformance checking strategies typically alter the implementation of an application, increasing its size and affecting its performance and maintainability. In this paper, we describe the design of a novel dynamic conformance-checking framework that is pluggable and non-intrusive, thereby limiting any overheads to those periods when checking is activated. An implementation of this framework with Java as the target language and its early evaluation are also presented.

1 Introduction

A key benefit of software architectures [9] is that they establish the basis for system implementation. The essential structure, interactions and quality attributes captured at the architectural level can guide the development of the system [4].

Architecture-driven development methodologies can ensure that a software system conforms to its prescribed static architecture at the outset. However, verifying the compliance of dynamic features of an implementation is not always possible until the system is deployed in its target operational environment. In addition, routine maintenance as well as changes to requirements and operating conditions can cause the behaviour of a deployed system to deviate from its intended architecture. Such erosion of the architecture [9] can lead to vital properties being violated and the software becoming unfit for use [14]. Both static and dynamic conformance checks are therefore required to ensure that an implementation and its architecture remain consistent with one another.

Dynamic architectural features include runtime instantiations, reflective method invocations, dynamic linking, online updates and patches, and quality of service measures. Detecting runtime violations requires system execution to be monitored and relevant runtime data be extracted, abstracted and checked against architectural constraints.

Most existing work in dynamic architectural conformance checking involves incorporating extra functionality, such as aspect weaving, or source code annotations of architectural properties in the target system. In both cases an external monitoring system reconstructs a runtime view of the architecture using data gathered from the added code

K. Drira (Ed.): ECSA 2013, LNCS 7957, pp. 240–248, 2013.

or annotations. The extracted architecture is then used for checking conformance against a prescriptive architecture using other tools [13]. Such conformance checking techniques are tightly coupled with the software product and cannot be invoked only when required. This limitation can lead to permanent degradation of application performance, inflexibility in conformance checking and poor maintainability [13].

This paper introduces PANDArch, a framework for checking conformance between software architectures and implementations that aims to solve these problems. The framework is designed to be automated, customisable, non-intrusive and pluggable, thus minimising overheads on applications. We outline its design, implementation and some early evaluation using architectures specified in the Grasp [12] architecture description language (ADL) and implementations in Java. The key contribution of this work is making dynamic architecture conformance checking a viable option for developers.

The paper is organised as follows. Section 2 outlines the concept of architectural conformance while Section 3 describes design principles that guided the framework. Key implementation details are discussed in Section 4 and preliminary evaluation results using an open source application are presented in Section 5. Section 6 describes related work and the paper concludes with thoughts on future work in Section 7.

2   Architecture Conformance Checking

An implementation that satisfies the constraints specified in its prescribed architecture is said to conform to it. Conformance can relate to a number of architectural properties relating to structure, interactions and quality of service (QoS) requirements. Our framework aims to check all these properties captured in the form of conformance rules.

2.1   Static and Dynamic Checking

An architecture specification may contain multiple views associated with static (such as code or development) or dynamic (execution) aspects of the system. As explained in Section 1, both static and dynamic checks are required to ensure full conformance.

Static checks are done while a system is being built or when taken offline for maintenance. They may relate to code structures and aspects of communication integrity.

Dynamic checks are carried out while the system executes and thus require access to runtime state and operations which are validated against architectural constraints. Such checks may relate to structures, communication integrity, component instances and quality of service thresholds at runtime. As method-level granularity is often required for dynamic checking, a key challenge is capturing relevant and useful data from system execution while still keeping any performance impact to a minimum.

2.2   Mapping between Architecture and Implementation

An architecture may be used to derive multiple system implementations. It exists at a higher level of abstraction and hence a single architectural feature can be implemented using a combination of programming constructs. Many implementation details are not significant at the architectural level. Therefore, a mapping between architectural and implementation abstractions is required to perform conformance checking. We categorise mechanisms for specifying such mappings as follows:

- **Naming Conventions from Architectural to Programming Constructs.** For example, a component in the architecture is implemented by a class of the same name. Although such a mapping primarily provides structural information, it may facilitate checking conformance of behavioural and QoS properties as well. This technique can be further extended by supplementing architectural elements with annotations having rich information about corresponding implementation constructs. Conversely, annotations in source code could identify relevant architectural entities. An annotation for a class, for example, can identify the component implemented by that class. Source code annotations, however, could be easily lost due to programmer activity.

- **Combining Architecture and Implementation in a Single Artefact, as in ArchJava [1] or ArchWare [7].** Conformance checks are minimised or not required in such systems since architecture and implementation are combined in one specification. However, current approaches either require a permanent runtime platform or that the application be implemented in a language that is not widely adopted in industry.

- **External (Outwith both Architecture and Implementation) Specification of the Mapping.** While this mechanism does constrain architecture and implementation representations, it does require a separate artefact having explicit mapping of all architecturally significant features. The DiscoTect [11] technique uses this approach.

PANDArch adopts the first strategy for dynamic conformance checking. This decision avoids a complex mapping scheme that could hinder adoption, while still allowing the dynamic checks noted earlier to be carried out. It also makes the framework more readily adaptable to both existing modelling notations and programming languages.

3   Design Principles

As motivated in Section 1, the following principles guided the design of the framework.

- **Pluggable.** Target application can execute with or without the monitoring framework; when the framework is unplugged, the binaries have no instrumentation or other code,
- **Automated.** Generation of conformance rules and their checking are automated,
- **Non-intrusive.** The source code of the target application is not changed,
- **Performance-centric.** Performance impact on target application is minimised as far as possible and limited to the period when the framework is plugged in, and
- **Extensible.** The framework can accommodate modifications to conformance rules.

We hypothesise that these principles lead to a more viable compliance checking framework that aligns well with industry practices. The conceptual process for checking conformance using the proposed framework is illustrated in Figure 1 below.

An architecture specification, containing required mapping annotations, drives both system development and the conformance process. Architectural constraints and mapping information are extracted from the specification after compilation, and used by

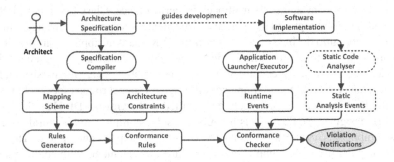

Fig. 1. Proposed conceptual process for checking architectural conformance

the rules generator to create a set of conformance rules. The mapping scheme is customised to the specific technology or language used for the target system. For instance, if the system is implemented in Java, then the mapping scheme is specific to Java and object-orientation. Rules are specified as Java objects exposing a specific interface.

The conformance checker takes the set of conformance rules and validates them against runtime events while the program executes. It may produce a series of violation notifications where appropriate. This is a continuous process while the framework is plugged in and the application is executing. If required, execution data is cached by the framework until there is sufficient information to validate an architectural rule. The same process is applicable to events generated through static analysis. Although currently not implemented, the design can accommodate a static analyser using an adaptor to transform code inspection notifications to PANDArch events.

4 Implementation

The architecture of the conformance checking framework reflects the design principles listed in section 3. The layered architecture of the framework is shown in Figure 2.

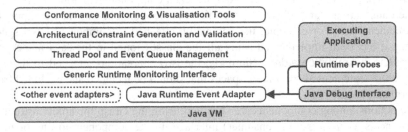

Fig. 2. Layered logical architecture of the conformance checking framework

PANDArch is implemented in Java and can currently check conformance of applications executed in the Java Virtual Machine (JVM). However, it is extensible to handle other event sources. Initially the JDI platform alone was used to capture events emitted by the JVM. However, due to their impact on performance, Class-Load and Method-Entry events are now captured using a Java instrumentation agent [8]. The agent injects optimised probes into the byte code whenever the JVM loads an application class. These probes are both additive and stateless and therefore do not alter application behaviour. Byte code streams are modified only in-memory, hence changes are not persistent. Raw data from probes are sent to the framework through an asynchronous socket channel.

Our implementation uses architectures specified in the Grasp ADL [12], though the framework design is not tied to this notation. Besides common architectural concepts such as components, connectors and layers, Grasp also supports annotations. These are name-value pairs useful for supplementing architectural elements with additional data without altering semantics. In our case, annotations carry crucial mapping information linking architectural entities to their implementation, as explained further in Section 5.

5 Evaluation

The initial evaluation focuses on two aspects: the ability of PANDArch to detect conformance violations and its impact on the performance of target applications. We chose version 2.4.2 of Apache Jackrabbit [2], a Java content repository application, for the initial evaluation of the framework primarily because it includes some architecture documentation. As a server application, Jackrabbit is also suitable for testing performance impact. However, the published runtime architecture is neither complete nor up to date, particularly with respect to interactions among architectural elements [3]. In order to generate useful and sufficient conformance rules, the source code was manually examined to discover interactions among a few key components. Filtering capabilities of PANDArch were configured to monitor only these components at runtime. For these parts, conformance is guaranteed since the architecture reflects the implementation. However, where appropriate conformance was deliberately broken to test the effectiveness of the framework. The extracted architecture is shown in Figure 3.

The Grasp specification for the extracted portion of the architecture is shown in Listing 1. The whole architecture is contained within an architecture block while the runtime view is described within the system block. Components are described using the component keyword and in this example, each component declaration has an associated annotation that begins with @confomn. These annotations map components to implementation. For example, the annotation attached to component Data specifies that it has been implemented using all the classes found in the Java namespace org.apache.jackrabbit.core.data. Similarly, the two annotations attached to the root architecture statement identify namespaces that should be included and excluded from conformance monitoring.

Interactions among components are specified using the Grasp the link construct. A link connects a *requires* (i.e. consumer) interface in one component to one or more *provides* interfaces in other components. However, in real-world software component interactions are not always through interfaces, as exemplified in Jackrabbit. Grasp overcomes this by equipping every component with an intrinsic *out* interface to model outgoing, non-interface method calls to other components. This is evinced in Listing 1.

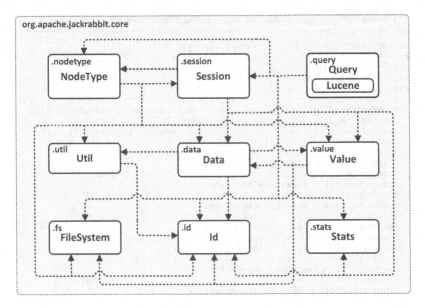

Fig. 3. Extracted architecture of Jackrabbit showing interactions among a few key components

5.1 Detecting Architecture Violations

The ability of the framework to detect architecture violations was evaluated using the above Grasp specification. Namespace filters were set to ignore components and interactions not included in this specification. Initial runtime tests were carried out using a modified version of the SecondHop program distributed with Jackrabbit. This program signs in to the content repository, performs a few content operations and signs out. As expected, the framework did not report any violations in the first instance as all components and their interactions were compliant with the architecture. The architecture and the implementation were then changed to cause mismatches. Particular attention was given to violations that could be detected only at runtime. For example, the AddNode-Operation class in the Session component was modified to instantiate a class in the Util component and invoke one of its methods using Java reflection. This interaction is not specified in the architecture and therefore should not be allowed. In addition, this reflective method invocation cannot be easily detected, if at all, through static analysis. As in all other cases, the framework correctly identified this violation when the test program was executed.

5.2 Performance Impact

The SecondHop program was also used to evaluate the performance of PANDArch. The program executes for ten iterations during a single run, and makes four such runs for each test case. The results of these tests are shown in Table 1. A significant performance gain is achieved by using instrumentation probes instead of JDI. Although

Listing 1. Grasp specification of modules and interactions shown in Figure 3

```
@confmon(include=["org.apache.jackrabbit.core"])
@confmon(exclude=["org.apache.jackrabbit.core.query.lucene"])
architecture Jackrabbit {
    template NamespaceComponent() {}
    system Core {
        // Components
        @confmon(ns=["org.apache.jackrabbit.core.nodetype"], classes=["*"])
        component NodeType = NamespaceComponent();
        @confmon(ns=["org.apache.jackrabbit.core.session"], classes=["*"])
        component Session = NamespaceComponent();
        @confmon(ns=["org.apache.jackrabbit.core.query"], classes=["*"])
        component Query = NamespaceComponent();
        @confmon(ns=["org.apache.jackrabbit.core.util"], classes=["*"])
        component Util = NamespaceComponent();
        @confmon(ns=["org.apache.jackrabbit.core.data"], classes=["*"])
        component Data = NamespaceComponent();
        @confmon(ns=["org.apache.jackrabbit.core.value"], classes=["*"])
        component Value = NamespaceComponent();
        @confmon(ns=["org.apache.jackrabbit.core.fs"], classes=["*"])
        component FileSystem = NamespaceComponent();
        @confmon(ns=["org.apache.jackrabbit.core.id"], classes=["*"])
        component Id = NamespaceComponent();
        @confmon(ns=["org.apache.jackrabbit.core.stats"], classes=["*"])
        component Stats = NamespaceComponent();
        // Interactions
        link NodeType.out to Session, Util, Data, Value, FileSystem, Id;
        link Session.out  to NodeType, Data, Value, Stats, Id;
        link Query.out    to NodeType, Session, FileSystem, Id, Stats;
        link Util.out     to Id, Util, Id, Value;
        link Value.out    to Data, FileSystem, Id;
    }
}
```

our test application still runs almost 31% slower with probes, this may be an acceptable compromise given that the framework can be easily unplugged when conformance testing is not required.

The framework allows users to choose between JDI or probes for the purpose of fine tuning conformance checks. In comparison to probes, the JDI mode offers a more thorough conformance validation at the cost of reduced performance. The choice between the two may be dependent on a number of factors including whether dynamic conformance checking takes place as part of system testing prior to deployment or while the system is in operation, and how often such checks are carried out.

We also verified that PANDArch generates conformance rules automatically, does not affect the source code, and can be unplugged without recompiling the target.

6   Related Work

DiscoTect [11] uses runtime events, state information and rules for known architectural styles to discover the architecture of an executing Java program. It uses a mapping language to bridge the abstraction gap between architecture and implementation and conformance is checked manually. In contrast, PANDArch automatically validates constraints extracted from an architecture, irrespective of style, against the implementation.

A later work by Ganesan et al. [6] adapts DiscoTect by replacing its mapping language with Coloured Petri nets to link architecture to implementation. This technique

Table 1. A comparison of performance impact between JDI and instrumention probes. Tests were executed in a system with 2.26 GHz Core 2 Duo processors and 8GB of memory.

Run	Framework unplugged (μs)	Framework using probes (μs)	Framework using JDI (μs)
1	107,762	139,091	472,472
2	107,254	137,622	486,169
3	101,573	135,551	449,602
4	104,677	139,057	468,763
Average	105,317	137,830 (+30.9%)	469,251 (+345.6%)

is pluggable, non-intrusive and some aspects of the discovered architecture can be verified automatically. However, its mappings are also distinct from the architecture specification and stylistic architectural properties must be manually pre-configured in the checker. PANDArch uses a single architecture specification with in-built mappings, from which constraints used by the conformance checker are automatically generated.

Popescu and Medvidovic [10] propose a semi-automatic approach for checking dynamic compliance between an event-based system and its architecture. This approach injects probes and recorders into components, extracts and filters runtime data on events and compares it to a prescriptive sequence of events. It focuses on communications in event-based systems and requires some human interpretation to decide conformance.

The SAVE tool [5] uses runtime events as well as source code to extract architectural views, though runtime compliance checking is not possible.

7 Conclusions and Future Work

We have introduced a dynamic architecture conformance checking framework that is pluggable, automated, non-intrusive, and minimises overhead on target applications. An implementation of the framework for Grasp and Java is currently being evaluated.

This work opens up many avenues for further research. Extensive evaluation using different types of applications under different loads is required to determine viability and effectiveness of the framework. Although the core design of the framework does not preclude them, the current implementation does not support distributed applications or static conformance checking. We intend to incorporate these functionalities to improve applicability. Furthermore, a challenge faced by any dynamic program monitoring tool is ensuring sufficient execution coverage. We plan to address this issue by employing static analysis to preconfigure the runtime checker, so that runtime architectural violations can be meaningfully interpreted with relation to the amount of code covered during execution.

Acknowledgment. This work is supported through a PhD studentship awarded by Scottish Informatics and Computer Science Alliance (SICSA) and University of St Andrews.

References

1. Aldrich, J., Chambers, C., Notkin, D.: ArchJava: Connecting software architecture to implementation. In: Proceedings of the 24th International Conference on Software Engineering, pp. 187–197. ACM (2002)
2. Apache Software Foundation: Apache Jackrabbit (2010), http://jackrabbit.apache.org/ (accessed April 2013)
3. Apache Software Foundation: Jackrabbit Architecture (2010), http://jackrabbit.apache.org/jackrabbit-architecture.html (accessed April 2013)
4. Bass, L., Clements, P., Kazman, R.: Software Architecture in Practice, 2nd edn. Addison-Wesley (2003)
5. Duszynski, S., Knodel, J., Lindvall, M.: SAVE: Software architecture visualization and evaluation. In: Proceedings of the 13th European Conference on Software Maintenance and Reengineering, pp. 323–324. IEEE (2009)
6. Ganesan, D., Keuler, T., Nishimura, Y.: Architecture compliance checking at run-time. Information and Software Technology 51(11), 1586–1600 (2009)
7. Morrison, R., Kirby, G., Balasubramaniam, D., Mickan, K., Oquendo, F., Cimpan, S., Warboys, B., Snowdon, B., Greenwood, R.M.: Support for evolving software architectures in the ArchWare ADL. In: Proceedings of the 4th Working IEEE/IFIP Conference on Software Architecture, pp. 69–78. IEEE (2004)
8. Oracle: Package java.lang.instrument (2013), http://docs.oracle.com/javase/7/docs/api/java/lang/instrument/package-summary.html (accessed April 2013)
9. Perry, D.E., Wolf, A.L.: Foundations for the study of software architecture. ACM SIGSOFT Software Engineering Notes 17(4), 40–52 (1992)
10. Popescu, D., Medvidovic, N.: Ensuring architectural conformance in message–based systems. In: Proceedings of the Workshop on Architecting Dependable Systems (2008)
11. Schmerl, B., Garlan, D., Yan, H.: Dynamically discovering architectures with DiscoTect. In: Proceedings of the 13th ACM International Symposium on Foundations Software Engineering, pp. 103–106. ACM (2005)
12. de Silva, L., Balasubramaniam, D.: A model for specifying rationale using an architecture description language. In: Crnkovic, I., Gruhn, V., Book, M. (eds.) ECSA 2011. LNCS, vol. 6903, pp. 319–327. Springer, Heidelberg (2011)
13. de Silva, L., Balasubramaniam, D.: Controlling software architecture erosion: A survey. Journal of Systems and Software 85(1), 132–151 (2012)
14. van Gurp, J., Bosch, J.: Design erosion: problems and causes. Journal of Systems and Software 61(2), 105–119 (2002)

Claims and Evidence for Architecture-Based Self-adaptation: A Systematic Literature Review

Danny Weyns and Tanvir Ahmad

Department of Computer Science
Linnaeus University, Vaxjo, Sweden
danny.weyns@lnu.se, ta222aw@gmail.com

Abstract. Engineering the upcoming generation of software systems and guaranteeing the required qualities is complex due to the inherent uncertainties at design time, such as new user needs and changing availability of resources. Architecture-based self-adaptation is a promising approach to tackle these challenges. In this approach, a system maintains a model of itself and adapts itself to realize particular quality objectives using a feedback loop. Despite a vast body of work, no systematic study has been performed on the claims associated with architecture-based self-adaptation and the evidence that exists for these claims. As such insight is important for researchers and engineers, we performed a systematic literature review covering 20 leading software engineering conferences and journals in the field, resulting in 121 studies used for data collection. The review shows that self-adaptation is primarily used to improve performance, reliability, and flexibility. The tradeoffs implied by self-adaptation have not received much attention, and evidence is mainly obtained from simple examples. From the study, we derive a number of recommendations for future research in architecture-based self-adaptive systems.

1 Introduction

Engineering the upcoming generation of software systems and guaranteeing the required qualities (performance, robustness, etc.) pose severe challenges due to the inherent uncertainty resulting from incomplete knowledge at design time. Examples of uncertainties are new user needs, subsystems that come and go at will, dynamically changing availability of resources, and faults that are difficult to predict. These challenges have motivated the need for self-adaptive software systems. Self-adaptation endows a system with the capability to adapt itself to internal changes and dynamics in the environment in order to achieve particular quality goals in the face of uncertainty.

Over the past fifteen years, researchers have developed a vast body of work on engineering self-adaptive systems. Two prominent loosely connected approaches to realize self-adaptation are architecture-based self-adaptation and control-based self-adaptation. Architecture-based self-adaptation [1–3] emphasizes software components for feedback loops, runtime models and mechanisms, and the interaction with the managed system. Control-based self-adaptation [4, 5] applies principles from control theory to design and analyze feedback control loops for computing systems. Our focus in this paper is on architecture-based self-adaptation.

K. Drira (Ed.): ECSA 2013, LNCS 7957, pp. 249–265, 2013.

Despite more than a decade of research on self-adaptation, it is not clear how the research results have actually contributed to improvements of engineering complex software systems. Recent efforts resulting from two Dagstuhl seminars summarize achievements in software engineering for self-adaptive systems and outline challenges for future research [6, 7]. But, to the best of our knowledge, no systematic study has been performed on the claims associated with self-adaptation and the evidence that exists for these claims. However, such an insight is crucial for researchers and engineers.

Recently, two related surveys have been conducted. Patikirikorala et al. [8] surveyed engineering approaches for control-based self-adaptation. The authors investigated control methodologies in self-adaptive systems and identified a set of design patterns. However, this survey did not investigate the evidence of self-adaptive systems. Moreover, the survey covered only 9 venues tailored to control-based approaches. In a previous effort [9], we performed a pilot study in which we investigated claimed benefits and supporting evidence for self-adaptation from studies published by the SEAMS community (http://www.self-adaptive.org/) between 2006 and 2012. Most of these studies focus on architecture-based self-adaptation. While this pilot provided useful insights for the SEAMS community, the survey was limited in scope and time and as such did not provide conclusive insights for the field as a whole.

The goal of the research presented in this paper is to perform a comprehensive study, aiming to identify:

1. The focus of research on architecture-based self-adaptation,
2. The claimed benefits of architecture-based self-adaptation,
3. The evidence that is provided for these claims.

To that end, we have performed a systematic literature review. In this review we searched 20 main software engineering venues and journals in the period 2000-2012, resulting in 121 primary studies for data collection. All material of the systematic literature review is available at the survey website.[1]

Paper Overview. Section 2 provides a short introduction of architecture-based self-adaptation. In Section 3, we describe the method we used in our research. In Section 4 we present and analyze the data extracted from the primary studies to answer the research questions. Section 5 discusses limitations of our study. Finally, we derive conclusions from the review and highlight a number of recommendations for future research in architecture-based self-adaptation in Section 6.

2 A Brief Introduction to Architecture-Based Self-adaptation

Figure 1 shows the primary elements of a self-adaptive system situated in an environment. We use the general terms *managed* subsystem and *managing* subsystem to denote the constituent parts of a self-adaptive software system [2, 3, 10].

The environment refers to the part of the external world with which the self-adaptive system interacts and in which the effects of the system will be observed and evaluated. The distinction between the environment and the self-adaptive system is made

---

[1] http://homepage.lnu.se/staff/daweaa/SLR/CESAS/CE-SAS.htm

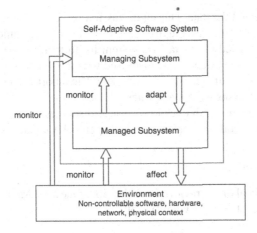

Fig. 1. Constituent parts of a self-adaptive software system

based on the extent of control. The managed subsystem comprises the application logic that provides the system's domain functionality. The managing subsystem manages the managed subsystem. The managing subsystem comprises the adaptation logic that deals with one or more concerns. To realize its goals, the managing subsystem monitors the environment and the managed subsystem and adapts the latter when necessary. Other layers can be added to the system where higher-level managing subsystems manage underlying subsystems, which can be managing subsystems themselves. One common approach to describe the functions of managing subsystems is by means of a Monitor-Analyze-Plan-Execute-Knowledge loop [2] (MAPE-K loop). The MAPE elements map to the basic functions of a feedback loop, while the K component maps to runtime models maintained by the managing system to support the MAPE functions [10].

It is important to note that the managed and managing subsystems can be deployed centralized or distributed, and both subsystems can be explicitly separated or they can be (partially) interwoven. Furthermore, the managing system can consist of one or more feedback loops, and the MAPE functions can be mapped to distinct components, or they can be integrated in one or more components.

3   Research Method

Our study uses a systematic literature review [11], which is a well-defined method to identify, evaluation and interpreting all relevant studies regarding a particular research question or topic of interest. A systematic literature review comprises three main phases: planning, executing, and reporting. In the planning phase, the protocol for the review is defined. This protocol describes the procedure that will be followed to conduct the review. In the execution phase, studies are selected, data is extracted, and the results are analyzed. In the reporting phase, the study results are documented.

Three researchers were involved in the systematic literature review. The team defined the protocol. To minimize bias, each primary study was assigned to two researchers that independently collected the data. During discussion sessions with the three reviewers, the collected data was compared and in case of differences, conflicts were resolved. The data was then entered in a data base system for further processing. Data analysis was performed by two researchers and discussed with the third researcher. Finally, two researchers produced the final report of the review. The report was checked by the third researcher and adjustments were made where needed.

We now discuss the research questions, searched sources, search strategy, inclusion and exclusion criteria, collected data items, and approach for data analysis.

3.1 Research Questions

We formulated the goal of the review using the Goal-Question-Metric (GQM) perspectives (purpose, issue, object, viewpoint) [12]:

Purpose: Analyze and characterize
Issue: the claims and evidence
Object: for architecture-based self-adaptive software systems
Viewpoint: from a researcher's viewpoint.

This overall goal can be translated to three concrete research questions:

RQ1: What is the focus of research in architecture-based self-adaptation?
RQ2: What are the claims made for self-adaptation and what are the tradeoffs implied by self-adaptation?
RQ3: How much evidence is available for the claims and what are the types of evidence?

With RQ1, we want to get insight in the trends of research on architecture-based self-adaptation and the current state of the art. RQ2 is motivated by the need to get clear understanding of the benefits of architecture-based self adaptation, that is, we are interested in identifying which concerns are addressed in self adaptive systems and what are the tradeoffs implied by applying self-adaptation. With RQ3 we aim to investigate what assessment methods have been used to obtain evidence for the research results and how much evidence is available for the applied methods.

3.2 Searched Sources

To guarantee high quality of the primary studies and obtain solid data to answer the research questions, we searched the main conferences and journals for publishing research results on self-adaptive systems, software architecture, and software engineering. The selected sources are listed in Table 1. Rank is based on the Australian Research Council ranking and H-index[2]. Instead of a general search, we opted for searching the main specialized venues and the premier software architecture and engineering venues, guaranteeing inclusion of high-quality primary studies for data collection.

---

[2] ARC: http://www.arc.gov.au/era/era_2010/archive/era_journal_list.htm, H-index: http://www.scimagojr.com and http://academic.research.microsoft.com/

Table 1. Searched Sources

ID	Conference/Journal	Rank	H-index
Adaptive	Adaptive and Self-adaptive Systems and Applications	n/a	n/a
ASE	International Conf. on Automated Software Engineering	A	24
DEAS	Design and Evolution of Autonomic Application Software	n/a	n/a
ECSA	European Conference on Software Architecture	n/a	8
FSE	Foundations of Software Engineering	A	31
ICAC	International Conference on Autonomic Computing	B	32
ICSE	International Conference on Software Engineering	A	63
ICSM	International Conference on Software Maintenance	A	57
ISARCS	International Symposium on Architecting Critical Systems	n/a	n/a
ISSTA	International Symposium on Software Testing and Analysis	A	35
SASO	Self-Adaptive and Self-Organizing Systems	n/a	9
SEAMS	Software Engineering for Adaptive & Self-Managing Systems	n/a	n/a
SefSAS	Software Engineering for Self-Adaptive Systems	n/a	n/a
WADS	Workshop on Architecting Dependable Systems	n/a	n/a
WICSA	Working International Conference on Software Architecture	A	n/a
WOSS	Workshop on Self-Healing	n/a	n/a
JSS	Journal of Systems and Software	A	48
TAAS	Transactions on Autonomous and Adaptive Systems	n/a	16
TOSEM	Transactions on Software Engineering and Methodology	A*	47
TSE	Transactions on Software Engineering	A*	93

3.3   Search Strategy

The search strategy combines automatic with manual search. In a first step we searched primary studies by automatic search using the following search string:

((Title:adaptive OR Title:adaptation OR Title:self OR Title:autonomic
OR Title:autonomous) OR
(Abstract:adaptive OR Abstract:adaptation OR Abstract:self OR Abstract:autonomic OR Abstract:autonomous))

We performed automated search on three data search engines: IEEE Explore, ACM Digital Library, and Springer for the respective venues. Search was based on title and abstract. To ensure that the search string provides the right scope of studies, we applied pilot searches on the set of studies from three venues: TAAS, ICAC, and SEAMS.

In the second step, two researchers read the abstracts, introduction and conclusions of all the primary studies selected in the first step and used the inclusion/exclusion criteria to filter out the studies that were not relevant for the review. For a number of papers, we further looked into other sections. We explain the selection criteria below.

3.4 Inclusion and Exclusion Criteria

We used the following inclusion criteria in our search:

- Studies which were published between January 2000 to December 2012. We used 2000 as starting date as self-adaptive systems have become subject of active research around that time.
- Studies on self-adaptive systems that at least partially separate the managing system (adaptation logic) from the managed system (domain logic).
- Studies that concern the engineering of self-adaptation, i.e. the realization of self-adaptation or parts of self-adaption.
- Studies that provide a minimal level of assessment of the research, which may be in the form of example application, simulation, rigorous analysis, empirical, or real world example.

We used the following exclusion criteria:

- Surveys and roadmap papers, as we are only interested in studies that provide a minimal level of assessment of research results.
- We also excluded tutorials, short papers, editorials etc. because these papers do not provide reasonable data.

A paper was selected as a primary study if it met all inclusion criteria and eliminated if it met any exclusion criterion.

3.5 Data Items

Table 2 shows the data items we extracted to answer the research questions. For each research question, we identified 3 to 4 data items that aim to provide data to answer the research question. Several of these data items are defined based on the insights derived from the pilot study [9].

We briefly discuss the different data items. The concrete options for each data item are further discussed in the next section. For a detailed description of the data items, we the protocol that is available at the survey website.

F1-F5: The data items author(s), year, title, venue, citation count are used for documentation.

F6: Quality score assesses the quality of study, which is important for data analysis and interpretation of results. Based on [13] and the pilot study, we assessed the following quality items: (1) problem definition of the study, (2) problem context, i.e., the way the study is related to other work, (3) research design, i.e., the way the study was organized, (4) contributions and study results, (5) insights derived from the study, (6) limitations of the study. For each item, we have quality levels: explicit description (2 points), general description (1 point), and no description (0 points). A quality assessment score (max 12) is calculated by summing up the scores for all the items for a study.

F7: Subject of the study refers to the software engineering field that is addressed in the study. We used the SWEBOK sub-disciplines [14] to define the options, including software requirements, software design, software construction, software testing, software maintenance, among others.

Table 2. Data Items

Item ID	Field	Use
F1	Author(s)	Documentation
F2	Year	Documentation
F3	Title	Documentation
F4	Venue	Documentation
F5	Citation count	Documentation
F6	Quality score	RQ1-3
F7	Subject of the study	RQ1
F8	Feedback loop architecture	RQ1
F9	Application domain (if applicable)	RQ1
F10	Quality concerns	RQ2
F11	Claimed benefits	RQ2
F12	Tradeoffs	RQ2
F13	Validation setting	RQ3
F14	Assessment approach	RQ3
F15	Evidence level	RQ3
F16	Repeatability	RQ3

F8: Feedback loop architecture refers to the structure of the feedback loop(s) (or parts of it) that are the focus of the study. Options range from: focus on particular MAPE functions, to single MAPE loop, and mutiple MAPE loops.

F9: Application domain refers to the kind of application for which self-adaptation is used. We started from the an initial list of application domains taken from our pilot study [9] and added additional domains when they appeared during the review.

F10: Quality concerns refer to the concerns related to self-adaptation. We defined the following option based on IEEE 9126 and ISO/IEC 25012: reliability, availability, usability, efficiency/performance, maintainability, portability, security, accuracy, flexibility, and other concern.

F11: Claimed benefits refer to the concerns of self-adaptation (identified in F10) with positive impact. Options are: preserving quality of the software, improving quality of the software, assuring quality of the software, and improving other concerns.

F12: Tradeoffs refer to the concerns of self-adaptation (identified in F10) with a negative impact. Option are: quality concerns that are negatively influenced due to self-adaptation, and other concerns that are negatively influenced due to self-adaptation.

F13: Validation setting refers to the context in which validation is performed, with the options: academic effort, academic/industry collaboration, and industrial effort.

F14: Assessment approach refers to the method used for evaluating the research results. Options are: example application, simulation (use of a model of the real world), rigorous analysis (typically based on formal methods), empirical study (case study, controlled experiment), and experience from real examples.

F15: Evidence level expresses the degree of evidence for the research results. Evidence can be obtained from: demonstration or application to simple examples, expert opinions or observations, empirical studies, and industrial evidence.

F16: Repeatability of the study is one of the following options: the study is not repeatable (no useful material is available to repeat the study), a partial description is available to repeat the study, the material to repeat the study is partially available, all the material is available to repeat the study.

3.6   Approach for Analysis

The data items of the primary studies was collated to answer the research questions. Analysis included: (i) obtaining consensus among the reviewers in case of conflicts, (ii) analyzing the data, for which we used descriptive analysis and multiple regression to identify correlations, and (iii) answering research questions. Based on the analysis results, we derived conclusions and recommendations for future research in the area of architecture-based self-adaptation, and we reflected on threats to validity of the review.

4   Results Analysis

We start by giving an overview of the primary studies selected for the review. Then we discuss the results for each research question.

4.1   Selected Primary Studies

From 7400 studies published at 20 conferences/journals we retrieved 1296 studies after applying the search string. From these studies we selected 121 primary studies after applying the inclusion/exclusion criteria. A list with the selected primary studies is available at the survey website. Figure 2 shows the number of selected studies per venue.

We see that JSS is the most popular journal to publish papers on architecture-based self adaptive systems with 21.5% of the studies, while SEAMS is the most prominent conference with 19.9% of the studies. TSE and TAAS represent 14.9% of the studies and the top software engineering conferences ICSE, FSE and ASE represent 9.9% of the studies. The architecture focused venues, WICSA, ECSA, and ISARCS represent 6.7% of the studies. 10.7% of the studies were published between 2000 and 2005 and 89.3% between 2006 and 2012, which shows the growing research interest in this area.

Figure 3 summarizes the quality scores for the selected primary studies.

The results show that researchers provide descriptions of the problem they tackle and how the problem relates to other efforts. Contributions and insights are also reported, although not always explicitly. However, the majority of studies do not describe research design, i.e. the way the research is organized, and most studies ignore reporting limitations of the results (although we notice that a growing number of researchers have started reporting limitations after 2008). Providing an explicit description of research design is common practice for empirical studies, but less common in software

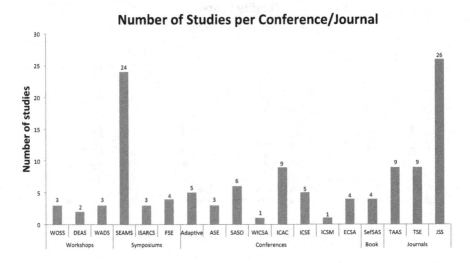

Fig. 2. Primary studies per venue/journal

Table 3. Number of studies and quality score for different publication fora

Venues	Regression Eq.	R	Mean	S.D.
Journals	y = -0,0672x + 2,3498	-0,11	6,11	1,7
Conferences	y = -0,1502x + 2,4545	-0,27	5,39	1,68
Symposia	y = -0,1067x + 1,998	-0,15	5,67	1,37
Book Chapters	y = -0,0178x + 0,2895	-0,16	5,38	1,75
Workshops	y = -0,0791x + 0,9051	-0,37	4,28	1,33

engineering in general. The results confirm this trend for the primary studies in this review. However, the poor treatment of limitations deserves attention as this should be a key part of any engineering study. Table 3 shows the regression analysis between the number of studies and quality score for different publication fora.

The values confirm common sense that the primary studies with the best quality scores are published in journals, while studies presented at workshops have lower quality scores. However, with a mean of the overall score of 5.6 (on a max of 12), the quality of the selected primary studies can be considered as reasonably good.

4.2   RQ1: What Is the Focus of Research in Self-adaptation?

Research focus is derived from data items: subject of the studies (F7), feedback loop architecture (F8), and application domain (F9).

Quality Scores

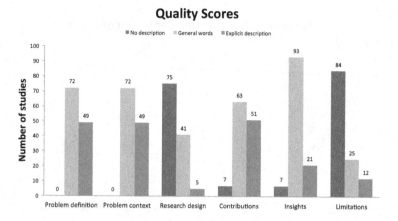

Fig. 3. Quality scores for the primary studies

The most popular subject of the studies (F7) in terms of SWEBOK software engineering fields is software design with 48% of the studies, followed by software quality with 17%, software requirements with 8% and software testing with 8%. Design activities are an evident focus of architecture-based self-adaptation. Requirements for self-adaptive systems have gained increasing attention during the last years (all studies on requirements are from 2006 onward), confirming that handling dynamic changing user needs is a topic of increasing importance in software engineering.

Figure 4 shows the frequency of feedback loop architecture (F8). The dominant focus has been on single feedback loops, with 37% of the studies using distinct components for each of the MAPE functions and 32% using components that mix (some of) the MAPE functions. 20% of the studies (24 in total) focus on multiple feedback loops. All studies directly or indirectly refer to the MAPE functions in their solutions, which shows that MAPE serves a *reference model* (i.e., a division of functionality together with flows between the pieces [15]). However, as a significant number of studies do not map these functions one-to-one to components, MAPE is not generally considered as a *reference architecture* (i.e., a reference model mapped to software elements). The numbers show that researchers have payed less attention to engineering self-adaptive systems with multiple control loops. However, we notice that 92% of these studies have been published in the last four years, which underpins the growing interest in this area.

Figure 5 shows the frequency of application domains (F9).

Only 69% of the studies do consider an explicit application domain. The remaining studies refer to abstract applications, such as resource management, service-based system, networking, etc. The dominant application domains are embedded systems (46%) and web applications (30%); the latter are e-commerce (such as travel planning, book store, etc.) and information systems (such as news services, social media, etc.). Embedded systems have always been an important domain in research on self-adaptation. In the last years, dynamic service composition has gained increasing attention. We found that 86% of the studies with multiple feedback loops are applied to the domains of

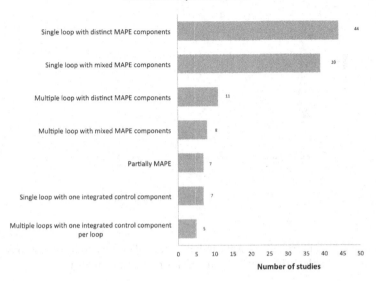

Fig. 4. Feedback loop architectures

embedded systems, traffic, and robotics, which can be explained by the fact that these domains are characterized by loosely coupled, physically distributed entities.

Summary for RQ1: The main focus of research in engineering architecture-based self-adaptation has been on software design of a single feedback loop, applied to the domains of embedded systems and web applications. Driven by the engineering challenges of future software systems, there is a growing interest in requirements for self-adaptive systems, dynamic service composition, and multiple feedback loops.

4.3 RQ2: What Are the Claims Made for Self-adaptation and What Are the Tradeoffs Implied by Self-adaptation?

The answer to RQ2 is derived from quality concerns (F10), claimed benefits (F11), and tradeoffs (F12).

The top three concerns related to self-adaption (F10) are efficiency/performance (55% of the studies), reliability (41%), and flexibility (28%). Accuracy, security, usability, maintainability, and availability account each for 6% or less of the studies. Other reported concerns are engineering effort, complexity, stability, and cost. These concerns are considered in only 6% of the studies (in total). This latter observation is remarkable as seminal papers in the area of self-adaptation use these other concerns as the primary arguments for the need of self-adaptation [1–3].

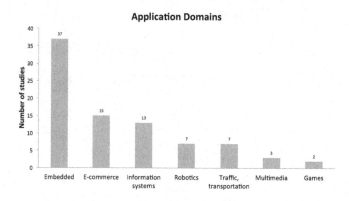

Fig. 5. Studied application domains

We analyzed the correlation between the main quality concerns and the main application domains. Table 4 shows the results of this regression analysis.

Table 4. Correlation between main quality concerns and application domains

Application Domains	Efficiency/Performance	Reliability	Flexibility
Embedded	0,89	0,84	0,59
Information Systems	0,88	0,68	0,78
E-commerce	0,75	0,63	0,81

The results tell us that efficiency/performance is relevant to self-adaptation in all primary domains, while reliability is more relevant to embedded systems and flexibility to web-based systems. Reliability is a classic quality concern in embedded systems. On the other hand, in web-based systems, flexibility provides an alternative for reliability tailored to open environments. For example, a common approach to deal with uncertainty about the availability of services is to exploit self-adaptation to replace dynamically a service that becomes unavailable.

We also looked at the number of concerns considered in individual studies and measured that 57% of the studies consider a single concern, 40% consider 2 concerns, the remaining 3% consider more concerns. We can conclude that most researchers take a narrow view on engineering self-adaptive systems, focusing on a particular concern, without considering the interplay with other concerns.

Figure 6 summarizes the data for claimed benefits (F11) and tradeoffs (F12). This important figure clearly shows that most studies focus on concerns with a positive effect, i.e., 91% of the concerns related to self-adaptation are claimed to be positively influenced. Broken down, 81% of the studies state that a quality of the software is improved by self-adaptation, 5% state that a quality is assured, and the remaining 5% state that a quality is preserved.

Claims versus Tradeoffs

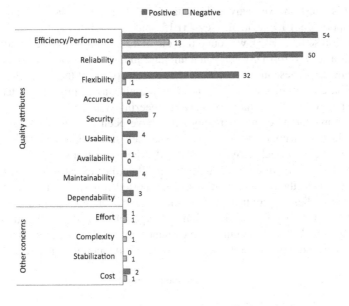

Fig. 6. Claims and tradeoffs of self-adaptation

On the other hand, little attention is given to concerns with a negative effect, i.e., the tradeoffs implied by self-adaptation. 10.7% of the studies state that self-adaptation has an efficiency/performance cost, a single study considers a negative effect on flexibility, and 3.3% of the studies state a negative effect on other engineering aspects (effort, complexity, stability and cost). Concretely, seven studies report an efficiency/performance tradeoff against flexibility and six studies against reliability. Three the four studies report negative effects to other concerns against performance, the other one against accuracy.

This analysis confirms that the majority of researchers focus on a single concern only (see F10). Even if multiple concerns are considered, they mainly look at the positive effects of self-adaptation. To further understand these observations, we looked into the studies and found that 80% of the studies that do not consider tradeoffs in their evaluation, simply ignore implications of self-adaptation. 13% of the studies recognize possible tradeoffs and acknowledge the limitations of their study in that respect, the other 7% of the studies postpone the issues related to tradeoffs to future work.

Summary for RQ2: Most researchers on self-adaptive systems claim improvements of software qualities, in particular for efficiency/performance, reliability, and flexibility. Tradeoffs are hardly considered at all, neither with respect to other qualities nor the effects on concerns such as effort and cost. A minority of researchers recognize the limitations of their work with respect to tradeoffs or they postpone it to future work.

4.4 RQ3: How Much Evidence Is Available for the Claims and What Are the Types of Evidence?

To answer this question, we analyze the data extracted from validation setting (F13), assessment approach (F14), evidence level (F15) and repeatability (F16).

For validation setting (F13), we found that out of 121 studies, only two studies were performed in a joint effort between academic and industry. No industry-only studies have been reported. These numbers give a strong indication that the research results of architecture-based self-adaptation have not found their way to practice (at least, they have not been reported in the main software engineering venues).

Figure 7 shows the assessment methods that have been used in the studies (F14). Example application accounts for 67.8% of the studies, simulation for 19.8%, rigorous analysis for 8.3%, empirical study for 2.5% and experience from real-world example for 1.7%. Closer examination reveals that almost all studies use simple basic example applications to assess the research findings. The reported empirical studies were in fact quasi empirical studies. No controlled experiments have been reported in the area of engineering architecture-based self-adaptation and experiences with real-world examples is very limited. The lack of both empirical evidence and studies with industry partners hampers industrial adoption of architecture-based self-adaptation in general.

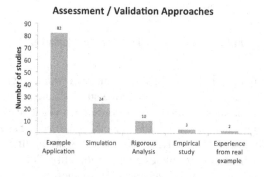

Fig. 7. Assessment approaches

Table 5 shows that example applications are used in all application domains. Simulation is mainly used in web-based systems (e-commerce and information systems), while rigorous analysis is mainly used for embedded systems and e-commerce.

Table 5. Correlation between assessment methods and application domains

Assessment Methods	Embedded	Robotics	E-commerce	Traffic and transport.	Information systems
Example Application	0,93	0,93	0,84	0,88	0,85
Simulation	0,78	0	0,84	0,14	0,82
Rigorous Analysis	0,73	0	0,86	0	0,20

Given the used assessment methods, it is not surprising that most studies have a low evidence level (F15). Concretely, 95.8% of the studies provide minimal evidence from demonstrations or simple/toy examples, 1.7% provide evidence from expert opinions or observation, and 2.5% provide (weak) empirical evidence.

Summary for RQ3: Most research on architecture-based self-adaptive systems is assessed using simple example applications with a minimal level of evidence. Few empirical studies exist and there is hardly any industrial application of architecture-based self-adaptation reported. Weak evidence and poor connection with practice shows that research in architecture-based self-adaptation is still more exploratory than exploitative.

5   Limitations of Study

Despite the sound methodology, this study has some limitations. First, our study is limited to 20 major venues in the field. While we believe that these are the most prominent venues for research on architecture-based self-adaptive systems, we may have missed a number of primary studies that have been published elsewhere. Second, we used common terms to formulate the search string. However, these terms may not fully cover all studies on architecture-based self-adaptation, as there is no generally agreed consensus on the key terms in the field. This limitation is inherent to a field where research is still in an exploratory phase. To minimize this threat, we performed a number of pilot searches to get optimal coverage of automatic search. Third, there is a potential bias of the reviewers. We believe that the comprehensive selection and data extraction process that involved two reviewers who cross-checked the search results, supported by a third reviewer to obtain consensus in case of conflicts, should minimize this threat of bias.

6   Conclusion

Research on architecture-based self-adaptation is widely recognized as key for tackling several of the hard challenges we currently face in software engineering. However, reflecting on the results and analysis of our study, we conclude that there are opportunities for improving coherence in research to move the field forward. We recommend coherence improvements in three dimensions.

First, coherence among the researchers can be improved. We observe that different groups follow specific lines of research that are only weakly connected. Researchers apply their results to specific applications and mostly ignore limitations. Furthermore, there is a lack of empirical studies. Clear and fair treatment of limitations and evidence for findings provide a basis for both consolidation of results and starting points for future research efforts in the field. However, there are some positive signs. First, we notice that researchers have started reporting limitations of their work. Over 85% of the studies that report limitations have been published since 2008. Furthermore, a recent study [16] reports the results of a first controlled experiment on design improvements of using external feedback loops to realize architecture-based self-adaptation.

Second, coherence of research that spans software engineering fields can be improved. We observe a clear dominance of attention for the design of self-adaptive systems. Clearly, there is a need to integrate design with other engineering activities of self-adaptive systems, including requirements, testing and engineering processes.

Here too, we observe some positive signs. During the last years, we notice a growing interest in the study of requirements for self-adaptive systems, lead by different groups in the world. We also notice a growing interest in other activities, e.g. the 10 studies on testing were all published since 2008. Finally, a recent publication [17] shows an interest of the community in engineering processes for self-adaptive systems.

Third, coherence of research with the surrounding world can be improved. Currently, research is primarily evaluated using simple applications without making the material available to others. Worse, collaborations with industry partners are very rare. Availability of experimental material and industrial involvement are essential to the field to obtain maturity. But again, there is some hope. The community took the initiative to establish *exemplars* that provide model problems for the community (http://seams.self-adapt.org/wiki/Exemplars). We also refer to a recent study [18] that reports experiences of an industrial application of architecture-based self-adaptation.

We performed a systematic literature review study that shed light on the claims that are made for architecture-based self-adaptation and evidence that is provided for these claims. We hope that this study can contribute to push this important field forward.

References

1. Oreizy, P., et al.: Architecture-based runtime software evolution. In: ICSE (1998)
2. Kephart, J., Chess, D.: The vision of autonomic computing. Computer 36(1) (2003)
3. Garlan, D., et al.: Rainbow: Architecture-based self-adaptation with reusable infrastructure. IEEE Computer 37, 46–54 (2004)
4. Hellerstein, J., et al.: Feedback Control of Computing Systems. Wiley (2004)
5. Filieri, A., et al.: Self-adaptive software meets control theory: A preliminary approach supporting reliability requirements. In: ASE (2011)
6. Cheng, B.H.C., de Lemos, R., Giese, H., Inverardi, P., Magee, J.: Software engineering for self-adaptive systems: A research roadmap. In: Cheng, B.H.C., de Lemos, R., Giese, H., Inverardi, P., Magee, J. (eds.) Self-Adaptive Systems. LNCS, vol. 5525, pp. 1–26. Springer, Heidelberg (2009)
7. de Lemos, R., et al.: Software engineering for self-adaptive systems: A second research roadmap. In: de Lemos, R., Giese, H., Müller, H.A., Shaw, M. (eds.) Self-Adaptive Systems. LNCS, vol. 7475, pp. 1–32. Springer, Heidelberg (2013)
8. Patikirikorala, T., et al.: Survey on the design of self-adaptive software systems using control engineering approaches. SEAMS (2012)
9. Weyns, D., et al.: Claims and supporting evidence for self-adaptive systems: A literature study. Software Engineering for Adaptive and Self-Managing Systems (2012)
10. Weyns, D., et al.: Forms: Unifying reference model for formal specification of distributed self-adaptive systems. ACM TAAS (2012)
11. Kitchenham, B., Charters, S.: Guidelines for performing systematic literature reviews in software engineering. In: EBSE 2007-001, Keele and Durham University (2007)
12. Basili, V., et al.: Goal question metric approach. In: Encyclopedia of Soft. Eng. (1994)
13. Dybå, T., Dingsøyr, T.: Empirical studies of agile software development: A systematic review. Inf. Software Technology 50, 833–859 (2008)
14. Abran, A., et al. (eds.): Guide to the Software Engineering Body of Knowledge - SWEBOK. IEEE Press, Piscataway (2001)

15. Bass, L., et al.: Software Architecture in Practice. Addison-Wesley (2003)
16. Weyns, D., et al.: Do external feedback loops improve the design of self-adaptive systems? a controlled experiment. In: SEAMS (2013)
17. Andersson, J., Baresi, L., Bencomo, N., de Lemos, R., Gorla, A., Inverardi, P., Vogel, T.: Software eng. processes for self-adaptive systems. In: de Lemos, R., Giese, H., Müller, H.A., Shaw, M. (eds.) Self-Adaptive Systems. LNCS, vol. 7475, pp. 51–75. Springer, Heidelberg (2013)
18. Camara, J., et al.: Evolving an adaptive industrial software system to use architecture-based self-adaptation. SEAMS (2013)

Towards an Optimized Software Architecture for Component Adaptation at Middleware Level

Thomas Pramsohler[1], Simon Schenk[2], and Uwe Baumgarten[2]

[1] BMW Forschung und Technik GmbH, München, Germany
thomas.pramsohler@bmw.de
[2] Technische Universität München, Lehrstuhl für Betriebssysteme,
Garching bei München, Germany
{schenksi,baumgaru}@in.tum.de

Abstract. The amount of software in the automotive domain is steadily increasing. Existing functions are adapted or enhanced on a regular basis. Often, such adaptations do not allow to keep the interfaces of the concerned components stable, leading to incompatibilities with former systems. In this contribution, we propose an optimized adaptation software architecture to deal with mismatching interfaces. We extend existing middleware solutions with transparent adapter loading capabilities. This enables for seamless adapter integration on those systems. As adapter model we use a finite-state machine aside with a domain specific language. By extracting static adaptations from the state machine we achieve state reduction and performance gain. The approach is evaluated using an automotive case-study.

Keywords: behavioral adaptation, adaptation architecture, software components, middleware adapter, software composition.

1 Introduction

A modern vehicle features a complex IT infrastructure: up to seventy electronic control units (ECUs) are forming the computational backbone of a car. They are interlinked with up to six different networking technologies. These ECUs host differently complex software components, ranging from chassis and engine control to computationally intensive tasks like visual traffic sign recognition.

Not only the in-car network is heterogeneous and distributed, but also single ECUs (for instance the headunit) are composed of different software components, which are connected via different inter-process comunication mechanisms. Sometimes software components are re-used from other product lines without modification to simplify the validation process and reduce costs. Furthermore, cars already in production are upgraded with components from newer products, meaning that a component must be able to correctly operate in different environments.

On the one hand, such component interfaces have to be stable in order to support development using common building blocks. On the other hand, the

K. Drira (Ed.): ECSA 2013, LNCS 7957, pp. 266–281, 2013.

software interface has to be flexible in order to operate in different environments. For this reason current automotive software components support several interfaces at the same time. Adding the requirement of backward compatibility, this results in ever-increasing interface size and complexity.

A promising solution to keep the component interface small, flexible, and backward compatible would be software adaptation. Thereby adaptation allows for the composition of components with mismatching interfaces [13] and the adapter acts as mediator [15] between these components. Adaptation is not completely new in the field of automotive software engineering. Current gateway ECUs for instance can be configured for signal adaptation and the AUTOSAR[1] runtime environment supports basic adaptation at design time.

The selection of a suitable adaptation technique depends on the target domain. Currently, in the infotainment domain, there is no sufficient solution to adapt software components. An adapter for infotainment components has to fulfill several requirements which arise from the domain specific properties. First, the hardware does not offer much headroom, because automotive hardware matches the software requirements very well. Second, most of the control flow is implemented using client-server communication. In contrast to the electrical system which uses cyclic broadcast signals, the client-server communication uses complex protocols and data. Finally, software components are developed by suppliers and thus are treated as black-boxes with a rigid interface. These properties lead to the following requirements:

- **Hardware limitations**: The execution of the adapter must not be computational intensive. Small interface changes should be adapted in a simple and efficient way.
- **Client-server Communication**: The adaptation approach has to be applied on client-server communication. This includes the adaptation of method calls, their responses, and broadcasts by the server. The adaptation approach should support rich behavioral models.
- **Black-box components**: The adapter has to be injected between the client and server without changing the respective black-boxes.

In this contribution we present an architecture for interface adaptation which suits these requirements. The presented approach puts current adaptation technologies into practice and adds the concepts needed for a efficient adaptation and seamless integration in the communication layer. We consider complex adaptation scenarios and support the adaptation of syntactical (signature) and behavioral (protocol) mismatches. We use a model-based interface and adapter definition which can be used for automatic adapter-code generation. The adapter is integrated in the middleware by delegation and can be loaded transparently. We describe the approach on an abstract level, hence it could be applied to other domains like web services.

The remainder of this paper is structured as follows. Section 2 presents our running example which will be used throughout the paper. Section 3 introduces

---

[1] http://www.autosar.org

an interface- and adapter-notation. Section 4 presents our software architecture and seamless adapter integration. In section 5 we show an example adaptation using our case study. Section 6 compares our approach to related work and section 7 will conclude the paper.

2   Case Study

In this section, we present our example of mismatching components. The target domain is the inter-process communication in an automotive infotainment system. We will use this example throughout the paper to explain the modeling approach and the software architecture. This is a fictitious example and real interfaces usually have more parameters and additional timing constraints. But even this small example shows the different adaptation cases that occur when adapting software interfaces.

At this point the basic functionality of both components is explained. The specification of the use case will be refined in the next chapters using our modeling approach.

ParkA1 defines a simple protocol, whereas ParkA2 is more sophisticated (see Table 1). To be able to receive any sensor values, the client has to start the ParkA1 first with an asynchronous boot procedure calling a `startup` method and waiting for a `started` broadcast. Once the ParkA1 is started the client can request sensor values, or shut down the ParkA1.

Table 1. Method overview of the ParkA interfaces in version 1 and 2

ParkA1	ParkA2
startup()	connect(retry, lastErr, errCode)
shutdown()	disconnect()
getSensors(f_l,f_m,f_r)	getSensorAndStatus(fl,fml,fmr,fr,status)
started	

The second version of the component, ParkA2, is capable of providing sensor values, even when it is in idle mode. Thereby the last measured sensor values are returned instead of starting the real-time measuring. To get real-time sensor values, the client has to connect to the ParkA2 with a synchronous `connect` procedure. Similar to ParkA1 the client can request new sensor values and terminate the connection. Additionally, the ParkA2 component will handle connected components with higher priority and adds a status parameter to the results indicating the quality of the current values. Table 2 gives an overview of the differences between ParkA1 and ParkA2:

Table 2. Feature comparison between ParkA1 and ParkA2

	ParkA1	ParkA2
sensor values when shut down	no	yes
sensor status	no	yes
startup procedure	asynchronous	synchronous
startup retry	no	yes
sensor count	3	4

3   Interface and Adapter Model

We distinguish between an *Interface Model* and an *Adapter Model*. Interface Models are related to a specific version of an interface and needed as input for the adapter construction. Each Interface Model has to provide three sub-models: A *Syntax Model*, an *Event Model*, and a *Behavior Model*. Figure 1 shows the different models and their relationships. We are constructing the adapter from the client point of view. That is, a client interface will be adapted to communicate with a different server interface. Each Adapter Model consists either of a *Static Adapter Model*, or a *Dynamic Adapter Model*, or both.

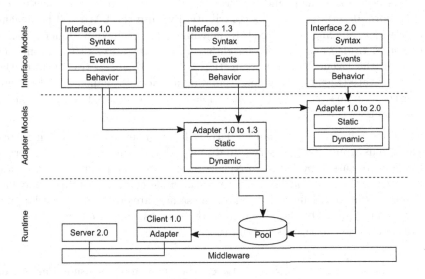

Fig. 1. Interface and Adapter models

3.1   Interface Model

The Interface Model consists of three parts. The *Syntax Model*, the *Behavior Model*, and the *Event Model*.

- **Syntax Model:** The Syntax Model includes information about the *interface name, interface version* and the *methods, broadcasts,* and *type definitions.* This model is usually provided in a middleware-specific Interface Definition Language (IDL) and can be used to generate server and client stubs.

- **Event Model:** The Event Model extends the Syntax Model with the definition of events. An event specifies an occurrence of a method execution or a broadcast execution. In case of a method the occurrence can be the method call or the method response. Therefore we distinguish between *InputEvent* (*CallEvent*) and *OutputEvent* (*ResponseEvent* and *BroadcastEvent*). Each event can specify a *constraint* with a logical expression using the parameters of the referenced method or broadcast. The InputEvent is constrained using the input parameters of the method and the OutputEvent using the output parameters of the method or broadcast.

  In order to generate an event, each argument has to be set in such way that the constraint evaluates to true. For this purpose we provide an *Emulation* field to the modeler. An Emulation for a CallEvent, for instance, defines a default value or a calculation rule for every input parameter of the referenced method. Using this definition the adapter can produce the event by executing the Emulation.

- **Behavior Model:** The Behavior Model specifies the valid sequences of events between a client and a server [2]. We use a finite-state machine for behavioral description. In this contribution we use the UML [14] nomenclature when referring to finite-state machines. The Behavior Model consists of *states, transitions,* and *initial states.* We use instances of the events defined in the Event Model as transition triggers. Hence, a transition of the current state triggers, if the corresponding method was called and the event constraint holds true. Event constraints can be compared to UML guard conditions.

  The direction of an event can be derived from the event itself. InputEvents are signals from client to server and OutputEvents are signals from server to client. In case a method or broadcast is executed, we need a deterministic behavior of the state machine. Therefore an implementation of this model has to ensure that outgoing transitions of the same state do not have overlapping event constraints. Overlapping means, that one parameter configuration will cause multiple constraints to hold true.

Figure 2 shows the relationships between the three models using ParkA2 of our example. The `connect` method is used to establish a connection to the server. The `disconnect` method releases the connection. If connecting fails, the client has to retry the connection process until the connection is successfully established. This has to be done calling the `connect` method with the `retry` parameter set to `true`. In order to retrieve the sensor values and the status the client has to call `getSensorsAndStatus`. This can be done with or without an established connection.

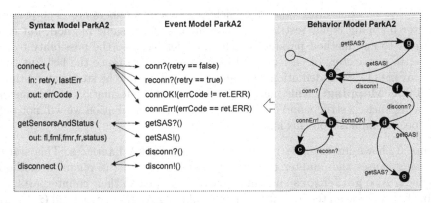

Fig. 2. Interface Models describing the ParkA2 service. InputEvents of the service are denoted using ? and OutputEvents using !

3.2   Adapter Model

For the model point of view it is not relevant whether the client or the server is adapted. Without loss of generality, we will always refer to client-adapters in this contribution. Hence, every client Interface Model can store adapters for several server Interface Models with different version. Each Adapter Model may have two submodels, a *Static Adapter Model* which describes adaptations that occur anytime and/or a *Dynamic Adapter Model* which specifies context-sensitive behavior depending on the current state of the communication between the components (communication state).

In this contribution we do not focus on automated adapter construction but there exist approaches for semi-automated adapter construction. The reader may refer to [4,16,6,11].

Static Adapter Model. The static adaptation is the most common case of adaptation. The *Static Adapter Model* describes all the adaptations which are not dependent on the current communication state. Hence, static adaptations for a concrete interface artifact will be executed each time the interface artifact is involved in the communication. The Static Adapter Model consists of three independently defined mappings: a *Method Mapping*, a *Parameter Mapping* and a *Type Mapping*.

- **Method Mapping:** Methods of the client interface are mapped to a sequence of methods in the server interface. Each time the client calls a method, its mapped server methods will be called by the adapter. If no Method Mapping exists, the adapter will handle the method call and return the value defined in the Parameter Mapping.
- **Parameter Mapping:** A parameter mapping can be defined for each output parameter of the adapter. This includes input parameters of the server-side interface and output parameters of the client-side interface. The parameter mapping is defined using a default value and an optional algebraic

expression containing other parameters, random numbers etc. The parameter mapping is not restricted to parameters of the same method, but can refer to any method parameter. The modeler has also the possibility to refer to parameters of past method invocations, for instance the last but two (param[1]). Such definition will cause the argument to be stored at runtime.

- **Type Mapping:** This mapping defines the transformation of parameter types such as structs and enumerations. In this contribution we will not put special emphasis on this kind of mapping.

Figure 3 shows an example mapping using the ParkA interfaces. This static mapping causes the adapter to redirect a start call to the renamed method connect. Also getSensors and shutdown are mapped to their counterparts.

In this example all the output parameters of the getSensors method (f_l, f_m, and f_r) are mapped to the parameters of the getSensorsAndStatus method (fl, fml, fmr and fr). The parameters for the front left (fl) and the front right (fr) sensor values are matched directly to the corresponding server parameters (f_l and f_r). The parameters for the middle sensors, fml and fmr, do not exist in the server interface and are calculated as mean value of other server parameters. If a parameter is not mapped statically it has to be set by the dynamic adapter. For simple one-to-one mappings with the same parameter types the Static Adapter Model can be generated and tested using the original unit test cases of the interfaces [10].

	client interface		server interface
Method mapping:	start	⟶	connect
Method mapping:	getSensors	⟶	getSensorsAndStatus
Method mapping:	shutdown	⟶	disconnect
Parameter mappping:	f_l	⟶	-1 | fl[0]
Parameter mappping:	f_m	⟶	-1 | (fml[0] + fmr[0]) /2
Parameter mappping:	f_r	⟶	-1 | fr[0]

Fig. 3. Static Adapter Model describing independent Method- and Parameter-Mappings

Dynamic Adapter Model. The Dynamic Adapter Model describes all the adaptations which are dependent on the current communication state. This model does not have to represent the whole behavior of the adapter component but only the behavioral differences between client and server which are not part of the Static Adapter Model. We use a finite-state machine for the notation and include additional *actions* which are executed by the adapter once the transition is triggered.

A trigger can be any event specified in the client or server Interface. This enables the Dynamic Adapter to perform additional actions in any communication state. The actions are events defined in the Event Model. In order to execute an action, the output arguments of the referenced method are assigned as defined in the corresponding Emulation definition of the event. Additionally each state specifies a *return flag* which is needed to define a rigorous execution semantics. The default value of the return flag is `true` and we use the *-Symbol to mark such a state in our models (see figure 4 and figure 8).

Figure 4 shows the Behavior Models for the ParkA use case. The client uses version one of the interface and the server implements version two with the corresponding behavior. The first task designing a Dynamic Adapter Model is to apply the mappings defined in the Static Adapter Model and the second is to identify the remaining mismatches.

In this example we use the Static Adapter Model presented in figure 3. The dashed arrows in figure 4 mark the transitions handled by the Static Adapter and the black colored states mark the deadlock situations which arise. A deadlock occurs, if the client and server are in a circular wait condition where the client expects an action from the server but the server expects a client action. The first deadlock situation occurs in state c of the server. In case the `connect` ResponseEvent of the server equals `connErr`, the server expects the client to invoke the `connect` method again and waits for the `reconn` event. In this case the Dynamic Adapter is used to resolve the mismatch. We use the incoming triggers of the deadlock state c (`connErr`) as trigger for the Dynamic Adapter to emulate the `reconn` event with an action.

The second deadlock situation occurs in state 3 of the client where the client awaits a `started` broadcast. Since the server does not provide the broadcast, we will resolve this mismatch with another transition in the Dynamic Adapter Model. In order to guarantee the server to be started, we use the server `connOK` event as trigger to execute the `started` Emulation on the client side. This leads to a Dynamic Adapter with only two transitions.

3.3   Execution Semantics

In order to understand the expressive power of the models we define the execution semantics of Static and Dynamic Adapter Models. The execution semantics is important if both, static and dynamic adaptations are performed for a method call or broadcast. The *Static Adapter* executes the Static Adapter Model and the *Dynamic Adapter* executes the state machine defined in the Dynamic Adapter Model.

The Static Adapter is the entry point for method calls from the client and broadcasts from the server. It forwards each incoming or outgoing event to the Dynamic Adapter. The event can easily be generated by evaluating the constraints defined in the Event Mapping. While the Dynamic Adapter processes the events, the Static Adapter has to pause. This processing may last for more then one transition. Thus the modeler has to define which states belong to one processing step which can be done using the return flag. If this flag is set, the state is a return state. Once the Dynamic Adapter has reached such a return state, it pauses and the Static Adapter resumes.

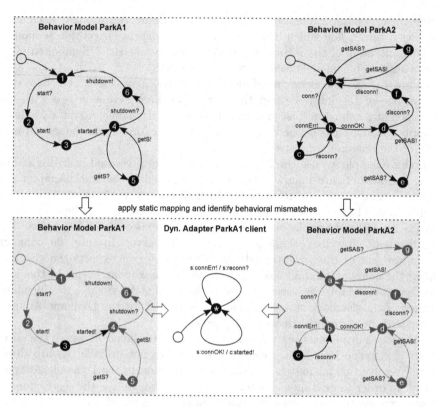

Fig. 4. Dynamic Adapter Model describing an additional broadcast and method call sent by the adapter. Return states are denoted using *

4   Runtime Architecture

In order to integrate the adapter in a transparent manner we suggest to extend the middleware with adapter loading capabilities. An adapter loading mechanism will be integrated into the software stack generated by the IDL code generator. The client invokes a function call to a proxy. The proxy itself should be middleware independent and uses a middleware specific serializer interface to access the messagebus. At startup the platform dependent serializer is loaded to split the method calls into messages. Figure 5 shows the overall architecture.

In the adaptation case we hook into the process with a different serializer. Each serializer implements the method `getServerVersion`. First, the default serializer is loaded, the `getServerVersion`-Method is called and the proxy checks whether the interface version of the server matches with the client (1), or not. In the latter case, a `SerializerAdapter` is loaded from a default directory (2). For the adaptation we use the design pattern adaptation by delegation [7]: Thus, the adapter implements the serializer interface of the client-side version and delegates the calls to a serializer instance of the server-side version (3). This serializer is then used to communicate with the server (4).

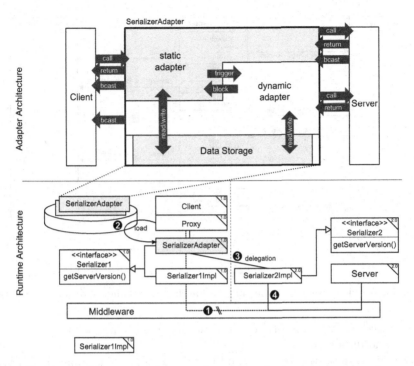

Fig. 5. Runtime architecture and integration of the adapter into a messagebus system

The architecture of the adapter itself is closely related to the adapter model. Thus the adapter is divided into two parts: the Static Adapter and the Dynamic Adapter (see figure 5). The Static Adapter provides the serializer interface and thus is responsible for communicating with the proxy. The Dynamic Adapter is implemented as finite-state machine that can be triggered using the **process_event** command. Since the Dynamic Adapter cannot be triggered by the proxy, the Static Adapter has to identify the current event by evaluating the event constraints (see section 3.1) and forward it to the Dynamic Adapter.

A data storage is used to store parameters. Storing is necessary in order to implement the parameter mapping defined in section 3.2. Both parts of the adapter interact directly with the serializer and the data storage.

4.1 Static Adapter

As shown, the Static Adapter is the module which is triggered by the client. Whenever a method is called by the client, two major actions have to be performed:

- any statically mapped server methods are called
- every Input- or OutputEvent is forwarded to the Dynamic Adapter

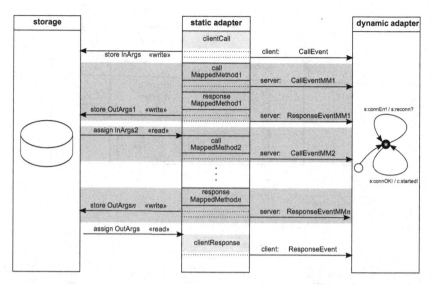

Fig. 6. An overview of what is happening inside the Static Adapter during a client call

Figure 6 gives an overview of the interaction between Static Adapter, Dynamic Adapter and data storage.

The first thing to do after a method is called is storing the input parameters. Then, the Dynamic Adapter is triggered by forwarding the CallEvent corresponding to the called method. Then the Static Adapter computes and assigns the input parameters for the mapped server methods using the parameter mappings defined in the adapter model. Once all arguments are assigned the server method is called and the Dynamic Adapter is informed about this call by triggering the corresponding CallEvent.

The actions of the Static Adapter after the server method has returned are similar to those after the client method has been called. First, the output arguments of the server method are stored, then a ResponseEvent is sent to the Dynamic Adapter. Before returning, the output arguments of the called client method have to be computed and assigned and the ResponseEvent of the client method has to be triggered inside the Dynamic Adapter.

4.2 Dynamic Adapter

As seen in section 3, each transition of the Dynamic Adapter Model has a trigger event and optional action events.

Triggering an event may cause the Dynamic Adapter to perform a transition. Thereby all action events corresponding to this transition have to be executed. In general there are three different types of actions caused by different action events:

- **CallEvent to the server:** The action computes the input parameters and calls the server method referenced by the event. Furthermore, it triggers the CallEvent of this method (an event can be both an action and a trigger). After the server method has returned, the output arguments are stored and the RespnseEvent is triggered.
- **ResponseEvent to the client:** The action evaluates the emulation field of the ResponseEvent and assigns the values to the output parameters of the referenced method. The method return itself will be handled by the static adapter.
- **BroadcastEvent to the client:** The action method computes the output arguments of the broadcast and executes the broadcast using the serializer.

As mentioned in section 3 the dynamic adapter remains active until he reaches a return state. At all other states, the adapter does not return and the static adapter has to be blocked, even though the processing of the triggered event finished. To block and unblock the static adapter, one of two additional actions – `blockSA` and `unblockSA` – is added to the transitions. `blockSA` puts the thread, the Static Adapter is running on to sleep, and thus blocks its execution until the `unblockSA` action wakes it up again. The outcome of this is the following execution trace:

$$\texttt{action1} \mid \ldots \mid \texttt{actionN} \mid \texttt{blockSA*} \mid \texttt{unblockSA*},$$

where the * means that executing this action is optional and not done by all transitions. A transition going into a return state has to unblock the static adapter. All other transitions have to block it.

5   Practical Realization

We implemented the Interface Model and the Adapter Model with a Domain Specific Language using the Eclipse Modeling Framework (EMF[2]). We used a textual notation for the Static Adapter Model and a graphical notation for the Dynamic Adapter Model.

Additionally we implemented a code generator to directly extract the adapter implementation from the model. The code generator is divided in an adapter specific and a middleware specific part. We implemented the middleware specific layer for the D-Bus middleware[3].

In order to get a more complex example, the interface versions of client and server are switched compared to the example used in section 3. As a result, the client uses the ParkA interface in version 2 whereas the server provides the same interface in version 1. The resulting adapters are shown in figure 7 and figure 8.

When the client calls the `connect` method, the call is received by the Static Adapter. Since there is no static mapping for the `connect` method, the Static Adapter has only to delegate the `connect` CallEvent to the Dynamic Adapter.

---

[2] http://www.eclipse.org/modeling/emf/
[3] http://dbus.freedesktop.org/

	client interface		server interface
Method mapping:	disconnect	⟶	shutdown
Parameter mappping:	fl	⟶	-1 | f_l[0]
Parameter mappping:	fml	⟶	-1 | (f_l[0] + f_m[0]) /2
Parameter mappping:	fmr	⟶	-1 | (f_r[0] + f_m[0]) /2
Parameter mappping:	fr	⟶	-1 | f_r[0]

Fig. 7. The Static Adapter of the evaluation example. The client using ParkA interface version 2 and the server using interface version 1.

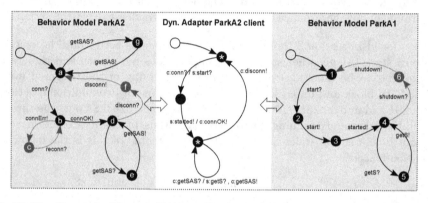

Fig. 8. The Dynamic Adapter of the evaluation example. The client uses the ParkA interface version 2 and the server interface version 1.

The Dynamic Adapter gets triggered by the CallEvent and calls the server's `starup` method. In this case the Dynamic Adapter has to remain active (return flag = false) until he receives the broadcast from the server. Once the `started` event is received, the server assigns OK to the result parameter of the `connect` method and unblocks the Static Adapter which returns the method call to the client.

When the `getSensorAndStatus` method is called and client and server are connected, the adaptation is performed by the Dynamic Adapter. In this case the `getSensorValues`-method gets called, the response parameters (sensor values) are stored in the data storage and the data is returned to the client.

When the client and the server are not connected, no transition is triggered inside the Dynamic Adapter. In this case only the Parameter Mapping is performed by getting the last sensor values from the storage and returning them to the client.

Since the `disconnect` method is statically mapped the Static Adapter, once the `disconnect` method is called, calls the `shutdown` method on the server. After the `shutdown` method returns, it returns the `disconnect` method and triggers the Dynamic Adapter causing it to go into disconnected state.

6   Related Work

The main goal of component based software engineering (CBSE) is the planned reuse of software artefacts. Component adaptation and adapter generation is a promising approach to extend the reuse of components even if their interfaces do not match. In this section we will refer to a variety of adapter modeling techniques and adaptation formalisms. We focus on horizontal adapters which adapt the communication between components.

Most of works addressing component adaptation deal with adapter generation approaches from formal service-descriptions [1,3,9,8,5,12]. Our Static Adapter Model can be compared to the approaches presented in [1,9,8]. Gierds et. al. specify *elementary activities* which include message creation, multiplication, deletion, transformation, message splitting, merging and recombination. The approach composes the adapter using this elementary activities and results in one adapter Petri-net. Dynamic adaptation can be achieved non-deterministic using alternative elementary activities.

Bracciali et. al. use dedicated non-deterministic actions [1] but no insight is given of how the adapter chooses which rule to take in a certain state.

Martin and Pimentel [12] present an approach for automatic adapter generation using a guided search with a heuristic. Their modeling formalism describes services in the mean of methods and parameters but does not facilitate the possibility to refine constraints for a transition. This means that a state with more than one leaving transition labeled with the same method will lead to non-deterministic behavior. The generation approach relies on the presumption that method parameters are already matched between the services.

Canal et. al. [5] also present an approach for adapter generation. They use finite-state machines with labeled transitions to describe the behavior of components. The formalism focuses on the behavioral aspects and is limited to the usage of events which are represented as strings.

Since the mentioned activities focus on the formal derivation of adaptation contracts they do not give special emphasis on the adaptation architecture. Our approach differs in various ways from the presented work on component adaptation.

All of the mentioned approaches use a monolithic behavioral model for the adaptation which usually results in a poor performance for large components. To improve the performance of the adapter, the classical partitioning of syntactical and behavioral mismatches could be converted to Static and Dynamic Adapter Model and implemented using our proposed architecture. A simple way to achieve this would be to identify elementary static mappings in the monolithic behavioral adapter model and to split it in a static and dynamic part.

The high-level protocol notation with string-based messages is not applicable to real infotainment interfaces and should be mapped to concrete methods, parameters and types. We define such an extension using the Event Model.

Additionally to the modeling part we describe an approach for dynamic adapter loading as part of the client-stub. This has two mayor benefits. The adapter is transparent for the communicating components and the adapter can be added or changed without changing the binary code of the communicating components. The direct loading of the adapter in the client has performance advantages compared to a dedicated mediator component on the messagebus. Only the adapter uses a serializer and the interface to the client can be realized using internal method-calls.

7 Conclusion and Future Work

In this paper we illustrated an adaptation technique for the composition of clients and services with mismatching interfaces. We focused on both, the syntactical interface and the protocol. In contrast to previous approaches we divide the adaptation contract into static and dynamic adaptations. Static adaptations are the most usual case when an interface evolves and can be implemented straight forward without triggering a state machine. Dynamic adaptations are needed if the adapter behavior for a certain event depends on the communication state between client and server. Partitioning the adapter into a static and a dynamic part enables us to reduce the complex adaptations which need a state machine execution.

We use an event definition model in order to link the adapter models to a concrete interface with methods, parameters, types and broadcasts. This model was precise enough to directly generate code for the DBUS middleware. We implemented a prototype for modeling and code generation and demonstrated the approach with an automotive example.

A first perspective of our work is the semi-automated adapter model generation and completely automated adapter model verification. A second perspective is to enhance the modeling approach with timing constraints and parallel regions. Parallel regions are needed, for instance, to model an adapter which mediates between a client which expects the server sending cyclic values and a server which provides a method for value retrieval. In this case one parallel region has to handle the cyclic broadcasts to the client and the other parallel region the sensor retrieval from the server.

References

1. Bracciali, A., Brogi, A., Canal, C.: A formal approach to component adaptation. Journal of Systems and Software 74(1), 45–54 (2005)
2. Brand, D., Zafiropulo, P.: On communicating finite-state machines. J. ACM 30(2), 323–342 (1983)
3. Brogi, A., Popescu, R.: Automated generation of BPEL adapters. In: Dan, A., Lamersdorf, W. (eds.) ICSOC 2006. LNCS, vol. 4294, pp. 27–39. Springer, Heidelberg (2006)
4. Camara, J., Salaun, G., Canal, C., Ouederni, M.: Interactive specification and verification of behavioural adaptation contracts. In: 9th International Conference on Quality Software, QSIC 2009, pp. 65–75 (2009)
5. Canal, C., Poizat, P., Salaun, G.: Model-based adaptation of behavioral mismatching components. IEEE Transactions on Software Engineering 34(4), 546–563 (2008)

6. Canal, C., Poizat, P., Salaün, G.: Synchronizing behavioural mismatch in software composition. In: Gorrieri, R., Wehrheim, H. (eds.) FMOODS 2006. LNCS, vol. 4037, pp. 63–77. Springer, Heidelberg (2006)

7. Gamma, E., Helm, R., Johnson, R., Vlissides, J.: Design patterns: elements of reusable object-oriented software. Addison-Wesley Longman Publishing Co., Inc., Boston (1995)

8. Gierds, C., Mooij, A.J., Wolf, K.: Reducing adapter synthesis to controller synthesis. IEEE Transactions on Services Computing 5(1), 72–85 (2012)

9. Gierds, C., Mooij, A.J., Wolf, K.: Specifying and generating behavioral service adapters based on transformation rules. Univ., Inst. fur Informatik (2008)

10. Hummel, O., Atkinson, C.: Automated creation and assessment of component adapters with test cases. In: Grunske, L., Reussner, R., Plasil, F. (eds.) CBSE 2010. LNCS, vol. 6092, pp. 166–181. Springer, Heidelberg (2010)

11. Inverardi, P., Tivoli, M.: Deadlock-free software architectures for COM/DCOM applications. Journal of Systems and Software 65(3), 173–183 (2003)

12. Martín, J.A., Pimentel, E.: Automatic generation of adaptation contracts. Electronic Notes in Theoretical Computer Science 229(2), 115–131 (2009)

13. Mateescu, R., Poizat, P., Salaün, G.: Adaptation of service protocols using process algebra and on-the-fly reduction techniques. IEEE Transactions on Software Engineering 38(4), 755–777 (2012)

14. OMG. UML version 2.2 superstructure. Technical report, OMG (2009)

15. Wiederhold, G.: Mediators in the architecture of future information systems. Computer 25(3), 38–49 (1992)

16. Yellin, D.M., Strom, R.E.: Protocol specifications and component adaptors. ACM Trans. Program. Lang. Syst. 19(2), 292–333 (1997)

Run-Time Support to Manage Architectural Variability Specified with CVL*

Gustavo G. Pascual, Mónica Pinto, and Lidia Fuentes

Departamento de Lenguajes y Ciencias de la Computación
University of Málaga, Málaga, Spain
CAOSD group
http://caosd.lcc.uma.es
{gustavo,pinto,lff}@lcc.uma.es

Abstract. The execution context in which pervasive systems or mobile computing run changes continuously. Hence, applications for these systems should be adapted at run-time according to the current context. In order to implement a context-aware dynamic reconfiguration service, most approaches usually require to model at design-time both the list of all possible configurations and the plans to switch among them. In this paper we present an alternative approach for the automatic run-time generation of application configurations and the reconfiguration plans. The generated configurations are optimal regarding different criteria, such as functionality or resource consumption (e.g. battery or memory). This is achieved by: (1) modelling architectural variability at design-time using Common Variability Language (CVL), and (2) using a genetic algorithm that finds at run-time nearly-optimal configurations using the information provided by the variability model. We also specify a case study and we use it to evaluate our approach, showing that it is efficient and suitable for devices with scarce resources.

Keywords: Architectural Variability, CVL, Dynamic Reconfiguration, Genetic Algorithm, Context, Pervasive Systems.

1 Introduction

Mobile applications demand runtime reconfiguration services that make it possible to adapt their behaviour to the continuous contextual changes that occur in their environment. One accepted approach to manage the runtime variability of applications is the Dynamic Software Product Line (DSPL) approach. DSPLs produce software capable of adapting to changes, by means of binding the variation points at runtime [1]. This means that the variants of the DSPL are generated at runtime.

Moreover, mobile applications run of lightweight devices with scarce resources (e.g. battery, memory, CPU, etc.), so they have the necessity of optimizing

---

* Work supported by Projects TIN2008-01942, P09-TIC-5231, TIN2012-34840 and INTER-TRUST FP7-317731.

K. Drira (Ed.): ECSA 2013, LNCS 7957, pp. 282–298, 2013.

their functionality to the continuous resource variations, and also to the user needs. Ideally, such optimization should be managed autonomously by the application, which should be self-adapted. In this sense, it is widely accepted by the distributed systems community the use of the Autonomic Computing (AC) paradigm [2] to endow distributed systems with self-management capacities.

Combining the ideas of DSPL with AC, the development of a software system with self-adaptation capacities implies the following steps: (1) modelling as part of the software architecture (SA) the variation points that the designer foresees that may change at runtime; (2) the runtime environment needs to be monitored to listen for contextual changes that may affect the variation points; (3) when a contextual change occurs, the system must analyse how the change affects the variation points, and if a reconfiguration is needed; (4) if so, a plan defined as the set of changes that need to be performed in the current configuration over the set of variation points must be generated, ideally at runtime, and finally (5) the architectural variation points that are affected by the reconfiguration must be modified according to the plan generated in the previous step.

For the first step, a language to model the system variability is needed. Variability is modeled at different abstraction levels, mostly using feature models (FM) [3] at the requirements level and UML profiles or Architecture Description Languages (ADLs) [4–6] at the architectural level. In our approach, we model variability at the architectural level using the Common Variability Language [7](CVL). The reasons for choosing CVL are twofold. First, it is a MOF-based variability language and this means that any MOF-based application model can be easily extended with variability information using CVL; second, it has been submitted to the OMG for its standardization and it is expected to be accepted soon as the standard for modelling and resolving variability.

For the rest of steps, we follow the typical MAPE-K loop of the AC paradigm, where "MAPE"' stands for Monitoring-Analysis-Plan-Execution and 'K' stands for Knowledge. Existing approaches [8–12, 3, 13] mainly consists on doing at design time the analysis of the contextual changes and the generation of the reconfiguration plans to meet the new environmental conditions. Then, the set of valid configurations are pre-calculated, as well as the differences between pairs of configurations and the conditions to adapt the system from one configuration to another one, loading them into the device as part of the knowledge base. This is a shortcoming which limits the number of possible configurations and avoid generating the optimal ones. The alternative of using models@runtime approaches [14, 15] has also limitations in mobile environments since these approaches normally demand high computing resources. Thus, one of the contributions of our approach is the generation of the application configurations and the reconfiguration plans automatically at runtime.

Moreover, most DSPL approaches do not consider the optimization of the used resources at runtime. However, when the availability of certain resources decreases or increases significantly, the ideal situation would be to be able to decide which architectural configuration provides the best functionality, while not exceeding the available resources. Thus, fast algorithms to calculate the optimum configuration at runtime are desirable. Since this can be formulated as an optimization problem, genetic algorithms (GAs) can be used to optimize the selection of architectural variation points that will conform to the new configuration. In this sense, a second contribution of our approach is the optimization of the used resources using genetic algorithms.

Specifically, our approach defines a *Context Monitoring* Service (CMS) for *monitoring* the environment and providing this information to a *Dynamic Reconfiguration Service* (DRS), which covers the *analysis* of the monitored information and the *generation* and *execution* of the reconfiguration *plans*. Both services are designed to be integrated in a middleware for adaptive applications development [16], although in this paper we focus on presenting the details of how the DRS accomplishes the runtime reconfiguration of mobile applications. On the one hand, our DRS has the SA with variability specified using CVL available at runtime as part of the knowledge base, using it to perform reconfiguration. On the other hand, when the availability of certain resources decreases or increases significantly, the DRS has to decide which architectural configuration provides the best functionality, while not exceeding the available resources. For this we use a GA [17] which have already been used in static SPL – i.e. the optimization is performed at design-time. Since our DRS is installed inside a mobile device, we present some evaluation results showing that our approach is feasible and efficient for being executed with the fairly limited resources of a mobile device, resulting in good response times and nearly-optimal architectural configurations.

The rest of the paper is organized as follows. The motivation of our approach, the main contributions and the case study used throughout the paper are presented in Section 2. Then, the approach is further described in Section 3. Evaluation results are presented in Section 4, related work discussed in Section 5 and finally our conclusions and on-going work are described in Section 6.

2 Motivation and Approach Overview

In this section we show the motivation for our work discussing challenges that have to be taken into account for specifying the DRS. The basics of CVL, an overview of our approach and a case study are also presented.

2.1 Common Variability Language (CVL)

CVL is a domain-independent language for specifying and resolving variability that allows the specification of variability over any model which has been defined using a MOF-based metamodel. The approach proposed by CVL can be seen in Figure 1. The *base model* of an application does not contain any information about variability. Instead, the variability information is separately specified in a *variability model*, according to the CVL metamodel. One of the main advantages of CVL is that it is *executable*, meaning that it is possible to automatically generate *resolved models*. To this end, *resolution models* are specified to decide the choices in the variability models that are selected in order to automatically

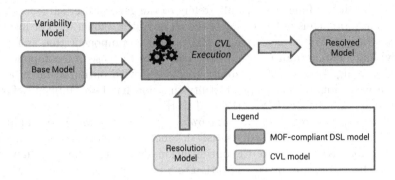

Fig. 1. CVL Approach

generate a fully specified product (i.e. without variability). In CVL, a variability model consists of three main parts:

1. **Variation points.** Define the points of the base model that are variable and can be modified during the CVL execution. For instance, some of the variation points supported by CVL are the existence of elements of the base model or the links among them, or the assignment of an attribute's value.
2. **Variability Specification Tree (VSpec tree).** Tree structures whose elements represent choices bound to variation points. These choices are resolved by a resolution model and propagated to variation points and the base model, generating the resolved model without variability. As it is explained in Section 2.4, VSpec trees show many commonalities with respect to FMs.
3. **OCL Constraints.** CVL supports the definition of OCL constraints among elements of a *VSpec tree*, providing a highly flexible mechanism for delimiting the bounds of variability, being able to discard invalid configurations.

2.2   Challenges

In order to achieve our goal of building a DRS that reacts to the runtime contextual changes by optimizing the configurations according to the availability of certain resources (e.g. battery, memory, CPU), we have identified a list of challenges that must be taken into account:

Challenge 1: Optimizing the architectural configuration. Mobile devices have scarce resources, so the challenge is to generate optimal configurations at runtime. We use an optimization algorithm that is able to find a nearly-optimal configuration taking into account the resource usage of the valid architectural configurations [1]. Concretely, the algorithm optimizes an *utility function* that quantify the architectural variation points according to a criterion specified by

---

[1] An exact algorithm cannot be used because the problem to be solved is NP-hard (non-deterministic polynomial-time hard).

the SA. This utility function typically refers to the general user satisfaction, although our approach is independent of the chosen utility function. For instance, the criterion can be the *precision* in the case of a component that is focused on providing location information, or the *quality* in the case of a component for video streaming. Because of its ability to fit well with optimization problems based on variability, the concept of utility function has been applied before in other proposals, such as MUSIC [12] and [11].

Challenge 2: Generating the reconfiguration plan at runtime. In our approach this challenge is straightforwardly satisfied. Since a configuration is specified as an array of bits (the output of the optimization algorithm), the reconfiguration plan to go from the running configuration to a new optimized one can be generated at runtime just by applying an XOR operation between the arrays of bits representing the source and target configurations (see Section 3).

Challenge 3: Executing the service in mobile environments. An important challenge of any service executing on a mobile environment is to reduce to the minimum the resources (time, memory, CPU, battery) consumed by the service itself. In particular, for a reconfiguration service, the time is critical since, in order to be useful, applications must be reconfigured without appreciating the extra time employed for the reconfiguration process. Regarding this, in Section 4 we demonstrate that our DRS is fast enough to avoid harming the user response time or the performance of the system.

2.3   Our Approach

All these challenges have been addressed in our approach, summarized in Figure 2. We propose a middleware in which the CMS and the DRS provide support for deploying adaptive applications by covering the steps of the MAPE-K loop.

Knowledge. As shown in Figure 2, in our approach the knowledge is represented by (1) the variation points; (2) the VSpecs tree; (3) the OCL constraints; (4) the software architecture; (5) the resource and utility information, and (6) the reconfiguration policy. The SA specifies the variability model in CVL, containing the variation points, the VSpecs tree and the OCL constraints, as well as an estimation of the resource usage and the utility provided by the components of the architecture. This information provides an optimization criterion for run-time reconfiguration and, therefore, using it we can generate different configurations at run-time which maximize the utility of the application without exceeding the availability of a concrete resource, addressing the *Challenge 1*.

Monitor. The CMS provides the DRS with information about the evolution of the availability of a certain resource, such as the battery level or the memory. When a change is detected, the DRS is notified.

Analyse. When a Context Change event is received, the DRS analyses if the change is significant enough to trigger the adaptation process –i.e. if the reconfiguration criteria is satisfied. There can be several criteria for measuring the significance of a context change. For instance, a change in the battery level can be significant if it has changed more than a 5% since the last measurement, or if it changes more than 10% per hour. Therefore, several reconfiguration policies can be defined, and the policy applied is part of the *Knowledge* base.

Plan. In case the analyser decides that the application needs to be adapted, the GA is executed in order to find a nearly-optimal configuration according to the current context. Then, the differences between the current realization model and the new one are calculated, generating a plan for switching between them (*Challenge 2*). As it has been explained in Section 2.2, calculating the difference between two configurations is quite straightforward since it is directly obtained by performing an XOR operation between both configurations.

Execute. Finally, the plan is executed in order to adapt the running architecture of the application.

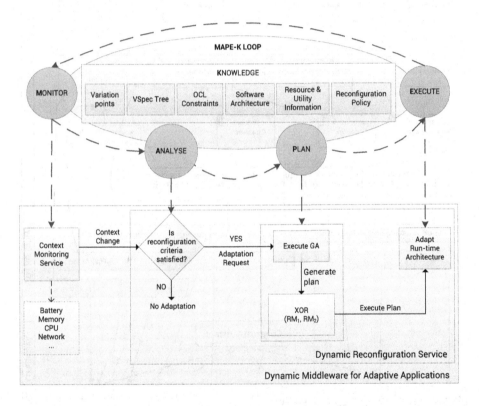

Fig. 2. Approach Overview

2.4   Case Study

In the following sections we use a case study that consists of an application that assists attendees of international congresses, keeping them up to date with the latest news and providing several social facilities. The application provides the following variable set of services:

1. Access to information about the events, stands and news about the congress.
2. Receive a video stream of keynotes or conferences in the mobile phone. The quality of the received video is variable (high, medium, low).
3. Check-in in the stands/events to track your activity. The technology used is variable and either NFC or Bluetooth may be used.
4. Access information about your friends: location, visited events and stands, agenda. Location is obtained using GPS or WLAN, and the measuring rate is variable (high, medium or low).
5. Exchange public messages or with your friends using a message board.

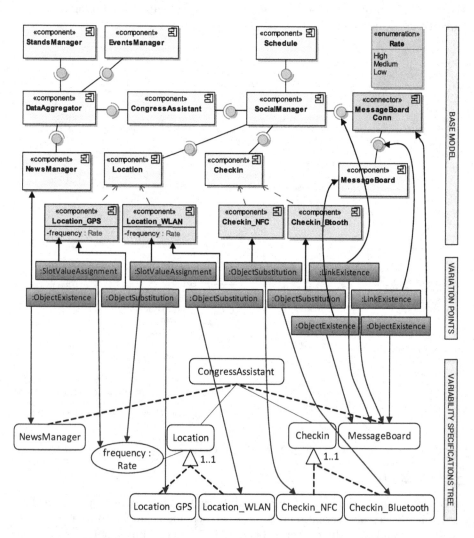

Fig. 3. Case study (Base model and variability model)

This application can be adapted according to user preferences (e.g. high quality of video is preferred), to the availability of the resources (e.g. WLAN is used because GPS is not available) or to the amount of consumed resources (e.g. use low quality of video because the mobile battery is low). In this paper we focus on this last kind of reconfiguration.

Figure 3 shows an excerpt of the component-and-connector view of the software architecture of our case study – i.e. components model the basic behaviour of the application and communicate with each other using connectors. All the connectors, except MessageBoardConn have been omitted from the figure for legibility reasons. The variability model is also shown in the Figure, including both the *variation points* and the *variability specifications tree*. For instance, using CVL we define *optional* components (ObjectExistence variation point), different variants for a component (ObjectSubstitution variation point), parametrizable components (SlotValueAssignment variation point) and optional links between elements (LinkExistence variation point).

The main component of the architectural model is the CongressAssistant. On the one hand, it communicates with the DataAggregator component for accessing information about events, stands, news or for receiving a video stream of a conference. On the other hand, it communicates with the SocialManager component in order to take advantage of the social facilities of the application. The Location component is responsible for providing the location of the owner of the mobile device for tracking his/her position, and can be realized either by the Location_GPS or the Location_WLAN variants. The GPS variant measurements are more precise but it is also much more expensive regarding battery consumption. On the other hand, the Checkin component can also be realized by Checkin_NFC and Checkin_Btooth components. As we can see in the figure, this is specified in the architectural model by applying the ObjectSubstitution variation points to the components and realizations. On the other hand, the components Location_GPS and Location_WLAN have a configurable parameter, frequency, which defines the measuring rate. To this end, the SlotValueAssignment variation point has been applied to the parameters of the components.

The architectural elements with an ObjectExistence variation point can be removed from the configuration. For instance, the Location component if the battery level is low. Then, the links between the SocialManager and Location components, which are not shown in detail in the figure, should be removed too. Our DRS detects when a connector or a component is not necessary and removes it automatically in order to ensure that the resulting configuration is always consistent. We can see that a LinkExistence variation point has been associated to the links which connect the SocialManager and the MessageBoard components because they are removed in case the connector is deleted from the architectural model.

Each variations point has to be bound to a VSpec of the VSpec tree. We use two different kinds of VSpecs: *choices* and *variables*. Choices, which are shown in the figure as rectangles with rounded corners, are evaluated to *true* or *false*. On the other hand, *variables* can be evaluated to values of different types. For instance, if the VSpec *NewsManager* is decided false, the linked ObjectExistence variation point is disabled and the NewsManager component is removed from the architectural configuration. On the other hand, the value provided to the variable frequency is propagated to the frequency attribute of the Location_WLAN and Location_GPS components because they are bound to this variable through SlotValueAssignment variation points. An Vspec can be bound to its parent by a solid or a dotted line. In the first case, it means that in case the parent has been decided true, a value has to be decided for that VSpec too. Then, a dotted line means that if the parent has been evaluated false, it is not necessary to decide a value for this VSpec. For instance, if the Location Vspec is decided false, it is not necessary to decide a value for Loaction_GPS or Location_WLAN.

The information about resource usage and utility is provided as a table in which each entry specifies the resource usage and the utility of different elements of the architectural model (components, variants or parameters). This information, together with the VSpec tree, are the input for the GA which is executed by the DRS in order to find a configuration of the application that fits the current context. In this case, the resource we are restricting is the battery usage. Some of these values are shown in Table 1.

Table 1. Resource usage and utility information table

Element	Battery	Utility
Location_GPS	60	35
Location_WLAN	30	15
Location_WLAN.frequency.High	15	9
Location_WLAN.frequency.Medium	10	7
Location_WLAN.frequency.Low	5	4

3 Dynamic Reconfiguration Service

As previously described, the DRS is responsible for adapting the applications at runtime according to the current context, while the CMS provides the DRS with context information. In this section we mainly focus on the plan stage of the MAPE-K loop (Plan Generator), which is part of the DRS and uses the variability model, the context information and the utility and resources information.

As Brataas et al. show in [18], the reconfiguration time is divided in three different tasks: (1) analyse the context data; (2) plan (decide) the new configuration and (3) execute the plan in order to deploy the new configuration. They prove that the cost of the first and third tasks can be considered fixed, while it is critical to make the plan task as efficient as possible because it depends on the number of configuration variants. Therefore, the challenge is finding the set of choices for the VSpecs Tree (i.e. the resolution model) that defines the optimal configuration (the one that provides the highest utility while not exceeding the resources limitations) in a very efficient way. However, it is an NP-hard problem [19] and, therefore, it is impossible to use exact techniques to solve this optimization problem for our purpose. Concretely, as shown in [17], exact techniques can only be applied to small cases at the cost of a very high execution time. Nevertheless, artificial intelligence algorithms can find nearly-optimal solutions in an efficient and scalable way. In this paper, we use a genetic algorithm based on the algorithm of Guo et al. [17], which focus on optimizing feature models configurations, for optimizing the Vspecs Tree, since it has been proven to be efficient and produces nearly-optimal results. Concretely, this algorithm is able to generate configurations with about 90% of optimality, which means that the utility of the solutions obtained using this algorithm is approximately the 90% of the utility of the optimal configuration that would be obtained using an exact algorithm. Although the algorithm by Guo et al. is not focused on a DSPL approach, we show in this paper that their algorithm is applicable to the DSPL domain. Furthermore, thanks to the great improvement in the processing and memory capacities of smartphones, using artificial intelligence algorithms in mobile devices is feasible and efficient, as it is proven in this paper.

Therefore, the plan generator of the DRS relies on a genetic algorithm to decide which configuration should be deployed according to the current context. In genetic algorithms, solutions are modelled as chromosomes. A chromosome consist of a sequence of genes, where each gene is a boolean value. In our case, VSpecs are mapped to genes in this way: (1) VSpec tree is traversed in a concrete order, which can be either breadth-first or depth-first; (2) each *choice* VSpec is modelled as a gen. In case the gen is evaluated as *true*, the VSpec is also decided true and (3) each *variable* VSpec is modelled as a set of genes. Concretely, a gen is added for each possible value of the VSpec. Only one of these genes can be evaluated as true simultaneously. Then, the gen whose value is true provides the value for the VSpec.

The steps taken during the execution of the algorithm are as follows:

1. *Population initialization.* A set of initial chromosomes (configurations) is generated. They are generated randomly, and therefore it is necessary to transform each one to get a valid solution from each randomly-generated one. The transformation process performs the necessary additions and exclusions of Vspecs from the randomly generated one, returning a chromosome which represents a valid configuration as a result which, in addition, does not exceed the available resources.

2. *Evolution through generations.* Once an initial population of valid configurations has been generated, the next step is evolving the population through generations in order to find better configurations, which provide a higher utility. In each generation, two chromosomes randomly chosen from the population are crossed. The resulting chromosome is transformed to get a a valid solution, and the worst chromosome of the population is replaced with the new one. This process is repeated until a stopping condition is reached. For instance, the evolution can be stopped once a maximum number of generations is reached or when the population has not evolved after a certain number of consecutive generations. In our case, we use both conditions, stopping the evolution when the first one is reached.

3. *Return the best chromosome.* The best chromosome, which represents the configuration which provides the highest utility, is returned as the solution to the optimization problem.

In the rest of this section, this approach is applied to our case study, as illustrated by Figure 4. First, before the application is started, it is necessary to deploy the initial configuration. An initial population of chromosomes that represent valid configurations and fit the resource constraints is generated. Our VSpec Tree is mapped to a chromosome that contains 81 genes but, due to the lack of space, we only show a reduced set (NewsManager, Location_WLAN, Location_GPS, Location.frequency.High, Location.frequency.Medium, Location.frequency.Low in Figure 4). Then, in every generation, two chromosomes are randomly selected for performing a *crossover*. A *crossover* between the two selected parents (...110100... and ...101010...) is performed taking genes randomly from both parents, and the resulting *offspring* (...110010...) is *mutated* by changing the value of one of its genes (...111010...). However, the *offspring* will probably be an invalid chromosome because it does not fit the constraints of the VSpec Tree. For instance, in our example, the *offspring* has the Location_GPS component selected (i.e. its bit is 1), but no location frequency is specified. Therefore, it is necessary to apply a *transformation* to the *offspring*, which adds all the missing decisions. The transformation mechanism adds them, and its output is a valid configuration where, in this case, the Location.frequency VSpec is set to *medium* (...110010...). Then, this new chromosome replaces the chromosome with lowest value of the population, and this process is repeated until the stopping condition is reached.

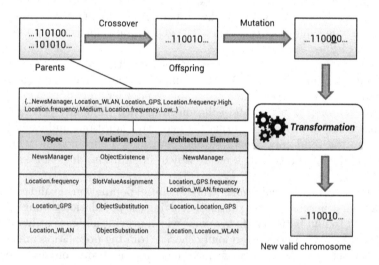

Fig. 4. Applying the genetic algorithm in the Dynamic Reconfiguration Service

4   Evaluation

In this section we evaluate the ability of the optimization algorithm to find nearly-optimal configurations according to the available resources. Furthermore, since the resources of mobile devices are very limited, it is very important to

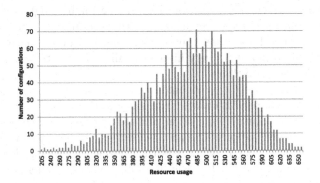

Fig. 5. Case Study configurations distribution

verify the efficiency of the algorithm. Concretely, the time elapsed by the algorithm during the optimization process has been measured. To this end, the optimization algorithm has been applied to our case study using an ASUS Nexus 7 device running Android 4.2.1.

The VSpec tree defined for the variability specification of our case study contain 2400 valid configurations that fulfill all the constraints. Figure 5 shows how these configurations are distributed according to their resource usage. Concretely, we can see that there is a peak in the distribution of configurations at around 500 units of resource usage. Therefore, we can expect a significant decrease in the execution time of the algorithm as the available resources increase and get closer to 500 units because it is increasingly easier to find a valid configuration. On the other hand, once the peak is exceeded, the number of new valid configurations decreases fast. Therefore, we can expect a nearly-constant execution time despite the increase in the available resources.

All the experiments have been repeated 100 times and the mean value and standard deviation (both for utility and time) has been calculated. The size of the population is 30, while the maximum number of generations for each repetition of the experiment is 20, stopping the algorithm if no better solutions are found after 3 consecutive generations. These settings have been proven to provide good results, although an exhaustive optimization of them, which will be addressed in future work, has not been performed. For the evaluation of the effectiveness of the algorithm we have compared the solutions obtained using the genetic algorithm with the optimal solutions. In order to find the optimal solutions we have generated a list of all the valid configurations, calculating then the resource usage and the utility of each one of them. This step (obtaining the optimal solutions) have been executed in a desktop computer since it is too expensive to be run in a mobile device.

Results are shown in Figure 6 and summarized in Table 2. If we use the concept of optimality presented in [17], which can be defined as the ratio between the utility of the solution obtained using the genetic algorithm and the one obtained using the exact method, the results show that the degree of optimality of the solutions obtained is always over 87%. The optimality slightly decreases as the available resources increase because there are much more valid configurations whose utility is much lower than the optimal one. However, even in the worst case the degree of optimality is very high, specially taking into account that the optimization problem is NP-hard.

On the other hand, we have evaluated the time elapsed in the execution of the algorithm. We distinguish between the initialization time, which is the time needed to generate the initial population, and the analysis time, elapsed iterating over the successive generations. The results for the initialization time are shown in Table 2. As it is expected, when the restrictions are harder (less resources are available) it is more difficult to obtain valid solutions. Therefore, the time elapsed in the generation of the initial population is higher. In the worst case, the initialization time is 334.584 ms. However, as the available resources are higher, it becomes much easier to find valid solutions and the initialization time drops significantly, falling below 100 ms when the available resources are higher than 380 units. Further optimizations can be introduced in the algorithm in order to minimize the initialization time. For instance, those elements of the population that remain valid can be reused along different executions of the optimization algorithm. However, it has not been still evaluated and will be addressed in future work. Regarding the analysis time, we can see that it is very low compared with the initialization time. Although its value does not vary significantly with respect to the available resources, we can see that it increases slightly as the number of available resources increase. This behaviour can be explained because, when there are less available resources, the algorithm usually stops before reaching 20 generations because no better solutions are found.

According to the results obtained, we consider that our approach is suitable for providing support for dynamic reconfiguration on mobiles devices, generating nearly-optimal configurations without introducing an excessive overhead.

Table 2. Evaluation Results Summary

Resource limit	Obtained utility	Optimality	Initialization time (ms)	Analysis time (ms)
205	425 ($\sigma = 0$)	100%	334.584 ($\sigma = 55.207$)	2.416 ($\sigma = 0.995$)
255	474.62 ($\sigma = 1.886$)	99.92%	177.312 ($\sigma = 29.056$)	3.224 ($\sigma = 2.697$)
300	524.59 ($\sigma = 10.755$)	96.79%	147.137 ($\sigma = 22$)	4.055 ($\sigma = 2.169$)
350	580.9 ($\sigma = 17.514$)	94.61%	115.03 ($\sigma = 17.483$)	4.321 ($\sigma = 2.419$)
400	614.52 ($\sigma = 19.865$)	92.13%	96.291 ($\sigma = 11.877$)	5.03 ($\sigma = 2.195$)
450	641.635 ($\sigma = 20.333$)	89.49%	81.319 ($\sigma = 8.577$)	6.055 ($\sigma = 3.738$)
500	665.075 ($\sigma = 23.652$)	90.24%	76.067 ($\sigma = 7.128$)	7.128 ($\sigma = 4.577$)
550	680.445 ($\sigma = 27.414$)	87.91%	74.043 ($\sigma = 6.316$)	8.013 ($\sigma = 5.52$)
600	692.66 ($\sigma = 32.322$)	87.68%	75.165 ($\sigma = 9.921$)	9.484 ($\sigma = 6.762$)
655	691.904 ($\sigma = 32.656$)	87.03%	73.682 ($\sigma = 6.091$)	8.83 ($\sigma = 6.381$)

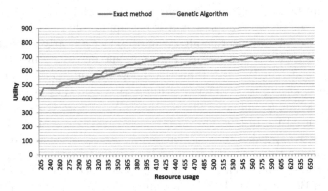

Fig. 6. Optimality Evaluation

5   Related Work

In this section we discuss those approaches comparable to the work presented in this paper. On the one hand, our approach is driven by the MAPE-K loop on which AC rely, providing the applications for mobile devices with the ability to reconfigure their architecture in an autonomic and optimal way according to the available resources. We can find several approaches in the literature which also rely on the same principals. For instance, Gamez et al. [3] propose a reconfiguration mechanism that switches among different architectural configurations at run-time. The valid configurations are manually specified and represented using FMs, while the reconfiguration plans are automatically generated from the differences among them. Therefore, both are specified at design-time, which leads to the deployment of sub-optimal configurations at run-time.

There are also many work that do not exactly follow the principals of AC but provide support for reconfiguration at the application level [8, 13], or also at the middleware layer [9–12]. However, they are not usually available for evaluation or they are not runnable on mobile devices. MUSIC [12] is an OSGi-based middleware for developing context-aware adaptive applications. It is a component based and service oriented approach which mainly consists of two different parts: the context and the adaptation middlewares. The adaptation middleware is responsible for adapting the applications, deploying the configuration that best fits the current context. The main difference between MUSIC (as well as the other existing approaches) and our approach is that they require having available at runtime all the valid configurations of an application, while in our approach this configuration is generated on demand using the optimization algorithm.

Other work use CVL to manage variability and provide reconfiguration support. For instance, Ayora et al. [15] propose a mechanism for managing variability in business processes. At design time, variability is modelled using CVL. Then, process variants are adapted following a *models@runtime* approach, which is not suitable for devices with scarce resources. In [20], Cetina et al. also model variability using CVL, applying it to smart-homes environments. Concretely, several mechanisms for applying the necessary model transformations are evaluated. However, as in the previous approach, it is not applicable to mobile devices.

Finally, we use an optimization algorithm to select a nearly-optimal configuration that satisfies the resource constraints and maximizes a utility function. In this sense, there are similar algorithms that allow the automatic generation of a *resolution model* according to different criteria. However, they are applied to (1) variability modelling techniques different than CVL VSpec trees, such as FMs, and (2) to static SPLs. In [19], an FM is transformed into a Multi-dimensional Multiple-choice Knapsack Problem that allows nearly-optimal FM configurations in polynomial-time to be found. This is also the objective of [17], but using genetic algorithms, being even faster than the previous one. On the other hand, the proposal of Benavides et al. [21] always finds the optimal configuration using Constraint Satisfaction Problems with exponential-time complexity, making it unsuitable for runtime optimization.

The main difference with our approach is that all these algorithms have been used in static SPLs, while we use it in DSPLs. In a static SPL a product configuration is generated during the design time in order to deploy one particular product from the family of products. This means that the algorithm is applied only once at design time. We use the algorithm to implement a DSPL, meaning that the optimization algorithm is used at runtime by the DRS in order to adapt the product. The most similar approach to ours is the work presented in [22], where an optimization algorithm is also used to improve user interface adaptation at runtime. An important difference is that their work is specific to a user interface architectural model, while our approach is more general because it can be applied to the architectural model of any kind of applications They use a different optimization algorithm although, as in our case, their approach does not depend on a particular optimization algorithm and is designed to work with other algorithms. Finally, the average adaptation time of our approach is considerable lower than the one reported in [22].

6   Conclusions

In this paper we have presented a novel approach that provides support for the dynamic reconfiguration of mobile applications, optimizing the system configuration according to the available resources. In order to do that we model the variability of the application architectural model using CVL. In this way, we take advantage of available algorithms to optimize the variability resolution. Concretely, the use of a GA has been proposed to obtain nearly-optimal configurations at runtime using the VSpec tree, the context information and the resource and utility information as input. In order to describe and evaluate our approach we have applied it to a case study. A set of experiments have been defined to evaluate the efficiency of the optimization algorithm applied to our case study in order to verify that it is suitable for resource-constrained devices. The results obtained show that it is efficient and can be used to provide dynamic reconfiguration in mobile devices without introducing an excessive overhead.

References

1. Hallsteinsen, S., Hinchey, M., Park, S., Schmid, K.: Dynamic software product lines. Computer 41(4), 93–95 (2008)
2. IBM: Autonomic Computing White Paper — An Architectural Blueprint for Autonomic Computing. IBM Corp. (2005)
3. Gamez, N., Fuentes, L., Aragüez, M.A.: Autonomic computing driven by feature models and architecture in famiware. In: Crnkovic, I., Gruhn, V., Book, M. (eds.) ECSA 2011. LNCS, vol. 6903, pp. 164–179. Springer, Heidelberg (2011)
4. Haber, A., Kutz, T., Rendel, H., Rumpe, B., Schaefer, I.: Delta-oriented architectural variability using monticore. In: Proceedings of the 5th European Conference on Software Architecture: Companion Volume, ECSA 2011, pp. 6:1–6:10. ACM, New York (2011)
5. Adachi Barbosa, E., Batista, T., Garcia, A., Silva, E.: Pl-aspectualacme: an aspect-oriented architectural description language for software product lines. In: Crnkovic, I., Gruhn, V., Book, M. (eds.) ECSA 2011. LNCS, vol. 6903, pp. 139–146. Springer, Heidelberg (2011)
6. Gomaa, H.: Designing software product lines with uml 2.0: From use cases to pattern-based software architectures. In: Morisio, M. (ed.) ICSR 2006. LNCS, vol. 4039, p. 440. Springer, Heidelberg (2006)
7. CVL: Common Variability Language, http://www.omgwiki.org/variability/
8. Chan, A., et al.: MobiPADS: a reflective middleware for context-aware mobile computing. IEEE Transactions on Software Engineering, 1072–1085 (2003)
9. Gu, T., et al.: A service-oriented middleware for building context-aware services. Journal of Network and Computer Applications 28(1), 1–18 (2005)
10. Janik, A., Zielinski, K.: AAOP-based dynamically reconfigurable monitoring system. Information and Software Technology 52(4), 380–396 (2010)
11. Paspallis, N.: Middleware-based development of context-aware applications with reusable components. University of Cyprus (2009)
12. Rouvoy, R., Barone, P., Ding, Y., Eliassen, F., Hallsteinsen, S., Lorenzo, J., Mamelli, A., Scholz, U.: MUSIC: Middleware support for self-adaptation in ubiquitous and service-oriented environments. In: Cheng, B.H.C., de Lemos, R., Giese, H., Inverardi, P., Magee, J. (eds.) Self-Adaptive Systems. LNCS, vol. 5525, pp. 164–182. Springer, Heidelberg (2009)
13. Cuervo, E., Balasubramanian, A., Cho, D., Wolman, A., Saroiu, S., Chandra, R., Bahl, P.: Maui: Making smartphones last longer with code offload. In: Proceedings of the 8th International Conference on Mobile Systems, Applications, and Services, pp. 49–62. ACM (2010)
14. Welsh, K., Bencomo, N.: Run-time model evaluation for requirements model-driven self-adaptation. In: 2012 20th IEEE International Requirements Engineering Conference (RE), pp. 329–330. IEEE (2012)
15. Ayora, C., Torres, V., Pelechano, V., Alférez, G.H.: Applying CVL to business process variability management. In: Proceedings of the VARiability for You Workshop: Variability Modeling Made Useful for Everyone, VARY 2012, pp. 26–31. ACM, New York (2012)
16. Pascual, G.: Aspect-oriented reconfigurable middleware for pervasive systems. In: Proceedings of the CAiSE Doctoral Consortium, vol. 731. CEUR-WS (2011)
17. Guo, J., White, J., Wang, G., Li, J., Wang, Y.: A genetic algorithm for optimized feature selection with resource constraints in software product lines. Journal of Systems and Software 84(12), 2208–2221 (2011)

18. Brataas, G., et al.: Scalability of decision models for dynamic product lines (2007)
19. White, J., et al.: Selecting highly optimal architectural feature sets with filtered cartesian flattening. Journal of Systems and Software 82(8), 1268–1284 (2009)
20. Cetina, C., Haugen, O., Zhang, X., Fleurey, F., Pelechano, V.: Strategies for variability transformation at run-time. In: Proceedings of the 13th International SPLC, SPLC 2009, pp. 61–70. Carnegie Mellon University, Pittsburgh (2009)
21. Benavides, D., Trinidad, P., Ruiz-Cortés, A.: Automated reasoning on feature models. In: Pastor, Ó., Falcão e Cunha, J. (eds.) CAiSE 2005. LNCS, vol. 3520, pp. 491–503. Springer, Heidelberg (2005)
22. Blouin, A., et al.: Combining Aspect-Oriented Modeling with Property-Based Reasoning to Improve User Interface Adaptation. In: ACM SIGCHI Symposium on Engineering Interactive Computing Systems, Pisa, Italy, pp. 85–94 (June 2011)

Towards Extensive Software Architecture Erosion Repairs

Matthias Mair and Sebastian Herold

Clausthal University of Technology, Department of Informatics
Julius-Albert-Strasse 4, 38678 Clausthal-Zellerfeld, Germany
{matthias.mair,sebastian.herold}@tu-clausthal.de

Abstract. Software architecture erosion can reduce the quality of software systems significantly. It is hence of great importance to repair erosion efficiently, for example, by means of refactoring. However, existing refactoring approaches do not address architecture erosion holistically.

In this paper, we describe the problem of optimally repairing software architecture erosion and investigate the applicability and limitations of current refactoring approaches. We argue that a heuristic search for adequate repairs using formalized and explicit knowledge of software engineers could overcome those limitations.

This paper outlines an approach we have been starting to investigate in our recent research and also aims at stimulating a discussion about further research challenges in repairing software architecture erosion.

Keywords: software architecture, software architecture erosion, refactoring, software maintenance.

1 Introduction

The more complex a software system is and the longer its lifetime is, the higher the risk is that software architecture erosion or architectural drifts occur [1,2]. Both terms describe the divergence of the intended software architecture and its realization. The reasons for architecture erosion and architectural drifts are manifold, e.g., changes in code for bug-fixing or adapting to new requirements [3]. In general, architecture erosion leads to a degradation of system quality attributes such as maintainability and reusability. In the long term, progressing erosion leads to software that requires to be replaced by completely and expensively redeveloped systems [4].

Approaches dealing with software architecture erosion can be divided into three categories [5]. Approaches to *avoid erosion* couple architecture design and implementation such that divergence is unlikely to happen. The second category concludes approaches to *minimize erosion* mainly based on consistency checking, e.g., reflexion modeling [6] or generative techniques to establish consistency (semi-)automatically, such as model-driven engineering (MDE) approaches.

Approaches of the third category try to *repair erosion* and become important if complete avoidance is impossible, or to complement minimizing approaches.

K. Drira (Ed.): ECSA 2013, LNCS 7957, pp. 299–306, 2013.

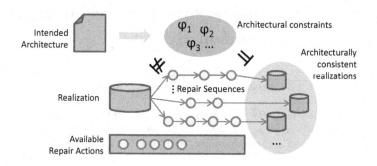

Fig. 1. The problem of finding optimal architecture erosion repair sequences

This group of approaches consists mostly of reengineering and refactoring techniques [7,8]. However, repairing architecture erosion requires a broad understanding of the—often rather complex—software system at hand. It might be difficult for software designers and programmers to find a good or even optimal way to refactor an eroded software system.

In this paper, we will investigate the problem of how to support software engineers in repairing eroded software systems. We will discuss how the state of the art in refactoring addresses this problem and propose an outline of a heuristic approach to determine good repair actions for a broad set of possible cases of erosion.

2   Problem Analysis

In an eroded software system, the realization of the system does not conform to the intended architecture. Repairing or reversing the erosion process can be understood as the task of transforming and manipulating the realization such that conformance is re-established. Finding the optimal way to do that is the task of finding a sequence of repair steps that is optimal regarding a measure of costs, e.g. least steps to perform, required time to perform, etc.

Following Eden et al. [9], a software architecture can be understood as a set of logical statements about possible realizations. A realization conforms to an architecture, if and only if it fulfills the set of logical statements given by the architecture. For example, the layers pattern [10] defines constraints about the allowed dependencies between components of the system. Only realizations in which dependencies are going from "upper" layers to "lower" layers conform to this pattern. Eden lists many different examples of architectural aspects, such as patterns, reference architecture, naming conventions, metrics that can be interpreted this way and expresses them as first-order logic statements.

Figure 1 illustrates the difficulty of finding optimal repair sequences to repair architectural erosion. Given is an intended software architecture represented as a set of first-order logic statements and a realization that does not fulfill these

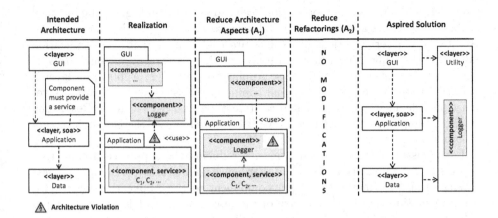

Fig. 2. Application scenario that shows current approaches and their deficits

statements. Furthermore, there is a set of atomic repair actions, such as a catalog of refactorings [8] defining how structures in a realization can be modified.

Due to the undecidability of first-order logic, the set of realizations conforming to the given architecture is not computable. Consequently, the set of sequences of repair actions is not computable as well. This implies that we have to perform an exhaustive search for the optimal sequence of repair actions that transforms the actual, non-conforming realization into a conforming one. Checking potential solutions hence means to perform first-order logic model checking.

Two issues have to be considered for this search: first, it is not clear that the search will terminate (is there a sequence transforming the current realization into architecturally conformable one at all?); second, the search-space of this problem is very "broad" depending on the number of available repair actions and possible places for application. For example, Fowler's catalog of refactorings consists of about 90 refactorings. The *Move Class* refactoring alone has c^{p-1} possible applications for c classes and p possible places to move classes.

Thus, the general problem of finding optimal repair sequences is very complex. Most applicable solutions from the field of automated refactorings in practice apply heuristic search techniques. There are several restrictions and possibilities to reduce complexity in order to provide practical solutions:

- Reduce architecture aspects. This reduces the complexity of checking solution candidates to something less complex (see Sec. 3) than general first-order logic model checking. On the other hand, flexibility is sacrificed by a certain degree because there are remaining architectural constraints that cannot be checked—hence, not every case of architecture erosion can be considered.
- Reduce available refactorings to decrease the size of the search space. This implies that not every way of how architecture erosion can be repaired, can be considered.

Consider, for example, the application scenario depicted in Fig. 2. The Intended Architecture follows a strict layered architecture with GUI, Application and Data. Additionally a service-oriented architecture (SOA) is used in the Application layer. More specific, this architecture implies three *architectural constraints* or *rules*: (1) GUI layer is allowed to use Application layer, (2) Application layer is allowed to use Data layer and (3) all components inside the Application layer must provide a service (represented as stereotype «service»). In the Realization a logger component is placed in the GUI layer and causes thereby architecture violations.

Let us assume that A_1 is an approach reducing the supported architecture aspects by not considering SOAs and that hence ignores rule (3). It could suggest a refactoring that moves the logger component to the Application layer. This is correct inside the restricted view of the approach A_1 but is not the aspired solution. An approach A_2 that supports only *Move Class* refactorings, would not find a better solution than the current realization. A possible aspired solution, however, with a more extensive set of refactorings and knowledge about both architectural aspects, would solve the problem by creating a new Utility layer and moving the logger component inside it.

In the following, we will discuss how current approaches address the complexity of the general problem of finding appropriate refactorings, and the restrictions they make.

3   State of the Art of Complex Refactoring

The following approaches do often not explicitly name architecture erosion as one of the motivating use cases. Nevertheless, most of them use heuristic techniques to find opportunities for applying refactorings in complex systems which includes somehow evaluating the "goodness" of an application in a certain context. This is comparable to the situation we are faced with if we are searching for a repair sequence.

As discussed in Sec. 2, one way to reduce the complexity of the general problem of finding repair sequences is focusing on architectural aspects. For example, many approaches are focusing on the evaluation of metrics to find opportunities in systems for the application of refactorings. Ouni et al. [11] use metrics for a multi-objective approach for Fowler's catalog of refactorings. Seng et al. [12] and in a similar way O'Keeffe et al. [13] restrict their approaches to metrics regarding class structures and support the relevant refactorings from the same catalog. Ivkovic et al. [14] refine softgoals to metrics to determine applications of refactorings. All these approaches are appropriate for using architectural principles as source for possible refactorings as far as those principles can be quantified by metrics. They do not consider architectural aspects like dependency constraints or other structural constraints.

Other approaches focus on single structural constraints such as simple graph patterns on program dependency graphs [15], or cycles in such graphs [16]. While the formalism—graphs—provides great expressiveness, the set of actual expressions they investigate is limited. The same holds for approaches focusing on other structural dependencies or properties, such as code clones [17], layering of systems [18,19], or a set of bad smells [20].

Most approaches limit also the set of supported refactorings. The already mentioned work described by Dietrich et al. [15], for example, detects unwanted graph patterns in program dependency graphs and uses the removal of edges only as refactoring. Shah et al. [16] use only the *Move Class* refactoring to resolve dependency cycles. Tsantalis et al. [21] identify *Move Method* refactoring opportunities, Hotta et al. [17] for *Form Template Method* refactorings. Other approaches mentioned above, consider 5–15 different refactorings [12,13,22,19,23]. The work of Terra et al. [24] allows to define user-specific refactorings by combining seven atomic refactorings. The considered architectural aspects are only limited by the *Dependency Constraint Language (DCL)*; however, they only detect opportunities of refactorings without searching for optimal solutions.

It must be concluded that the current state of the art provides appropriate support for finding solutions for single kinds of architectural erosion. The restrictions that the approaches exhibit, however, are too strong to let them address the general problem of repairing software architecture erosion adequately. Especially the restrictions to single or few architectural aspects do not allow a seamless support to the general problem; erosion especially occurs if different, potentially conflicting architectural aspects are applied.

4   Solution Outline

The application scenario in Fig. 2 illustrates that current approaches cannot address the general problem satisfyingly, thus a new and more powerful approach with the following properties is needed:

- Support of many architecture aspects
- Support of many, possibly user-specific, atomic and composite repair actions
- Search for and recommend optimal repair sequences
- Formalize software engineering expertise to keep the heuristic search focused

An overall process of a new approach is depicted in Fig. 3. The Architecture Checking process transforms the intended architecture and the realization into logical facts of a Knowledge Representation and Reasoning (KRR) system. Furthermore, the architecture rules are represented as queries that can be executed by the KRR system; results returned by executing these queries indicate architectural violations; these are tuples of violated architecture rules and the binding of variables causing the violation.

Afterwards, the Repair Recommendation process tries to find and recommend optimal repair sequences. Inside the process the Heuristic Search is supported by the Rating process which computes after each step—adding a new repair action to the repair sequence—if the current solution is closer to the demanded optimum. The result of the repair recommendation process is a set of ranked repair sequences, i.e. ranked system solutions by remaining architecture violations.

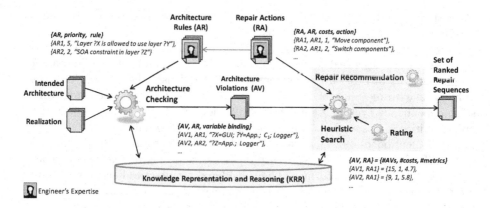

Fig. 3. Overview and process of the proposed approach

The heuristic search operates on the facts in the KRR system, the previously identified architecture violations and the repair actions. The repair actions are possible solutions for violations and extended by their costs. In addition, the architecture rules are prioritized, for example, by their negative influence on the system and thereby candidates that should be repaired first. Prioritization is not easy and should be done well with software engineering expertise. Executing the heuristic search computes the next step by choosing all violations with the same highest priority and apply their repair actions. The result are tuples of architecture violations and repair actions which the rating process can evaluate and rank.

The optimum is a vector with values which includes but is not limited to: number of violations, costs and metrics (e.g., coupling, cohesion, etc.). Furthermore, it might be useful to assign weights to the values in the vector to specify a demanded optimum. The overall goal is to get rid of violations, but through changing the factors the heuristic search can be controlled to focus on, for example, costs or metric values.

Inside the rating process for each tuple of architecture violation and repair action the number of violations are determined by executing the architecture checking process again. The cost value is taken from the repair action and the metric values are calculated in the KRR system. Afterwards the ranking is done on basis of the demanded optimum. If there are still violations, the heuristic search chooses an arbitrary number of repair sequences and continues with the next step, otherwise the algorithm terminates. Due to the fact that first-order logic is undecidable, the heuristic search algorithm terminates alternatively by setting a cost limit or a maximal step depth.

A big advantage of this approach and the main distinction to other approaches is the more extensive usage of explicitly modeled engineering expertise. The knowledge, for example, is used in prioritization of architecture rules and the connection of them with repair actions. Additionally the vector values can be extended through new software engineering aspects, for example, new metrics which bring up better system solutions. Furthermore, the knowledge is used to model new repair actions that resolve architecture violations, for example, creating a new layer to resolve a layer dependency violation (see Fig. 2).

The focus of the current work is on the repair recommendation process. For the architecture checking process the approach uses the tool *Architecture Checker* (ArCh) [25] which can handle different architecture aspects formalized as first-order logic statements. The output of ArCh are architecture violations that the approach can use directly.

A first evaluation of the approach is currently in progress which tries to find optimal repair sequences for dependency violations in layered architectures. As case study serves the open source software *jEdit*. Within the evaluation different heuristic search algorithms are tested that try to find an optimum in regard to the number of violations and costs.

5   Conclusion

Software architecture erosion happens very likely during the lifetime of complex software systems and cannot be avoided completely in general. Repairing eroded software architectures is therefore an important task. Refactoring techniques are an important puzzle piece to tackle this task.

Existing approaches limit the set of considered architectural aspects or the set of possible repairs to deal with the overall complexity of the task. Both limitations lead to approaches that do not address the overall problem holistically as shown by a simple application scenario. Instead, we suggest to formalize more existing engineering knowledge of how to repair architecture violation to realize a more effective heuristic search for good architectural repairs in complex eroded systems, and outline a possible approach to extensive architecture erosion detection.

In the future, we will further elaborate this approach and plan to conduct extensive industrial case studies to show the applicability to "real life" erosion cases and the usefulness for dealing with software architecture erosion.

References

1. Perry, D.E., Wolf, A.L.: Foundations for the study of software architecture. ACM SIGSOFT Softw. Eng. Notes 17, 40–52 (1992)
2. van Gurp, J., Bosch, J.: Design erosion: problems and causes. J. Syst. Softw. 61(2), 105–119 (2002)
3. Lindvall, M., Muthig, D.: Bridging the software architecture gap. IEEE Computer 41, 98–101 (2008)
4. Sarkar, S., Ramachandran, S., Kumar, G.S., Iyengar, M.K., Rangarajan, K., Sivagnanam, S.: Modularization of a large-scale business application: A case study. IEEE Softw. 26(2), 28–35 (2009)
5. de Silva, L., Balasubramaniam, D.: Controlling software architecture erosion: A survey. J. Syst. Softw. 85(1), 132–151 (2012)
6. Murphy, G.C., Notkin, D., Sullivan, K.J.: Software reflexion models: bridging the gap between design and implementation. IEEE Trans. Softw. Eng. 27(4), 364–380 (2001)

7. Opdyke, W.F.: Refactoring object-oriented frameworks. PhD thesis, University of Illinois at Urbana-Champaign (1992)
8. Fowler, M.: Refactoring: Improving the Design of Existing Code. Addison-Wesley (1999)
9. Eden, A., Hirshfeld, Y., Kazman, R.: Abstraction classes in software design. IEE Proc. - Softw. 153(4), 163–182 (2006)
10. Buschmann, F., Meunier, R., Rohnert, H., Sommerlad, P.: A System of Patterns: Pattern-Oriented Software Architecture, vol. 1. John Wiley & Sons (1996)
11. Ouni, A., Kessentini, M., Sahraoui, H., Boukadoum, M.: Maintainability defects detection and correction: a multi-objective approach. Automated Software Engineering 20, 47–79 (2013)
12. Seng, O., Stammel, J., Burkhart, D.: Search-based determination of refactorings for improving the class structure of object-oriented systems. In: Proc. of the 8th Conf. on Genetic and Evolutionary Computation, pp. 1909–1916. ACM (2006)
13. O'Keeffe, M., Cinneide, M.: Search-based software maintenance. In: Proc. of the 10th Europ. Conf. on Software Maintenance and Reengineering (2006)
14. Ivkovic, I., Kontogiannis, K.: A framework for software architecture refactoring using model transformations and semantic annotations. In: Proc. of the 10th Europ. Conf. on Software Maintenance and Reengineering, pp. 135–144. IEEE (2006)
15. Dietrich, J., McCartin, J., Tempero, E., Shah, S.M.A.: On the existence of high-impact refactoring opportunities in programs. In: Australasian Computer Science Conf., vol. 122, pp. 37–48. ACS (2012)
16. Shah, S.M.A., Dietrich, J., McCartin, C.: Making smart moves to untangle programs. In: Proc. of the 2012 16th Europ. Conf. on Software Maintenance and Reengineering, pp. 359–364. IEEE (2012)
17. Hotta, K., Higo, Y., Kusumoto, S.: Identifying, tailoring, and suggesting form template method refactoring opportunities with program dependence graph. In: 16th Europ. Conf. on Software Maintenance and Reengineering, pp. 53–62 (2012)
18. Bourqun, F., Keller, R.K.: High-impact refactoring based on architecture violations. In: Proc. of the 11th Europ. Conf. on Software Maintenance and Reengineering, pp. 149–158. IEEE (2007)
19. Schmidt, F., MacDonell, S.G., Connor, A.M.: An automatic architecture reconstruction and refactoring framework. In: Lee, R. (ed.) Software Eng. Research, Management & Appl. 2011. SCI, vol. 377, pp. 95–111. Springer, Heidelberg (2012)
20. Pérez, J., Crespo, Y.: Computation of refactoring plans from refactoring strategies using htn planning. In: Proc. of the Fifth Workshop on Refactoring Tools, pp. 24–31. ACM (2012)
21. Tsantalis, N., Chatzigeorgiou, A.: Identification of move method refactoring opportunities. IEEE Trans. Softw. Eng. 35(3), 347–367 (2009)
22. Ouni, A., Kessentini, M., Sahraoui, H., Hamdi, M.: Search-based refactoring: Towards semantics preservation. In: 28th IEEE Int. Conf. on Software Maintenance, pp. 347–356 (2012)
23. Moghadam, I.H., Cinneide, M.O.: Automated refactoring using design differencing. In: Proc. of the 16th Europ. Conf. on Software Maintenance and Reengineering, pp. 43–52. IEEE Computer Society (2012)
24. Terra, R., Valente, M.T., Czarnecki, K., da Silva Bigonha, R.: Recommending refactorings to reverse software architecture erosion. In: Proc. of the 16th Europ. Conf. on Software Maintenance and Reengineering, pp. 335–340. IEEE (2012)
25. Herold, S.: Architectural Compliance in Component-Based Systems. Foundations, Specification, and Checking of Architectural Rules. PhD thesis, Clausthal University of Technology (2011)

Benefits and Drawbacks of Reference Architectures

Silverio Martínez-Fernández[1], Claudia P. Ayala[1], Xavier Franch[1],
and Helena Martins Marques[2]

[1] GESSI Research Group, Universitat Politècnica de Catalunya, Barcelona, Spain
{smartinez,cayala,franch}@essi.upc.edu
[2] *everis*, Barcelona, Spain
hmartinm@everis.com

Abstract. Reference architectures (RA) have been studied to create a consistent notion of what constitutes them as well as their benefits and drawbacks. However, few empirical studies have been conducted to provide evidence that support the claims made. To increase this evidence, this paper investigates the actual industrial practice of using RAs. The study consists of a survey with 28 stakeholders from *everis*, a multinational consulting company based in Spain. We report the findings and contextualize them with previous research.

Keywords: Software reference architecture, empirical software engineering.

1 Introduction

Software reference architectures (RA) have emerged as an approach to guide the development, standardization and evolution of concrete software architectures for new systems [5]. As in [1], we refer to the definition of RA as stated by Bass et al.: "a reference model mapped onto software elements and the data flows between them".

RAs have become widely studied and used in research and practice [1], as they are claimed to increase speed, reduce operational expenses and improve quality in software systems development mainly due to reuse [6]. Nonetheless, limited evidence exists to support these claims [7]. Therefore, the goal of this study is to investigate:

> How practitioners perceive the potential benefits and drawbacks of RAs?

Industrial Context. This study is part of an ongoing action-research initiative among *everis* and our research group, aimed to improve *everis*' architectural practices. *everis* is a software consulting company that offers solutions for big businesses that provide a wide spectrum of services to their customers. The solution that *everis* provides them is based on the deployment of an RA in their company, from which concrete software architectures are derived and used in a wide spectrum of applications. In this context, *everis* commissioned our research group to systematically gather empirical evidence about the benefits and drawbacks of the adoption of RAs for their clients, in order to avoid just relying on anecdotal evidences.

K. Drira (Ed.): ECSA 2013, LNCS 7957, pp. 307–310, 2013.
© Springer-Verlag Berlin Heidelberg 2013

2   Benefits and Drawbacks of RAs from the Literature

We identified the following benefits (B) and drawbacks (D) from the literature:

- (B1) Standardization of concrete architectures of systems [1][4][5][7][8].
- (B2) Facilitation of the design of concrete architectures for system development and evolution [1][5], improving the productivity of system developers [3][4][8].
- (B3) Systematic reuse of common functionalities and configurations in systems generation [2][4][5], implying shorter time-to-market and reduced cost [3][4].
- (B4) Risk reduction through the use of proven and partly prequalified architectural elements [2][4].
- (B5) Better quality by facilitating the achievement of quality attributes [3][8].
- (B6) Interoperability of different systems [2][4][5].
- (B7) Creation of a knowledge repository that allows knowledge transfer [2][7].
- (B8) Flexibility and a lower risk in the choice of multiple suppliers [2].
- (B9) Elaboration of the organization mission, vision and strategy [2].
- (D1) The need for an initial investment [6].
- (D2) Inefficient instantiation for the organization's systems [5].

3   Benefits and Drawbacks of RAs from Our Study

9 RA projects executed in 9 different organizations that were clients of *everis* were analyzed. 28 stakeholders from these projects participated in the study. They covered 3 essential roles: 9 software architects and 9 architecture developers that designed and implemented RAs for the 9 client organizations; and 10 application builders who created RA-based applications. We report the benefits and drawbacks of RAs for the development of systems as seen by these practitioners. Fig. 1 includes a bar chart that shows the frequency in which stakeholders mentioned RA benefits and drawbacks. The reader is encouraged to see how this study was conducted in www.essi.upc.edu/~gessi/papers/ecsa13-annex.pdf .

Main Benefits of RA Adoption. We report benefits for RA acquisition organizations with the code "Ben" whereas we use the code "Ven" for the benefits to RA vendors.

- (Ben-A) Reduced development costs. Mainly due to software component reuse that facilitate functionality and speed up the process, leading to shorter time-to-market.
- (Ben-B) Reduced maintenance costs. Because of: better understandability of systems derived from the RA; the fact that RA common elements have fewer errors.
- (Ben-C) Easier development and increased productivity of application builders by architecturally-significant requirements already addressed and RA artifacts.
- (Ben-D) Incorporation of latest technologies, which among other things facilitates the recruitment of professionals with the required technological skills.
- (Ben-E) Applications more aligned with business needs.
- (Ben-F) Homogenization (or standardization) of the development and maintenance of a family of applications by defining procedures and methodologies.

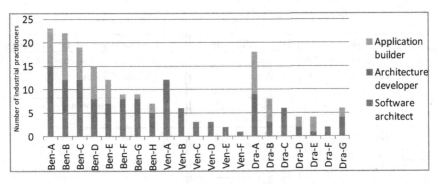

Fig. 1. Benefits and Drawbacks of RA adoption in organizations as seen by practitioners

- (Ben-G) Increased reliability of RAs software elements, which are common for applications, that have been tested and matured, with the reliability that it implies.
- (Ben-H) Others benefits.
- (Ven-A) The consulting company harvests experience for prospective RA projects. The main reason is that requirements are very similar between client organizations.
- (Ven-B) Reusing architectural knowledge can speed up prospective RA projects and reduce time-to-market (e.g., by reducing their planning and development time).
- (Ven-C) They gain reputation for prospective client organizations and gain organizational competence.
- (Ven-D) Previous experience reduces the risks in future projects because a "to-be" model exists. It can be used in projects without very specific requirements.
- (Ven-E) It provides a shared architectural mindset.
- (Ven-F) It turns tacit knowledge into explicit knowledge in the reference model. Some tool support (e.g., wiki technologies) helps in managing such knowledge.

Main Drawbacks of Using RAs.

- (Dra-A) Additional high or medium learning curve for using the RA features.
- (Dra-B) Limited innovation by giving prescriptive guidelines for applications.
- (Dra-C) Applications' dependency over the RA. When applications have requirements that the RA does not offer yet, applications development is stopped.
- (Dra-D) Complexity. Participants who indicated that the use of the RA is complex.
- (Dra-E) None. Responders who indicated that RA adoption presents no drawbacks.
- (Dra-F) Wrong decisions about the technologies to be used in all the applications.
- (Dra-G) Other drawbacks.

4   Discussion of Main Findings and Conclusions

Table 1 summarizes the benefits and drawbacks of RAs respectively. Its columns respectively indicate: 1) benefits or drawbacks from the literature and uncovered ones by our survey that we could not match to the former ones; 2) the extent to which the results from our survey confirm ($\sqrt{}$), partially support or help to understand ($\pm$), do not

Table 1. Summary of benefits and drawbacks of RAs

Benefits	D[1]	Findings	Drawbacks	D[1]	Findings
Standardization (B1)	√	Ben-F	Investment (D1)	±	Dra-G
Facilitation (B2)	√	Ben-C	Inefficient instantiation (D2)	±	Imp-C
Reuse (B3)	√	Ben-A, Ben-B, Ven-B	Learning curve	new	Dra-A
Risk reduction (B4)	√	Ben-G, Ven-D	Limited innovation	new	Dra-B
Enhanced quality (B5)	±	Ben-E	RA dependency	new	Dra-C
Interoperability (B6)	°	[2]	Complexity	new	Dra-D
Knowledge repository (B7)	√	Ven-A, Ven-F	Wrong decisions	new	Dra-F
Flexibility for suppliers (B8)	±	Ven-E			
Mission, vision, strategy (B9)	×	[3]			
Latest technologies used	new	Ben-D			
Reputation	new	Ven-C			

a. Notes: 1) diagnostic; 2) not mentioned as a benefit; 3) mentioned as enterprise architecture benefit.

explicitly mention (°), refuse theoretical evidences (×) or uncover new results (new); and 3) survey findings related to such benefits or drawbacks.

In conclusion, a survey was conducted to analyze benefits and drawbacks of RAs in the industrial practice. It provides evidence to corroborate or refuse existing research. The main findings were: 1) the support of already known RAs benefits, mainly cost savings in the development and evolution of software systems, and the facilitation of the design of concrete software architectures; 2) new risks of adopting RAs emerged, such as additional learning curve, less room for innovation and complexity. As future work, we plan to perform further analysis of this survey.

Acknowledgements. This work has been supported by "Cátedra *everis*" and the Spanish project TIN2010-19130-C02-00. We thank all participants of the survey.

References

1. Angelov, S., Grefen, P., Greefhorst, D.: A framework for analysis and design of software reference architectures. Information and Software Technology 54(4), 417–431 (2012)
2. Cloutier, R., Muller, G., Verma, D., Nilchiani, R., Hole, E., Bone, M.: The concept of reference architectures. Systems Engineering 13(1), 14–27 (2010)
3. Dobrica, L., Ovaska, E.: Analysis of a Cross-Domain Reference Architecture using Change Scenarios. SAVA@ECSA (2011)
4. Gallagher, B.: Using the architecture tradeoff analysis method sm to evaluate a reference architecture: A case study. SEI CMU Tech. rep., DTIC Document (2000)
5. Galster, M., Avgeriou, P.: Empirically-grounded reference architectures: A proposal. In: QoSA-ISARCS, pp. 153–158 (2011)
6. Martínez-Fernández, S., Ayala, C., Franch, X., Martins, H.: REARM: A Reused-Based Economic Model for Software Reference Architectures. In: ICSR (2013)
7. Muller, G., Laar, P.: Researching reference architectures. In: CSER (2009)
8. Nakagawa, E.Y., Antonino, P.O., Becker, M.: Reference architecture and product line architecture: A subtle but critical difference. In: Crnkovic, I., Gruhn, V., Book, M. (eds.) ECSA 2011. LNCS, vol. 6903, pp. 207–211. Springer, Heidelberg (2011)

Swap Fairness for Thrashing Mitigation

François Goichon, Guillaume Salagnac, and Stéphane Frénot

University of Lyon
INSA-Lyon, CITI-INRIA
F-69621, Villeurbanne

Abstract. The swap mechanism allows an operating system to work with more memory than available RAM space, by temporarily flushing some data to disk. However, the system sometimes ends up spending more time swapping data in and out of disk than performing actual computation. This state is called thrashing. Classical strategies against thrashing rely on reducing system load, so as to decrease memory pressure and increase global throughput. Those approaches may however be counterproductive when tricked into advantaging malicious or long-standing processes. This is particularly true in the context of shared hosting or virtualization, where multiple users run uncoordinated and selfish workloads.

To address this challenge, we propose an accounting layer that forces swap fairness among processes competing for main memory. It ensures that a process cannot monopolize the swap subsystem by delaying the swap operations of abusive processes, reducing the number of system-wide page faults while maximizing memory utilization.

1 Introduction

When the operating system is under memory pressure, the virtual memory manager picks some arbitrary memory pages and temporarily moves them out of RAM, to free up some space. Whenever such a page is later requested, the hardware generates a *page fault*, i.e. an event informing the OS that the page needs to be reloaded –*swapped in*– again in RAM. While swapping gives applications the illusion of an "infinite" memory, it may turn into a severe performance bottleneck, as accessing secondary storage is several orders of magnitude slower than main memory. Under high memory pressure from multiple tasks, the system has to constantly swap pages in and out, yielding low CPU utilization. This state is called thrashing, and is a common issue on shared systems, where the activity of a unique user may have a significant impact on the system behavior [5].

Classical strategies [1,3,4,11] to avoid thrashing either reduce global memory utilization or are very expensive to implement. More recently, Jiang et al.'s *token-ordered LRU* policy [9] proposes to protect the most memory-intensive task by keeping all its pages in main memory. This approach expects a quicker termination of that task and release of its memory pressure.

However, modern systems are typically running uncoordinated workloads, from multiple users. In this context, trying to favour the most memory-hungry task

K. Drira (Ed.): ECSA 2013, LNCS 7957, pp. 311–315, 2013.

may obliterate lighter tasks performance, especially when heavier tasks are long-standing. An obvious solution to this issue would be to use memory quotas. However, figuring out suitable settings is challenging, and even impossible when the workloads are not known in advance. Moreover, statically pre-allocating space leads to poor memory utilization.

On the contrary, our approach tries to dynamically minimize the impact of deviant behaviors, while still maximizing memory utilization. Our idea is to intercept and manipulate page faults: if N users contend for memory, then we restrict each one to be causing no more than a $\frac{1}{N}$ fraction of the overall swapping time. Delaying swap-in requests of abusive users reduces the total number of page faults and allow other tasks to run more smoothly.

2   Related Work

This section first reviews existing approaches aiming at detecting or preventing thrashing. We then discuss past work on fairness for disk usage, which is an important topic in the real-time systems community.

Thrashing Mitigation. Past proposals mainly focus on reducing system-wide load. The idea is to first try and evaluate the needs of each task, and then to take appropriate actions when memory pressure arises, from task suspension to bin-packing and memory-aware scheduling [3,4,11]. Even though they were implemented [6,12], such approaches increase overall throughput at the expense of increased latency for individual tasks, and cannot adapt to fluctuating memory demands [10].

To cope with dynamicity, Jiang and Zhang [8,9] propose to temporary protect the most memory-intensive task: while protected, the task's pages cannot be swapped out. If the process finishes faster, its memory is freed, reducing system-wide memory pressure and early thrashing peaks. The Linux kernel implements this idea, starting with v2.6.9, with the name *swap token*. The main limitation of this approach is the hypothesis that memory-hungry tasks are transient. If several long-running tasks compete for memory, the swap token is of no help, and can even make things worse.

On the contrary, the local page replacement policy [1] aims at isolating tasks performance, as it restricts every process to only swap out its own pages. However, this idea requires specific memory allocations schemes [2,7], which are difficult to fine-tune, and do not maximize memory space utilization.

Disk Usage Fairness. To improve performance, the OS typically interposes several software layers between user programs and hardware devices. Each layer reorders requests to increase overall throughput. Unfortunately, this enables adverse effects caused by one task to have a significant impact on other tasks. For instance, abusing filesystem locality may cause request starvation, as both the operating system's I/O scheduler and on-disk schedulers try to minimize disk head movement [15]. Many techniques have been proposed to address request starvation, such as draining the request queue [13], or dynamically adapting the number of best-effort requests allowed to be passed to the I/O scheduler, considering missed deadlines by real-time requests [14]. Whereas these ideas are designed for real-time environments, they apply the idea of sporadic scheduling as a fairness mechanism for device requests, focusing on delaying requests that can negatively impact the reponse time of others.

Discussion. While most approaches to mitigate thrashing ignore individual performance, others [1] bring up the idea of performance isolation, a requirement on shared platforms. On the other hand, researchers from the real-time community have developped dynamic approaches to reduce or bound the maximum duration of disk requests. In the next section, we propose an approach aiming at controlling the fairness of swap usage, to reduce page faults from memory heavy processes, thus bounding the impact of deviant workloads while still maximizing memory utilization.

3   Our Approach

Our approach to mitigate thrashing is to enforce fairness among the different users requesting memory. We refer to those users as *swapping domains*. A swapping domain may consist of one process, or of all the processes of a system user or system group. In this section, we present our approach with further detail and argue why fairness on swap operations can help to mitigate thrashing.

Fairness on Swap Operations to Mitigate Thrashing. The natural circumventions to domains monopolizing main memory - quotas or local page replacement [2] - do not use the system's space at its full potential and are hard to setup in practice. Our approach to deal with this problem is to disregard space usage, and instead to account for the amount of *work* that each domain induces on the swapping subsystem. When the system is thrashing, it means that one swapping domain must be preventing others to establish their working sets. This implies that this domain has to constantly produce page faults to keep its own pages in main memory. Therefore, the system spends more time in swapping operations on behalf of this particular domain than for other domains. Our approach aims at detecting this situation, and reacting by delaying requests from abusive domains until other domains have had their share of swapping time. This may increase the actual execution time of memory-heavy processes but reduces global page faults rate, while providing non-abusive domains with guaranteed periods of time where their pages will remain available. This strategy is almost the opposite of the swap-token approach, in which a process causing more page faults becomes less likely to have its pages swapped out.

Approach Formalization. We consider a set of N swapping domains $\{D_i\}_{i\in\{1..N\}}$, and we write $S(D_i)$ to denote the cumulated duration of swapping operations caused by domain D_i. A domain D is said to be abusive if $S(D) > \frac{1}{N}\sum S(D_i)$.

In other words, a domain is abusive when it induces more, or longer, swapping operations than other competing domains. Whenever a swapping domain is detected as being abusive, we delay all its future swap-in operations until $S(D) \leq \frac{1}{N} \sum S(D_i)$ holds again.

The main OS events required to calculate the $S(D_i)$ are the swap request issue dates and completion dates: by calculating the time difference between these two events we can deduce the precise duration of each swap-in operation. The sum of these durations reflects the pressure that a particular swapping domain is putting on the virtual memory subsystem. Please note however that neither the disk devices nor the software I/O layers have a FIFO behavior. As a result, multiple disk requests sometimes cost less than a single one. Therefore, computing the duration of the requests and not just counting them provides a sounder basis for the accounting. Implementing such an approach in a monolithic kernel brings up many efficiency concerns, that we detail and address in a companion technical report [5].

Prototype. To evaluate our idea, we implemented our accounting layer within the Linux kernel, and compared its performance and its fairness to the Linux swap-token implementation. As expected, when a memory-hungry (maybe malicious) process runs for a long enough time, then the swap token makes it harder for other legitimate processes to execute smoothly. With our swap accounting layer, legit workloads that are intensive in memory are allocated more swap time than with the swap token, and their performance is improved significantly as a result. Moreover, forcing fairness on the swap-in operations is equivalent to force a general fairness in terms of computation, and induces a better predictability of execution duration. More details on our experiments results can be found in [5].

4   Conclusion

The problem of physical memory shortage, with thrashing as its side effect, has been an open problem for more than 50 years. As a result, the virtual memory subsystem has been widely studied and many improvements over the existing page replacement policies have been presented to allow concurrent processes to run more smoothly. The most recent step is the introduction of the token-ordered LRU, or swap token, which selects processes for LRU evasion. This mechanism allows processes with important memory demands to keep their pages in main memory and hopefully finish quickly enough to reduce system pressure.

In this paper, we highlight the fact that the swap token may be counterproductive when in presence of malicious or uncoordinated workloads that do not end their execution quickly. As an alternative, we propose a lightweight accounting layer that delays swap requests from processes monopolizing the virtual memory subsystem without any preliminary configuration. Such a system allows processes with legit memory needs to have normal access to the swap space at the expense of abusive processes. Our first results show that the approach is promising in terms of performance and fairness, and is well adapted to shared hosting platforms.

References

1. Aho, A.V., Denning, P.J., Ullman, J.D.: Principles of optimal page replacement. Journal of the ACM 18(1), 80–93 (1971)
2. Alderson, A.: Thrashing in a multiprogrammed paging system. Technical report, University of Newcastle (1972)
3. Denning, P.J.: Thrashing: its causes and prevention. In: 1968 Fall Joint Computer Conference, pp. 915–922. ACM (1968)
4. Denning, P.J.: The working set model for program behavior. Commun. ACM 11(5), 323–333 (1968)
5. Goichon, F., Salagnac, G., Frnot, S.: Swap fairness for thrashing mitigation. Technical report, INRIA (2013)
6. Hewlett-Packard. HP-UX 11i Version 3: serialize(1) (2010)
7. Iyer, S.: Advanced memory management and disk scheduling techniques for general-purpose operating systems. PhD thesis, Rice University (2005)
8. Jiang, S., Zhang, X.: TPF: a dynamic system thrashing protection facility. Software: Practice and Experience 32, 295–318 (2002)
9. Jiang, S., Zhang, X.: Token-ordered LRU: An effective page replacement policy and its implementation in Linux systems. Perform. Eval. 60(1-4), 5–29 (2005)
10. Morris, J.B.: Demand paging through utilization of working sets on the MANIAC II. Commun. ACM 15(10), 867–872 (1972)
11. Reuven, M., Wiseman, Y.: Medium-term scheduler as a solution for the thrashing effect. Computer J. 49(3), 297–309 (2006)
12. Rodriguez-Rosell, J., Dupuy, J.-P.: The design, implementation, and evaluation of a working set dispatcher. Commun. ACM 16(4), 247–253 (1973)
13. Stanovich, M.J., Baker, T.P., Wang, A.I.: Throttling on-disk schedulers to meet soft-real-time requirements. In: Real-Time and Embedded Technology and Applications Symposium, RTAS 2008 (2008)
14. Wu, J., Brandt, S.: Storage access support for soft real-time applications. In: Real-Time and Embedded Technology and Applications Symposium, RTAS 2004 (2004)
15. Yu, Y.J., Shin, D.I., Eom, H., Yeom, H.Y.: NCQ vs. I/O scheduler: Preventing unexpected misbehaviors. ACM Transactions Storage 6(1), 2 (2010)

Architectural Slicing: Towards Automatic Harvesting of Architectural Prototypes

Henrik Bærbak Christensen[1] and Klaus Marius Hansen[2]

[1] Department of Computer Science, Aarhus University, Aarhus, Denmark
hbc@cs.au.dk
[2] Department of Computer Science (DIKU), University of Copenhagen,
Copenhagen, Denmark
klausmh@diku.dk

Abstract. Architectural prototyping is a widely used practice, concerned with taking architectural decisions through experiments with lightweight implementations. However, many architectural decisions are only taken when systems are already (partially) implemented. This is problematic in the context of architectural prototyping since experiments with full systems are complex and expensive and thus architectural learning is hindered. In this paper, we propose a novel technique for harvesting architectural prototypes from existing systems, "architectural slicing", based on dynamic program slicing. Given a system and a slicing criterion, architectural slicing produces an architectural prototype that contains the elements in the architecture that are dependent on the elements in the slicing criterion.

1 Motivation

Software architecture work does not stop once a systems has been deployed. New quality attribute demands may trigger the wish to change the software architecture to better accommodate such requirements. However, experimenting with architectural changes in large systems is usually prohibitively expensive as even minor changes have ripple effects that are costly to fix even though they are unrelated to the architectural challenge.

Architectural prototypes (APs) [1] constitute a lightweight and cost efficient approach to explore changes to software architecture: an AP is a minimal executing system that only contains the core architectural elements relevant for the architectural issue explored, but of course the AP must be valid in the sense that architectural knowledge gained from the AP will be true also for the original system (e.g., that a certain communication component architecture change indeed improves performance). As the AP has a much smaller codebase, the software architect can explore the architectural design space much more freely and faster. Christensen [3] describes *harvesting* as the process of extracting a valid AP from an existing system.

However, the apparent appeal is somewhat offset by the cost of the harvesting process itself: core elements must be copied from the host system to form the AP,

K. Drira (Ed.): ECSA 2013, LNCS 7957, pp. 316–319, 2013.

usually trimmed for irrelevant methods, the dependency graph analyzed in order
to include dependent elements while stubbing others deemed irrelevant for the
architectural issue. This cost results in a reluctance to harvest and a tendency
to either experiment within the original system itself or even worse avoid the
experiments all together.

In this research challenge paper we propose to take the ideas of *program
slicing* [7,5] and apply them in an software architectural context i.e. viewing
the process of harvesting an AP from a host system as an *architectural slicing*
process.

1.1 Example

In a research project related to CO_2 emission monitoring, the readings from 3,180
sensors in a student apartment complex are uploaded to a database every five
seconds. The software architecture is a three tier system in which the complex's
sensor collector gateway publishes raw data to a message queue. A server side
consumes raw data from the queue and stores them in a MongoDB database.
The producer API is tested through a small set of end-to-end JUnit test cases
as outlined in the pseudo code:

```
1   @Test public void shouldSupportEnd2EndScenario() {
2       readings = new SensorReadings();
3       [insert sensor readings 0..3180 into 'readings']
4       chr = new ClientRequestHandler(); // POSA Vol 4 p 246
5       chr.send(readings);
6       // validate that 'readings' are safely stored
7       query = new Query( [last inserted reading of sensor 0] );
8       double value = chr.retrieve( query );
9       assertEquals( readings.getValueOfSensor(0), value );
10  }
```

The ClientRequestHandler is responsible for serializing the SensorReadings object
and publishing it on a message queue.

Now, the software architect is requested to improve the architecture's *modifiability*, by making the ClientRequestHandler more flexible with respect to the
type of data transmitted, so third-party developers can develop Android apps
for sending GPS and motion sensor data to the database.

However, it is difficult to experiment because the above test case relies on a
running test environment (message queue and MongoDB) and has dependencies
on many server side abstractions (MongoDB schemas, server side deserializers,
etc.). Changing the client API will require changes in a lot of places that are not
really relevant for the architectural issue but required just to keep the test case
running.

A harvested AP would consist of the above test case, the ClientRequest-
Handler's **send** and **retrieve** methods, transitively dependent methods and
components (serializer, SensorReadings) and just a test stub implementation of
the message queue library. This allow experimentation without changes rippling

into the server and database tiers. It is this harvesting process we propose to automate.

2 Background

Weiser [7] originally introduced the concept of a "program slice" as pieces of a program decomposed by dataflow and provided algorithms for calculating slices from procedural programs ("slicing"). Generally, a distinction is made between "static slicing" (in which slicing is performed without making assumptions on a program's input) and "dynamic slicing" (in which slicing relies on test cases) [6].

Program slicing has been applied in numerous areas including debugging, software maintenance, and testing [6,5]. Furthermore, program slicing techniques have been applied to software architecture descriptions (in particular in ACME and Rapide) [4]. In this paper, we propose to slice system on an architectural level, but based on the implementation of the system, so as to support software architects in architectural prototyping.

Christensen [3] defined an operational conceptual framework for architectural prototyping including the concepts of "harvesting" and "retrofitting". Harvesting refers to the process of extracting an AP from an existing system, whereas retrofitting refers to changing an existing system to accommodate architectural decisions made in an architectural prototype. Our contribution relates to the automation of these processes.

3 Approach

Based on the definition of software architecture by Bass et al. [2], we informally define an *architectural slice* as

> An *architectural slice* of a system is an executable subset of the system. The software architecture of the architectural slice comprises a subset of the software elements and relations of the software architecture of the system, selected according to a *slicing criterion*

Architectural slicing is then the tasks of computing an architectural slice, essentially automating the harvesting of an architectural prototype. The slicing criterion may statically select elements of interest or dynamically select elements of interest based on executions of a system. In the following, we are concerned with dynamic slicing, using test cases to select elements and relations of interest.

We currently consider Java-based systems and their execution, but the ideas should generalize to any language with strong instrumentation and code generation tools. In the Java case, elements are packages, interfaces, classes from which objects are constructed, and the methods that are exercised by test case executions. We envision a process in which the test cases are executed on the host system(s) while architectural harvesting processes are monitoring and collecting execution data, the *harvested element set*. The harvest element set records information on executing methods and objects, type and package relationships, return values, etc. Once the tests cases have finished execution, the architect is presented with an overview that allows him/her to optionally *annotate* elements in the set. Annotations may mark elements to ignore or elements to replace with stubs. As an example, the message queue client library used in the example above would be annotated as "stub" as we want real calls to the message queue to be stubbed/replaced with simple replay of return values recorded in the harvesting phase. In a final step, the annotated element set is used to construct an AP that is faithful to the host system, passes the selection criteria test case(s), but only include elements as defined by the architect's annotations. Thus the AP will have a significantly (orders of magnitude) smaller code base allowing much easier experimentation.

Note that the harvesting processes must coordinate across machine boundaries in the most likely case of distributed systems, as client calls must be matched by server invocations.

3.1 Initial Experiments

We have designed and implemented an experimental architectural slicer, *APHarvest*, for Java. The slicer is implemented as a Java agent (that may, e.g., be added as an argument in an Ant java task). The agent traces a program execution dynamically through a *sensor* implemented using AspectJ. The events of the sensor are received by a *harvester* that collects information on elements (methods, classes and packages) that are affected by execution. Subsequently, a *generator* uses CodeModel to generate a Java project containing the slice.

References

1. Bardram, J., Christensen, H.B., Hansen, K.M.: Architectural Prototyping: An Approach for Grounding Architectural Design and Learning. In: WICSA, pp. 15–24 (2004)
2. Bass, L., Clements, P., Kazman, R.: Software Architecture in Practice, 3rd edn. Addison-Wesley (2012)
3. Christensen, H.: Towards an Operational Framework for Architectural Prototyping. In: 5th Working IEEE/IFIP Conference on Software Architecture (WICSA 2005), pp. 301–302 (2005)
4. Kim, T., Song, Y.-T., Chung, L., Huynh, D.T.: Dynamic Software Architecture Slicing. In: Proceedings of the Twenty-Third Annual International Computer Software and Applications Conference, COMPSAC 1999, pp. 61–66. IEEE (1999)
5. Silva, J.: A vocabulary of program slicing-based techniques. ACM Computing Surveys 44(3), 1–41 (2012)
6. Tip, F.: A Survey of Program Slicing Techniques. Journal of Programming Languages 3(3), 121–189 (1995)
7. Weiser, M.: Program Slicing. IEEE Transactions on Software Engineering 10(4), 352–357 (1984)

Describing Cloud Applications Architectures

Everton Cavalcante, Ana Luisa Medeiros, and Thais Batista

DIMAp – Department of Informatics and Applied Mathematics
UFRN – Federal University of Rio Grande do Norte
Natal, Brazil
evertonrsc@ppgsc.ufrn.br, analuisafdm@gmail.com, thais@ufrnet.br

Abstract. The architecture of cloud applications differs from traditional software architectures mainly regarding their basic architectural elements, the *services*, the *metadata* about the services for expressing information related to quality parameters and pricing models, and the *constraints* over the applications and the used services. This paper presents Cloud-ADL, a seamless extension of the ACME ADL to support the architectural representation of cloud applications by relying on the existing ACME abstractions. In addition, it defines *contracts* to modularly encapsulate typical contract information of cloud applications, such as quality parameters, pricing model of the services, and constraints. Finally, Cloud-ADL also supports the dynamic reconfiguration of cloud applications through programmed changes, which can be foreseen at design time and specified at the ADL level.

1 Introduction

Cloud Computing is a new computing paradigm that enables ubiquitous, convenient, on-demand network access to a shared pool of resources (e.g. networks, servers, applications, and services) that can be rapidly provisioned and released with minimal management effort or interaction with the service provider [1]. The emergence of this paradigm brings several new challenges to be addressed in the Cloud Computing context, and one of them is related to methods, tools, and techniques to support developers to design, project, and deploy new software systems that make use of the cloud technology. In fact, building cloud-based applications is a challenging task as they are significantly more complex due to the intrinsic complexity of using cloud service providers. The particular nature of Cloud Computing applications creates specific requirements that also demand changes in terms of the development of such applications, which encompass methodologies and techniques for requirements elicitation, architecture, implementation, deployment, testing, and evolution of software [2,3].

In terms of software architecture, architectures of service-oriented applications (such as cloud applications) differ from the architecture of traditional applications mainly re- garding their basic architectural elements, the *services*, and their dynamic behavior, thus dealing with issues related to heterogeneity interoperability, and changing requirements [4,5]. As most of the works addressing

K. Drira (Ed.): ECSA 2013, LNCS 7957, pp. 320–323, 2013.

cloud-related challenges focus on the underlying infrastructure or on discussions about the cloud services provided by third-party providers, there is an important gap in terms of architectural support in order to enable the use of the cloud technology in a systematic way. For instance, it is reasonable to think that software architectures need to be described in a different way if they are deployed on the cloud. Therefore, it is necessary to provide an architectural support to their project and means to model them and capture important elements regarding the Cloud Computing paradigm.

In this perspective, this paper gives an overview of Cloud-ADL (see Section 2), a customized architecture description language (ADL) [6] that takes advantage of ACME [7] elements to model the architecture of a cloud application, thus relying on the existing abstractions and avoiding the addition of many new ones. In this perspective, Cloud-ADL enables to specify the resources (cloud services) to be used by the applications, as well as to define their relationships, metadata about the services, constraints, and dynamic reconfiguration actions according to QoS and resource provisioning constraints.

2   Cloud-ADL: An Overview

ADLs [6] usually provide both a conceptual framework as a concrete syntactic notation to characterize software architectures in terms of components, connectors, and configurations. Although there is a myriad of ADLs in the literature, the architectural features of cloud applications goes beyond what is currently supported by the existing ADLs, so that it is missing models that capture specific and important aspects always present in the Cloud Computing context, such as: (i) the logical separation between the cloud platforms and the applications that use the provided services; (ii) the agreed contract between these players, and; (iii) the QoS model for the services. To the best of our knowledge, there are no proposals in the literature for modeling cloud-based applications, and despite of they are service-oriented, there are very few proposals for describing service-oriented software architectures [4,5].

Cloud-ADL is a seamless extension of the ACME [7] general-purpose ADL for modeling Cloud Computing applications. The philosophy of Cloud-ADL is to take advantage of ACME elements to describe architectures of a cloud application, thus relying on existing abstractions and avoiding the addition of many new abstractions and maintaining characteristics related to generality, simplicity, and expressiveness inherited from ACME. Cloud-ADL enables to describe the architecture of the applications and: (i) the *services* provided by cloud platforms and that are used by the applications, thus making a clear and modular separation between the definition of the cloud services and the specification of the applications that use them; (ii) the agreed *contracts* between service providers and clients, in terms of quality metadata, pricing models, and constraints regarding the services; (iii) application-level *constraints*, and; (iv) *dynamic reconfiguration actions* according to QoS and resource provisioning constraints.

The complete specification of a cloud application in Cloud-ADL encompasses:

1) Definition of Cloud Services Provided by Cloud Computing Platforms and Essential Characteristics Related to This Context. In this step, the ACME *Family* element is customized to the cloud scenario for representing the set of services provided by a cloud platform, so that a new *Family* abstraction must be created for each cloud platform. In the *Family* element, each service provided by a cloud platform is represented by a *Type* associated to a *Component* element, similarly to the specification of component types in ACME. In the architectural description of the application, the component types that represent provided cloud services can be instantiated in order to indicate which services are being used by the application.

Furthermore, Cloud-ADL comes with a novel mandatory first-class primitive called *Contract* for specifying the agreed contract of service providers in terms of cloud both static and/or quality attributes and constraints over them, and also the pricing model of the services. Within such element associated to a given service, there are four main elements: (i) the *QualityParameters* element, in which the properties regarding the quality parameters are specified; (ii) the *Pricing-Model* element, which defines details about the pricing model of the service; (iii) a *constraints* section specified in Armani [8], which determinate the minimal warranties offered by the service provider related to the quality parameters, and; (iv) a section in which the software architect can *annotate* any additional information using the conventional *Property* element defined in ACME. In addition, Cloud-ADL introduces the *Dynamic* clause associated to elements of the *Contract* that enables to specify monitorable parameters at runtime.

2) Specification of a Cloud Application Itself in Cloud-ADL. The specification of an application in Cloud-ADL is very similar to the ACME architectural description of systems by using the same basic architectural elements defined in such ADL. In a Cloud-ADL architectural description of an application, cloud services (represented by *Component* elements) are instances of the services (represented by *Component Type* elements) defined in the *Family* elements that abstract the cloud platforms. In this perspective, a *System* element that describes a cloud application must extend (adhere) the *Family* element that represent the cloud platforms that are providers of the services used by the application. For instance, in the statement *System A : B, C*, the application *A* uses services provided by the cloud platforms represented by the *B* and *C Family* elements. In Cloud-ADL, describing a component *x* in a *System* element as an instance of a component type *y* defined within a *Family* element means that the application component *x* uses the cloud service defined by the component type *y*.

As the *Dynamic* clause present in Cloud-ADL supports the specification of monitorable parameters at runtime and these dynamic attributes can change over time, a *reconfiguration action* is required in order to better satisfy the application needs. In this perspective, Cloud-ADL currently addresses dynamic reconfiguration in terms of architectural *programmed changes*, which can be foreseen at design time, thus following ideas proposed in the Plastik framework [9], which extends the ACME/Armani ADL to enable this dynamic reconfiguration support.

3 Final Remarks

In this paper we briefly introduced Cloud-ADL, a simple, seamless extension of the ACME ADL that relies on the existing ACME abstractions and their associated extensions (e.g. Armani and Plastik) and avoids adding many new abstractions. Cloud-ADL makes a clear and modular separation between the definition of the cloud services and the specification of cloud applications that use them. By relying on the ACME/Armani ADL, it is possible to specify the high-level architectural representation of cloud service providers and cloud applications, as well as the related constraints. In this perspective, our philosophy in the design of Cloud-ADL was to avoid reinventing the wheel by taking advantage of existing abstractions, reusing and adapting them to the fit the needs of the cloud domain, and to offer a simple and small language. As far as we are concerned, this is the first proposal in terms of provisioning a customized ADL for modeling cloud domain specificities. Furthermore, an important issue considered by Cloud-ADL is the dynamic reconfiguration of cloud applications at the ADL level combined with the specification of monitorable parameters at runtime.

References

1. Mell, P., Grance, T.: The NIST Definition of Cloud Computing. Technical report, National Institute of Standards and Technology, USA (2011)
2. Chhabra, B., et al.: Software Engineering issues from the cloud application perspective. International Journal of Information Technology and Knowledge Management 2(2), 669–673 (2010)
3. Sriram, I., Khajeh-Hosseini, A.: Research agenda in cloud technologies. Computing Research Repository. Cornell University, USA (2010)
4. Xie, D., et al.: An approach for describing SOA. In: 2006 IEEE International Conference on Wireless Communications, Networking and Mobile Computing, pp. 1–4. IEEE Computer Society, USA (2006)
5. Jia, X., et al.: A new architecture description language for service-oriented architecture. In: 6th International Conference on Grid and Cooperative Computing, pp. 96–103. IEEE Computer Society, USA (2007)
6. Medvidovic, N., Taylor, R.N.: A classification and comparison framework for software architecture description languages. IEEE Transactions on Software Engineering 26(1), 70–93 (2000)
7. Garlan, D., et al.: ACME: An architecture description interchange language. In: 1997 Conference of the Centre for Advanced Studies on Collaborative Research, pp. 169–189. IBM Press, USA (1997)
8. Monroe, R.: Capturing software architecture expertise with Armani. Technical report, Carnegie Mellon University, USA (1998)
9. Batista, T.V., Joolia, A., Coulson, G.: Managing dynamic reconfiguration in component-based systems. In: Morrison, R., Oquendo, F. (eds.) EWSA 2005. LNCS, vol. 3527, pp. 1–17. Springer, Heidelberg (2005)

MVIC – An MVC Extension for Interactive, Multimodal Applications

Marc Hesenius and Volker Gruhn

paluno - The Ruhr Institute for Software Technology
University of Duisburg-Essen
Gerlingstr. 16, 45127 Essen, Germany
{marc.hesenius,volker.gruhn}@paluno.uni-due.de
http://www.paluno.de

Abstract. MVC is considered an important architectural patterns when it comes to interactive applications since its invention in the days of Smalltalk. However, interaction with computers has changed. Touch-screens are as natural to users nowadays as mouse and keyboard have been for the past decades of computing and HCI-researchers keep on developing more interaction modalities. Multimodal applications pose major challenges to software engineers who have to deal with different ways for users to express the same intention. MVC does not incorporate the flexibility needed to cope with multimodal applications as it makes the controller component responsible for interaction interpretation and managing the application flow. We propose MVIC, an extension to MVC dedicated to provide a solid software architecture for multimodal, interactive applications by introducing a dedicated interaction component.

1 Introduction

Software engineers have been optimising and refining the incorporation of classic interaction modalities like mouse and keyboard into software products for decades. Model-View-Controller (MVC), *the* architectural pattern for interactive applications, was introduced with Smalltalk-80 [1,5] and has ever since been used by different applications in different contexts. But with the appearance of smartphones and tablets, interaction with computers has changed. Surface gestures have become a common interaction modality and HCI-Researchers keep on adding new technologies to the existing portfolio, increasing and improving interaction possibilities.

Often, the same functionality can be accessed in different ways depending on the current situation – for example, a ringing phone can be turned off by either pressing a button or turning the device upside down. The reasons to incorporate different interaction modalities are manifold, from situational reasons to personal preferences and cultural background. Different schemes of the same interaction modality, like novice and expert gestures, may improve usability and applications could be easily adapted to the customs of different cultures.

But what maybe a wonderful new world full of possibilities to users poses major challenges to software engineers. The new interaction modalities are often highly ambiguous and not easily interpreted – interaction has evolved from basic concepts to a

K. Drira (Ed.): ECSA 2013, LNCS 7957, pp. 324–327, 2013.

highly complex matter in the last years. Recent mobile devices equipped with different sensors allow developers to implement a variety of interaction modalities. Operating systems like Android typically give support by providing recognition functions for a basic set of gestures. However, the implementation of custom gestures requires developers to work on raw sensor data. In a typical MVC setup, the controller is in charge of tracking user actions and inferring the meaning for the application, which requires developers to implement recognition and maintenance code for several input sources at one place. As applications may change often and quickly, maintenance is made difficult. Developers aim for using agile development methodologies, short release cycles and be able to extend and adapt applications to current needs. The foundation for this goal is always a sound and solid software architecture. MVC has provided this base for many years but is reaching limits when it comes to multimodal technologies.

We describe an extension to the well-known MVC pattern named Model-View-Interaction-Controller (MVIC) focused on separating *controller* and *interaction* concerns. The software's architecture should reflect the flexibility that results from the advances in HCI and allow developers to add new interaction modalities without the risk of breaking existing ways of interaction. In standard MVC, the controller is responsible for interpreting *any* kind of input and mapping it to the application's functionality, hence breaking *separation of concerns*.

Our contribution to the field of software architecture for interactive applications is twofold. One the one hand, MVIC slims down code written in the controller and introduces a dedicated interaction component, thus increasing separation of concerns. On the other hand, MVIC adapts the reliable and familiar MVC pattern to recent needs, making it easier to learn and implement in existing frameworks. This paper is structured as follows: Section 2 will introduce MVIC, its concepts and ideas and how the media player implementation can be optimized. Related work is discussed in section 3. The paper is concluded in section 4.

2 Model-View-Interaction-Controller

MVIC consists of the basic MVC elements and adds a dedicated interaction component. It is oriented towards more recent variants of MVC, removing any relationship between view and model. The components and their tasks are:

Model. The model in MVIC remains unchanged from its role in MVC. Its main task is to provide the core functionality, map real world objects into the application and provide a place to store and manipulate their current state.

View. The view has the same function in MVIC as in MVC as well – it presents data from the model to the user and is therefore in charge of the application's *output*. Different descriptions of MVC also interpret the view role in a distinct way, adding or removing *input* responsibilites (cf. [4] for a narrow and in contrast [2,5] for a wide interpretation). In MVIC this makes no difference as any input task should be delegated to the interaction component, no matter where the input information comes from.

Interaction. Here processing of all interaction takes place. In MVC, the controller solely is responsible for this task, which involves identification as well as interpretation of input. Whatever the user did is transferred to the controller and it decides how

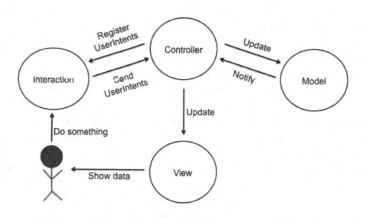

Fig. 1. MVIC Structure

the application should react. In MVIC, the interaction component is in charge of interpreting the user input: It receives input data from any device sensor, tries to figure out what the user wants to do, and sends a message to the controller containing the user's intention; hence we call this message a *UserIntent*. UserIntents should be designed to carry additional information needed for the controller to perform actions (e. g. touch coordinates). The interaction component will usually consist of several smaller components called *InteractionHandlers*, each of them dedicated to processing a certain input modality. All code previously crammed up in the controller is now distributed over various dedicated components, enforcing separation of concerns and leading to a more structured architecture. Although the InteractionHandlers map a certain kind of input to a specific UserIntent, they are oblivious to its meaning. Mapping the UserIntent to functionality and calling the model is still the controller's task.

Controller. The main purpose of the controller remains unchanged. As in MVC, the controller is in charge of the whole application flow. However, it does not receive detailed input information from sensors anymore and is completely oblivious to how interaction processing is implemented. Instead, it waits for the arrival of *UserIntents*. As a consequence, the application needs a precise *interaction concept*, which maps user input to UserIntents to specific functionality.

Summarized, MVIC strips the controller of any detailed user input recognition, sensor data is transferred to the interaction component. This component is in charge of identifying the user's intention and inform the controller about it. Whatever actions within the application are necessary to satisfy the user's wishes is up to the controller, who will call the appropiate functions on the model.

3   Related Work

Another architecture for multimodal applications strictly following the MVC pattern is the W3C recommendation *Multimodal Architecture and Interfaces*[1] (MMI). MMI is

---
[1] http://www.w3.org/TR/mmi-arch/, Feb. 2013

divided into three components, each representing one part of MVC, and all components are interconnected via a *Runtime Framework* providing infrastructure which is not defined by the W3C recommendation and left to platform specific implementations.

MMI and MVIC share common goals and target the same class of applications but differ in details. MVIC is more oriented towards recent technology like Android and iOS, while MMI is more loosely coupled and takes e.g. distribution of components into account. MMI emphasises the use of markup and scripting, which is not specifically defined in MVIC. However, using markup for configuration of InteractionHandlers is an interesting option to define an interaction concept and is part of our future research.

How to use MMI in a mobile environment is demonstrated by Cutugno et al. in [3]. They present a framework for multimodal mobile applications with focus on the possibility to configure MMI's controller via an XML file, but they extend MMI by adding *Input Recognizers* and *Semantic Interpretation Components* for each interaction modality, providing an interesting alternative to MVIC.

The idea of UserIntents is closely related to the typical way of calling other applications in Android. When an Android application needs to trigger e.g. a phone call it will do this by invoking an `Intent` without actually knowing what application will answer. Android will answer to the user's intention by bringing up its phone app. UserIntents bring this concepts deeper into applications on a much finer level.

4 Conclusion

We presented MVIC, an extension to the well-known MVC pattern targeting multimodal applications. We expect MVIC to make interactive applications more flexible and easier to extend and maintain. MVIC is build around the idea that dedicated interaction components for the different interaction modalities are in charge of interpreting the user input and identifying his or her intentions – a task left solely to the controller in MVC. Identified *UserIntents* are then send to the controller for further processing, so in MVIC the controller is still in charge of managing the application flow. Taking the interaction matters out of the controller will decrease the chance of breaking the UI when making changes to existing or adding new interaction modalities.

References

1. Burbeck, S.: Applications programming in smalltalk-80 (tm): How to use model-view-controller (mvc). Smalltalk-80 v2. 5. ParcPlace (1992)
2. Buschmann, F., Meunier, R., Rohnert, H., Sommerlad, P., Stal, M.: Pattern-Oriented Software Architecture, vol.1 - A system of patterns. Wiley, Chichester (1996)
3. Cutugno, F., Leano, V.A., Rinaldi, R., Mignini, G.: Multimodal framework for mobile interaction. In: Proceedings of the International Working Conference on Advanced Visual Interfaces, AVI 2012, pp. 197–203 (2012)
4. Freeman, E., Robson, E., Sierra, K., Bates, B.: Head First Design Patterns. O'Reilly, Sebastopol (2004)
5. Krasner, G.E., Pope, S.T.: A description of the model-view-controller user interface paradigm in the smalltalk-80 system. Journal of object oriented programming 1(3), 26–49 (1988)

Toward Industry Friendly Software Architecture Evaluation

Zhao Li and Jiang Zheng

ABB US Corporate Research Center
940 Main Campus Drive, Raleigh, NC, USA 27606
{Zhao.Li,Jiang.Zheng}@us.abb.com

Abstract. Due to the increasingly complexity of industry software products, software architecture evaluation is getting important to effectively identify potential risks and ensure the quality goals of the resulting system are well addressed in the design phase. However, despite the plethora of evaluation approaches proposed in academia, few of them have proven suitable to evaluate architecture designs of wide spread industry applications. As the initial efforts of addressing this issue, this paper identifies the gaps between an ideal industry friendly software architecture evaluation approach and existing evaluation methods.

Keywords: Software Architecture, Architecture Evaluation, Architecture Analysis.

1 Introduction

Nowadays, most industry software products have become increasingly complex: Externally, they are network-based, large-scaled, and distributed; internally, they are multi-threaded. This results in the complexity of software architecture and deeply hidden defects. Since detecting potential defects and risks in the architecture design phase effectively reduces the waste resulting from an unsuitable design in the early stages of the life cycle of a software product, identifying an industry friendly software evaluation approach becomes the focal point of the recent industry research.

The objectives of this paper are to briefly review software architecture evaluation approaches in state of the art and identify the gaps between an ideal industry friendly software architecture evaluation approach and these evaluation methods. The rest of the paper is organized as follows: Section 2 highlights the characteristics of software architecture evaluation. Section 3 reviews primary software architecture evaluation approaches in state of the art and identifies the gaps between an ideal industry friendly software architecture evaluation approach and those in state of the art. Section 4 concludes the paper.

2 Essentials of Software Architecture Evaluation

As a ubiquitous process found everywhere in our daily life, the evaluation activity has been well addressed by researchers primarily from the disciplines of sociology

K. Drira (Ed.): ECSA 2013, LNCS 7957, pp. 328–331, 2013.

and psychology [1]. The software architecture evaluation is the application of the above evaluation activities to the software engineering discipline. Based on the set of architectural design decisions as the evaluation target and the functional and non-functional requirements as the evaluation criteria, the activities of the software architecture evaluation are formulated as follows [2]:

- Elaborate the precise statements of an architectural design decision
- Elaborate the precise statements of the functional requirements and its related quality attribute requirements
- Evaluate the architecture design decisions to determine whether they address the quality attribute requirements

Practically, as shown in Fig. 1, the above software architecture evaluation process, uniquely triggers a series of activities, including checklists, interviews, scenarios, questionnaires, workshops, simulations, metrics architecture patterns, prototypes, and brainstorming. The effectiveness of these activities is determined by four factors: 1) existing knowledge of the software architecture, 2) the experience and expertise of the evaluator, 3) the inputs of stakeholders, and 4) the impact of the business factors.

The above four underground factors permeate every corner of the software architecture evaluation, directly influencing the qualities of evaluation results and the software architecture evaluation is a process of dealing with these factors via a series of activities and methods (e.g., interviews and brainstorming). An effective software architecture evaluation process should organize the above factors systematically to maximize their contributions to the evaluation.

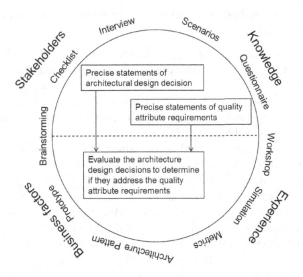

Fig. 1. Factors that influence software architecture evaluation

3 Research Challenges

3.1 Architecture Evaluation in State of the Practice

In literature, software architecture evaluation methods fall into two categories: the quantitative evaluation and the qualitative evaluation. The quantitative evaluation consists of metrics, simulation, and prototype; while the qualitative evaluation includes scenario-based and attribute-model-based evaluation.

The quantitative evaluation is an experimental-oriented method. It is based on a prototype and/or a simulation of a software architecture design and provides more insights of the resulting system. However, the high cost of the quantitative evaluation prevent it from widely adoption. The qualitative evaluation is experience oriented, mostly relying on the experience and expertise of participants. As the major technologies used in the qualitative evaluation are questionnaires, checklists and scenarios, it is relatively cheaper to assess a large system or a group of quality attributes using qualitative methods. However, over dependency on the experiences and expertise of the evaluators makes the qualitative evaluation more subjective and its results are generally non-repeatable. Practically, to enhance the evaluation results, quantitative evaluation is generally used as a complementary approach to the qualitative evaluation method.

In industry, besides the design review, a lightweight ATAM [3] with a formal evaluation framework is a typical solution for software architecture evaluation. Recently, to avoid the subjectiveness of the existing evaluation methods, some new methods (e.g., TARA [4]) are proposed, which utilizes existing artifacts (e.g., source code) to improve the objectiveness of the evaluation.

3.2 Developing an Industry Friendly Software Architecture Evaluation Method

After 20 years examination, software architecture evaluation has been fully discussed in academia. Theoretically, proposed evaluation methods can identify most of the hidden defects and potential risks in an ideal situation. However, in practice, the evaluation process is primarily constrained by factors that do not always surface in academic research (e.g., limited budgets, geographically distributed evaluator, and different schedule of the evaluator), applying academic methods to industry applications does not always produce expected results.

The development of an efficient industry friendly method of evaluating software architecture can be facilitated in the following ways: First, guaranteeing the quality of the evaluation results requires a formal evaluation framework that can temporally organize events and activities associated with the evaluation process. Second, the most effective way to collect evaluation data is face-to-face negotiation/workshop with stakeholders, but it is prohibitively expensive, and therefore, is impractical for a general industry application. A less costly solution for industry applications is a lightweight workshop or interviews (e.g., a network-based forum and individual interviews with stakeholders). However, compared to the face-to-face methods, the lightweight methods unavoidably lose some effectiveness. Third, bypassing the expensive scenario collection process and instead fully relying on an evaluators subjective judgments is a risky venture but obviously is the most cost saving approach affordable by industry applications. However, the tradeoff is it causes the evaluation more subjective. In practice, mitigating the subjectivity calls for remedial actions such as TARA, which lends objectivity to the process by adding a new step: checking the collected data against source code. Finally, as the budget for the software architecture evaluation varies case by case, mostly, the architecture evaluation is launched with limited budgets will end up at the certain point without generating any useful results. Under this situation, adapting the evaluation process to the wide range of budgets and producing the corresponding results per the provided budget become important.

4   Conclusion

Because the evaluation environment in industry differs considerably from that in academia, the results of evaluation method (e.g., ATAM) applied in one environment do not necessarily apply to the other. Hence, even though the plethora of the evaluation methods in academia, few of them have been successfully applied to real industry situations. On the other hand, in industry, the design review is widely used to assess the quality of software architecture design. However, design reviews cannot generate high quality and reproduced assessment results due to lacking of a formal evaluation framework and over-dependency on the evaluators.

Regardless an evaluation method from academia or industry, it consists of subjective factors and objective factors. The more objective factors an evaluation method has, the better its evaluation results. Hence, adding objective factors extracted from the research in academia into the industry design review becomes a promising direction. A more recently proposed approach, TARA, demonstrates the trend along this direction.

References

1. Lopez, M.: Application of an evaluation framework for analyzing the architecture tradeoff analysis method. The J. of System and Software 68(3) (December 2003)
2. Clements, P., Kazman, R., Klein, M.: Evaluating Software Architectures, methods and case studies. Addison-Wesley (2002)
3. Kazman, R., Klein, M., Barbacci, M., Lipson, H., Longstaff, T., Carriere, S.J.: The Architecture Tradeoff Analysis method. In: Proc. Fourth Intl Conf. Eng. Of Complex Computer Systems (ICECCS 1998) (August 1998)
4. Woods, E.: Industrial Architectural Assessment using TARA. In: 2011 Ninth Working IEEE/IFIP Conference on Software Architecture (2011)

Towards Continuous Reference Architecture Conformance Analysis

Georg Buchgeher[1] and Rainer Weinreich[2]

[1] Software Competence Center Hagenberg, Austria
georg.buchgeher@scch.at
[2] Johannes Kepler University Linz, Austria
rainer.weinreich@jku.at

Abstract. Reference architectures (RA) are reusable architectures for artifacts in a particular domain. They can serve as a basis for designing new architectures, but also as a means for quality control during system development. Quality control is performed through checking the conformance of systems in development to (company-wide) reference architectures. If performed manually, reference architecture conformance checking is a time- and resource-intensive process. In this paper we outline an approach for reference architecture conformance checking of application architectures in the banking domain. Reference architectures are defined on the basis of reusable rules, consisting of roles and of constraints on roles and role relationships. Conformance checking can be performed semi-automatically and continuously by automating important steps like the extraction of the actual application architecture, the binding of reference architecture roles to the elements of a specific application architecture, and the evaluation of the reference architecture rules for an application architecture.

Keywords: Software Architecture, Reference Architectures, Conformance Analysis.

1 Introduction

Multiple definitions have been provided for the term reference architecture both in the context of software architecture[1][2][3] and beyond [4][5]. While the perspective on what constitutes a reference architecture and how it is represented still varies quite a bit [5], there is a consensus on some defining characteristics. First, there is a focus on reuse [5][1]. Reference architectures are defined to be reused for the definition of concrete architectures of specific systems. This means they are more generic [2][4] and sometimes at a higher level of abstraction [2] than concrete architectures. Second, they encode important design decisions for applications in a particular domain. This means they are usually domain-specific [3][1], though this may depend on how one defines a domain [5]. Third, reference architectures can take different roles in software development [4]. They can take an instructive role for designing new application architectures, an informative

K. Drira (Ed.): ECSA 2013, LNCS 7957, pp. 332–335, 2013.

role for sharing architectural knowledge, and a regulative role for restricting the design space of systems in development. A reference architecture can take all three roles, though it depends on how it is actually represented.

In this paper we focus on the regulative role of reference architectures and propose an approach for continuous reference architecture conformance checking. Reference architectures are specified as a set of rules that consist of roles and constraints among these roles and their relationships. Roles defined in a reference architecture specification are mapped onto elements of an existing architecture (model), which is then automatically checked against the defined reference architecture rules. Main contributions of the proposed approach are a way for defining and storing reference architectures as a reusable set of rules, and for automatically binding these rules to and evaluating them for specific application architectures. Since binding and evaluation activities are mostly automated, the approach can be used as a means for continuous quality control. The approach is currently being used for checking the architecture of service-oriented applications to company-wide reference architectures in the banking domain and is based on previous work on architecture extraction and review support [6] in this domain.

2   Approach

The main aim of the proposed approach is support for automatically analyzing the architecture of existing enterprise application systems for conformance to company-wide reference architectures. The approach consists of the two main activities shown in Figure 1: The definition of reusable reference architecture specifications, and the actual use of such a specification for checking the conformance of existing application architectures to the constraints of the reference architecture specification.

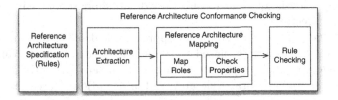

Fig. 1. Approach Overview

A reference architecture is defined as a set of rules. Conceptually a rule consists of roles, required and/or forbidden relationships between these roles, and a set of constraints on both roles and relationships. During the checking process roles are mapped onto elements of the architecture of the checked system. These elements are then analyzed for conformance to relationships and constraints defined in the rules of the reference architecture. Roles and constraints can be specified using a structured editor, which works directly on the constraint model representing the reference architecture specification. The actual conformance checking is performed in three steps:

- In the first step the actually implemented architecture is automatically extracted from the system implementation. For a description of the extraction process we refer to [6].
- In the second step roles are assigned to elements of the extracted architecture model. Role assignment is performed semi-automatically. For each role it is possible to specify so-called role assignment rules. For example, a role assignment rule might specify to assign a role to all components based on a specific technology (e.g., EJB) or using a specific naming convention (e.g., to all components containing *Service* in their name). Roles may have additional properties, which are required for analysis. During role assignment we check whether elements with this role are able to provide the required properties. If properties cannot by provided by the elements themselves, they can be provided manually by the user or through extensions to the conformance checker.
- The final step of the checking process is the actual conformance checking. In this step the rules of the reference architecture are evaluated for an application architecture with assigned roles.

3   Related Work

Software architecture conformance checking is addressed by numerous approaches in both research and practice. Dependency analysis approaches like Lattix, Structure 101 and SonarJ support architecture/implementation conformance checking at the programming language abstraction level by analyzing source code dependencies. Analysis at higher abstraction levels, and analysis of information beyond static dependencies (e.g., communication protocols used) is not supported. Dependency analysis approaches also provide no support for defining reusable reference architectures.

Schmerl and Garlan [7] describe an approach for defining and automatically analyzing architectural styles based on the ACME/Armani architecture description language [8]. Their approach consists of two separate activities. (1) The definition of an architectural style and (2) the definition of architecture design models based on a previously defined architectural style. Their work is targeted at defining and checking new architectures based on architectural styles, and not at the continuous conformance checking of already implemented systems as supported in our approach.

Deiters et al. [9] present an approach with similar concepts to ours, which is based on so-called architectural building blocks (ABBs). Rules and constraints are Prolog-like fact bases which are defined textually in their approach, while we use a projectional editor on a constraint model. Their architecture model is simpler (entities and dependencies) and automatic role assignment is not supported in their approach. The differences are mainly because their approach is also more targeted at supporting composition during design than at continuous conformance checking during system evolution and development.

4 Conclusion

We have presented an approach for reference architecture conformance checking. The approach is currently being used by architects as a means for continuous quality control for enterprise applications in the banking domain. However, the developed concepts and tools are not limited to this domain. The basic concepts for defining reference architectures like roles, properties, relationships, and constraints are quite general and could also be used for checking the conformance to reference architectures in other domains, to patterns, and to architectural styles. We are currently investigating the use of the approach for automatically checking the correct application of security patterns. We are also working on strategies for eliminating human intervention during the checking process, which might currently still be required in some cases (like the provisioning of missing property values during role assignment).

References

1. Nakagawa, E.Y., Oliveira Antonino, P., Becker, M.: Reference Architecture and Product Line Architecture: A Subtle But Critical Difference. In: Crnkovic, I., Gruhn, V., Book, M. (eds.) ECSA 2011. LNCS, vol. 6903, pp. 207–211. Springer, Heidelberg (2011)
2. Angelov, S., Trienekens, J.J.M., Grefen, P.W.P.J.: Towards a method for the evaluation of reference architectures: Experiences from a case. In: Morrison, R., Balasubramaniam, D., Falkner, K. (eds.) ECSA 2008. LNCS, vol. 5292, pp. 225–240. Springer, Heidelberg (2008)
3. Hofmeister, C., Nord, R., Soni, D.: Applied Software Architecture. Addison-Wesley Professional (November 1999)
4. Greefhorst, D., Proper, E.: Architecture Principles: The Cornerstones of Enterprise Architecture, vol. 4. Springer (2011)
5. Cloutier, R., Muller, G., Verma, D., Nilchiani, R., Hole, E., Bone, M.: The concept of reference architectures. Systems Engineering, 14–27 (2009)
6. Weinreich, R., Miesbauer, C., Buchgeher, G., Kriechbaum, T.: Extracting and facilitating architecture in service-oriented software systems. In: 2012 Joint 10th IEEE/IFIP Working Conference on Software Architecture & 6th European Conference on Software Architecture (WICSA-ECSA 2012). IEEE (2012)
7. Schmerl, B., Garlan, D.: Acmestudio: supporting style-centered architecture development. In: Proceedings of 26th International Conference on Software Engineering, ICSE 2004, pp. 704–705 (2004)
8. Monroe, R.T.: Capturing Software Architecture Design Expertise with Armani. Carnegie-mellon univ pittsburgh pa school of computer Science (October 2001)
9. Deiters, C., Rausch, A.: A constructive approach to compositional architecture design. In: Crnkovic, I., Gruhn, V., Book, M. (eds.) ECSA 2011. LNCS, vol. 6903, pp. 75–82. Springer, Heidelberg (2011)

Towards Automated Deployment of Distributed Adaptation Systems

Mohamed Zouari[1,2] and Ismael Bouassida Rodriguez[1,2,3]

[1] CNRS, LAAS, 7 Avenue du Colonel Roche, F-31400 Toulouse, France
[2] Univ de Toulouse, LAAS, F-31400 Toulouse, France
[3] ReDCAD, University of Sfax, B.P. 1173, 3038 Sfax, Tunisia
{mohamed.zouari,bouassida}@laas.fr

Abstract. The development of a single software product is inefficient when groups of product are related since the development cost could be high. In addition, some products need to be self-adaptive in order to take into account the execution context changes. In this case, the implementation and management of the adaptation mechanisms variability is challenging especially for distributed systems due to the distribution issues. We address in this paper such issues by proposing a method for the software engineering of distributed adaptation systems. We propose an architectural model for distributed management of dynamic adaptation. We define also a graph grammar based approach to automate the tasks needed to construct and configure the adaptation system[1].

Keywords: Distributed adaptation, Software architectural model, Automated deployment, Graph grammar.

1   Introduction

Several applications running in fluctuating and heterogeneous environments require dynamic adaptation [1]. This is especially necessary when users may have different and variable QoS requirements and resources are highly dynamic and unpredictable. The adaptation approach enables to deal with the different fluctuations in available resources, to meet new user requirements, and to improve the application services.

In general, an adaptation engine monitors the execution context (resources characteristics, user profile, terminal capabilities, etc) in order to trigger dynamic adaptation whenever it detects significant variations. Then, it makes decisions regarding the adaptation and controls the modification of the application in order to achieve the appropriate configuration. When a decentralized application is running in heterogeneous environments, distributed adaptation system may be required in order to improve the adaptation mechanisms quality such as efficiency, robustness, and scalability. The distributed management of adaptation leads to the concurrent execution of multiple adaptation processes performed

---

[1] This work is partially funded by the IMAGINE IP European project.

K. Drira (Ed.): ECSA 2013, LNCS 7957, pp. 336–339, 2013.

by several engines. The customization and the deployment of the engines may need to perform complex dedicated tasks and be time consuming. Facilitating these tasks and reducing the development cost of distributed adaptation systems is challenging. In fact, current approaches do not offer development facilities of distributed adaptation systems where the activities of several adaptation engines are coordinated without a central control entity.

In this paper, we propose an approach for easy customization and deployment of distributed adaptation systems.The aim of this approach is to provide facilities for the elaboration of the system configuration and for its deployment in automated way. Actually, we provide firstly an architectural model of distributed adaptation systems. Secondly, we offer a tool called factory that performs the deployment tasks. The factory processes the appropriate system configuration using a graph grammar-based approach and then, it sets up the system. Our case study concerns data management in medical environments for collaborative remote care delivery. We enable to make self-adaptive data replication systems in order to improve the data availability and response times for data requests.

The remainder of the paper is organized as follows. We present our method to build distributed adaptation systems in Section 2. Then, we conclude and discuss future work in Section 3.

2   Method to Build Self-adaptive Applications

Our approach aims at facilitating the component-based development of distributed self-adaptive applications. We follow the separation of concerns principle between the adaptation concerns and the business aspects. Moreover, we externalize the mechanisms of adaptation control for reusability. Some application components provide well defined control interfaces that define primitive operations to observe and modify them (see Figure 1). The adaptation system is connected to the application trough such interfaces to produce a *self-adaptive application*.

We design the adaptation mechanisms in a modular way and we offer facilities for adaptation system building. In fact, we define an tool called factory to facilitate the customization of the adaptation system according to the target application and to ensure the automatic deployment of the system. As shown in Figure 1, an architect provides a software architectural model of adaptation systems and an expert in deployment provides a set of deployment strategies for the set up of concrete systems. This architectural model specifies a set of component types, the possible connections among them and several constraints that must be meet when constructing a concrete system. Each deployment strategy is a set of graph grammars processed to choose the distribution of the adaptation system according to targeted application to adapt and specific required quality criteria of the adaptation system. The configuration manager determinates the adaptation system architecture description that specifies the components that compose the adaptation system, the connections among them, the values of configuration parameters, and the connections with the application

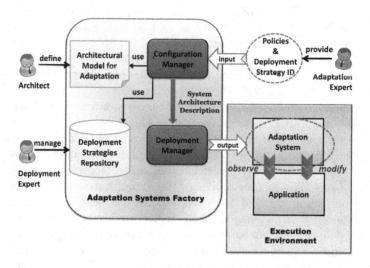

Fig. 1. Building a self-adaptive application

components. The architecture is expressed in the GraphML language which is an XML dialect for representing graphs [2]. For that, the configuration manager applies the grammars related to a chosen deployment strategy and verifies that the constraints of the architectural model are well respected. The selection of the suitable strategy is done by the adaptation expert. We use GMTE[2] in order to process the graph grammars. In addition, the configuration manager uses a set of policies provided by the adaptation expert. These policies enable the configuration manager to customize the behaviour of some adaptation system components. Then, the deployment manager sets up the adaptation system and connect it with the application according to the architecture description provided by the configuration manager. The connections are realized through the dedicated control interfaces provided by the application. The outcome is a self-adaptive application deployed in a decentralized execution environment.

Our architectural model [3] specifies two component types *ContextManager* and *AdaptationManager* to perform the adaptation steps. An adaptation system is composed of several context managers and adaptation managers. A component type *ContextManager* collects, interprets, and aggregates some contextual data. A component type *AdaptationManager* determines which components of the application must be adapted and the means to achieve it.

The factory allows several strategies for deploying the adaptation system. The strategies are divided based on the expected load of the adaptation system, the customization requirements of managers' behaviour, and the distribution requirements. We are currently evaluating the different strategies in order to provide a guide that allows the adaptation expert to choose the appropriate

---

[2] Graph Matching and Transformation Engine (GMTE),
available at http://homepages.laas.fr/khalil/GMTE.

strategy based on many factors. We are particularly interested in the following deployment strategies: (**1**) *Centralized deployment* : In this situation, a single context manager and a single adaptation manager control the adaptation of all the application components. (**2**) *Location-based deployment* : The difference is the use of multiple context managers and adaptation managers. The distribution is based on geographic location of the application components. Each manager controls a group of components hosted by machines in a specific site (organization, department, vehicle, etc). (**3**) *Service centric deployment* : This deployment strategy is characterized by the consideration of the different services provided by the application components. An adaptation manager (resp., context manager) is associated with a component or group of components that offers specific service (the data consistency achievement, the replica placement, etc). (**4**) *Hybrid deployment* : This strategy combines the two previous strategies: location-based and service centric deployment. The goal is to combine the best of both. (**5**)*Distributed deployment* : This strategy is characterized by a fully distributed system where an adaptation manager (resp., context manager) is associated with a single application component.

3 Conclusion

In this paper, we addressed how to manage effectively and in a structured way variability in distributed adaptation systems. We enable variable configuration for distributed adaptation systems in order to meet specific requirements regarding the adaptation system QoS. We presented a systematic approach to model, implant and manage the variability of such systems based on the architectural model. Among the benefits of this model are reusability and the support of several types of variations like the behaviour and the distribution of the system. Our experience shows that our factory provides an effective and easy way to manage variability that turns up during the construction of an adaptation system.

There are several possible directions for future work. We are interested in facilitating more the customization process. Currently, human actor makes decision related to the deployment strategy. It will possible to extend the factory in order to allow choosing automatically the appropriate strategy. Moreover, we are exploring the connection between the architectural model and the existing components models. Our vision is to make the factory able to support several components models and service oriented architectures.

References

1. Cheng, B.H., Lemos, R., Giese, H.: Inverardi: Software engineering for self-adaptive systems, pp. 1–26. Springer, Heidelberg (2009)
2. Brandes, U., Eiglsperger, M., Herman, I., Himsolt, M., Marshall, M.S.: GraphML progress report. In: Mutzel, P., Jünger, M., Leipert, S. (eds.) GD 2001. LNCS, vol. 2265, p. 501. Springer, Heidelberg (2002)
3. Zouari, M., Segarra, M.T., André, F., Thépaut, A.: An architectural model for building distributed adaptation systems. In: IDC 2011, pp. 153–158 (2011)

Towards a Bigraph-Based Model for Context-Aware Adaptive Systems

Taha Abdelmoutaleb Cherfia and Faïza Belala

Department of Software Technologies and Information Systems,
University of Constantine II, Constantine, Algeria
taha.cherfia@gmail.com, belalafaiza@hotmail.com

Abstract. In the last decade, context-aware computing has become the central focus of the ubiquitous computing where computers disappear in the background of people's everyday life activities. Context-aware adaptive systems are able to adapt themselves according to the gathered context information. In this context, many approaches have been proposed in order to model the former systems but only few of them tackle at the same time all the features of these systems. This paper presents a formal modeling approach based on Bigraphical Reactive Systems to deal with both the structural and behavioral aspects of context-aware adaptive systems. It provides a clear separation between the context-aware information that affect the system and the system itself. Indeed, we specify the context and the system using two distinct bigraphs, then we combine them using the bigraphs composition operation to represent the whole system.

1   Introduction

Context-aware adaptive systems are able to dynamically adapt their behavior at runtime in response to changes on the context information without an explicit user intervention. In the literature, there are many definitions of the term "context" but until now there is no universal one. Dey and Abowd [1] gave a generic definition which encompasses the existing ones given by previous authors where context is referred as "any information that can be used to characterize the situation of an entity. An entity is a person, place or object that is considered relevant to the interaction between a user and an application, including location, time, activities and the preferences of each entity". However, the lack of a solid formal foundation in the most existing definitions represents a clear challenge to the context-aware systems community. Hence, the modeling of context-aware adaptive systems represents an essential task for capturing and managing the changes of these systems.

In this context, graph-based approaches are commonly used within this field. Authors in [2] introduced a modeling framework of context-awareness for ubiquitous computing based on contextual graphs. Moreover, according to [3], one of the principal aims for the theory of Bigraphical Reactive Systems (or BRS in short) is to model ubiquitous systems, capturing mobile locality in the place graph and mobile connectivity in the link graph. Within the same line of thought, two classes of work

K. Drira (Ed.): ECSA 2013, LNCS 7957, pp. 340–343, 2013.

have arisen. The first class consists of extending and combining BRS with other models in order to formalize some aspects of context-aware systems. Authors of the relevant works [4], [5] argued that BRS in their current form, as introduced by Milner [3], are not suitable for directly modeling context queries. The second class of work used directly bigraphs to formalize the context-aware systems. The proposed approaches [6], [7] introduced different types of nodes to model context-awareness.

In the above work, authors only used the graphical presentation of BRS formalism to model context-aware systems and their evolution. They did not give any information or formal definition of the relationship between the context changes and the system reactions. With the objective to gain a better understanding on how to model, process, and manage the context information, and how a system adapts itself in response to (unanticipated) changes in the context information; the idea presented in this paper is quite similar to the previous ones since it is based on the same used formalism, but it models separately the context-aware information and the system. Furthermore, it exploits the operation of composition in bigraphs to define the whole context-aware system. Thus, it enriches the existing BRS model by appending the context information to a new set of reaction rules, in order to capture the relationship between the context changes and the system reactions.

2   Bigraphs and Context-Aware Adaptive Systems

According to Milner and co-workers, a Bigraphical Reactive System is a graphical model which emphasizes both locality and connectivity. A BRS comprises a category of bigraphs and a set of reaction rules that maybe applied to rewrite these bigraphs. Structurally, a bigraph consists of two independent sub-graphs; a place graph expressing usually the physical location of nodes whereas the link graph represents the mobile connectivity among them. Moreover, BRS defines various operations derived from categorical theory. In this paper, we particularly focus on the operation of *composition*. Basic definitions used in this paper can be found in [3].

Context-awareness is a central aspect in the modeling of adaptive systems. It provides detailed information about entities such as people, places, and things. Each entity is characterized by an identity, location, status and time. Identity refers to the ability to embed a unique identifier for each entity. Location represents the spatial information of an entity. Status (or activity) represents the intrinsic properties of an entity. Finally, time refers to the relative ordering of events. Furthermore, context always changes resulting in behavioral modifications of context-aware adaptive systems. These latter can be able to control and adapt themselves in response to the context transitions.

Hence, in order to clarify the formalization task of the structure and behavior of context-aware adaptive systems, we propose a set of formal mapping rules defining correspondences between context-aware adaptive system elements and bigraph concepts (see Table 1). First, we model solely both the context and the system using two distinct bigraphs (C and S) and then, we combine them together with the operation of composition ($S \circ C$) to represent the entire system S_C. Thus, each context entity (i.e. person, place, or object) is specified by a bigraph node v_i assigned with a control K

to represent its identity. Also, the interaction among entities is formalized by bigraph hyper-edges e_i. Then, we propose a new bigraphical reaction rules category to formalize the behavioral aspect of the context-aware adaptive system.

Table 1. Mapping context-aware elements to Bigraphs

Context elements	Bigraphical semantics
Context-aware structure	
Context	Bigraph: $C = (V_C, E_C, ctrl_C, G_C^P, G_C^L): I \rightarrow K$
System	Bigraph: $S = (V_S, E_S, ctrl_S, G_S^P, G_S^L): K \rightarrow J$
Context-aware System	Bigraph: $S_C: I \rightarrow J \overset{\text{def}}{=} S \circ C$
Entity	Node: $v_i \in V_C^S / V_C^S = V_S \uplus V_C$ and $V_S \cap V_C = \emptyset$
Identity of entity	Control: $K \in \mathcal{K}_C^S / \mathcal{K}_C^S = \mathcal{K}_S \uplus \mathcal{K}_C$
Interaction	Hyper-edge: $e_i \in E_C^S / E_C^S = E_S \uplus E_C$ and $E_S \cap E_C = \emptyset$
Context-aware behavior	
Context transition	Context Reaction rule: $S_C \overset{\mathcal{R}}{\rightarrow} S_{C'}$, where $\mathcal{R} = (R_C, R'_{C'}, \eta)$

Definition 1. A bigraph S_C modeling a context-aware adaptive system S in a context C over a signature $\mathcal{K}_C^S$ takes the form $S_C \overset{\text{def}}{=} S \circ C$ where:

$$S_C = (V_C^S, E_C^S, ctrl_C^S, GP_C^S, GL_C^S): I \rightarrow J$$

- $V_C^S = V_S \uplus V_C$ and $V_S \cap V_C = \emptyset$ is a finite set of nodes in a current context C.
- $E_C^S = E_S \uplus E_C$ and $E_S \cap E_C = \emptyset$ is a finite set of edges.
- $\mathcal{K}_C^S = \mathcal{K}_S \uplus \mathcal{K}_C$ is an extended signature defined by a set of controls where each control indicates how many *fixed-ports* and *context-ports* the node has.
- $ctrl_C^S: V_C^S \rightarrow \mathcal{K}_C^S$ is a new control map assigning to each node $v_i \in V_C^S$ a control $K \in \mathcal{K}_C^S$.
- $GP_C^S = G_S^P \circ G_C^P$ and $GL_C^S = G_S^L \circ G_C^L$ represent respectively the place graph and the link graph of S_C.
- $I = (m, X)$ and $J = (n, Y)$ represent respectively the inner face and the outer face of S_C; where m represents the number of sites, X is a set of inner names, n represents the number of regions and finally, Y is the set of outer names.

Definition 2. A bigraph C modeling a context over a signature $\mathcal{K}_C$ takes the form

$$C = (V_C, E_C, ctrl_C, G_C^P, G_C^L): I \rightarrow K$$

- V_C is a finite set of *context-nodes* where each node defines a context entity.
- E_C is a finite set of *context-edges* where each edge connects different *context-nodes*.
- $\mathcal{K}_C$ is a *context-signature* whose elements are controls, and a map $ctrl_C: V_C \rightarrow E_C$ assigns a control to each node dictating how many *context-ports* the node has.
- G_C^P and G_C^L represent *context-place graph* and *context-link graph* respectively.

Now, let S be a bigraph modeling an adaptive system. Formally S takes the form

$$S = (V_S, E_S, ctrl_S, G_S^P, G_S^L): K \rightarrow J$$

Unlike an ordinary bigraph, $K = \langle k, Z \rangle$ is the inner face of the bigraph S in which k represents the number of sites where each region i of C containing *context-nodes* can be planted into the ith site of S. Z is the set of inner names where each inner name is linked to its related outer name of C to form a *context-edge*.

Finally, a *context transition* which takes the form $S_C \overset{\mathcal{R}}{\to} S_{C'}$, is defined by a *Context Reaction Rule* given by $\mathcal{R}$, where S_C models the *current state* of a context-aware adaptive system and $S_{C'}$ models the *next state* of the system in a new context.

3   Conclusion

This paper presents an idea of a new formal modeling approach based on bigraphs for context-aware adaptive systems. Bigraph is more than a graphical representation; it is a unifying theory of process models for distributed, concurrent and ubiquitous computing. In the present paper, we have shown the convenience of this formalism to provide a high level modeling of context-aware adaptive systems. Our contribution consists in providing an extended BRS-based approach to formalize the structure and behavior of context-aware adaptive systems. It provides a clear separation between the context and the system. In other words, each one is modeled separately using a bigraph. Hence, their composition yields a new bigraph representing the structure of context-aware adaptive system. Besides, a new set of bigraphical reaction rules, called context reaction rules, to deal with context changes is proposed. These rules adopt the context-aware information resulting from any context change to formalize the behavior of context-aware adaptive systems.

References

1. Dey, A., Abowd, G.: Towards a better understanding of context and context-awareness. In: Proceedings of the Workshop on the What, Who, Where, When and How of Context-Awareness. ACM Press, New York (2000)
2. Nguyen, T.V., Lim, W., Choi, D.: Context Awareness Framework based on Contextual Graph. In: IEEE 8th International Conference on Computer and Information Technology Workshops, CIT 2008 Workshops, pp. 488–493 (2008)
3. Milner, R.: The Space and Motion of Communicating Agents. Cambridge University Press, Cambridge (2009)
4. Pereira, E., Kirsch, C., Sengupta, R.: BiAgents – A Bigraphical Agent Model for Structure-aware Computation. In: Cyber-Physical Cloud Computing Working Papers, CPCC Berkeley (2012)
5. Birkedal, L., Debois, S., Elsborg, E., Hildebrandt, T., Niss, H.: Bigraphical Models of Context-Aware Systems. In: Aceto, L., Ingólfsdóttir, A. (eds.) FOSSACS 2006. LNCS, vol. 3921, pp. 187–201. Springer, Heidelberg (2006)
6. Wang, J., Xu, D., Lei, Z.: Formalizing the Structure and Behaviour of Context-aware Systems in Bigraphs. In: First ACIS International Symposium on Software and Network Engineering (2011)
7. Xu, D.Z., Xu, D.: Bigraphical Model of Context-aware in Ubiquitous Computing Environments. In: Pacific Services Computing Conference. IEEE, Asia (2011)

Characterising Software Platforms from an Architectural Perspective

Ulrik Eklund[1,2], Carl Magnus Olsson[2], and Marcus Ljungblad[2]

[1] Volvo Car Group, Sweden
ulrik.eklund@volvocars.com
[2] Malmö University, Sweden

Abstract. With demands of speed in software development it is of interest to build on available software platforms that incorporate the necessary non-competitive functionalities and focus the development effort on adding features to a competitive product. This paper proposes that we move from an API-oriented focus and instead suggest four architectural concerns for describing software platforms as more relevant.

1 Introduction: An Empirical Reflection

Using three empirical cases from the embedded domain, this paper reflects on the challenge for future research for new product and feature development based on existing platforms and the architectural concerns this brings. The need for this is motivated by the current trend in software engineering towards extending and integrating existing platforms to further the supported functionality [1].

1.1 Case 1: Platform Development in a Heterogeneous Domain

Home automation is attracting increasing attention from commercial actors such as energy suppliers, infrastructure providers, construction companies, third party software and hardware vendors. As there are no accepted reference architectures or software platforms we see multiple vertical solutions where companies strive to support the whole chain - from the sensors and devices to gateways and servers, with whatever dedicated software that is of particular interest to the company. This creates a situation where it is difficult to avoid lock-in for third party service developers and customers, which subsequently may limit their willingness to commit and develop services for each specific platform. One example of this problem is in a major project with one of Europe's largest energy suppliers (henceforth referred to as EnergyCorp), where the desire is to overcome the problem of heterogeneous technologies. In this case, three concerns stand out from an architect's and developer's perspective:

- What assumptions can be made about the components supporting the API?
- What limitations regarding the data and communication paths can be inferred from the API? I.e. what guarantees does a developer have when changing state on an actuator?

K. Drira (Ed.): ECSA 2013, LNCS 7957, pp. 344–347, 2013.

– What are the run-time dependencies and functionalities not attached to a
device initially? This is not obvious since the exposed API is a composition of data from several sources within the platform, and the contextual
information about where a device is located is added by the user.

1.2   Case 2: Implementation Based on an Existing Platform

Volvo Car Corporation has a strategy to use the AUTOSAR [2] architecture and
platform as a basis for the software in new vehicle platforms. To use a platform-
based approach is not only deciding on the infrastructure configuration, but
also to maintain a selection of functionalities the platform shall support when
developing new innovations enabled by software. This caused a need for the
architects to:

– Define the scope of the platform that is easy to communicate to managers
  and developers and roadmapping the platform to meet long term demands.
– Configure the selected subset of basic software in the AUTOSAR platform.
– Focus on platform definition and evolution rather than integration of separately developed applications towards model year changes.
– Separate slow evolving platform development from fast application development in general, and to allow differentiated lead-times for novel features.

1.3   Case 3: Adaptation of a Platform to a Different Context

The Open Infotainment Labs is a previously published case [3][4] of a prototype
development of an in-vehicle infotainment systems in cooperation between Volvo
Car Corporation and EIS by Semcon. The project had two goals: First, to establish whether it was possible to do feature development with extremely short
leadtimes from decision to implementation compared to present automotive industry standard, from a nominal leadtime of 1-3 years to 4-12 weeks. From an
architect's perspective there was a need to:

– Analyse the Android platform to identify additional needed services and
  behaviour when used in a car compared to a mobile phone.
– Break down any change or addition to the platform to fit as a single user
  story in the product backlog (an effect of the project using Scrum).
– Focus on platform development and deemphasize application development.

2   Research Challenge

The case of EnergyCorp suggests the difficulties to see, on an API level alone,
how combined heterogeneous hardware and software from several platforms
complement and contradict each other from an architectural perspective. For
AUTOSAR, both long and short term product management is concerned with
how the functionalities provided by a platform are combined and extended to
realise new customer-discernible features. In these situations, it is desirable to

scope the platform both in terms of what domain-specific services/functions it provides and what commodity components it contains to build products and product families. Finally, when developing on top of an Android platform it is important to separate the concerns between what services/functions are available and how these services are used. It is impractical for an architect or product manager to incorporate updates in platform backlog user stories in terms of API changes, instead a higher abstraction of the platform capabilities is necessary. Overall, this hints towards a working hypothesis that the API-level may not be appropriate for discussing architectural concerns of software platforms.

Our challenge for future research therefore becomes how to characterise software platforms from an architect's perspective and what views or dimension are important to capture. Found factors of relevance include building products based on a combination of multiple platforms (case 1), long-term product planning (case 2), or addressing various non-functional properties (case 3). In the four subsections below, we put this working hypothesis to initial scrutiny by reviewing which architectural concerns stand out in our three empirical cases.

2.1 Infrastructure

According to [5] a platform infrastructure consists of the operating system and commodity components, with database management and GUI being two examples. In case 1 and 2 this concern is present, as application developers often have to make implicit assumptions about the available hardware and software services available to be able to efficiently build applications on top of the platform. It is thus important that the infrastructure is communicated properly. Based on our three cases, this should from an infrastructure perspective include at least a list and description of the available hardware devices and commodity components.

2.2 Run-Time Dependencies

Simply being aware of the platform infrastructure, however, does not enable application developers to build efficient applications (case 1 and case 2). The type of communication, asynchronous or synchronous, between application and platform components is not easily discernible from the API as functionalities may be physically separated with respect to dependencies on data. An API request to modify a device's state says little about consistency guarantees among the platform components. Highlighting platform communication paths as well as their respective guarantees is thus needed.

2.3 Functionalities

Functionalities are those domain-specific services, attributes, and operations that are part of the platform which can be used for feature and application development. In an embedded system they are usually an abstraction of available hardware sensors and actuators. In a car in case 2, functionalities could be status and control of the interior lights, which can be utilised in development of various convenience features.

2.4   Construction Principle

There are two fundamental approaches to platform construction: monolithic vs. componentised platforms [6]. These affect the construction principle that guides system design and architecture. The monolithic type of platform have a static structure for every instantiation and variation is achieved by variation points in the components. In the componentised platform, the platform instantiation allows for a creative selection and configuration of components and most of the tailoring towards specific products is achieved through different component configurations.

3   Conclusion

This paper has presented three cases of typical platform usage; development of a new platform for a domain, product family implementation based on an existing platform, and adaptation of an existing platform to a different need. In the discussion of our empirical cases, it becomes clear that none of the main concerns are appropriate to discuss on an API level, which lends further support to the working hypothesis we started from, i.e. that there is a need to establish a suitable level of abstraction. To this end, we identified four suitable architectural concerns to describe software platforms: infrastructure, run-time dependencies, functionalities and construction principle.

Acknowledgements. We would like to thank the following supporting organizations: VINNOVA, Energimyndigheten, EnergyComp, ResearchGroup, Volvo Car Group, and Semcon.

References

1. Evans, D.D.S., Hagiu, A., Schmalensee, R.L.: Invisible Engines. MIT Press (2006)
2. AUTOSAR: Technical overview v2.2.2 (August 2008)
3. Eklund, U., Bosch, J.: Introducing software ecosystems for mass-produced embedded systems. In: Cusumano, M.A., Iyer, B., Venkatraman, N. (eds.) ICSOB 2012. LNBIP, vol. 114, pp. 248–254. Springer, Heidelberg (2012)
4. Eklund, U., Bosch, J.: Using architecture for multiple levels of access to an ecosystem platform. In: Proceedings of the ACM Sigsoft conference on Quality of Software Architectures, pp. 143–148. ACM, Bertinoro (2012)
5. van der Linden, F.J., Dannenberg, R.B., Kamsties, E., Känsälä, K., Obbink, H.: Software product family evaluation. In: Nord, R.L. (ed.) SPLC 2004. LNCS, vol. 3154, pp. 110–129. Springer, Heidelberg (2004)
6. van Ommering, R.: Roadmapping a product population architecture. In: van der Linden, F.J. (ed.) PFE 2002. LNCS, vol. 2290, pp. 51–63. Springer, Heidelberg (2002)

Specifying System Architecture from SysML Requirements and Component Interfaces

Samir Chouali, Oscar Carrillo, and Hassan Mountassir

Femto-ST Institute, University of Franche-Comté, Besançon, France
{schouali,ocarrill,hmountas}@femto-st.fr

Abstract. We propose to map functional system requirements, specified with SysML, directly into system architecture, by exploiting the composition relation between component interfaces. Our research challenge is to guarantee formally that the final system fulfill the set of all requirements. Our approach is based on component-based systems (CBS) specified with SysML models and Interface Automata (IA) to capture their behaviors. From a SysML Requirement Diagram (RD), we build a Block Definition Diagram (BDD) to specify system architecture, by taking, one by one, the lowest level of requirements. At each new added requirement, we add a new component satisfying this requirement, by the composition, in the partial architecture obtained in a precedent step. Then we verify whether the new component is compatible with the components in the partial architecture, and if the requirements are preserved.

Keywords: System architecture, Composition, Requirements, SysML, Interface Automata.

1   Introduction

CBS are built by assembling various reusable components (third party components), which reduces their development cost. However, the development CBS is a hard task, because the compatibility must hold between the components that compose the system, and all the requirements related to these components must be preserved in the final system. To construct systems from requirements, several approaches have been proposed. In [1], the authors takes into account all the requirements at once, and in [2], the authors propose an incremental approach by adding properties to system architecture. Others approaches like [3,4], are based on the translation of atomic requirements into a behavior tree,which allows to specify the system structure. In [5], the authors construct CBS incrementally starting from raw requirements described in a natural language. Nevertheless, these models are restrictive compared to our model, because they do not deal with component interfaces specifying component behaviors, and the compatibility verification between components is not clearly discussed. Our paper discusses the relationship between system requirements and CBS architecture specification. Our goal is to guide, by the requirements, the CBS specifier to build the system architecture that fulfills all requirements. We propose to exploit SysML [6], by specifying functional system requirements with SysML RD, and BDD

K. Drira (Ed.): ECSA 2013, LNCS 7957, pp. 348–352, 2013.

and Internal Block Diagram (IBD) to specify system architecture [1]. We exploit
the IA approach [7] to specify component interfaces and to verify the compatibility between components and also the preservation of the requirements. In
our previous works [8],[9], we exploited BDD, IBD, and sequences diagrams to
verify compatibility between SysML blocks and to analyze the relation between
composite blocks and atomic blocks. The originality of this new contribution is
the exploitation of the SysML RD with BDD and IBD, in the context of the
development of CBS.

2   Incremental Specification of System Architecture from SysML Requirements

In this work, we propose to specify incrementally CBS architecture directly from
functional SysML requirements, in order to guarantee the architecture consistency. This consistency is guaranteed when the compatibility between the components holds, and when the requirements are preserved in the final system.
Thus, we propose to analyze a SysML RD, that specifies CBS requirements, in
order to extract its atomic requirements, because they are more precise, and it
is easier to find components that satisfy them. We specify components interfaces with IA and we exploit the composition of IA to verify the preservation of
the requirements. The composition of two interfaces is achieved by synchronizing their shared output and input actions. An interesting verification approach
(called optimistic) was also proposed in [7], to detect interface incompatibilities
that may occur when, from some states in the synchronized product, one automaton issues a shared action as output which is not accepted as input in the
other. These states are called illegal.

The main steps of our approach are described in the following:
(1) Start by analyzing SysML RD to obtain the atomic requirements. **(2)** *Repeat until all the requirements are treated.* **(2-a)** Let R_i be an atomic
requirement, let C_i be a component satisfying R_i, and A_i is the interface automaton describing the component protocol. Identify the set of input and output
actions in A_i related to R_i. **(2-b)** Let R_{i+1} be the next atomic requirement, let
C_{i+1} be a component satisfying R_{i+1}, and A_{i+1} is the interface automaton describing the component protocol. Identify the set of input and output actions
in A_{i+1} related to R_{i+1}. **(2-c)** Verify that C_i and C_{i+1} are compatible thanks
to their interface automata, so verify that $A_i \parallel A_{i+1} \neq \emptyset$. **(2-d)** Verify that the
requirements R_i and R_{i+1} are preserved by the composition, so they are satisfied
by the composite $C = C_i \parallel C_{i+1}$. We verify that the input and the output actions
related to the requirements are preserved by the composition. **(2-e)** Define the
partial architecture of the system by the composite $C = C_i \parallel C_{i+1}$: we specify
the BDD diagram in order to relate C with C_i and C_{i+1}, and we specify also
the IBD diagram which identifies the interaction between C_i and C_{i+1} through
ports. **(3)** *End repeat.*

---

[1] We note that the term used in SysML for components is blocks.

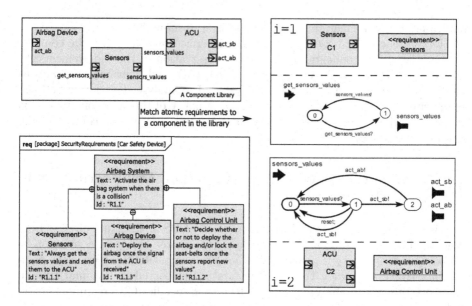

Fig. 1. Matching atomic requirements to components

To illustrate our approach, we propose to build the SysML structure that specifies the implementation of a vehicle safety system. Figure 1 shows the first two iterations of our approach. First, we analyze the RD to obtain the atomic requirements. The initial requirement $R1$ indicates that the airbag system must be deployed whenever the car is in a collision. $R1$ is decomposed into $R1.1.1$, $R1.1.2$, and $R1.1.3$ which are atomic. The requirement $R1.1.1$ indicates that the sensors must capture and send the sensors values to the Airbag Control Unit (ACU). And according to $R1.1.2$, the ACU component must decide whether or not to deploy the airbag and lock the seat belts as soon as the sensors report new values. Finally, $R1.1.3$ indicates the airbag device component must deploy the airbag, once the signal from the ACU is received. Our approach consists to take one by one these requirements to match them to reusable components. We start the first iteration ($i = 1$) with $R1.1.1$ which is matched to a *sensors* component and with its associated interface automaton shown in figure 1 (see iteration $i = 1$). The sensor component gets information from sensors at each call of **get_sensors_values** service, and sends them through a **sensors_values** service. These services are respectively the input $\{get\_sensors\_values\}$ and output actions $\{sensors\_values\}$ related to $R1.1.1$. In the next iteration ($i = 2$) we match the requirement $R1.1.2$ to the ACU component and to its associated interface automaton (see figure 1 on $i = 2$), that responds to the request of the requirement with the input action $\{sensors\_values\}$ and the output actions $\{act\_sb, act\_ab\}$ to lock seat belts and deploy an airbag respectively. Then, to link the components that satisfy requirements $R1.1.1$ and $R1.1.2$, we verify that they are compatible by composing their IA, so we obtain their composite automaton with Ptolemy tool [10]. The result is the composite automaton shown in figure 2, this automaton is not empty, so the components Sensors and ACU are compatible.

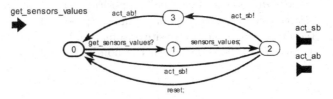

Fig. 2. IA for the composition of Sensors and ACU blocks

Despite the compatibility of these two components, this composition had illegal states that were eliminated automatically by Ptolemy tool by applying the steps of the IA approach, therefore transitions are also eliminated. So, to guarantee preservation of the requirements over the composition, we have to verify that the actions related to the requirements are still present on the transitions of the composite automaton. Following the transitions in the composite automaton, we find that the set of input/output actions, related to the requirements, are still present, so the the requirements are preserved over the composition. After that, we can proceed to define a partial architecture of the system by specifying the BDD with the refinement of a composite block into the blocks Sensors and ACU. This diagram is presented in figure 3 with its corresponding IBD which describes the connections between the composed blocks through the ports representing the shared actions between the IA of ACU and Sensors. For the lack of space we will not show the next iteration ($i = 3$) concerning the requirement $R1.1.3$.

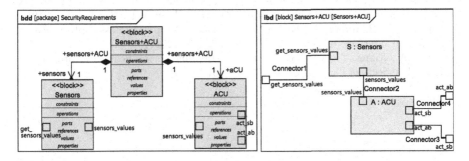

Fig. 3. SysML BDD and IBD for the second iteration

3   Conclusion

In this paper we proposed an approach to specify system architecture directly from functional requirements. System requirements were specified with SysML RD, which was analyzed to extract atomic requirements. These requirements were then associated, one by one, to reusable components, which satisfy them. These components were then added to a partial architecture by the composition of their component interfaces described through interface automata. The preservation of the requirements over the composition was guaranteed by the compatibility between the interface automata, and the preservation of the actions related to the requirements in the composite automaton. For future research, we plan to extend our approach to deal with the non-functional requirements in CBS.

References

1. Van Lamsweerde, A.: From system goals to software architecture. Formal Methods for Software Architectures, 25–43 (2003)
2. Barais, O., Duchien, L., Le Meur, A.F.: A framework to specify incremental software architecture transformations. In: EUROMICRO Conference SEAA, pp. 62–69 (2005)
3. Dromey, R.G.: From requirements to design: Formalizing the key steps. In: Software Engineering and Formal Methods, pp. 2–11 (2003)
4. Dromey, R.G.: Architecture as an emergent property of requirements integration. In: Second International SofTware Requirements to Architectures Workshop, pp. 77–84 (2003)
5. Lau, K.-K., Nordin, A., Rana, T., Taweel, F.: Constructing component-based systems directly from requirements using incremental composition. In: Proc. 36th EUROMICRO Conference SEAA, pp. 85–93. IEEE (2010)
6. The Object Mangagement Group (OMG): OMG Systems Modeling Language Specification Version 1.2. (2010), http://www.omg.org/spec/SysML/1.2/
7. de Alfaro, L., Henzinger, T.A.: Interface automata. In: ESEC/SIGSOFT FSE, pp. 109–120 (2001)
8. Carrillo, O., Chouali, S., Mountassir, H.: Formalizing and verifying compatibility and consistency of sysml blocks. SIGSOFT Softw. Eng. Notes 37(4), 1–8 (2012)
9. Chouali, S., Hammad, A.: Formal verification of components assembly based on sysml and interface automata. ISSE 7(4), 265–274 (2011)
10. Lee, E.A., Xiong, Y.: A behavioral type system and its application in ptolemy II. Formal Aspects of Computing 16(3), 210–237 (2004)

Author Index